Learning PowerCLI

Second Edition

Learn to leverage the power of PowerCLI to automate your VMware vSphere environment with ease

Robert van den Nieuwendijk

BIRMINGHAM - MUMBAI

Learning PowerCLI

Second Edition

First published: February 2014

Second edition: February 2017

Production reference: 1200217

Published by Packt Publishing Ltd.
Livery Place
35 Livery Street
Birmingham
B3 2PB, UK.
ISBN 978-1-78646-801-7

www.packtpub.com

Credits

Author
Robert van den Nieuwendijk

Reviewer
Kim Bottu

Commissioning Editor
Vijin Boricha

Acquisition Editor
Prachi Bisht

Content Development Editor
Abhishek Jadhav

Technical Editor
Gaurav Suri

Copy Editors
Safis Editing
Dipti Mankame

Project Coordinator
Shweta H. Birwatkar

Proofreader
Safis Editing

Indexer
Pratik Shirodkar

Graphics
Kirk D'Penha

Production Coordinator
Shantanu N. Zagade

About the Author

Robert van den Nieuwendijk is an IT veteran from the Netherlands with over thirty years of experience in Information Technology. He holds a bachelor degree in software engineering. After working a few years as a programmer of air traffic control and vessel traffic management systems, he started his own company Van den Nieuwendijk Informatica in 1988. Since then he has worked as a freelance systems administrator of OpenVMS, Windows Server, Linux, and VMware vSphere systems, for Dutch governmental organizations and cloud providers. During winter he is also a ski and snowboard instructor at an indoor ski school.

With his background as a programmer, he always tries to make his job easier by writing programs or scripts to perform repeating tasks. In the past, he used the C programming language, OpenVMS DCL, Visual Basic Script and KiXtart to do this. Now, he uses Microsoft PowerShell and VMware PowerCLI for all of his scripting work.

Robert is a frequent contributor and moderator at the VMware VMTN Communities. Since 2012 VMware awarded him the vExpert title for his *significant contributions to the community and a willingness to share his expertise with others*.

He has a blog at `http://rvdnieuwendijk.com` where he writes mainly about VMware PowerCLI, Microsoft PowerShell, and VMware vSphere.

If you want to get in touch with Robert, then you can find him on Twitter. His username is `@rvdnieuwendijk`.

Robert is also the author of *Learning PowerCLI, Packt Publishing*.

I would like to thank my wife Ali for supporting me writing this second book.

I also want to thank the people at Packt Publishing for giving me the opportunity to update the Learning PowerCLI book and write this second edition.

About the Reviewer

Kim Bottu is the virtualization engineer in the EMEA region for an international Biglaw firm, where he focuses on virtual datacenter operations, optimization, and design.

In his current role, he takes care of the consolidated virtual datacenters in Asia and Europe, and he is the SME for the EMEA Litigation virtual datacenters.

He holds the following certifications and honors: VCA-NV, VCP5-DCV, VCP6-DCV, VCAP5-DCD, VCAP6-DCV Design, and TOGAF 9 certified. He has also been named vExpert 2016 and vExpert 2017.

Kim currently lives in Belgium and is a proud dad of a daughter named Zoey. In his spare time you might find him playing with his daughter, reading books, or riding his mountain bike.

Kim can be reached at www.vMusketeers.com.

www.PacktPub.com

For support files and downloads related to your book, please visit www.PacktPub.com.

Did you know that Packt offers eBook versions of every book published, with PDF and ePub files available? You can upgrade to the eBook version at www.PacktPub.com and as a print book customer, you are entitled to a discount on the eBook copy. Get in touch with us at service@packtpub.com for more details.

At www.PacktPub.com, you can also read a collection of free technical articles, sign up for a range of free newsletters and receive exclusive discounts and offers on Packt books and eBooks.

https://www.packtpub.com/mapt

Get the most in-demand software skills with Mapt. Mapt gives you full access to all Packt books and video courses, as well as industry-leading tools to help you plan your personal development and advance your career.

Why subscribe?

- Fully searchable across every book published by Packt
- Copy and paste, print, and bookmark content
- On demand and accessible via a web browser

Customer Feedback

Thanks for purchasing this Packt book. At Packt, quality is at the heart of our editorial process. To help us improve, please leave us an honest review on this book's Amazon page at `https://www.amazon.com/dp/1786468018`.

If you'd like to join our team of regular reviewers, you can e-mail us at `customerreviews@packtpub.com`. We award our regular reviewers with free eBooks and videos in exchange for their valuable feedback. Help us be relentless in improving our products!

Table of Contents

Preface

VMware PowerCLI is a command-line automation and scripting tool that provides a Microsoft PowerShell interface to the VMware vSphere and vCloud products. Learning PowerCLI shows you how to install and use PowerCLI to automate the management of your VMware vSphere environment. With lots of examples, this book will teach you how to manage vSphere from the command line and how to create advanced PowerCLI scripts.

What this book covers

`Chapter 1`, *Introduction to PowerCLI*, gets you started using PowerCLI. First, you will see how to download and install PowerCLI. Then, you will learn to connect to and disconnect from the vCenter and ESXi servers and retrieve a list of all of your hosts and virtual machines.

`Chapter 2`, *Learning Basic PowerCLI Concepts*, introduces the Get-Help, Get-Command, and Get-Member cmdlets. It explains the difference between PowerShell Providers and PSdrives. You will see how you can use the raw vSphere API objects from PowerCLI and how to use the New-VIProperty cmdlet to extend a PowerCLI object.

`Chapter 3`, *Working with Objects in PowerShell*, concentrates on objects, properties, and methods. This chapter shows how you can use the pipeline to use the output of one command as the input of another command. You will learn how to use the PowerShell object cmdlets and how to create PowerShell objects.

`Chapter 4`, *Managing vSphere Hosts with PowerCLI*, covers the management of the vSphere ESXi servers. You will see how to add hosts to the vCenter server and how to remove them. You will work with host profiles, host services, Image Builder, and Auto Deploy, as well as with the esxcli command and the vSphere CLI commands from PowerCLI.

`Chapter 5`, *Managing Virtual Machines with PowerCLI*, examines the lifecycle of virtual machines-from creating to removing them. Creating templates, updating VMware Tools and upgrading virtual hardware, running commands in the guest OS, and configuring fault tolerance are some of the topics discussed in this chapter.

Chapter 6, *Managing Virtual Networks with PowerCLI*, walks you through vSphere Standard Switches and vSphere Distributed Switches, port groups, and network adapters. It shows you how to configure host networking and how to configure the network of a virtual machine.

Chapter 7, *Managing Storage*, explores creating and removing datastores and datastore clusters, working with Raw Device Mapping, configuring software iSCSI initiators, Storage I/O Control, and Storage DRS.

Chapter 8, *Managing High Availability and Clustering*, covers HA and DRS clusters, DRS rules and DRS groups, resource pools, and Distributed Power Management.

Chapter 9, *Managing vCenter Server*, shows you how to work with privileges, work with roles and permissions, manage licenses, configure alarm definitions, alarm action triggers, and retrieve events.

Chapter 10, *Patching ESXi Hosts and Upgrading Virtual Machines*, focusses on using VMware vSphere Update Manager to download patches, creating baselines and baseline groups, testing virtual machines and hosts for compliance, staging patches, and remediating inventory objects.

Chapter 11, *Managing VMware vCloud Director and vCloud Air*, covers connecting to vCloud servers, retrieving organizations, virtual datacenters, organization networks, and users, using vCloud virtual machines and appliances, and using snapshots.

Chapter 12, *Using Site Recovery Manager*, explores the Meadowcroft.SRM module to manage SRM protection groups, protecting virtual machines and running recovery plans to migrate or fail-over virtual machines from the protected site to the recovery site.

Chapter 13, *Using vRealize Operations Manager*, shows you to use alerts, retrieve recommendations, statistical data, solutions, and traversalSpecs, manage local user accounts and user roles and create and retrieve reports.

Chapter 14, *Using REST API to Manage NSX and vRealize Automation*, walks you through REST APIs with examples from VMware NSX and vRealize Automation using basic authentication and bearer tokens, XML, and JSON.

Chapter 15, *Reporting with PowerCLI*, concentrates on retrieving log files and log bundles, performance reporting, exporting reports to CSV files, generating HTML reports, sending reports by e-mail, and reporting the health of your vSphere environment with the vCheck script.

What you need for this book

To run the example PowerCLI scripts given in this book, you need the following software:

- VMware PowerCLI
- Microsoft PowerShell
- VMware vCenter Server
- VMware ESXi
- VMware vSphere Update Manager
- VMware vCloud Director
- VMware Site Recovery Manager
- VMware vSphere Replication
- VMware vRealize Operations Manager
- VMware NSX
- VMware vRealize Automation

If you don't have specific software installed, you can use the VMware Hands-on Labs at `https://labs.hol.vmware.com/` to test the scripts.

The scripts in this book are tested using VMware PowerCLI 6.5 Release 1, VMware vCenter Server 6.5, and VMware ESXi 6.5. Microsoft PowerShell and VMware PowerCLI are free. You can download a free 60-day evaluation of VMware vCenter Server and VMware ESXi from the VMware website. It is not possible to modify the settings on the free VMware vSphere Hypervisor using PowerCLI.

Who this book is for

This book is written for VMware vSphere administrators who want to automate their vSphere environment using PowerCLI. It is assumed that you have at least a basic knowledge of VMware vSphere. If you are not a vSphere administrator, but you are interested in learning more about PowerCLI, then this book will also give you some basic knowledge of vSphere.

Conventions

In this book, you will find a number of text styles that distinguish between different kinds of information. Here are some examples of these styles and an explanation of their meaning.

Code words in text, database table names, folder names, filenames, file extensions, pathnames, dummy URLs, user input, and Twitter handles are shown as follows: "The script uses the `Get-Cluster` cmdlet to retrieve all the clusters."

A block of code is set as follows:

```
$HostName = '192.168.0.133'
$iSCSITarget = '192.168.0.157'
$VirtualSwitchName = 'vSwitch2'
$NicName = 'vmnic3'
$PortGroupName = 'iSCSI Port group 1'
$ChapType = 'Preferred'
$ChapUser = 'Cluster01User'
$ChapPassword = ' Cluster01Pwd'
$DatastoreName = 'Cluster01_iSCSI01'
```

Any command-line input or output is written as follows:

```
PowerCLI C:\> New-VM -Name VM1 -ResourcePool (Get-Cluster
-Name Cluster01)
```

New terms and **important words** are shown in bold. Words that you see on the screen, for example, in menus or dialog boxes, appear in the text like this: "If your cluster is incorrectly configured, the vSphere Web Client will show you the issues in the **Summary** tab."

Warnings or important notes appear in a box like this.

Tips and tricks appear like this.

Reader feedback

Feedback from our readers is always welcome. Let us know what you think about this book-what you liked or disliked. Reader feedback is important to us as it helps us develop titles that you will really get the most out of.

To send us general feedback, simply e-mail feedback@packtpub.com, and mention the book's title in the subject of your message.

If there is a topic that you have expertise in and you are interested in either writing or contributing to a book, see our author guide at www.packtpub.com/authors.

Customer support

Now that you are the proud owner of a Packt book, we have a number of things to help you to get the most from your purchase.

Downloading the example code

You can download the example code files for this book from your account at http://www.packtpub.com. If you purchased this book elsewhere, you can visit http://www.packtpub.com/support and register to have the files e-mailed directly to you.

You can download the code files by following these steps:

1. Log in or register to our website using your e-mail address and password.
2. Hover the mouse pointer on the **SUPPORT** tab at the top.
3. Click on **Code Downloads & Errata**.
4. Enter the name of the book in the **Search** box.
5. Select the book for which you're looking to download the code files.
6. Choose from the drop-down menu where you purchased this book from.
7. Click on **Code Download**.

Once the file is downloaded, please make sure that you unzip or extract the folder using the latest version of:

- WinRAR / 7-Zip for Windows
- Zipeg / iZip / UnRarX for Mac
- 7-Zip / PeaZip for Linux

The code bundle for the book is also hosted on GitHub at `https://github.com/PacktPubl ishing/Learning-PowerCLI-Second-Edition`. We also have other code bundles from our rich catalog of books and videos available at `https://github.com/PacktPublishing/`. Check them out!

Errata

Although we have taken every care to ensure the accuracy of our content, mistakes do happen. If you find a mistake in one of our books-maybe a mistake in the text or the code-we would be grateful if you could report this to us. By doing so, you can save other readers from frustration and help us improve subsequent versions of this book. If you find any errata, please report them by visiting `http://www.packtpub.com/submit-errata`, selecting your book, clicking on the **Errata Submission Form** link, and entering the details of your errata. Once your errata are verified, your submission will be accepted, and the errata will be uploaded to our website or added to any list of existing errata under the Errata section of that title.

To view the previously submitted errata, go to `https://www.packtpub.com/books/content/support` and enter the name of the book in the search field. The required information will appear under the **Errata** section.

Piracy

Piracy of copyrighted material on the Internet is an ongoing problem across all media. At Packt, we take the protection of our copyright and licenses very seriously. If you come across any illegal copies of our works in any form on the Internet, please provide us with the location address or website name immediately so that we can pursue a remedy.

Please contact us at `copyright@packtpub.com` with a link to the suspected pirated material.

We appreciate your help in protecting our authors and our ability to bring you valuable content.

Questions

If you have a problem with any aspect of this book, you can contact us at `questions@packtpub.com`, and we will do our best to address the problem.

1
Introduction to PowerCLI

Have you ever had to create 200 virtual machines in a short period of time, change a setting on all of your hosts, or make an advanced report for your boss to show how full the hard disks of your virtual machines are? If you have, you know that performing these tasks using the vSphere web client will take a lot of time. This is where automation can make your job easier. **VMware PowerCLI** is a powerful tool that can perform these tasks and much more. And the best thing is that it is free!

VMware PowerCLI is a **command-line interface (CLI)** distributed as a collection of Microsoft PowerShell modules and snap-ins. **Microsoft PowerShell** is Microsoft's command shell and scripting language, designed with the systems administrator in mind. Microsoft PowerShell is available on every Microsoft Windows server or workstation since Windows Server 2008 R2 and Windows 7. VMware PowerCLI is an extension to Microsoft PowerShell. This means that all of the features of PowerShell can be used in PowerCLI. You can use PowerCLI to automate your vSphere hosts, virtual machines, virtual networks, storage, clusters, vCenter Servers, and more.

In this chapter, you will learn:

- Downloading and installing PowerCLI
- Participating in the VMware Customer Improvement Program
- Modifying the PowerShell execution policy
- Creating a PowerShell profile
- Connecting and disconnecting servers
- Using the credential store
- Retrieving a list of all of your virtual machines
- Retrieving a list of all of your hosts

Downloading and installing PowerCLI

In this section, you will learn how to download and install **PowerCLI 6.5 Release 1**. First, we will list the requirements for PowerCLI 6.5 Release 1. After downloading PowerCLI from the VMware website, we will install PowerCLI on your system.

Requirements for using PowerCLI 6.5 Release 1

You can install VMware PowerCLI 6.5 Release 1, the version used for writing this book, on the following 64-bit operating systems:

- Windows Server 2012 R2
- Windows Server 2008 R2 Service Pack 1
- Windows 10
- Windows 8.1
- Windows 7 Service Pack 1

VMware PowerCLI 6.5 Release 1 is compatible with the following PowerShell versions:

- Microsoft PowerShell 3.0
- Microsoft PowerShell 4.0
- Microsoft PowerShell 5.0
- Microsoft PowerShell 5.1

If you want to work with VMware PowerCLI 6.5 Release 1, make sure that the following software is present on your system:

- Microsoft PowerShell 3.0, 4.0, 5.0, or 5.1
- NET Framework 4.5, 4.5.x, 4.6, or 4.6.x

Downloading PowerCLI 6.5 Release 1

Before you can install PowerCLI, you have to download the PowerCLI installer from the VMware website. You will need a **My VMware account** to do this.

Perform the following steps to download PowerCLI:

1. Visit `http://www.vmware.com/go/powercli`. On this page, you will find a **Resources** section.

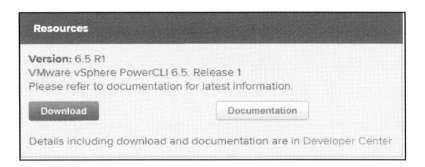

2. Click on the **Download** button to download PowerCLI.
3. You have to log in with a My VMware account. If you don't have a My VMware account, you can register for free.

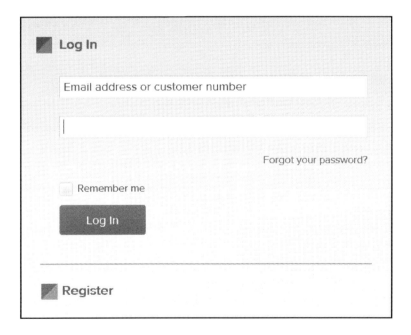

4. After you log in, you will be taken to the **VMware PowerCLI** download page. Click on the **Download Now** button to start downloading PowerCLI.

Installing PowerCLI

Perform the following steps to install PowerCLI:

1. Run the PowerCLI installer that you just downloaded.
2. Click **Yes** in the **User Account Control** window to accept the **Do you want to allow this app to make changes to your device?** option.
3. If the **PowerShell execution policy** on your computer is not set to **RemoteSigned**, you will get a warning that tells you **It is recommended that you set the execution policy to "RemoteSigned" in order to be able to execute scripts**. After the installation of PowerCLI, I will show you how to set the execution policy. Click on **Continue** to continue to the installation of PowerCLI.

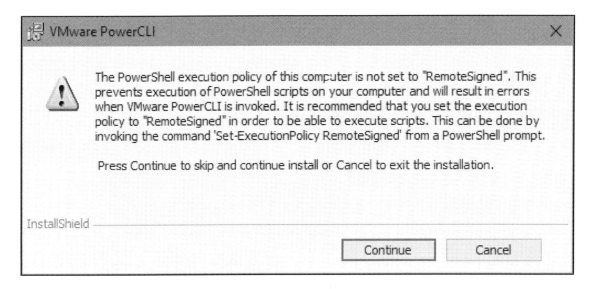

4. Click on **Next >** in the **Welcome to the InstallShield Wizard for VMware PowerCLI** window.

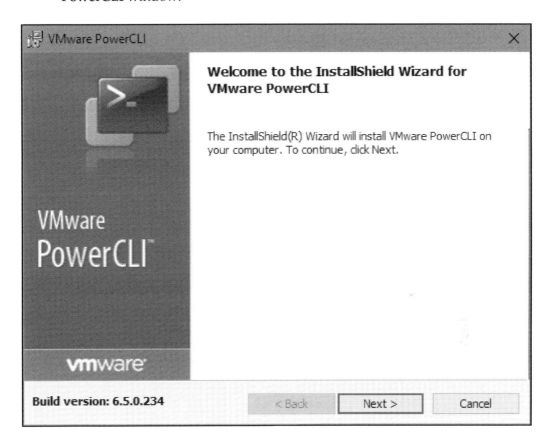

5. Select **I accept the terms in the license agreement** and click on **Next >**.

6. If you are not using **vCloud Air**, **VMware vCloud Director**, **vSphere Update Manager**, **vRealize Operations Manager**, or **Horizon View**, you can click on the little arrow to the left of a feature and select **This feature will not be available**. I recommend installing all of the features, to be able to run the scripts in all of the chapters in this book. If you want, you can change the installation directory by clicking on **Change…**. Click on **Next >**.

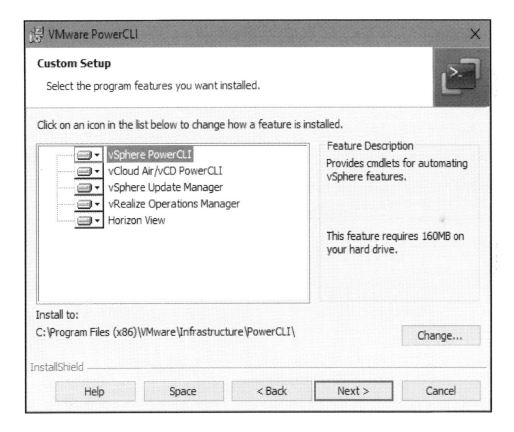

7. Click on **Install** to begin the installation.

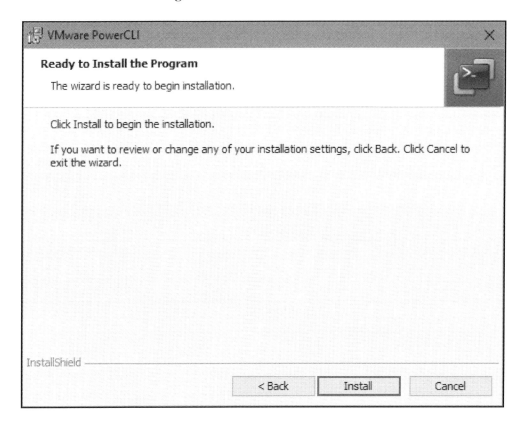

8. Click on **Finish** to exit the installation wizard.

After installing PowerCLI, you will have a **VMware PowerCLI** icon on your desktop. If you installed PowerCLI on a 64-bit computer, you will also have a **VMware PowerCLI (32-Bit)** icon. Some PowerCLI commands only work in the 32-bit version of PowerCLI. So keep both versions.

Participating in the VMware Customer Improvement Program

When you start PowerCLI for the first time, you will get the following screen:

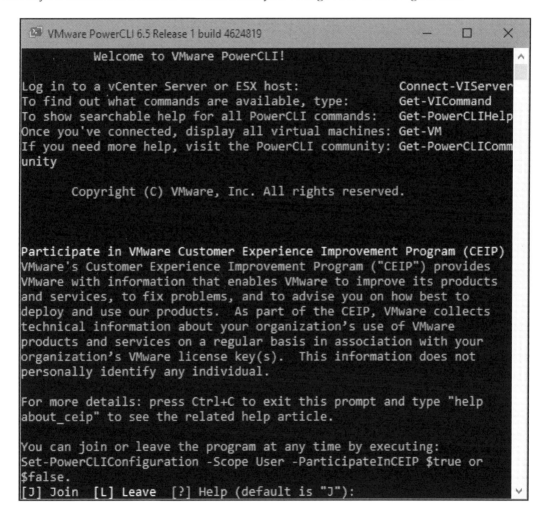

You are asked to participate in the **VMware Customer Improvement Program** (CEIP). Type *J* to participate in the CEIP or type *L* to leave.

If you didn't get the text from the preceding screenshot, you may get the following error message:

. : File C:\Program Files (x86)\VMware\Infrastructure\vSphere PowerCLI\Scripts\Initialize-PowerCLIEnvironment.ps1 cannot be loaded because running scripts is disabled on this system. For more information, see about_Execution_Policies at http://go.microsoft.com/fwlink/?LinkID=135170.

Then, read the following section, *Modifying the PowerShell execution policy*, to solve this problem.

Modifying the PowerShell execution policy

If this is the first time that you are using Microsoft PowerShell on the computer on which you installed PowerCLI, you have to change the **execution policy** to be able to start PowerCLI.

The Microsoft PowerShell execution policies define when you can run scripts or load configuration files. The possible values for the execution policy are Restricted, AllSigned, RemoteSigned, Unrestricted, Bypass, and Undefined.

Policy	Description
Restricted	This is the default execution policy. It allows you to run commands at the Command Prompt, but disables the execution of scripts. It will also disable the start of PowerCLI.
AllSigned	With the AllSigned execution policy, scripts can run, but they must be signed by a trusted publisher. If you run a script by a publisher that is not trusted yet, you will see a prompt asking whether you trust the publisher of the script.
RemoteSigned	The RemoteSigned execution policy allows you to run scripts that you have written on the local computer. Any script downloaded from the Internet must be signed by a trusted publisher or must be unblocked.
Unrestricted	When the execution policy is set to Unrestricted, unsigned scripts can run. If you run a script that has been downloaded from the Internet, you will get a security warning saying that this script can potentially harm your computer and asking whether you want to run this script.

Bypass	The Bypass execution policy blocks nothing and displays no warnings or prompts. This execution policy is designed for configurations in which a Microsoft PowerShell script is built into a larger application that has its own security model.
Undefined	The Undefined execution policy removes the execution policy from the current scope. If the execution policy in all scopes is Undefined, the effective execution policy is Restricted, which is the default execution policy. The Undefined execution policy will not remove an execution policy that is set in a **Group Policy** scope.

You can check the current execution policy setting with the following command:

```
PowerCLI C:\> Get-ExecutionPolicy
```

Get-ExecutionPolicy is a Microsoft PowerShell **commandlet (cmdlet)**. Cmdlets are commands built into PowerShell or PowerCLI. They follow a verb-noun naming convention. The get cmdlets retrieve information about the item that is specified as the noun part of the cmdlet.

Set the execution policy to RemoteSigned to be able to start PowerCLI and run scripts written on the local computer with the Set-ExecutionPolicy -ExecutionPolicy RemoteSigned command.

> You have to run the Set-ExecutionPolicy -ExecutionPolicy RemoteSigned command from a PowerShell or PowerCLI session that you started using the **Run as Administrator** option, or you will get the following error message:
>
> **Set-ExecutionPolicy : Access to the registry key 'HKEY_LOCAL_MACHINE\SOFTWARE\Microsoft\PowerShell\1\ShellIds\Microsoft.PowerShell' is denied.**
>
> If you are using both the 32-bit and the 64-bit versions of PowerCLI, you have to run this command in both versions.

In the following screenshot of the PowerCLI console, you will see the output of the Set-ExecutionPolicy -ExecutionPolicy RemoteSigned command if you run this command in a PowerCLI session started with **Run as Administrator**.

```
VMware PowerCLI 6.5 Release 1 build 4624819                    —    □    ✕
PowerCLI C:\> Set-ExecutionPolicy -ExecutionPolicy RemoteSigned

Execution Policy Change
The execution policy helps protect you from scripts that you do not
trust. Changing the execution policy might expose you to the
security risks described in the about_Execution_Policies help topic
at http://go.microsoft.com/fwlink/?LinkID=135170. Do you want to
change the execution policy?
[Y] Yes  [A] Yes to All  [N] No  [L] No to All  [S] Suspend
[?] Help(default is "N"): Y
PowerCLI C:\>
```

You can get more information about execution policies by typing the following command:

```
PowerCLI C:\> Get-Help about_Execution_Policies
```

To get more information about signing your scripts, type the following command:

```
PowerCLI C:\> Get-Help about_signing
```

If you get an error message saying **Get-Help could not find about_Execution_Policies in a help file**, you have to run the Update-Help cmdlet in a PowerShell, or PowerCLI session started with **Run as Administrator** first. The Update-Help cmdlet downloads the newest help files for Microsoft PowerShell modules and installs them on your computer. Because Microsoft updates the Microsoft PowerShell help files on a regular basis, it is recommended to run the Update-Help cmdlet on a regular basis also.

Creating a PowerShell profile

If you want certain PowerCLI commands to be executed every time you start a PowerCLI session, you can put these commands in a **PowerShell profile**. The commands in a PowerShell profile will be executed every time you start a new PowerCLI session. There are six PowerShell profiles, two specific for the PowerShell console, two specific for the PowerShell **Integrated Scripting Environment** (**ISE**), and two used by both the PowerShell console and the PowerShell ISE. The PowerShell console and the PowerShell ISE have their own profiles for:

- All users, current host
- Current user, current host

The two profiles used by both the PowerShell console and the PowerShell ISE are:

- All users, all hosts
- Current user, all hosts

You can retrieve the locations for the different profiles of the PowerShell console by executing the following command in the PowerShell console. In this command, the `$PROFILE` variable is a standard PowerShell variable that returns an object containing the locations of the PowerShell profiles. This object is piped to the `Format-List -Force` command to display all of the properties of the `$PROFILE` object in a list:

```
PowerCLI C:\> $PROFILE | Format-List -Force

AllUsersAllHosts        : C:\Windows\System32\WindowsPowerShell\v1.0\p
                          rofile.ps1
AllUsersCurrentHost     : C:\Windows\System32\WindowsPowerShell\v1.0\M
                          icrosoft.PowerShell_profile.ps1
CurrentUserAllHosts     : C:\Users\robert\Documents\WindowsPowerShell\
                          profile.ps1
CurrentUserCurrentHost  : C:\Users\robert\Documents\WindowsPowerShell\
                          Microsoft.PowerShell_profile.ps1
Length                  : 76
```

Downloading the example code

Detailed steps to download the code bundle are mentioned in the Preface of this book. Please have a look.

The code bundle for the book is also hosted on GitHub at: `https://github.com/rosbook/effective_robotics_programming_wit` `h_ros`. We also have other code bundles from our rich catalog of books and videos available at `https://github.com/PacktPublishing/`. Check them out!

As you can see in the output of the preceding command, the `$PROFILE` object has four properties `AllUsersAllHosts`, `AllUsersCurrentHost`, `CurrentUserAllHosts`, and `CurrentUserCurrentHost` that contain the locations of the different profiles.

To list the locations of the PowerShell profiles of the PowerShell ISE, you have to execute the preceding command in the PowerShell ISE. This gives the following output:

```
PS C:\> $PROFILE | Format-List -Force

AllUsersAllHosts        : C:\Windows\System32\WindowsPowerShell\v1.0\p
                          rofile.ps1
AllUsersCurrentHost     : C:\Windows\System32\WindowsPowerShell\v1.0\M
                          icrosoft.PowerShellISE_profile.ps1
```

```
CurrentUserAllHosts      : C:\Users\robert\Documents\WindowsPowerShell\
                           profile.ps1
CurrentUserCurrentHost : C:\Users\robert\Documents\WindowsPowerShell\
                           Microsoft.PowerShellISE_profile.ps1
Length                   : 79
```

 You can start the PowerShell ISE from a Command Prompt by running `powershell_ise.exe`. You can start the PowerShell ISE from within a PowerShell console with the alias `ise`.

The default value for the $PROFILE variable is the value of the $PROFILE.CurrentUserCurrentHost property. So you can use $PROFILE instead of $PROFILE.CurrentUserCurrentHost.

You can determine if a specific profile exists by using the Test-Path cmdlet. The following command will test if the profile specified by $PROFILE exists:

```
PowerCLI C:\> Test-Path -Path $PROFILE
False
```

If a profile does not exist, as in the preceding example, you can create the profile using the New-Item cmdlet. If the directories in the path do not exist, by using the -Force parameter the New-Item cmdlet will create the directories. The following command will create the current user/current host profile and will also create the missing directories in the path:

```
PowerCLI C:\> New-Item -Path $PROFILE -ItemType file -Force
    Directory: C:\Users\robert\Documents\WindowsPowerShell
Mode            LastWriteTime       Length  Name
----            -------------       ------  ----
-a--         1/7/2017   2:01 PM          0  Microsoft.PowerShell_pro
                                            file.ps1
```

After creating the PowerShell profile, you can edit the profile using the PowerShell ISE with the following command:

```
PowerCLI C:\> ise $PROFILE
```

If you put the commands from the preceding section, *Modifying the PowerShell execution policy*, the new colors of the messages will be used in all of your PowerCLI sessions.

Connecting and disconnecting servers

Before you can do useful things with PowerCLI, you have to connect to a vCenter Server or an ESXi server. And if you are finished, it is a good practice to disconnect your session. We will discuss how to do this in the following sections *Connecting to a server*, *Connecting to multiple servers*, *Suppressing certificate warnings*, and *Disconnecting from a server*.

Connecting to a server

If you are not connected to a vCenter or an ESXi server, you will get an error message if you try to run a PowerCLI cmdlet. Let's try to retrieve a list of all of your data centers using the following command:

```
PowerCLI C:\> Get-Datacenter
```

The output of the preceding command is as follows:

```
Get-Datacenter : 1/7/2017 1:37:17 PM     Get-Datacenter          You are
not currently connected to any servers. Please connect first using a
Connect cmdlet.
At line:1 char:1
+ Get-Datacenter
+ ~~~~~~~~~~~~~~
    + CategoryInfo          : ResourceUnavailable: (:) [Get-
                              Datacenter], ViServerConnectionException
    + FullyQualifiedErrorId : Core_BaseCmdlet_NotConnectedError,
                              VMware.VimAutomation.ViCore.Cmdlets.
                              Commands.GetDatacenter
```

You can see that this gives an error message. You first have to connect to a vCenter Server or an ESXi server using the Connect-VIServer cmdlet. If you have a vCenter Server, you only need to connect to the vCenter Server and not to the individual ESXi servers. It is possible to connect to multiple vCenter Servers or ESXi servers at once. The Connect-VIServer cmdlet has the following syntax. The syntax contains two parameter sets. The first parameter set is the default:

```
Connect-VIServer [-Server] <String[]> [-Port <Int32>] [-Protocol
<String>] [-Credential <PSCredential>] [-User <String>] [-Password
<String>] [-Session <String>] [-NotDefault] [-SaveCredentials]
[-AllLinked] [-Force] [<CommonParameters>]
```

In the Default parameter set, the -Server parameter is required. The second parameter set can be used to select a server from a list of recently connected servers:

```
Connect-VIServer -Menu [<CommonParameters>]
```

In the Menu parameter set, the -Menu parameter is required. You cannot combine parameters from the Default parameter set with the Menu parameter set.

Let's first try to connect to a vCenter Server with the following command:

```
PowerCLI C:\> Connect-VIServer -Server 192.168.0.132
```

192.168.0.132 is the IP address of the vCenter Server in my home lab. Replace this IP address with the IP address or DNS name of your vCenter or ESXi server.

The preceding command will pop up a window in which you have to specify server credentials to connect to your server if your Windows session credentials don't have rights on your server. Enter values for **User name** and **Password** and click on **OK**.

If you specified valid credentials, you would get output similar to the following:

```
Name                              Port  User
----                              ----  ----
192.168.0.132                     443   root
```

You can also specify a username and password on the command line as follows:

```
PowerCLI C:\> Connect-VIServer -Server 192.168.0.132 -User admin
-Password pass
```

You can also save the credentials in a variable with the following command:

```
PowerCLI C:\> $Credential = Get-Credential
```

The preceding command will pop up a window in which you can type the username and password.

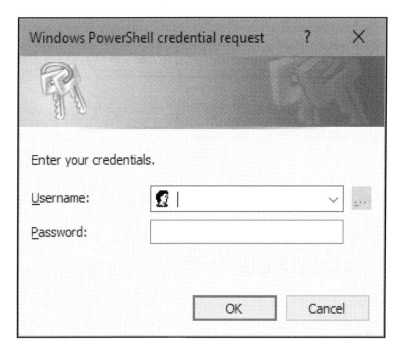

You can now use the $Credential variable to connect to a server using the -Credential parameter, as follows:

```
PowerCLI C:\> Connect-VIServer -Server 192.168.0.132 -Credential
$Credential
```

You can also use the PowerCLI credential store. This will be discussed in the *Using the credential store* section, later in this chapter.

The default protocol that the Connect-VIServer cmdlet uses is HTTPS. If you want to make a connection with the HTTP protocol, you can do that with the following command:

```
PowerCLI C:\> Connect-VIServer -Server 192.168.0.132 -Protocol HTTP
```

If you have multiple vCenter Servers in **Linked Mode**, you can use the `Connect-VIServer` `-AllLinked` parameter to connect all of these vCenter Servers at once, as follows:

```
PowerCLI C:\> Connect-VIserver -Server 192.168.0.132 -Credential
$Credential -AllLinked
```

The `Connect-VIServer -Menu` command gives you a list of previously connected servers from which you can pick one, as shown in the following command line:

```
PowerCLI C:\> Connect-VIServer -Menu
Select a server from the list (by typing its number and pressing
Enter):
[1] 192.168.0.132
[2] 192.168.0.133
```

Type the number of the server you want to connect to.

Connecting to multiple servers

It is possible in PowerCLI to connect to multiple servers at once. You can do this by specifying more than one server, as follows:

```
PowerCLI C:\> Connect-VIServer -Server vCenter1,vCenter2
```

The first time you try to do this, you will get the following message:

```
Working with multiple default servers?

    Select [Y] if you want to work with more than one default
servers. In this case, every time when you connect to a different
server using Connect-VIServer, the new server connection is stored in
 an array variable together with the previously connected servers.
When you run a cmdlet and the target servers cannot be determined
from the specified parameters, the cmdlet runs against all servers
stored in the array variable.
    Select [N] if you want to work with a single default server. In
this case, when you run a cmdlet and the target servers cannot be
determined from the specified parameters, the cmdlet runs against the
 last connected server.
    WARNING: WORKING WITH MULTIPLE DEFAULT SERVERS WILL BE ENABLED BY
 DEFAULT IN A FUTURE RELEASE. You can explicitly set your own
preference at any time by using the DefaultServerMode parameter of
Set-PowerCLIConfiguration.
    [Y] Yes   [N] No   [S] Suspend   [?] Help (default is "Y"):
```

Press *Enter* or type *Y* to work with multiple default servers.

As the message says, you can always connect to multiple servers, but your commands will only work against the last server you connected to unless you have enabled working with multiple servers.

You can see the current value of `DefaultVIServerMode` with the `Get-PowerCLIConfiguration` cmdlet:

```
PowerCLI C:\> Get-PowerCLIConfiguration

Scope      ProxyPolicy     DefaultVIServerMode InvalidCertificateAction
-----      -----------     ------------------- ------------------------
Session    UseSystemProxy  Multiple            Unset
User                       Multiple
AllUsers
```

If you want to change `DefaultVIServerMode` from single to multiple, you can do that with the `Set-PowerCLIConfiguration` cmdlet. This cmdlet has the following syntax:

```
Set-PowerCLIConfiguration [-ProxyPolicy <ProxyPolicy>]
[-DefaultVIServerMode <DefaultVIServerMode>] [-InvalidCertificateAction
<BadCertificateAction>] [-ParticipateInCeip <Boolean>]
[-CEIPDataTransferProxyPolicy <ProxyPolicy>] [-
DisplayDeprecationWarnings <Boolean>] [-WebOperationTimeoutSeconds
<Int32>] [-VMConsoleWindowBrowser <String>] [-Scope
<ConfigurationScope>] [-WhatIf] [-Confirm] [<CommonParameters>]
```

You can change `DefaultVIServerMode` from single to multiple with the following command:

```
PowerCLI C:\> Set-PowerCLIConfiguration -DefaultVIServerMode Multiple
-Scope User
```

All of the servers that you are currently connected to are stored in the variable `$global:DefaultVIServers`. If `DefaultVIServerMode` is set to `multiple`, your PowerCLI cmdlets will run against all servers stored in the `$global:DefaultVIServers` variable.

The last server you are connected to is stored in the variable `$global:DefaultVIServer`. If `DefaultVIServerMode` is set to `single`, your PowerCLI cmdlets will only run against the server stored in the `$global:DefaultVIServer` variable.

Suppressing certificate warnings

If your vCenter Server does not have valid server certificates, the `Connect-VIserver` cmdlet will display some warning messages, as shown in the following screenshot:

It is a good practice to supply your vCenter Server and ESXi servers with certificates signed by a **certificate authority (CA)**. You can find information on how to do this in the VMware Knowledge Base article, *Replacing default certificates with CA signed SSL certificates in vSphere 6.x (2111219)* at `http://kb.vmware.com/kb/2111219`.

If you don't have valid certificates, you can suppress the warning messages using the `Set-PowerCLIConfiguration` cmdlet with the following command:

```
PowerCLI C:\ > Set-PowerCLIConfiguration -InvalidCertificateAction
Ignore
```

The preceding command will modify `InvalidCertificationAction` in the `AllUsers` scope. You have to run this command using the **Run as Administrator** PowerCLI session. Otherwise, you will get the following error message:

```
Set-PowerCLIConfiguration : Only administrators can change settings for
all users.
At line:1 char:1
+ Set-PowerCLIConfiguration -InvalidCertificateAction Ignore
+ ~~~~~~~~~~~~~~~~~~~~~~~~~~~~~~~~~~~~~~~~~~~~~~~~~~~~~~~~~~~~~
    + CategoryInfo          : NotSpecified: (:)
                              [Set-PowerCLIConfiguration],
                              InvalidArgument
    + FullyQualifiedErrorId : VMware.VimAutomation.ViCore.Types.V1.
                              ErrorHandling.InvalidArgument, VMware.
                              VimAutomation.ViCore.Cmdlets.Commands.
                              SetVIToolkitConfiguration
```

Disconnecting from a server

To disconnect from a vSphere server, you have to use the `Disconnect-VIServer` cmdlet. The `Disconnect-VIServer` cmdlet has the following syntax:

```
Disconnect-VIServer [[-Server] <VIServer[]>] [-Force]
[-WhatIf] [-Confirm] [<CommonParameters>]
```

To disconnect all of your server connections, type the following command:

```
PowerCLI C:\> Disconnect-VIServer -Server * -Force
```

The output of the preceding command is as follows:

```
Confirm
Are you sure you want to perform this action?
Performing operation "Disconnect VIServer" on Target "User:
VSPHERE.LOCAL\Administrator, Server: 192.168.0.132, Port: 443".
[Y] Yes  [A] Yes to All  [N] No  [L] No to All  [S] Suspend
[?]  Help (default is "Y"):
```

Type *Y* or *Enter* to disconnect from the server.

If you don't want to be prompted with **Are you sure you want to perform this action?**, you can use the `-Confirm:$false` option as follows:

```
PowerCLI C:\> Disconnect-VIServer -Server * -Force
-Confirm:$false
```

It may be that you want to disconnect only one session and not all. In that case, specify the server name or IP address of the server you want to disconnect. The following command only disconnects the latest session from server `192.168.0.132`:

```
PowerCLI C:\> Disconnect-VIServer -Server 192.168.0.132
```

Disconnecting one or more sessions will also change the value of the `$global:DefaultVIServers` and `$global:DefaultVIServer` variables.

Retrieving the PowerCLI configuration

To see the current setting of `InvalidCertificationAction`, you can use the `Get-PowerCLIConfiguration` cmdlet. The syntax of this cmdlet is as follows:

```
Get-PowerCLIConfiguration [-Scope <ConfigurationScope>]
[<CommonParameters>]
```

The following example will retrieve the PowerCLI configuration and shows the `InvalidCertificateAction` value for all scopes:

```
PowerCLI C:\> Get-PowerCLIConfiguration |
>> Select-Object -Property Scope, InvalidCertificateAction,
DisplayDeprecationWarnings |
>> Format-Table -AutoSize
>>

    Scope InvalidCertificateAction DisplayDeprecationWarnings
    ----- ------------------------ --------------------------
  Session                    Unset                       True
     User
  AllUsers
```

As you can see in the output, there are three different scopes for which you can modify the PowerCLI configuration: `Session`, `User`, and `AllUsers`. The `Set-PowerCLIConfiguration` cmdlet will modify the `AllUser` scope if you don't specify a scope.

The `DisplayDeprecationWarnings` property shown in the preceding output will be discussed in the section, *Suppressing deprecated warnings*, later in this chapter.

Using the credential store

If you are logged in to your computer with a domain account, you can use your Windows session credentials to connect to a vCenter or ESXi server. If you are not logged in to your computer with a domain account or your domain account has no rights in vSphere, you have to supply account information every time you connect to a vCenter or ESXi server.

To prevent yourself from having to do this, you can store credentials in the credential store. These stored credentials will be used as default if you connect to a server that is stored in the credential store. You can use the `-SaveCredentials` parameter of the `Connect-VIServer` cmdlet to indicate that you want to save the specified credentials in the local credential store, as follows:

```
PowerCLI C:\> Connect-VIServer -Server 192.168.0.132 -User admin
-Password pass -SaveCredentials
```

You can also create a new entry in the credential store with the `New-VICredentialStoreItem` cmdlet:

```
PowerCLI C:\> New-VICredentialStoreItem -Host 192.168.0.132
-User Admin -Password pass
```

You can not only store credentials for vCenter Servers but also for ESXi servers, using the following command:

```
PowerCLI C:\> New-VICredentialStoreItem -Host ESX1 -User root
-Password VMware1!
```

To get a listing of all of your stored credentials, type the following command:

```
PowerCLI C:\> Get-VICredentialStoreItem
```

And to remove a stored credential you can use the following command:

```
PowerCLI C:\> Remove-VICredentialStoreItem -Host ESX1 -User root
```

The stored credentials are stored in a file on your computer. The default credential store file location is: `%APPDATA%\VMware\credstore\vicredentials.xml`. But it is also possible to create other credential store files. You can see the contents of the default credential store file with the following command:

```
PowerCLI C:\> Get-Content -Path $env:APPDATA\VMware\credstore
\vicredentials.xml
```

The passwords stored in a credential store file are encrypted. But you can easily retrieve the stored passwords with the following command:

```
PowerCLI C:\> Get-VICredentialStoreItem |
>> Select-Object -Property Host,User,Password
```

> The passwords in the stored credentials are encrypted. Only the user who created the item can decrypt the password.

Retrieving a list of all of your virtual machines

Now that we know how to connect to a server, let's do something useful with PowerCLI. Most of the people who begin using PowerCLI create reports, so create a list of all of your virtual machines as your first report. You have to use the `Get-VM` cmdlet to retrieve a list of your virtual machines. The syntax of the `Get-VM` cmdlet is as follows. The first parameter set is the default:

```
Get-VM [[-Name] <String[]>] [-Server <VIServer[]>]
[-Datastore <StorageResource[]>] [-Location <VIContainer[]>]
[-Tag <Tag[]>] [-NoRecursion] [<CommonParameters>]
```

The second parameter set is for retrieving virtual machines connected to specific virtual switches:

```
Get-VM [[-Name] <String[]>] [-Server <VIServer[]>] [-VirtualSwitch
<VirtualSwitchBase[]>] [-Tag <Tag[]>] [<CommonParameters>]
```

The third parameter set is for retrieving virtual machines by ID:

```
Get-VM [-Server <VIServer[]>] -Id <String[]> [<CommonParameters>]
```

The `-Id` parameter is required. The fourth parameter set is for retrieving virtual machines by related object:

```
Get-VM -RelatedObject <VmRelatedObjectBase[]> [<CommonParameters>]
```

The `-RelatedObject` parameter is required. You can use these four parameter sets to filter the virtual machines based on name, server, datastore, location, distributed switch, ID, or related object.

Create your first report with the following command:

```
PowerCLI C:\> Get-VM
```

This will create a list of all of your virtual machines. You will see the name, power state, the number of CPU's, and the amount of memory in GB for each virtual machine, as shown in the following command-line output:

```
Name                  PowerState NumCPUs MemoryGB
----                  ---------- ------- --------
Dc1                   PoweredOn  2          4.000
VM1                   PoweredOn  1          0.250
DNS1                  PoweredOn  2          8.000
```

The `Name`, `PowerState`, `NumCPU`, and `MemoryGB` properties are the properties that you will see by default if you use the `Get-VM` cmdlet. However, the virtual machine object in PowerCLI has a lot of other properties that are not shown by default. You can see them all by piping the output of the `Get-VM` cmdlet to the `Format-List` cmdlet using the pipe character `|`. The `Format-List` cmdlet displays object properties and their values in a list format, as shown in the following command-line output:

```
PowerCLI C:\> Get-VM -Name DC1 | Format-List -Property *

Name                    : DC1
PowerState              : PoweredOff
Notes                   :
Guest                   : DC1:
NumCPU                  : 1
CoresPerSocket          : 1
MemoryMB                : 4096
MemoryGB                : 4
VMHostId                : HostSystem-host-10
VMHost                  : 192.168.0.133
VApp                    :
FolderId                : Folder-group-v9
Folder                  : Discovered virtual machine
ResourcePoolId          : ResourcePool-resgroup-8
ResourcePool            : Resources
```

```
HARestartPriority            : ClusterRestartPriority
HAIsolationResponse          : AsSpecifiedByCluster
DrsAutomationLevel           : AsSpecifiedByCluster
VMSwapfilePolicy             : Inherit
VMResourceConfiguration      : CpuShares:Normal/1000
                               MemShares:Normal/40960
Version                      : v13
PersistentId                 : 50399fa1-6d65-a26f-1fd2-b635d0e8610f
GuestId                      : windows9Server64Guest
UsedSpaceGB                  : 30.0000018076971173286437988828
ProvisionedSpaceGB           : 34.17544779740273952484130859 4
DatastoreIdList              : {Datastore-datastore-11}
ExtensionData                : VMware.Vim.VirtualMachine
CustomFields                 : {}
Id                           : VirtualMachine-vm-46
Uid                          : /VIServer=vsphere.local\administrator@192.
                               168.0.132:443/VirtualMachine=VirtualMachin
                               e-vm-46/
Client                       : VMware.VimAutomation.ViCore.Impl.V1.VimCli
                               Ent
```

You can select specific properties with the Select-Object cmdlet. Say you want to make a report that shows the Name, Notes, VMHost, and Guest properties for all your virtual machines. You can do that with the following command:

```
PowerCLI C:\> Get-VM | Select-Object -Property Name,Notes,VMHost,Guest
```

The output of the preceding command is as follows:

```
Name              Notes        VMHost         Guest
----              -----        ------         -----
DC1                            192.168.0.133 DC1:
VM1                            192.168.0.134 VM1:
DNS1              DNS Server   192.168.0.134 DNS1:
```

In PowerShell, parameters can be positional. This means that you can omit the parameter name if you put the parameter values in the right order. In the preceding example, the -Property parameter of the Select-Object cmdlet can be omitted. So the preceding command can also be written as:

```
PowerCLI C:\> Get-VM | Select-Object Name,Notes,VMHost,Guest
```

In the examples in this book, I will always use the parameter names.

Suppressing deprecated warnings

You will probably have also seen the following warning messages:

```
WARNING: The 'Description' property of VirtualMachine type is
deprecated. Use the 'Notes' property instead.
WARNING: The 'HardDisks' property of VirtualMachine type is
deprecated. Use 'Get-HardDisk' cmdlet instead.
WARNING: The 'NetworkAdapters' property of VirtualMachine type is
deprecated. Use 'Get-NetworkAdapter' cmdlet instead.
WARNING: The 'UsbDevices' property of VirtualMachine type is
deprecated. Use 'Get-UsbDevice' cmdlet instead.
WARNING: The 'CDDrives' property of VirtualMachine type is
deprecated. Use 'Get-CDDrive' cmdlet instead.
WARNING: The 'FloppyDrives' property of VirtualMachine type is
deprecated. Use 'Get-FloppyDrive' cmdlet instead.
WARNING: The 'Host' property of VirtualMachine type is deprecated.
Use the 'VMHost' property instead.
WARNING: The 'HostId' property of VirtualMachine type is deprecated.
Use the 'VMHostId' property instead.
WARNING: PowerCLI scripts should not use the 'Client' property. The
property will be removed in a future release.
```

These warning messages show the properties that should not be used in your scripts because they are deprecated and might be removed in a future PowerCLI release. Personally, I like these warnings because they remind me of the properties that I should not use anymore. But if you don't like these warnings, you can stop them from appearing with the following command:

```
PowerCLI C:\> Set-PowerCLIConfiguration -DisplayDeprecationWarnings
$false -Scope User
```

Using wildcard characters

You can also use **wildcard characters** to select specific virtual machines. To display only the virtual machines that have names that start with an A or a, type the following command:

```
PowerCLI C:\> Get-VM -Name A*
```

Parameter values are not case sensitive. The asterisk (*) is a wildcard character that matches zero or more characters, starting at the specified position. Another wildcard character is the question mark (?), which matches any character at the specified position. To get all virtual machines with a three-letter name that ends with e, use the following command:

```
PowerCLI C:\> Get-VM -Name ??e
```

You can also specify some specific characters, as shown in the following command:

```
PowerCLI C:\> Get-VM -Name [bc]*
```

The preceding command displays all of the virtual machines that have names starting with b or c. You can also specify a range of characters, as shown in the following command:

```
PowerCLI C:\> Get-VM -Name *[0-4]
```

The preceding command lists all of the virtual machines that have names ending with 0, 1, 2, 3, or 4.

Filtering objects

If you want to filter properties that don't have their own Get-VM parameter, you can pipe the output of the Get-VM cmdlet to the Where-Object cmdlet. Using the Where-Object cmdlet, you can set the filter on any property. Let's display a list of all of your virtual machines that have more than one virtual CPU using the following command:

```
PowerCLI C:\> Get-VM | Where-Object {$_.NumCPU -gt 1}
```

In this example, the Where-Object cmdlet has a PowerShell scriptblock as a parameter. A **scriptblock** is a PowerShell script surrounded by braces. In this scriptblock, you see $_. When using commands in the pipeline, $_ represents the current object. In the preceding example, $_ represents the virtual machine object that is passed through the pipeline. $_.NumCPU is the NumCPU property of the current virtual machine in the pipeline. -gt means greater than, so the preceding command shows all virtual machines' objects where the NumCPU property has a value greater than 1.

PowerShell V3 introduced a new, easier syntax for the Where-Object cmdlet. You don't have to use a scriptblock anymore. You can now use the following command:

```
PowerCLI C:\> Get-VM | Where-Object NumCPU -gt 1
```

Isn't the preceding command much more like simple English?

 In the rest of this book, the PowerShell V2 syntax will be used by default because the V2 syntax will also work in PowerShell V3 and higher versions of PowerShell. If PowerShell V3 syntax is used anywhere, it will be specifically mentioned.

Using comparison operators

In the preceding section, *Filtering objects*, you saw an example of the -gt comparison operator. In the following table, we will show you all of the PowerShell comparison operators:

Operator	Description
-eq, -ceq, and -ieq	Equal to.
-ne, -cne, and -ine	Not equal to.
-gt, -cgt, and -igt	Greater than.
-ge, -cge, and -ige	Greater than or equal to.
-lt, -clt, and -ilt	Less than.
-le, -cle, and -ile	Less than or equal to.
-Like	Match using the wildcard character (*).
-NotLike	Does not match using the wildcard character (*).
-Match	Matches a string using regular expressions.
-NotMatch	Does not match a string. Uses regular expressions.
-Contains	Tells whether a collection of reference values includes a single test value.
-NotContains	Tells whether a collection of reference values does not include a single test value.
-In	Tells whether a test value appears in a collection of reference values.
-NotIn	Tells whether a test value does not appear in a collection of reference values.

In the preceding table, you see three different operators for some functions. So what is the difference? The `c` variant is case sensitive. The two-letter variant and the `i` variant are case-insensitive. The `i` variant is made to make it clear that you want to use the case insensitive operator.

Using aliases

The `Where-Object` cmdlet has two aliases: `?` and `where`. Therefore, both the following commands will display a list of all your virtual machines that have more than one virtual CPU:

```
PowerCLI C:\> Get-VM | ? {$_.NumCPU –gt 1}
```

```
PowerCLI C:\> Get-VM | Where NumCPU –gt 1
```

Using aliases will save you from the trouble of typing in the PowerCLI console. However, it is good practice to use the full cmdlet names when you write a script. This will make the script much more readable and easier to understand.

To see a list of all of the aliases that are defined for cmdlets, type the following command:

```
PowerCLI C:\> Get-Alias
```

You can create aliases using the `New-Alias` cmdlet. For example, to create an alias `childs` for the `Get-ChildItem` cmdlet, you can use the following command:

```
PowerCLI C:\> New-Alias –Name childs –Value Get-ChildItem
```

Retrieving a list of all of your hosts

Similar to the `Get-VM` cmdlet, which retrieves your virtual machines, is the `Get-VMHost` cmdlet, which displays your hosts. The `Get-VMHost` cmdlet has the following syntax. The first parameter set is the default:

```
Get-VMHost [[-Name] <String[]>] [-NoRecursion] [-Datastore
<StorageResource[]>] [-State <VMHostState[]>] [-Location
<VIContainer[]>]
[-Tag <Tag[]>] [-Server <VIServer[]>][<CommonParameters>]
```

The second parameter set is for retrieving hosts connected to specific distributed virtual switches:

```
Get-VMHost [[-Name] <String[]>] [-DistributedSwitch
<DistributedSwitch[]>] [-Tag <Tag[]>] [-Server <VIServer[]>]
[<CommonParameters>]
```

The third parameter set is for retrieving hosts by virtual machine or resource pool:

```
Get-VMHost [[-Name] <String[]>] [-NoRecursion] [-VM <VirtualMachine[]>]
[-ResourcePool <ResourcePool[]>] [-Datastore <StorageResource[]>]
[-Location <VIContainer[]>] [-Tag<Tag[]>] [-Server <VIServer[]>]
[<CommonParameters>]
```

The fourth parameter set is for retrieving hosts by ID:

```
Get-VMHost [-Server <VIServer[]>] -Id <String[]> [<CommonParameters>]
```

The -Id parameter is required. The fifth parameter set is for retrieving hosts by related object:

```
Get-VMHost [-RelatedObject] <VMHostRelatedObjectBase[]>
[<CommonParameters>]
```

The -RelatedObject parameter is required.

Don't mix parameters from different sets or you will get an error as follows:

```
PowerCLI C:\> Get-VMHost -Id HostSystem-host-22 -Name 192.168.0.133
Get-VMHost : Parameter set cannot be resolved using the specified named
parameters.
At line:1 char:1
+ Get-VMHost -Id HostSystem-host-22 -Name 192.168.0.133
+ ~~~~~~~~~~~~~~~~~~~~~~~~~~~~~~~~~~~~~~~~~~~~~~~~~~~~~~~
    + CategoryInfo          : InvalidArgument: (:) [Get-VMHost],
                              ParameterBindingException
    + FullyQualifiedErrorId : AmbiguousParameterSet,
                              VMware.VimAutomation
                              .ViCore.Cmdlets.Commands.GetVMHost
```

To get a list of all of your hosts, type the following command:

```
PowerCLI C:\> Get-VMHost
```

By default, only the Name, ConnectionState, PowerState, NumCPU, CpuUsageMhz, CpuTotalMhz, MemoryUsageGB, MemoryTotalGB, and Version properties are shown. To get a list of all of the properties, type the following command:

```
PowerCLI C:\> Get-VMHost | Format-List -Property *
```

The output of this command can be seen in the following screenshot:

You can use the `Get-VMHost` parameters or the `Where-Object` cmdlet to filter the hosts you want to display, as we did with the `Get-VM` cmdlet.

Displaying the output in a grid view

Instead of displaying the output of your PowerCLI commands in the PowerCLI console, you can also display the output in a grid view. A grid view is a popup that looks like a spreadsheet with rows and columns. To display the output of the `Get-VMHost` cmdlet in a grid view, type the following command:

```
PowerCLI C:\> Get-VMHost | Out-GridView
```

The preceding command opens the window of the following screenshot:

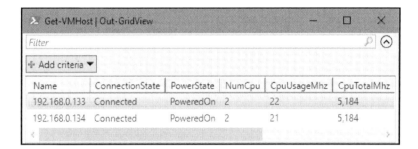

You can create filters to display only certain rows, and you can sort columns by clicking on the column header. You can also reorder columns by dragging and dropping them. In the following screenshot, we created a filter to show only the hosts with a **CpuUsageMhz** value greater than or equal to **22**. We also changed the order of the **ConnectionState** and **PowerState** columns.

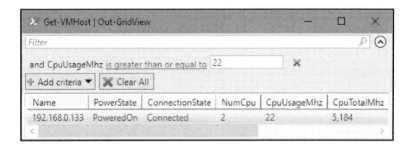

Isn't that cool?

Summary

In this chapter, we looked at downloading and installing PowerCLI, participating in the VMware CEIP, and modifying the PowerShell execution policy to be able to start PowerCLI. You learned to create a PowerShell profile containing commands that run every time you start PowerShell or PowerCLI. We showed you how to connect to and disconnect from a server and introduced the credential store to save you from having to specify credentials when you connect to a server. You also learned how to get a list of your virtual machines or hosts and how to stop deprecated warnings. You learned to filter objects by using the PowerShell comparison operators and found out about aliases for cmdlets. Finally, we concluded the chapter with grid views.

In the next chapter, we will introduce some basic PowerCLI concepts.

2
Learning Basic PowerCLI Concepts

While learning something new, you always have to learn the basics first. In this chapter, you will learn some basic PowerShell and PowerCLI concepts. Knowing these concepts will make it easier for you to learn the advanced topics. We will cover the following topics in this chapter:

- Using the `Get-Command`, `Get-Help`, and `Get-Member` cmdlets
- Using providers and PSdrives
- Using arrays and hash tables
- Creating calculated properties
- Using raw API objects with `ExtensionData` or `Get-View`
- Extending PowerCLI objects with the `New-VIProperty` cmdlet
- Working with vSphere folders

Using the Get-Command, Get-Help, and Get-Member cmdlets

There are some PowerShell cmdlets that everyone should know. Knowing these cmdlets will help you discover other cmdlets, their functions, parameters, and returned objects.

Using Get-Command

The first cmdlet that you should know is `Get-Command`. This cmdlet returns all the commands that are installed on your computer. The `Get-Command` cmdlet has the following syntax. The first parameter set is named `CmdletSet`:

```
Get-Command [[-Name] <String[]>] [[-ArgumentList] <Object[]>] [-All] [-
CommandType {Alias | Function | Filter | Cmdlet | ExternalScript |
Application | Script | Workflow | Configuration | All}] [-
FullyQualifiedModule <ModuleSpecification[]>] [-ListImported] [-Module
<String[]>] [-ParameterName <String[]>] [-ParameterType <PSTypeName[]>] [-
ShowCommandInfo] [-Syntax] [-TotalCount <Int32>] [<CommonParameters>]
```

The second parameter set is named `AllCommandSet`:

```
Get-Command [[-ArgumentList] <Object[]>] [-All] [-FullyQualifiedModule
<ModuleSpecification[]>] [-ListImported] [-Module <String[]>] [-Noun
<String[]>] [-ParameterName <String[]>] [-ParameterType <PSTypeName[]>] [-
ShowCommandInfo] [-Syntax] [-TotalCount <Int32>] [-Verb <String[]>]
[<CommonParameters>]
```

If you type the following command, you will get a list of commands installed on your computer, including cmdlets, aliases, functions, workflows, filters, scripts, and applications:

```
PowerCLI C:\> Get-Command
```

You can also specify the name of a specific cmdlet to get information about that cmdlet, as shown in the following command:

```
PowerCLI C:\> Get-Command -Name Get-VM | Format-Table -AutoSize
```

The preceding command returns the following information about the `Get-VM` cmdlet:

```
CommandType Name    Version       Source
----------- ----    -------       ------
Cmdlet      Get-VM  6.5.0.2604913 VMware.VimAutomation.Core
```

You see that the command returns the command type and the name of the module that contains the `Get-VM` cmdlet. `CommandType`, `Name`, `Version`, and `Source` are the properties that the `Get-Command` cmdlet returns by default. You will get more properties if you pipe the output to the `Format-List` cmdlet. The following screenshot will show you the output of the `Get-Command -Name Get-VM | Format-List *` command:

```
VMware PowerCLI 6.5 Release 1 build 4624819                    —    □    ×

PowerCLI C:\> Get-Command -Name Get-VM | Format-List *


HelpUri                 : http://www.vmware.com/support/developer/PowerC
                          LI/PowerCLI65R1/html/Get-VM.html
DLL                     : C:\Program Files (x86)\VMware\Infrastructure\P
                          owerCLI\Modules\VMware.VimAutomation.Core\VMwa
                          re.VimAutomation.ViCore.Cmdlets.dll
Verb                    : Get
Noun                    : VM
HelpFile                : C:\Program Files (x86)\VMware\Infrastructure\P
                          owerCLI\Modules\VMware.VimAutomation.Core\VMwa
                          re.VimAutomation.ViCore.Cmdlets.dll-Help.xml
PSSnapIn                :
Version                 : 6.5.0.2604913
ImplementingType        : VMware.VimAutomation.ViCore.Cmdlets.Commands.G
                          etVM
Definition              :
                          Get-VM [[-Name] <string[]>] [-Server
                          <VIServer[]>] [-Datastore
                          <StorageResource[]>] [-Location
                          <VIContainer[]>] [-Tag <Tag[]>]
                          [-NoRecursion] [<CommonParameters>]

                          Get-VM [[-Name] <string[]>] [-Server
                          <VIServer[]>] [-VirtualSwitch
                          <VirtualSwitchBase[]>] [-Tag <Tag[]>]
                          [<CommonParameters>]

                          Get-VM [-Server <VIServer[]>] [-Id
                          <string[]>] [<CommonParameters>]

                          Get-VM -RelatedObject <VmRelatedObjectBase[]>
                          [<CommonParameters>]

DefaultParameterSet     : Default
OutputType              : {VMware.VimAutomation.ViCore.Types.V1.Inventor
                          y.VirtualMachine}
Options                 : ReadOnly
Name                    : Get-VM
CommandType             : Cmdlet
Source                  : VMware.VimAutomation.Core
Visibility              : Public
ModuleName              : VMware.VimAutomation.Core
Module                  : VMware.VimAutomation.Core
RemotingCapability      : PowerShell
Parameters              : {[Name, System.Management.Automation.Parameter
                          Metadata], [Server, System.Management.Automati
                          on.ParameterMetadata], [Datastore, System.Mana
                          gement.Automation.ParameterMetadata],
                          [VirtualSwitch, System.Management.Automation.P
                          arameterMetadata]...}
ParameterSets           : {[[-Name] <string[]>] [-Server <VIServer[]>]
                          [-Datastore <StorageResource[]>] [-Location
                          <VIContainer[]>] [-Tag <Tag[]>]
                          [-NoRecursion] [<CommonParameters>], [[-Name]
                          <string[]>] [-Server <VIServer[]>]
                          [-VirtualSwitch <VirtualSwitchBase[]>] [-Tag
                          <Tag[]>] [<CommonParameters>], [-Server
                          <VIServer[]>] [-Id <string[]>]
                          [<CommonParameters>], -RelatedObject
                          <VmRelatedObjectBase[]> [<CommonParameters>]}
```

You can use the Get-Command cmdlet to search for cmdlets. For example, if necessary, search for the cmdlets that are used for vSphere hosts. Type the following command:

```
PowerCLI C:\> Get-Command -Name *VMHost*
```

If you are searching for the cmdlets to work with networks, use the following command:

```
PowerCLI C:\> Get-Command -Name *network*
```

Using Get-VICommand

PowerCLI has a Get-VICommand cmdlet that is similar to the Get-Command cmdlet. The Get-VICommand cmdlet is a function that creates a filter on the Get-Command output, and it returns only PowerCLI commands. Type the following command to list all the PowerCLI commands:

```
PowerCLI C:\> Get-VICommand
```

The Get-VICommand cmdlet has only one parameter -Name. So, you can also type, for example, the following command to get information only about the Get-VM cmdlet:

```
PowerCLI C:\> Get-VICommand -Name Get-VM
```

Using Get-Help

To discover more information about cmdlets, you can use the Get-Help cmdlet. For example:

```
PowerCLI C:\> Get-Help Get-VM
```

This will display the following information about the `Get-VM` cmdlet:

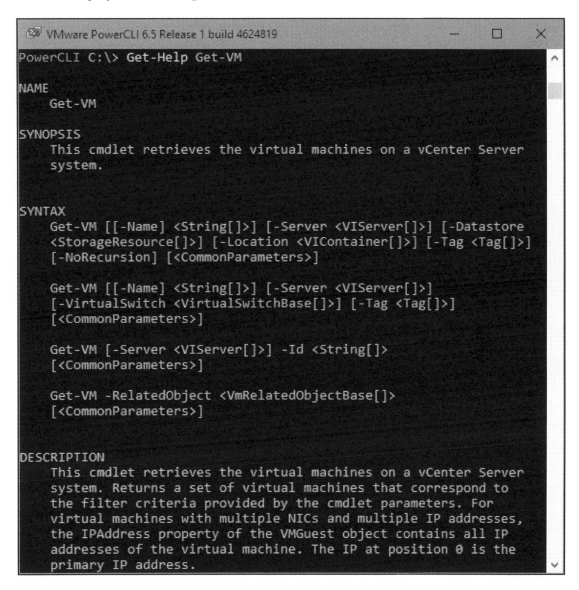

The Get-Help cmdlet has some parameters that you can use to get more information. The -Examples parameter shows examples of the cmdlet. The -Detailed parameter adds parameter descriptions and examples to the basic help display. The -Full parameter displays all the information available about the cmdlet. And the -Online parameter retrieves online help information available about the cmdlet and displays it in a web browser. Since PowerShell V3, there is a new Get-Help parameter -ShowWindow. This displays the output of Get-Help in a new window. The Get-Help -ShowWindow command opens the window in the following screenshot:

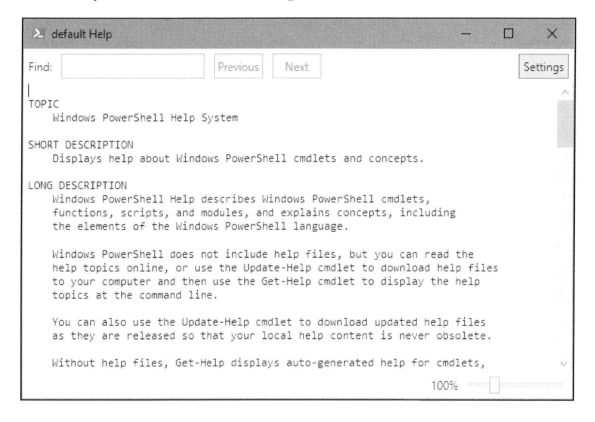

Using Get-PowerCLIHelp

The PowerCLI `Get-PowerCLIHelp` cmdlet opens the **VMware PowerCLI Documentation** website in a browser. You can find the PowerCLI documentation at the following URL: `htt ps://www.vmware.com/support/developer/PowerCLI/`. You will have access to the **Release Notes, User's Guide**, and the **Cmdlet Reference | Previous HTML interface**. The following screenshot shows the window opened by the `Get-PowerCLIHelp` cmdlet:

Support > Documentation

VMware PowerCLI Documentation

Community | Technical Papers | Knowledge Base | SDK Support

 Visit the vSphere 6.5 Documentation Center to learn more about VMware products.

Select a release: PowerCLI 6.5 Release 1 ▼

VMware PowerCLI 6.5 Release 1

Released 17 NOV 2016 | Download | Change Log

Documentation Resources:

Release Notes
User's Guide (pdf 🗋)
Cmdlet Reference | Previous HTML interface

Using Get-PowerCLICommunity

If you have a question about PowerCLI and you cannot find the answer in this book, use the `Get-PowerCLICommunity` cmdlet to open the VMware PowerCLI section of the VMware VMTN Communities. You can log in to the VMware VMTN Communities using the same **My VMware** account that you used to download PowerCLI. First, search the community for an answer to your question. If you still cannot find the answer, go to the **Discussions** tab and ask your question by clicking on the **Start a Discussion** button, as shown later. You might receive an answer to your question in a few minutes.

Using Get-Member

In PowerCLI, you work with objects. Even a string is an object. An object contains properties and methods, which are called members in PowerShell. To see which members an object contains, you can use the `Get-Member` cmdlet. To see the members of a string, type the following command:

```
PowerCLI C:\> "Learning PowerCLI" | Get-Member
```

Pipe an instance of a PowerCLI object to `Get-Member` to retrieve the members of that PowerCLI object. For example, to see the members of a virtual machine object, you can use the following command:

```
PowerCLI C:\> Get-VM | Get-Member
```

The preceding command returns the following output:

```
    TypeName:
VMware.VimAutomation.ViCore.Impl.V1.VM.UniversalVirtualMachineImpl

Name                     MemberType Definition
----                     ---------- ----------
ConvertToVersion         Method     T VersionedObjectInterop.Conve...
Equals                   Method     bool Equals(System.Object obj)
GetConnectionParameters  Method     VMware.VimAutomation.ViCore.In...
GetHashCode              Method     int GetHashCode()
GetType                  Method     type GetType()
IsConvertableTo          Method     bool VersionedObjectInterop.Is...
LockUpdates              Method     void ExtensionData.LockUpdates()
ObtainExportLease        Method     VMware.Vim.ManagedObjectRefere...
```

```
ToString                     Method       string ToString()
UnlockUpdates                Method       void ExtensionData.UnlockUpdat...
Client                       Property     VMware.VimAutomation.ViCore.In...
CoresPerSocket               Property     int CoresPerSocket {get;}
CustomFields                 Property     System.Collections.Generic.IDi...
DatastoreIdList              Property     string[] DatastoreIdList {get;}
DrsAutomationLevel           Property     System.Nullable[VMware.VimAuto...
ExtensionData                Property     System.Object ExtensionData {g...
Folder                       Property     VMware.VimAutomation.ViCore.Ty...
FolderId                     Property     string FolderId {get;}
Guest                        Property     VMware.VimAutomation.ViCore.Ty...
GuestId                      Property     string GuestId {get;}
HAIsolationResponse          Property     System.Nullable[VMware.VimAuto...
HARestartPriority            Property     System.Nullable[VMware.VimAuto...
Id                           Property     string Id {get;}
MemoryGB                     Property     decimal MemoryGB {get;}
MemoryMB                     Property     decimal MemoryMB {get;}
Name                         Property     string Name {get;}
Notes                        Property     string Notes {get;}
NumCpu                       Property     int NumCpu {get;}
PersistentId                 Property     string PersistentId {get;}
PowerState                   Property     VMware.VimAutomation.ViCore.Ty...
ProvisionedSpaceGB           Property     decimal ProvisionedSpaceGB {get;}
ResourcePool                 Property     VMware.VimAutomation.ViCore.Ty...
ResourcePoolId               Property     string ResourcePoolId {get;}
Uid                          Property     string Uid {get;}
UsedSpaceGB                  Property     decimal UsedSpaceGB {get;}
VApp                         Property     VMware.VimAutomation.ViCore.Ty...
Version                      Property     VMware.VimAutomation.ViCore.Ty...
VMHost                       Property     VMware.VimAutomation.ViCore.Ty...
VMHostId                     Property     string VMHostId {get;}
VMResourceConfiguration Property         VMware.VimAutomation.ViCore.Ty...
VMSwapfilePolicy             Property     System.Nullable[VMware.VimAuto...
```

The command returns the full type name of the `VirtualMachineImpl` object and all its methods and properties.

 Remember that the properties are objects themselves. You can also use `Get-Member` to get the members of the properties. For example, the following command line will give you the members of the `VMGuestImpl` object:

```
PowerCLI C:\> $VM = Get-VM -Name vCenter
PowerCLI C:\> $VM.Guest | Get-Member
```

Using providers and PSDrives

Until now, you have only seen cmdlets. Cmdlets are PowerShell commands. PowerShell has another import concept named **providers**. Providers are accessed through named drives or **PSDrives**. In the following sections, *Using providers* and *Using PSDrives*, providers and PSDrives will be explained.

Using providers

A PowerShell provider is a piece of software that makes datastores look like filesystems. PowerShell providers are usually part of a snap-in or a module-like PowerCLI. The advantage of providers is that you can use the same cmdlets for all the providers. These cmdlets have the following nouns: `Item`, `ChildItem`, `Content`, and `ItemProperty`. You can use the `Get-Command` cmdlet to get a list of all the cmdlets with these nouns:

```
PowerCLI C:> Get-Command -Noun Item,ChildItem,Content,ItemProperty |
Format-Table -AutoSize
```

The preceding command gives the following output:

```
CommandType Name                  Version Source
----------- ----                  ------- ------
Cmdlet      Add-Content           3.1.0.0 Microsoft.PowerShell.Mana...
Cmdlet      Clear-Content         3.1.0.0 Microsoft.PowerShell.Mana...
Cmdlet      Clear-Item            3.1.0.0 Microsoft.PowerShell.Mana...
Cmdlet      Clear-ItemProperty    3.1.0.0 Microsoft.PowerShell.Mana...
Cmdlet      Copy-Item             3.1.0.0 Microsoft.PowerShell.Mana...
Cmdlet      Copy-ItemProperty     3.1.0.0 Microsoft.PowerShell.Mana...
Cmdlet      Get-ChildItem         3.1.0.0 Microsoft.PowerShell.Mana...
Cmdlet      Get-Content           3.1.0.0 Microsoft.PowerShell.Mana...
Cmdlet      Get-Item              3.1.0.0 Microsoft.PowerShell.Mana...
Cmdlet      Get-ItemProperty      3.1.0.0 Microsoft.PowerShell.Mana...
Cmdlet      Invoke-Item           3.1.0.0 Microsoft.PowerShell.Mana...
Cmdlet      Move-Item             3.1.0.0 Microsoft.PowerShell.Mana...
Cmdlet      Move-ItemProperty     3.1.0.0 Microsoft.PowerShell.Mana...
Cmdlet      New-Item              3.1.0.0 Microsoft.PowerShell.Mana...
Cmdlet      New-ItemProperty      3.1.0.0 Microsoft.PowerShell.Mana...
Cmdlet      Remove-Item           3.1.0.0 Microsoft.PowerShell.Mana...
Cmdlet      Remove-ItemProperty   3.1.0.0 Microsoft.PowerShell.Mana...
Cmdlet      Rename-Item           3.1.0.0 Microsoft.PowerShell.Mana...
Cmdlet      Rename-ItemProperty   3.1.0.0 Microsoft.PowerShell.Mana...
Cmdlet      Set-Content           3.1.0.0 Microsoft.PowerShell.Mana...
Cmdlet      Set-Item              3.1.0.0 Microsoft.PowerShell.Mana...
Cmdlet      Set-ItemProperty      3.1.0.0 Microsoft.PowerShell.Mana...
```

To display a list of all the providers in your PowerCLI session, you can use the `Get-PSProvider` cmdlet:

```
PowerCLI C:\> Get-PSProvider
Name            Capabilities                         Drives
----            ------------                         ------
Alias           ShouldProcess                        {Alias}
Environment     ShouldProcess                        {Env}
FileSystem      Filter, ShouldProcess, Credentials   {C, A, D, Z}
Function        ShouldProcess                        {Function}
Registry        ShouldProcess, Transactions          {HKLM, HKCU}
Variable        ShouldProcess                        {Variable}
VimDatastore    Filter, ShouldProcess                {vmstores, vmstore}
VimInventory    None                                 {vis, vi}
```

The `VimDatastore` and `VimInventory` providers are part of PowerCLI. You will soon learn more about the `VimDatastore` and `VimInventory` providers.

Using PSDrives

Each provider has one or more drives. For example, the `FileSystem` provider has drives named `C`, `A`, `D`, and `Z`, which are hard disks on my PC. You can use the drives to access the providers. Microsoft calls these drives PSDrives to prevent confusing the drives with physical drives in your computer. For instance, to get a listing of all the files and folders in the root of `C:` on your PC, type the following command:

```
PowerCLI C:\> Get-ChildItem C:\
```

The `Get-ChildItem` cmdlet has aliases `dir`, `gci` and `ls` that give you the same result:

```
PowerCLI C:\> dir C:\
PowerCLI C:\> ls C:\
```

You can use the same `Get-ChildItem` cmdlet to get a list of all your cmdlet aliases by typing the following command:

```
PowerCLI C:\> Get-ChildItem alias:
```

The `Registry` PSDrive can be used to browse through the registry on your PC. The following command will list all the keys and values in the `HKEY_LOCAL_MACHINE\SOFTWARE` registry hive:

```
PowerCLI C:\> Get-ChildItem HKLM:\SOFTWARE
```

Using the PowerCLI Inventory Provider

The **Inventory Provider** gives you a filesystem-like view of the inventory items from a vCenter Server or an ESXi server. You can use this provider to view, move, rename, or delete objects by running PowerCLI commands.

When you connect to a server with the `Connect-VIServer` cmdlet, two PSDrives are created: `vi` and `vis`. The `vi` PSDrive contains the inventory of the last connected server. The `vis` PSDrive contains the inventory of all currently connected servers in your PowerCLI session.

You can set the location to the `vis` PSDrive using the `Set-Location` cmdlet:

```
PowerCLI C:\> Set-Location vis:
PowerCLI vis:\>
```

Use the `Get-ChildItem` cmdlet to display the items in the current location of the `vis` PSDrive:

```
PowerCLI vis:\> Get-ChildItem
Name                Type       Id
----                ----       --
192.168.0.132@443   VIServer    /VIServer=vsphere.local\administrator@...
```

Use the `Get-ChildItem -Recurse` parameter to display all the items in the Inventory Provider:

```
PowerCLI vis:\> Get-ChildItem -Recurse
```

Using the PowerCLI Datastore Provider

The Datastore Provider gives you access to the content of your vSphere datastores.

When you connect to a server with the `Connect-VIServer` cmdlet, two PSDrives are created: `vmstore` and `vmstores`. The `vmstore` PSDrive contains the datastores of the last connected server. The `vmstores` PSDrive contains the datastores of all the currently connected servers in your PowerCLI session. You can use these two default PSDrives or you can create custom PSDrives using the `New-PSDrive` cmdlet.

Set the location to the `vmstore` PSDrive with the following command:

```
PowerCLI C:\> Set-Location vmstore:
PowerCLI vmstore:\>
```

Display the content of the root directory of the `vmstore` PSDrive with the following command:

```
PowerCLI vmstore:\> Get-ChildItem
Name      Type       Id
----      ----       --
New York Datacenter Datacenter-datacenter-2
```

You can also create a custom PSDrive for a datastore using the `New-PSDrive` cmdlet. Start with getting a datastore object and save it in the `$Datastore` variable:

```
PowerCLI C:\> $Datastore = Get-Datastore -Name Datastore1
```

Create a new PowerShell PSDrive named `ds`, which maps to the `$Datastore` variable:

```
PowerCLI C:\> New-PSDrive -Location $Datastore -Name ds -PSProvider
VimDatastore -Root ""
```

Now, you can change your location into the PowerShell PSDrive using the `Set-Location` cmdlet:

```
PowerCLI C:\> Set-Location ds:
```

You can get a listing of the files and directories on the datastore using the `Get-ChildItem` cmdlet:

```
PowerCLI ds:\> Get-ChildItem
```

You will see an output similar to the following:

```
Name                            Type                    Id
----                            ----                    --
DC1                             DatastoreFolder
.sdd.sf                         DatastoreFolder
```

Copying files between a datastore and your PC

You can use the vSphere Datastore Provider to copy files between a datastore and your PC using the `Copy-DatastoreItem` cmdlet.

Change the location to a subfolder using the `Set-Location` cmdlet with the help of the following command line:

```
PowerCLI ds:\> Set-Location "virtualmachine1"
```

Copy a file or directory to the destination using the `Copy-DatastoreItem` cmdlet, as follows:

```
PowerCLI ds:\virtualmachine1> Copy-DatastoreItem -Item
ds:\virtualmachine1\virtualmachine1.vmx -Destination $env:USERPROFILE
```

Now, you can view the content of the `virtualmachine1.vmx` file with the following command:

```
PowerCLI C:\> Get-Content $env:USERPROFILE\virtualmachine1.vmx
```

`$env:USERPROFILE` is the path to your user profile, for example, `C:\users\username`.

> Files cannot be copied directly between vSphere datastores in different vCenter Servers using `Copy-DatastoreItem`. Copy the files to the PowerCLI host's local filesystem temporarily and then copy them to the destination.

Using arrays and hash tables

In PowerCLI, you can create a list of objects. For example, `red`, `white`, and `blue` is a list of strings. In PowerShell, a list of terms is named an **array**. An array can have zero or more objects. You can create an empty array and assign it to a variable:

```
PowerCLI C:\> $Array = @()
```

You can fill the array during creation using the following command line:

```
PowerCLI C:\> $Array = @("red","white")
```

You can use the `+=` operator to add an element to an array:

```
PowerCLI C:\> $Array += "blue"
PowerCLI C:\> $Array
red
white
blue
```

If you want to retrieve a specific element of an array, you can use an index starting with 0 for the first element, 1 for the second element, and so on. If you want to retrieve an element from the tail of the array, you have to use −1 for the last element, −2 for the second to last, and so on. You have to use square brackets around the index number. In the next example, the first element of the array is retrieved using the following command line:

```
PowerCLI C:\> $Array[0]
Red
```

If you want to test if an object is an array, you can use the following command:

```
PowerCLI C:\> $Array -is [array]
True
```

There is a different kind of an array called a **hash table**. In a hash table, you map a set of keys to a set of values. You can create an empty hash table using the following command line:

```
PowerCLI C:\> $HashTable = @{}
```

You can fill the hash table during creation using the following command line:

```
PowerCLI C:\> $HashTable = @{LastName='Doe';FirstName='John'}
```

To add a key-value pair to a hash table, you can use the following command line:

```
PowerCLI C:\> $HashTable["Company"]='VMware'
```

To show the contents of the hash table, just display the variable:

```
PowerCLI C:\> $HashTable
Name                        Value
----                        -----
Company                     VMware
FirstName                   John
LastName                    Doe
```

If you want to retrieve a specific key-value pair, you can use the following command:

```
PowerCLI C:\> $HashTable["FirstName"]
John
```

To retrieve all of the hash table's keys, you can use the `Keys` property:

```
PowerCLI C:\> $HashTable.Keys
Company
FirstName
LastName
```

To retrieve all the values in the hash table, you can use the `Values` property:

```
PowerCLI C:\> $HashTable.Values
VMware
John
Doe
```

If you want to test whether an object is a hash table, you can use the following command:

```
PowerCLI C:\> $HashTable -is [hashtable]
True
```

In the next section, hash tables will be used to create calculated properties.

Creating calculated properties

You can use the `Select-Object` cmdlet to select certain properties of the objects that you want to return. For example, you can use the following code to return the name and the used space, in GB, of your virtual machines:

```
PowerCLI C:\> Get-VM | Select-Object -Property Name,UsedSpaceGB
```

But what if you want to return the used space in MB? The PowerCLI `VirtualMachineImpl` object has no `UsedSpaceMB` property. This is where you can use a **calculated property**. A calculated property is a PowerShell hash table with two elements: `Name` and `Expression`. The `Name` element contains the name that you want to give the calculated property. The `Expression` element contains a scriptblock with PowerCLI code to calculate the value of the property. To return the name and the used space in MB for all your virtual machines, run the following command:

```
PowerCLI C:\> Get-VM |
>> Select-Object -Property Name,
>> @{Name="UsedSpaceMB";Expression={1KB*$_.UsedSpaceGB}}
>>
```

The hash table contains two key-value pairs:

- In the first element, the key is `Name` and the value is `UsedSpaceMB`
- In the other element, the key is `Expression`, and the value is `{1KB*$_.UsedSpaceGB}`

The special variable `$_` is used to represent the current object in the pipeline. `1KB` is a PowerShell constant that has the value `1024`. In calculated properties, you can abbreviate the `Name` and `Expression` names to `N` and `E`.

Another example of a calculated property shows you how to return the aliases of all the cmdlets that are the same for all the providers:

```
PowerCLI C:\> Get-Command -Noun Item,ChildItem,Content,ItemProperty |
>> Select-Object -Property Name,
>> @{Name="Aliases";Expression={Get-Alias -Definition $_.Name}}
>>

Name                    Aliases
----                    -------
Add-Content             ac
Clear-Content           clc
Clear-Item              cli
Clear-ItemProperty      clp
Copy-Item               {copy, cp, cpi}
Copy-ItemProperty       cpp
Get-ChildItem           {dir, gci, ls}
Get-Content             {cat, gc, type}
Get-Item                gi
Get-ItemProperty        gp
Invoke-Item             ii
Move-Item               {mi, move, mv}
Move-ItemProperty       mp
New-Item                ni
New-ItemProperty
Remove-Item             {del, erase, rd, ri...}
Remove-ItemProperty     rp
Rename-Item             {ren, rni}
Rename-ItemProperty     rnp
Set-Content             sc
Set-Item                si
Set-ItemProperty        sp
```

The first command is the `Get-Command` statement that you have seen before; this returns the cmdlets that are the same for all the providers. In the calculated property, the `Get-Alias` cmdlet is used to get the aliases of these commands.

Using raw API objects with ExtensionData or Get-View

PowerCLI makes it easy to use the VMware vSphere **application programming interface (API)**. There are two ways to do this. The first one is by using the `ExtensionData` property that most of the PowerCLI objects have. The `ExtensionData` property is a direct link to the vSphere API object related to the PowerCLI object. The second way is by using the `Get-View` cmdlet to retrieve the vSphere API object related to a PowerCLI object. Both these ways will be discussed in the following sections.

Using the ExtensionData property

Most PowerCLI objects, such as `VirtualMachineImpl` and `VMHostImpl`, have a property named `ExtensionData`. This property is a reference to a view of a VMware vSphere object as described in the *VMware vSphere API Reference* documentation. For example, the `ExtensionData` property of the PowerCLI's `VirtualMachineImpl` object links to a vSphere `VirtualMachine` object view. `ExtensionData` is a very powerful property because it allows you to use all the properties and methods of the VMware vSphere API. For example, to check whether the VMware Tools are running in your virtual machines, you can run the following command:

```
PowerCLI C:\> Get-VM |
>> Select-Object -Property Name,
>> @{Name = "ToolsRunningStatus";
>>    Expression = {$_.ExtensionData.Guest.ToolsRunningStatus}
>> }
>>
```

If VMware Tools are not installed in a virtual machine, the `ExtensionData.Guest.ToolsStatus` property will have the value `toolsNotInstalled`. You can check the tool's status with the following command:

```
PowerCLI C:\> Get-VM |
>> Select-Object -Property Name,
>> @{Name = "ToolsStatus"
>>    Expression = {$_.ExtensionData.Guest.ToolsStatus}
```

```
>> }
>>
Name                                    ToolsStatus
----                                    -----------
VM1                                     toolsNotInstalled
DNS1                                             toolsOk
DC1                                     toolsNotRunning
WindowsServer2012                               toolsOld
```

Using the Get-View cmdlet

Another way to get the vSphere API objects is by using the `Get-View` cmdlet. This cmdlet returns a vSphere object view, which is the same object you can retrieve via the `ExtensionData` property. For example, the following two PowerCLI commands will give you the same result:

```
PowerCLI C:\> (Get-VM –Name vCenter).ExtensionData
PowerCLI C:\> Get-VIew -VIObject (Get-VM –Name vCenter)
```

The `Get-View` cmdlet has the following syntax:

```
Get-View [-VIObject] <VIObject[]> [-Property <String[]>]
[<CommonParameters>]
Get-View [-Server <VIServer[]>] [-Id] <ManagedObjectReference[]>
[-Property <String[]>] [<CommonParameters>]
Get-View [-Server <VIServer[]>] [-SearchRoot <ManagedObjectReference>]
-ViewType <Type> [-Filter <Hashtable>] [-Property <String[]>]
[<CommonParameters>] Get-View [-Property <String[]>] -RelatedObject
<ViewBaseMirroredObject[]> [<CommonParameters>]
```

The names of the parameter sets are `GetViewByVIObject`, `GetView`, `GetEntity`, and `GetViewByRelatedObject`. The third parameter set, `GetEntity`, is very powerful and will allow you to create PowerCLI commands or scripts that are optimized for speed. For example, the following command will give you the vSphere object views of all virtual machines and templates:

```
PowerCLI C:\> Get-View –ViewType VirtualMachine
```

Possible argument values for the `-ViewType` parameter are `ClusterComputeResource`, `ComputeResource`, `Datacenter`, `Datastore`, `DistributedVirtualPortgroup`, `DistributedVirtualSwitch`, `Folder`, `HostSystem`, `Network`, `OpaqueNetwork`, `ResourcePool`, `StoragePod`, `VirtualApp`, `VirtualMachine`, and `VmwareDistributedVirtualSwitch`.

If you require only the virtual machines and not the templates, you need to specify a filter:

```
PowerCLI C:\> Get-View -ViewType VirtualMachine -Filter
@{" Config.Template" = "false"}
```

The filter is in the form of a hash table in which you specify that the value of the `Config.Template` property needs to be false to get only the virtual machines.

To make your command run faster, you need to specify the properties that you want to return. Otherwise, all the properties are returned, and it will make your command run slower.

Let's retrieve only the name and the overall status of your virtual machines:

```
PowerCLI C:\> Get-View -ViewType VirtualMachine -Filter
@{"Config.Template" = "false"} -Property Name,OverallStatus |
>> Select-Object -Property Name,OverAllStatus
>>
```

This command runs in my test environment about 23 times faster than the equivalent:

```
PowerCLI C:\> Get-VM | Select-Object -Property Name,
@{Name="OverallStatus";Expression={$_.ExtensionData.OverallStatus}}
```

The conclusion is if you need your script to run faster, try to find a solution using the `Get-View` cmdlet.

> You should always make a trade-off between the time it takes you to write a script and the time it takes you to run the script. If you spend 10 minutes to create a script that takes 1 hour to run, you will have your work done in 70 minutes. If you spend 2 hours to create a faster script that runs in 10 minutes, you will have your work done in 130 minutes. I would prefer the first solution. Of course, if you intend to run the script more than once, the time you spend to improve the speed of your script is spent better.

Using managed object references

If you look at a vSphere object view using the `Get-Member` cmdlet, you will see that a lot of properties are from the type `VMware.Vim.ManagedObjectReference`:

```
PowerCLI C:\> Get-VM -Name vCenter | Get-View | Get-Member |
>> Where-Object {$_.Name -eq 'Parent'}
>>

    TypeName: VMware.Vim.VirtualMachine
```

```
Name      MemberType  Definition
----      ----------  ----------
Parent    Property    VMware.Vim.ManagedObjectReference Parent {get;}
```

A **Managed Object Reference** (**MoRef**) is a unique value that is generated by the vCenter Server and is guaranteed to be unique for a given entity in a single vCenter instance.

 The vSphere object views returned by the `ExtensionData` property or the `Get-View` cmdlet are not the actual vSphere objects. The objects returned are copies or views of the actual objects that represent the actual objects at the time the view was made.

Using the Get-VIObjectByVIView cmdlet

The `Get-View` cmdlet gives you a way to go from a PowerCLI object to a vSphere object view. If you want to go back from a vSphere object view to a PowerCLI object, you can use the `Get-VIObjectByVIView` cmdlet. Take a look at the following example:

```
PowerCLI C:\> $VMView = Get-VM -Name vCenter | Get-View
PowerCLI C:\> $VM = $VMView | Get-VIObjectByVIView
```

In the preceding example, the first line will give you a vSphere object view from a PowerCLI `VirtualMachineImpl` object. The second line will convert the vSphere object view back to a PowerCLI `VirtualMachineImpl` object.

The `Get-VIObjectByVIView` cmdlet has the following syntax:

```
Get-VIObjectByVIView [-VIView] <ViewBase[]> [<CommonParameters>]
Get-VIObjectByVIView [-Server <VIServer[]>] [-MORef]
<ManagedObjectReference[]> [<CommonParameters>]
```

You can see that the `Get-VIObjectByVIView` cmdlet has two parameter sets. The first parameter set contains the `-VIView` parameter. The second parameter set contains the `-Server` and `-MORef` parameters.

 Remember that parameters from different parameter sets cannot be mixed in one command.

If you are connected to multiple vCenter Servers, the `Get-VIObjectByVIView` cmdlet might return objects from multiple vCenter Servers because MoRefs are only unique on a single vCenter Server instance. You can use the `-Server` parameter of the `Get-VIObjectByVIView` cmdlet to solve this problem by specifying the vCenter Server for which you want to return objects. Because the `-Server` parameter is in another parameter set and not in the `-VIView` parameter, you cannot use the `-VIView` parameter that is used in the pipeline. You have to use the `ForEach-Object` cmdlet and the `-MORef` parameter of the `Get-VIObjectByVIView` cmdlet:

```
PowerCLI C:\> $VMView |
>> ForEach-Object {
>>    Get-VIObjectByVIView -Server vCenter1 -MoRef $_.MoRef
>> }
>>
```

In the name of the `Get-VIObjectByVIView` cmdlet, you can see a piece of the history of PowerCLI. VMware vSphere was named VMware Infrastructure before VMware vSphere 4. The earlier VMware PowerCLI versions were named VI Toolkit. In the name of this cmdlet, you see that a PowerCLI object is still named a `VIObject` and a vSphere object view is named a `VIView`.

Extending PowerCLI objects with the New-VIProperty cmdlet

Sometimes, you can have the feeling that a PowerCLI object is missing a property. Although the VMware PowerCLI team tried to include the most useful properties in the objects, you can have the need for an extra property. Luckily, PowerCLI has a way to extend a PowerCLI object using the `New-VIProperty` cmdlet. This cmdlet has the following syntax:

```
New-VIProperty [-Name] <String> [-ObjectType] <String[]> [-Value]
<ScriptBlock> [-Force] [-BasedOnExtensionProperty <String[]>] [-WhatIf]
[-Confirm] [<CommonParameters>]
New-VIProperty [-Name] <String> [-ObjectType] <String[]> [-Force]
[-ValueFromExtensionProperty] <String> [-WhatIf] [-Confirm]
[<CommonParameters>]
```

Let's start with an example. You will add the VMware Tools' running statuses used in a previous example to the `VirtualMachineImpl` object using the `New-VIProperty` cmdlet:

```
PowerCLI C:\> New-VIProperty -ObjectType VirtualMachine -Name
ToolsRunningStatus -ValueFromExtensionProperty
```

```
'Guest.ToolsRunningStatus'

Name                 RetrievingType DeclaringType  Value
----                 -------------- -------------  -----
ToolsRunning... VirtualMachine VirtualMachine Guest.ToolsRunningStatus
```

Now you can get the tools' running statuses of all of your virtual machines with the following command:

```
PowerCLI C:\> Get-VM | Select-Object -Property Name, ToolsRunningStatus
```

Isn't this much easier?

In the next example, you will add the vCenterServer property to the VirtualMachineImpl object. The name of the vCenter Server is part of the VirtualMachineImpl Uid property. The Uid property is a string that looks like /VIServer=domain\account@vCenter:443/VirtualMachine=VirtualMachine-vm-239/.

You can use the Split() method to split the string. For example, the following command splits the string 192.168.0.1 at the dots into an array with four elements:

```
PowerCLI C:\> "192.168.0.1".Split('.')
192
168
0
1
```

The first element is 192, the second element is 168, the third element is 0, and the fourth and last element is 1. If you assign the array to a variable, then you can use an index to specify a certain element of the array:

```
PowerCLI C:\> $Array = "192.168.0.1".Split('.')
```

The index is 0 for the first element, 1 for the second element, and so on. If you want to specify the last element of the array, you can use the index –1. Take a look at the following example:

```
PowerCLI C:\> $Array[0]
192
```

In the `Uid` property, the name of the vCenter Server is between the @ sign and the colon. So, you can use those two characters to split the string. First, you split the string at the colon and take the part before the colon. That is the first element of the resulting array:

```
PowerCLI C:\> $Uid =
'/VIServer=domain\account@vCenter:443/VirtualMachine=
VirtualMachine-vm-239/'
PowerCLI C:\> $Uid.Split(':')[0]
/VIServer=domain\account@vCenter
```

Split the resulting part at the @ sign and take the second element of the resulting array to get the name of the vCenter Server:

```
PowerCLI C:\> $String = '/VIServer=domain\account@vCenter'
PowerCLI C:\> $String.Split('@')[1]
vCenter
```

You can do this splitting with one line of code:

```
PowerCLI C:\> $Uid =
'/VIServer=domain\account@vCenter:443/VirtualMachine=
VirtualMachine-vm-239/'
PowerCLI C:\> $Uid.Split(':')[0].Split('@')[1]
vCenter
```

Use the `-Value` parameter of the `New-VIProperty` cmdlet to specify a scriptblock. In this scriptblock, `$Args[0]` is the object with which you want to retrieve the name of the vCenter Server:

```
PowerCLI C:\> New-VIProperty -Name vCenterServer -ObjectType
VirtualMachine -Value {$Args[0].Uid.Split(":")[0].Split("@")[1]} -Force
```

The `New-VIProperty -Force` parameter indicates that you want to create the new property even if another property with the same name already exists for the specified object type.

Now you can get a list of all of your virtual machines and their vCenter Servers with the following command:

```
PowerCLI C:\> Get-VM | Select-Object -Property Name,vCenterServer
```

Working with vSphere folders

In a VMware vSphere environment, you can use folders to organize your infrastructure. In the vSphere web client, you can create folders in the `Hosts and Clusters`, `VMs and Templates`, `Storage`, and `Networking` inventories. The following screenshot shows an example of folders in the `VMs and Templates` inventory:

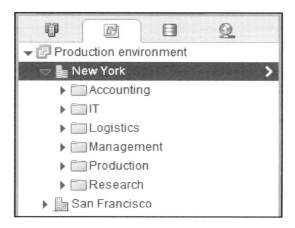

You can browse through these folders using the PowerCLI Inventory Provider. PowerCLI also has a set of cmdlets to work with these folders: `Get-Folder`, `Move-Folder`, `New-Folder`, `Remove-Folder`, and `Set-Folder`.

You can use the `Get-Folder` cmdlet to get a list of all of your folders:

```
PowerCLI C:\> Get-Folder
```

Otherwise, you can select specific folders by their name using the following command line:

```
PowerCLI C:\> Get-Folder -Name "Accounting"
```

All folders are organized in a tree structure under the root folder. You can retrieve the root folder with the following command:

```
PowerCLI C:\> Get-Folder -NoRecursion

Name                        Type
----                        ----
Datacenters                 Datacenter
```

The root folder is always named `Datacenters`. In this folder, you can only create subfolders or data centers.

Folders in vSphere are of a certain type. Valid folder types are `VM`, `HostAndCluster`, `Datastore`, `Network`, and `Datacenter`. You can use this to specify the type of folders you want to retrieve. For example, to retrieve only folders of type `VM`, use the following command:

```
PowerCLI C:\> Get-Folder -Type VM
```

A problem with folders is that you don't get the full path from the root if you retrieve a folder. Using the `New-VIProperty` cmdlet, you can easily add a `Path` property to a PowerCLI `Folder` object:

```
PowerCLI C:\> New-VIProperty -Name Path -ObjectType Folder -Value {
  # $FolderView contains the view of the current folder object
  $FolderView = $Args[0].Extensiondata

  # $Server is the name of the vCenter Server
  $Server = $Args[0].Uid.Split(":")[0].Split("@")[1]

  # We build the path from the right to the left
  # Start with the folder name
  $Path = $FolderView.Name

  # While we are not in the root folder
  while ($FolderView.Parent){
    # Get the parent folder
    $FolderView = Get-View -Id $FolderView.Parent -Server $Server

    # Extend the path with the name of the parent folder
    $Path = $FolderView.Name + "" + $Path
  }
  # Return the path
  $Path
} -Force # Create the property even if a property with this name exists
```

In this example, you see that the # character in PowerShell is used to comment.

Using the new `Path` property, you can now get the path for all the folders with the following command:

```
PowerCLI C:\> Get-Folder | Select-Object -Property Name,Path
```

You can use the `Path` property to find a folder by its complete path. Take a look at the following example:

```
PowerCLI C:\> Get-Folder |
>> Where-Object {$_.Path -eq 'Datacenters\Dallas\vm\Templates'}
>>
```

Summary

In this chapter, you looked at the `Get-Help`, `Get-Command`, and `Get-Member` cmdlets. You learned how to use providers and PSDrives. You also saw how to create a calculated property. Using the raw API objects with the `ExtensionData` property or the `Get-View` cmdlet was discussed, and you looked at extending PowerCLI objects with the `New-VIProperty` cmdlet. At the end, you learned to work with folders, and you saw how you can use the `New-VIProperty` cmdlet to extend the `Folder` object of PowerCLI with a `Path` property.

In the next chapter, you will learn more about working with objects in PowerCLI.

3
Working with Objects in PowerShell

PowerShell is an object-oriented shell. Don't let this scare you because if you know how to work with PowerShell objects, it will make your life much easier. Objects in PowerShell have properties and methods, just like objects in real life. For example, let's take a computer and try to see it as an object. It has properties such as the manufacturer, the number of CPUs, the amount of memory, and the type of computer (for example, server, workstation, desktop, or laptop). The computer also has methods, for example, you can switch the computer on and off. Properties and methods together are called **members** in PowerShell. In `Chapter 2`, *Learning Basic PowerCLI Concepts*, you already saw the `Get-Member` cmdlet that lists the properties and methods of a PowerShell object. In this chapter, you will learn all of the ins and outs of PowerShell objects. We will focus on the following topics:

- Using objects, properties, and methods
- Expanding variables and subexpressions in strings
- Using here-strings
- Using the pipeline
- Using the PowerShell object cmdlets
- Creating your own objects
- Using COM objects

Using objects, properties, and methods

In PowerCLI, even a string is an object. You can list the members of a string object using the `Get-Member` cmdlet that you have seen before. Let's go back to our example from `Chapter 2`, *Learning Basic PowerCLI Concepts*. First, we create a string `Learning PowerCLI` and put it in a variable named `$String`. Then, we take the `$String` variable and execute the `Get-Member` cmdlet using the `$String` variable as the input:

```
PowerCLI C:\> $String = "Learning PowerCLI"
PowerCLI C:\> Get-Member -Inputobject $String
```

You can also use the pipeline and do it in a one-liner:

```
PowerCLI C:\> "Learning PowerCLI" | Get-Member
```

The output will be as follows:

```
   TypeName: System.String
Name              MemberType        Definition
----              ----------        ----------
Clone             Method            System.Object Clone(), Syst...
CompareTo         Method            int CompareTo(System.Object...
Contains          Method            bool Contains(string value)
CopyTo            Method            void CopyTo(int sourceIndex...
EndsWith          Method            bool EndsWith(string value)...
Equals            Method            bool Equals(System.Object o...
GetEnumerator     Method            System.CharEnumerator GetEn...
GetHashCode       Method            int GetHashCode()
GetType           Method            type GetType()
GetTypeCode       Method            System.TypeCode GetTypeCode...
IndexOf           Method            int IndexOf(char value), in...
IndexOfAny        Method            int IndexOfAny(char[] anyOf...
Insert            Method            string Insert(int startInde...
IsNormalized      Method            bool IsNormalized(), bool I...
LastIndexOf       Method            int LastIndexOf(char value)...
LastIndexOfAny    Method            int LastIndexOfAny(char[] a...
Normalize         Method            string Normalize(), string ...
PadLeft           Method            string PadLeft(int totalWid...
PadRight          Method            string PadRight(int totalWi...
Remove            Method            string Remove(int startInde...
Replace           Method            string Replace(char oldChar...
Split             Method            string[] Split(Params char[...
StartsWith        Method            bool StartsWith(string valu...
Substring         Method            string Substring(int startI...
ToBoolean         Method            bool IConvertible.ToBoolean...
ToByte            Method            byte IConvertible.ToByte(Sy...
ToChar            Method            char IConvertible.ToChar(Sy...
```

ToCharArray	Method	char[] ToCharArray(), char[...
ToDateTime	Method	datetime IConvertible.ToDat...
ToDecimal	Method	decimal IConvertible.ToDeci...
ToDouble	Method	double IConvertible.ToDoubl...
ToInt16	Method	int16 IConvertible.ToInt16(...
ToInt32	Method	int IConvertible.ToInt32(Sy...
ToInt64	Method	long IConvertible.ToInt64(S...
ToLower	Method	string ToLower(), string To...
ToLowerInvariant	Method	string ToLowerInvariant()
ToSByte	Method	sbyte IConvertible.ToSByte(...
ToSingle	Method	float IConvertible.ToSingle...
ToString	Method	string ToString(), string T...
ToType	Method	System.Object IConvertible....
ToUInt16	Method	uint16 IConvertible.ToUInt1...
ToUInt32	Method	uint32 IConvertible.ToUInt3...
ToUInt64	Method	uint64 IConvertible.ToUInt6...
ToUpper	Method	string ToUpper(), string To...
ToUpperInvariant	Method	string ToUpperInvariant()
Trim	Method	string Trim(Params char[] t...
TrimEnd	Method	string TrimEnd(Params char[...
TrimStart	Method	string TrimStart(Params cha...
Chars	ParameterizedProperty	char Chars(int index) {get;}
Length	Property	int Length {get;}

You may see that a string has a lot of methods, one property, and a special type of property named `ParameterizedProperty`. Let's first use the `Length` property. To use a property, type the object name or the name of the variable containing the object, then type a dot, and finally type the property name. So, for the string, you could use any of the following command lines:

```
PowerCLI C:\> "Learning PowerCLI".Length
17
```

Or:

```
PowerCLI C:\> $String.Length
17
```

You may see that the `Length` property contains the number of characters of the string `Learning PowerCLI`; 17 in this case.

Property names in PowerShell are not case-sensitive. So, you could type the following command as well:

```
PowerCLI C:\> $String.length
17
```

`ParameterizedProperty` is a property that accepts a parameter value. The `ParameterizedProperty char Chars` property can be used to return the character at a specific position in the string. You have to specify the position, also named the **index**, as a parameter to `Chars`. Indexes in PowerShell start with `0`. So, to get the first character of the string, type the following command:

```
PowerCLI C:\> $String.Chars(0)
L
```

To get the second character of the string, type the following command:

```
PowerCLI C:\> $String.Chars(1)
e
```

You cannot use −1 to get the last character of the string, as you can do with indexing in a PowerShell array. You have to calculate the last index yourself, and it is calculated by subtracting 1 from the length of the string. So, to get the last character of the string, you can type the following command:

```
PowerCLI C:\> $String.Chars($String.Length − 1)
I
```

PowerShell has more types of properties, such as `AliasProperty`, `CodeProperty`, `NoteProperty`, and `ScriptProperty`:

- `AliasProperty` is an alias name for an existing property
- `CodeProperty` is a property that maps to a static method on a .NET class
- `NoteProperty` is a property that contains data
- `ScriptProperty` is a property whose value is returned from executing a PowerShell scriptblock

Using methods

Using `methods` is as easy as using properties. You can type the name of a variable containing the object, then you type a dot, and after the dot, you type the name of the method. For methods, you always have to use parentheses after the method name. For example, to modify a string to all uppercase letters type in the following command:

```
PowerCLI C:\> $String.ToUpper()
LEARNING POWERCLI
```

Some methods require parameters. For example, to find the index of the P character in the string, you can use the following command:

```
PowerCLI C:\> $String.IndexOf('P')
9
```

The character P is the tenth character in the `Learning PowerCLI` string. But because indexes in PowerShell start with 0 and not 1, the index of the P character in the string is 9 and not 10.

A very useful method is `Replace` that you can use to replace a character or a substring with another character, string, or nothing. For example, let's replace all e characters in the string with a u character:

```
PowerCLI C:\> $String.Replace('e','u')
Luarning PowurCLI
```

The characters in the method are case-sensitive. If you use an uppercase E, it won't find the letter and will replace nothing. See the following command:

```
PowerCLI C:\> $String.Replace('E','U')
Learning PowerCLI
```

You can also replace a substring with another string. Let's replace the word `PowerCLI` with `VMware PowerCLI`:

```
PowerCLI C:\> $String.Replace('PowerCLI','VMware PowerCLI')
Learning VMware PowerCLI
```

There is also a –Replace operator in PowerShell. You can use the –Replace operator to do a regular expression-based text substitution on a string or a collection of strings:

```
PowerCLI C:\> $string -Replace 'e','u'
Luarning PowurCLI
```

Although both have the same name, the string Replace method and the –Replace operator are two different things. There is no –ToUpper operator, as you can see in the following screenshot that gives an error message:

You can use more than one method in the same command. Say, you want to replace the word Learning with Gaining, and that you want to remove the characters C, L, and I from the end of the string using the TrimEnd method. Then, you can use the following command:

```
PowerCLI C:\> $String.Replace('Learning','Gaining').TrimEnd('CLI')
Gaining Power
```

Expanding variables and subexpressions in strings

In PowerShell, you can define a string with single or double quotes. There is a difference between these two methods. In a single-quoted string, variables and subexpressions are not expanded, whereas, in a double-quoted string, they are expanded.

Let's look at an example of variable expansion in a double-quoted string:

```
PowerCLI C:\> $Number = 3
PowerCLI C:\> "The number is: $Number"
The number is: 3
```

In the preceding example, the string is defined with double quotes, and the $Number variable is expanded. Let's see what happens if you use single quotes:

```
PowerCLI C:\> $Number = 3
PowerCLI C:\> 'The number is: $Number'
The number is: $Number
```

Using a single-quoted string, PowerShell doesn't expand the $Number variable. Let's try to put the number of virtual CPUs of a virtual machine in a double-quoted string:

```
PowerCLI C:\> $vm = Get-VM -Name dc1
PowerCLI C:\> "The number of vCPU's of the vm is: $vm.NumCpu"
The number of vCPU's of the vm is: dc1.NumCpu
```

The output is not what you intended. What happened? The $ sign in front of a variable name tells PowerShell to evaluate the variable. In the string that is used in the preceding example, $vm evaluates the variable vm. But it does not evaluate $vm.NumCpu. To evaluate $vm.NumCpu, you have to use another $ sign before and parentheses around the code that you want to evaluate: $($vm.NumCpu). This is called a **subexpression** notation.

In the corrected example, you will get the number of virtual CPUs:

```
PowerCLI C:\> $vm = Get-VM -Name dc1
PowerCLI C:\> "The number of vCPU's of the vm is: $($vm.NumCpu)"
The number of vCPU's of the vm is: 2
```

You can use subexpression evaluation to evaluate any PowerShell code. In the following example, you will use PowerShell to calculate the sum of 3 and 4:

```
PowerCLI C:\> "3 + 4 = $(3+4)"
3 + 4 = 7
```

When will a string be expanded?

A string will be expanded when it is assigned to a variable. It will not be re-evaluated when the variable is used later. The following example shows this behavior:

```
PowerCLI C:\> $Number = 3
PowerCLI C:\> $String = "The number is: $Number"
PowerCLI C:\> $String
The number is: 3
PowerCLI C:\> $Number = 4
PowerCLI C:\> $String
The number is: 3
```

As you can see, $String is assigned before $Number gets the value 4. The $String variable says The number is: 3.

Expanding a string when it is used

How can you delay the expansion of the string until you use it? PowerShell has a predefined variable named $ExecutionContext. You can use the InvokeCommand.ExpandString() method of this variable to expand the string:

```
PowerCLI C:\> $Number = 3
PowerCLI C:\> $String = 'The number is: $Number'
PowerCLI C:\> $ExecutionContext.InvokeCommand.ExpandString($String)
The number is: 3
PowerCLI C:\> $Number = 4
PowerCLI C:\> $ExecutionContext.InvokeCommand.ExpandString($String)
The number is: 4
```

The preceding example defines $String as a single-quoted string, so $Number is not expanded at the assignment of $String. The $ExecutionContext.InvokeCommand.ExpandString($String) command expands the string every time the command is executed.

Using here-strings

Until now, you have only seen single-line strings in this book. PowerShell has a so-called **here-string** that spans multiple lines. You use @" or @' to start the here-string and "@ or '@ to finish the here-string. The @" or @' must be at the end of a line and the "@ or '@ must be at the beginning of the line that terminates the here-string. As in single-line strings, variables and subexpressions are expanded in double-quoted here-strings and are not expanded in single-quoted here-strings.

The following command creates a here-string that spans two lines and puts the here-string in the $s variable:

```
PowerCLI C:\> $s = @"
>> Learning PowerCLI
>> is a lot of fun!
>> "@
>> $s
>>
Learning PowerCLI
is a lot of fun!
```

Using the pipeline

In PowerShell, you can use the output of one command as input for another command by using the vertical bar (|) character. This is called using the pipeline. The vertical bar character, in PowerShell, is called the **pipe** character. In PowerShell, complete objects pass through the pipeline. This is different from cmd.exe or a Linux shell where only strings pass through the pipeline. The advantage of passing complete objects through the pipeline is that you don't have to perform string manipulations to retrieve property values.

Using the ByValue parameter binding

You have already seen some examples of using the pipeline in preceding sections of this book. For example:

```
PowerCLI C:\> Get-VM | Get-Member
```

In this example, the output of the Get-VM cmdlet is used as the input for the Get-Member cmdlet. This is much simpler than the following command, which gives you the same result:

```
PowerCLI C:\> Get-Member -InputObject (Get-VM)
```

You can see that the Get-Member cmdlet accepts inputs from the pipeline if you look at the help for the Get-Member -Parameter InputObject using the following command:

```
PowerCLI C:\> Get-Help Get-Member -Parameter InputObject
```

The output will be the following:

```
-InputObject <PSObject>
Specifies the object whose members are retrieved.
Using the InputObject parameter is not the same as piping an object
to Get-Member. The differences are as follows:
-- When you pipe a collection of objects to Get-Member, Get-Member
gets the members of the individual objects in the collection, such as
the properties of each string in an array of strings.
-- When you use InputObject to submit a collection of objects,
Get-Member gets the members of the collection, such as the
properties of the array in an array of strings.

    Required?                      false
    Position?                      named
    Default value
    Accept pipeline input?         true (ByValue)
    Accept wildcard characters?    false
```

You can see that in the description it says `Accept pipeline input? true (ByValue)`. This means that the `Get-Member -InputObject` parameter accepts inputs from the pipeline.

The `ByValue` parameter binding means that PowerShell binds the entire input object to the parameter.

In the following figure, you will see that the pipeline binds the output of the `Get-Member` cmdlet to the `-InputObject` parameter of the `Get-Member` cmdlet:

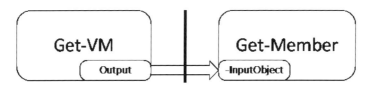

Using the ByPropertyName parameter binding

If PowerShell can't find a parameter that accepts pipeline inputs using `ByValue`, it tries to find parameters that accept pipeline inputs using `ByPropertyName`. When a parameter accepts pipeline inputs using `ByPropertyName`, it means that the value of a property of the input object is bound to a cmdlet parameter with the same name as the property.

An example of a PowerShell cmdlet that accepts inputs from the pipeline using the `ByPropertyName` parameter binding is the `Get-Date` cmdlet that returns a `System.DateTime` object. The `-Date` parameter of this cmdlet accepts pipeline inputs using both `ByValue` and `ByPropertyName`. The PowerCLI `Get-VIEvent` cmdlet retrieves information about the events on a vCenter Server system. Take a look at the following example:

```
PowerCLI C:\> Get-VIEvent | Select-Object -First 1
```

The preceding command has the following output:

```
ScheduledTask     : VMware.Vim.ScheduledTaskEventArgument
Entity            : VMware.Vim.ManagedEntityEventArgument
Key               : 64835
ChainId           : 64835

CreatedTime       : 1/7/2017 9:04:01 PM
UserName          :
Datacenter        :
ComputeResource   :
```

```
Host                    :
Vm                      :
Ds                      :
Net                     :
Dvs                     :
FullFormattedMessage :  Running task VMware vCenter Update Manager
                        Check Notification on Datacenters in
                        datacenter
ChangeTag               :
```

The output has a property `CreatedTime`. The value of the `CreatedTime` property has a `DateTime` object type.

Let's try to pipe the output of the preceding command into the `Get-Date` cmdlet:

This gives an error message because the output of the `Get-VIEvent` cmdlet does not have a `Date` property that matches the `-Date` parameter of the `Get-Date` cmdlet. We will now use a calculated property to rename the `CreatedTime` property into `Date`:

```
PowerCLI C:\> Get-VIEvent | Select-Object -First 1 |
>> Select-Object @{Name="Date";Expression={$_.CreatedTime}} |
>> Get-Date
>>
Saturday, January 7, 2017 9:14:51 PM
```

Because the output of the `Select-Object` cmdlet has a `Date` property and this property matches the `Get-Date` parameter `-Date` using the `ByPropertyName` parameter binding, the pipeline now works.

The following figure shows that the pipeline binds the value of the `Date` property in the output of the `Select-Object` cmdlet to the `-Date` property of the `Get-Date` cmdlet:

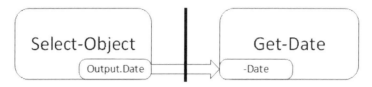

Most PowerCLI cmdlets will accept input from the pipeline using the `ByValue` parameter binding. However, only a few PowerCLI cmdlets will accept input from the pipeline using the `ByPropertyName` parameter binding. You can find these cmdlets with the following PowerShell code:

```
PowerCLI C:\> Get-VICommand |
>> Where-Object {$_.ParameterSets.Parameters |
>> Where-Object {
>> $_.ValueFromPipeline -and $_.ValueFromPipelineByPropertyName}}
>>
```

The preceding command has the following output:

```
CommandType Name                           Version Source
----------- ----                           ------- ------
Cmdlet      Add-EsxSoftwareDepot           6.0.0.0 VMware.ImageBuilder
Cmdlet      Add-EsxSoftwarePackage         6.0.0.0 VMware.ImageBuilder
Cmdlet      Compare-EsxImageProfile        6.0.0.0 VMware.ImageBuilder
Cmdlet      Export-EsxImageProfile         6.0.0.0 VMware.ImageBuilder
Cmdlet      New-EsxImageProfile            6.0.0.0 VMware.ImageBuilder
Cmdlet      Remove-EsxImageProfile         6.0.0.0 VMware.ImageBuilder
Cmdlet      Remove-EsxSoftwareDepot        6.0.0.0 VMware.ImageBuilder
Cmdlet      Remove-EsxSoftwarePackage      6.0.0.0 VMware.ImageBuilder
Cmdlet      Set-EsxImageProfile            6.0.0.0 VMware.ImageBuilder
```

The script uses the `Get-VICommand` cmdlet to get all of the PowerCLI cmdlets. It then filters only those cmdlets that have parameters that accept pipeline inputs using `ByPropertyName`. As you see, when writing this book, only cmdlets from the PowerCLI `VMware.ImageBuilder` module accept pipeline inputs using `ByPropertyName`.

Using the PowerShell object cmdlets

PowerShell has some cmdlets that are designed to work with all kinds of objects. You can easily recognize them because they all have the noun `Object`. You can use the `Get-Command` cmdlet `-Noun` parameter to find them:

```
PowerCLI C:\> Get-Command -Noun Object
```

The preceding command has the following output:

```
CommandType Name           Version Source
----------- ----           ------- ------
Cmdlet      Compare-Object 3.1.0.0 Microsoft.PowerShell.Utility
Cmdlet      ForEach-Object 3.0.0.0 Microsoft.PowerShell.Core
Cmdlet      Group-Object   3.1.0.0 Microsoft.PowerShell.Utility
Cmdlet      Measure-Object 3.1.0.0 Microsoft.PowerShell.Utility
Cmdlet      New-Object     3.1.0.0 Microsoft.PowerShell.Utility
Cmdlet      Select-Object  3.1.0.0 Microsoft.PowerShell.Utility
Cmdlet      Sort-Object    3.1.0.0 Microsoft.PowerShell.Utility
Cmdlet      Tee-Object     3.1.0.0 Microsoft.PowerShell.Utility
Cmdlet      Where-Object   3.0.0.0 Microsoft.PowerShell.Core
```

In the following section, we will discuss the `Object` cmdlets.

Using the Select-Object cmdlet

If you want to retrieve a subset of the properties of an object, select unique objects or a specific number of objects or specific objects from an array, you can use the `Select-Object` cmdlet. You can also use the `Select-Object` cmdlet to add properties to an object using calculated properties, as you have seen in `Chapter 2`, *Learning Basic PowerCLI Concepts*.

The `Select-Object` cmdlet has the following syntax. The first parameter set is the default:

```
Select-Object [[-Property] <Object[]>] [-ExcludeProperty <String[]>] [-
ExpandProperty <String>] [-First <Int32>] [-InputObject <PSObject>] [-Last
<Int32>] [-Skip <Int32>] [-Unique] [-Wait] [<CommonParameters>]
```

The second parameter set can be used to skip the last part of the output:

```
Select-Object [[-Property] <Object[]>] [-ExcludeProperty <String[]>] [-
ExpandProperty <String>] [-InputObject <PSObject>] [-SkipLast <Int32>] [-
Unique] [<CommonParameters>]
```

The third parameter set can be used to specify an array of objects to return based on their index values:

```
Select-Object [-Index <Int32[]>] [-InputObject <PSObject>] [-Unique] [-
Wait] [<CommonParameters>]
```

You can use `Select` as an alias for the `Select-Object` cmdlet.

The `Get-VM` cmdlet returns the `Name`, `PowerState`, `NumCpu`, and `MemoryGB` properties of the virtual machines by default. But what if you want to return the `Name`, `VMHost`, and `Cluster` properties instead? If you look at the properties of a virtual machine object, you will see the `VMhost` property. But you will not see a `Cluster` property. However, if you look at a `VMHostImpl` object, you will find a `Parent` property. The `Parent` property of a `VMhostImpl` object contains the cluster that the host is a member of.

You can use this information to create a `PowerCLI` one-liner to get the host and cluster of all of the virtual machines:

```
PowerCLI C:\> Get-VM | Select-Object -Property
Name,VMHost,
@{Name="Cluster";Expression={$_.VMHost.Parent}}
Name VMHost          Cluster
---- ------          -------
DC1  192.168.0.133 Cluster01
```

The preceding command uses the `Select-Object` cmdlet to select the `Name` and `VMHost` properties of the virtual machine objects, and it creates a calculated property named `Cluster` that retrieves the cluster via the `VMHost.Parent` property.

You can create a one-liner from all of your PowerShell scripts by using the semicolon as a separator between the commands. Use this only on the command line. It makes your scripts hard to read.

You can use the `Select-Object -First` parameter to specify the number of objects to select from the beginning of an array of input objects. For example, to retrieve the first three host types, use the following command:

```
PowerCLI C:\> Get-VMHost | Select-Object -First 3
```

If you are typing commands at the pipeline, you can also use their aliases. For `Select-Object`, the alias is `Select`. So, the next example will give the same result as the preceding one:

```
PowerCLI C:\> Get-VMHost | Select -First 3
```

To select a number of objects starting from the end of an array of objects, use the `Select-Object -Last` parameter. The following command retrieves the last cluster:

```
PowerCLI C:\> Get-Cluster | Select-Object -Last 1
```

You can also skip objects from the beginning or the end of an array using the `Select-Object -Skip` parameter. The following command returns all of the folder objects except the first two:

```
PowerCLI C:\> Get-Folder | Select-Object -Skip 2
```

A very interesting parameter of the `Select-Object` cmdlet is the `-ExpandProperty` parameter. You can use this parameter to expand the object if the property contains an object. For example, if you want to get the `VMHostImpl` object of the virtual machine named `dc1`, you can execute the following command:

```
PowerCLI C:\> Get-VM -Name dc1 | Select-Object
-ExpandProperty VMHost
```

Using the Where-Object cmdlet

If you only want a subset of all of the objects that a command returns, you can use the `Where-Object` cmdlet to filter the output of a command and only return the objects that match the criteria of the filter.

The `Where-Object` cmdlet syntax definition is so long that it'll take too much space in this book. You can easily get the `Where-Object` cmdlet syntax with the following command:

```
PowerCLI C:\> Get-Help Where-Object
```

PowerShell V3 introduced a new, easier syntax for the `Where-Object` cmdlet. I will show you both the V2 and V3 syntaxes. First, let's see the new PowerShell V3 syntax.

Let's try to find all virtual machines that have only one virtual CPU. You can do this by searching for virtual machines that have a NumCPU property with a value of 1:

```
PowerCLI C:\> Get-VM | Where-Object NumCpu -eq 1
Name     PowerState  Num CPUs  MemoryGB
----     ----------  --------  --------
DC1      PoweredOff   1         0.250
```

If you use the alias Where, the command looks more like a natural language:

```
PowerCLI C:\> Get-VM | Where NumCpu -eq 1
```

You can also use the alias ? if you want to type less on the command line:

```
PowerCLI C:\> Get-VM | ? NumCpu -eq 1
```

The **PowerShell V2** syntax is a bit more obscure. You have to use a script block as the value of the Where-Object -FilterScript parameter:

```
PowerCLI C:\> Get-VM | Where-Object -FilterScript {$_.NumCpu -eq 1}
```

Because the -FilterScript parameter is the first positional parameter of the Where-Object cmdlet, nobody uses the parameter name, and you will always see one of the following command lines being used:

```
PowerCLI C:\> Get-VM | Where-Object {$_.NumCpu -eq 1}
PowerCLI C:\> Get-VM | where {$_.NumCpu -eq 1}
```

The advantage of the PowerShell V2 syntax over the V3 syntax is that you can create complex filtering scripts. For example:

```
PowerCLI C:\> Get-VM |
>> Where-Object {$_.NumCpu -gt 2 -and $_.MemoryGB -lt 16}
>>
```

The preceding command will show you all of the virtual machines with more than two virtual CPUs and less than 16 GB of memory. If you want to create the same filter using the PowerShell V3 syntax, you have to use two filters: one for the number of CPUs and one for the memory:

```
PowerCLI C:\> Get-VM | Where NumCpu -gt 2 | Where MemoryGB -lt 16
```

Using the ForEach-Object cmdlet

Some cmdlets don't accept properties from the pipeline. On the other hand, you would like to use a cmdlet in the pipeline, but the property you want to use in the pipeline doesn't accept pipeline input. This is where the PowerShell `ForEach-Object` cmdlet will help you.

The `ForEach-Object` cmdlet has the following syntax. The first parameter set is for manipulating properties of the input objects:

```
ForEach-Object [-MemberName] <String> [-ArgumentList <Object[]>] [-Confirm]
[-InputObject <PSObject>] [-WhatIf] [<CommonParameters>]
```

The `-MemberName` parameter is required.

The second parameter set is for processing script blocks for each object in the input:

```
ForEach-Object [-Process] <ScriptBlock[]> [-Begin <ScriptBlock>] [-Confirm]
[-End <ScriptBlock>] [-InputObject <PSObject>] [-RemainingScripts
<ScriptBlock[]>] [-WhatIf] [<CommonParameters>]
```

The `-Process` parameter is required.

The default first parameter is `-Process`, and that parameter name is most of the time omitted when using the cmdlet. The `-Process` parameter has a scriptblock as its parameter value, and this scriptblock will run for every object that passes the pipeline. For example:

```
PowerCLI C:\> Get-VM | ForEach-Object {$_.Name}
```

The preceding command will retrieve the names of all of your virtual machines. In the scriptblock, the special variable `$_` is used. The `$_` variable is the current object that passes through the pipeline. So, `$_.Name` will return the value of the name property of the current object.

You can also use the alias `foreach`:

```
PowerCLI C:\> Get-VM | foreach {$_.Name}
```

In PowerShell V3, the command is even simpler:

```
PowerCLI C:\> Get-VM | foreach Name
```

If you want the `ForEach-Object` cmdlet to execute code before the objects start to pass through the pipeline, for example, to initialize a variable, you can create a scriptblock and use it as an argument value for the `-Begin` parameter. If you want the `ForEach-Object` cmdlet to execute code after the objects finish passing through the pipeline, for example, to return a result of a calculation you did on all of the objects in the pipeline, you can create a scriptblock and use it as an argument value for the `-End` parameter. For example:

```
PowerCLI C:\> 1,2,3,4 |
>> ForEach-Object -Begin {"Start of the Script"; $Sum = 0} `
>> -Process {$Sum += $_} -End {"Sum of the elements: $Sum"}
>>
Start of the Script
Sum of the elements: 10
```

The preceding example was just to demonstrate the `ForEach-Object` cmdlet. If you want to take the sum of the objects in the pipeline, it is better to use the `Measure-Object` cmdlet that will be discussed in one of the following sections.

 In the example, you can see that the semicolon character is used to separate PowerShell commands. The **backtick** character (`) used as the last character of a line is used to escape the newline character and treat the newline character as a space. This enables you to break long lines of code and continue them on the next line.

To specify 1, 2, 3, 4, you can also use the PowerShell range operator (`..`):

```
1..4
```

The preceding operator is equivalent to the following:

```
1, 2, 3, 4
```

The `ForEach-Object -Process` scriptblock is run at least once even if the input object is `$null`, as you can see in the following example:

```
PowerCLI C:\> $null | ForEach-Object -Process {"Hello world."}
Hello world.
```

You probably don't want to return anything if the input object is `$null`. You can solve this problem by testing inside the scriptblock if the input object exists with `if ($_)`:

```
PowerCLI C:\> $null | ForEach-Object -Process {if ($_) {"Hello."}}
```

Using the Sort-Object cmdlet

PowerCLI returns objects in a random order. If you want the objects to be sorted, you can use the `Sort-Object` cmdlet to sort them.

The `Sort-Object` cmdlet has the following syntax:

```
Sort-Object [[-Property] <Object[]>] [-CaseSensitive] [-Culture <String>]
[-Descending] [-InputObject <PSObject>] [-Unique] [<CommonParameters>]
```

The `Sort-Object` cmdlet sorts objects in ascending or descending order based on the values of the properties of the object.

You can specify a single property or multiple properties (for a multi-key sort), and you can select a case-sensitive or case-insensitive sort. You can also direct `Sort-Object` to display only the objects with a unique value for a particular property.

The following example will give a list of all of your virtual machines, and their hosts sorted in ascending order on the hostname and the virtual machine name:

```
PowerCLI C:\> Get-VM | Select-Object -Property VMHost,Name |
>> Sort-Object -Property VMHost,Name
>>
```

Using the aliases `select` for `Select-Object` and `sort` for `Sort-Object` and also using positional parameters, the preceding example can be shortened into:

```
PowerCLI C:\> Get-VM | select VMHost,Name | sort VMHost,Name
```

Using the Measure-Object cmdlet

If you want to count objects or calculate the minimum, maximum, sum, and average of the numeric values of properties, you can use the `Measure-Object` cmdlet. For text objects, it can count and calculate the number of lines, words, and characters.

The `Measure-Object` cmdlet has the following syntax. The first parameter set is for counting the input objects and displaying the minimum, and maximum values, the sum, and average values of the input objects:

```
Measure-Object [[-Property] <String[]>] [-Average] [-InputObject
<PSObject>] [-Maximum] [-Minimum] [-Sum] [<CommonParameters>]
```

The second parameter set is for counting characters, lines, and words in the input objects:

```
Measure-Object [[-Property] <String[]>] [-Character] [-IgnoreWhiteSpace] [-
InputObject <PSObject>] [-Line] [-Word] [<CommonParameters>]
```

There are no required parameters.

Let's get back to our example from the `ForEach-Object` cmdlet where we counted the sum of the numbers 1, 2, 3, and 4. You can do this in an easier way using the `Measure-Object` cmdlet with the following command:

```
PowerCLI C:\> (1..4 | Measure-Object -Sum).Sum
10
```

The only output property that the `Measure-Object` cmdlet fills by default is the `Count` property. To count the number of virtual machines in your environment, type the following command:

```
PowerCLI C:\> Get-VM | Measure-Object

Count    : 12
Average  :
Sum      :
Maximum  :
Minimum  :
Property :
```

If you just want the count value, you can specify the `Count` property:

```
PowerCLI C:\> (Get-VM | Measure-Object).Count
12
```

Otherwise, you can use the `Select-Object -ExpandProperty` parameter as follows:

```
PowerCLI C:\> Get-VM | Measure-Object |
>> Select-Object -ExpandProperty Count
>>
12
```

You can also use the alias `measure` for `Measure-Object`:

```
PowerCLI C:\> (Get-VM | measure).Count
12
```

 To get the average, sum, maximum, and minimum values of a property, you have to specify the property name and the parameters for the values that you want to retrieve.

The following command will retrieve the average, sum, maximum, and minimum values of the `ProvisionedSpaceGB` property of all of your virtual machines:

```
PowerCLI C:\> Get-VM | Measure-Object -Property
ProvisionedSpaceGB -Average -Sum -Maximum -Minimum

Count    : 12
Average  : 60.590376389601
Sum      : 727.084516675211
Maximum  : 221.090891393833
Minimum  : 2.58988594077528
Property : ProvisionedSpaceGB
```

To count the number of characters, words, and lines in a string, you can use the `-Line`, `-Word`, and `-Character` parameters:

```
PowerCLI C:\> "Learning PowerCLI" |
>> Measure-Object -Line -Word -Character
>>
```

Lines	Words	Characters	Property
1	2	17	

You can also use the `Measure-Object` cmdlet to count the number of lines, words, and characters in the here-string:

```
PowerCLI C:\> @"
>> Every vSphere admin should
>> Learn PowerCLI!
>> "@ | Measure-Object -Line -Word -Character
>>
```

Lines	Words	Characters	Property
2	6	42	

Rounding a value

If you don't want a value to have several fractional digits, you can use the .NET `Math.Round` method to round a value to the nearest integer or the specified number of fractional digits:

- The first parameter of the `Math.Round` method is the value that you want to round
- The optional second parameter is the number of fractional digits that you want the value to round to

If you don't specify the second parameter, the value will be rounded to the nearest integer. For example:

```
PowerCLI C:\> [math]::Round(60.590376389601,2)
60.59
```

You can use the `Math.Round` method in a calculated property. For example:

```
PowerCLI C:\> Get-VM | Measure-Object -Property
ProvisionedSpaceGB -Average -Sum -Maximum -Minimum |

>> Select-Object -Property Count,
>> @{Name="Average";Expression={[math]::Round($_.Average,2)}}
>>

Count          Average
-----          -------
   12            60.59
```

Using the Group-Object cmdlet

The `Group-Object` cmdlet group's objects contain the same value for the specified properties. Using the `Group-Object` cmdlet can be very useful, for example, when you want to count the number of instances of a specific value of a property.

The `Group-Object` cmdlet has the following syntax:

```
Group-Object [[-Property] <Object[]>] [-AsHashTable] [-AsString] [-
CaseSensitive] [-Culture <String>] [-InputObject <PSObject>] [-NoElement]
[<CommonParameters>]
```

Let's create a PowerCLI command to count the number of instances of each operating system installed on a virtual machine. In a traditional scripting language, you would have to loop through all of your virtual machines and increment counters for each operating system. In PowerCLI, you can achieve this much easier using the `Group-Object` cmdlet. The name of the guest operating system is in a virtual machine's `Guest.OSFullName` property. You can use the `Group-Object` cmdlet to group the objects on the `Guest.OSFullName` property using a calculated property. The `Group-Object` cmdlet will return the `Count`, `Name`, and `Group` properties by default. Using the `-NoElement` parameter will remove the `Group` property from the output. The following example groups the virtual machines on the `Guest.OSFullname` property and returns the `Count` and `Name` properties for each `Guest.OSFullName`:

```
PowerCLI C:\> Get-VM |
>> Group-Object -Property @{Expression=
{$_.Guest.OSFullName}} -NoElement    |
>> Format-Table -AutoSize
>>

Count Name
----- ----
    1 Microsoft Windows Server 2012 (64-bit)
    1 SUSE Linux Enterprise 11 (32-bit)
    3 SUSE Linux Enterprise 11 (64-bit)
    1
    2 Microsoft Windows Server 2008 R2 (64-bit)
    1 CentOS 4/5/6 (32-bit)
    2 Other (64-bit)
    1 CentOS 4/5/6 (64-bit)
    1 CentOS 4/5/6 (64-bit)
```

 The one virtual machine that does not have a guest operating system name is powered off for a long time. The guest operating system is determined using the VMware Tools. **VMware vSphere** can't find the guest operating system for this virtual machine while it is powered off.

The `Format-Table -AutoSize` command formats the output, so that you will get the full operating system name.

Using the Compare-Object cmdlet

If you want to compare two objects or sets of objects, you have to use the `Compare-Object` cmdlet.

The `Compare-Object` cmdlet has the following syntax:

```
Compare-Object [-ReferenceObject] <PSObject[]> [-DifferenceObject]
<PSObject[]> [-CaseSensitive] [-Culture <String>] [-ExcludeDifferent] [-
IncludeEqual] [-PassThru] [-Property <Object[]>] [-SyncWindow <Int32>]
[<CommonParameters>]
```

From the sets of objects that the `Compare-Object` cmdlet compares one set of objects is named the **reference set**, and the other set is named the **difference set**.

Let's compare two strings:

```
PowerCLI C:\> $string1 = "Learning PowerCLI"
PowerCLI C:\> $string2 = "Learning PowerCLI!"
PowerCLI C:\> Compare-Object -ReferenceObject $string1 `
>> -DifferenceObject $string2
>>
InputObject                    SideIndicator
-----------                    -------------
Learning PowerCLI!             =>
Learning PowerCLI              <=
```

The output shows that the strings are not the same. The `<=` symbol indicates objects from the reference set. The `=>` symbol indicates objects from the difference set. If you use the `-IncludeEqual` parameter, the `Compare-Object` cmdlet will also show objects that are equal in both sets. These objects are indicated by the `==` symbol.

Using the Tee-Object cmdlet

The `Tee-Object` cmdlet saves the command output in a file or a variable and also sends it down the pipeline. If `Tee-Object` is the last command in the pipeline, the command output is displayed at the prompt.

The `Tee-Object` cmdlet has the following syntax. The first parameter set is for saving the output in a file:

```
Tee-Object [-FilePath] <String> [-Append] [-InputObject <PSObject>]
[<CommonParameters>]
```

The `-FilePath` parameter is required. The second parameter set is for saving the output in a file using a literal path:

```
Tee-Object [-InputObject <PSObject>] -LiteralPath <String>
[<CommonParameters>]
```

The -LiteralPath parameter is required. The third parameter set is for saving the output in a variable:

```
Tee-Object [-InputObject <PSObject>] -Variable <String>
[<CommonParameters>]
```

The -Variable parameter is required.

The following example retrieves all of your virtual machines and saves the virtual machine objects in a variable named VMs. It also sends the objects down the pipeline and displays the Name and PowerState properties of the virtual machines:

```
PowerCLI C:\> Get-VM | Tee-Object -Variable VMs |
>> Select-Object -Property Name,PowerState
>>
```

The following figure shows that the Tee-Object cmdlet writes its output to the variable $VMs and pipes its output to the Select-Object cmdlet in the pipeline:

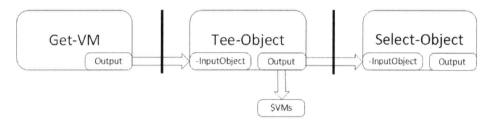

The Tee-Object cmdlet is named after the **T-splitter** used in plumbing. Doesn't the Tee-Object cmdlet in the figure look like a T-splitter?

Creating your own objects

There are several ways to create new objects in PowerCLI. In fact, you have already been creating new objects by using the Select-Object -Property command. In the following section, you will learn more ways to create new objects.

Using the New-Object cmdlet

PowerShell has its own cmdlet to create objects: New-Object. You can use this cmdlet to create a Microsoft .NET Framework or COM object.

The `New-Object` cmdlet has the following syntax. The first parameter set is for creating a Microsoft .NET Framework object:

```
New-Object [-TypeName] <String> [[-ArgumentList] <Object[]>]
[-Property <IDictionary>] [<CommonParameters>]
```

The `-TypeName` parameter is required.

The second parameter set is for creating a COM object:

```
New-Object [-ComObject] <String> [-Property <IDictionary>]
[-Strict] [<CommonParameters>]
```

The `-ComObject` parameter is required.

Using a hash table to create an object

One way to create a Microsoft .NET Framework object as the output of your `PowerCLI` scripts is to create a `PSObject` type object using a hash table. The following example creates an object with two members of member type `NoteProperty`: `Name` and `VMHost` :

```
PowerCLI C:\> $Object = New-Object -TypeName PSObject -Property @{
>> Name = "VM1"
>> VMHost = "ESX1"
>> }
>>
PowerCLI C:\> $Object
Name                              VMHost
----                              ------
VM1                               ESX1
```

If you look at the object with `Get-Member`, you will see four standard methods, along with `Name`, `VMHost`, and `NoteProperty`:

```
PowerCLI C:\> $Object | Get-Member
TypeName: System.Management.Automation.PSCustomObject
Name          MemberType    Definition
----          ----------    ----------
Equals        Method        bool Equals(System.Object obj)
GetHashCode   Method        int GetHashCode()
GetType       Method        type GetType()
ToString      Method        string ToString()
Name          NoteProperty  System.String Name=VM1
VMHost        NoteProperty  System.String VMHost=ESX1
```

The four methods `Equals`, `GetHashCode`, `GetType`, and `ToString` are methods that every PowerShell object has.

This technique is fast and easy-to-use. It has a disadvantage that PowerShell might output the properties in a different order than you added them. You can solve this problem by piping the object to `Select-Object` and specifying the properties there in the right order. For example:

```
PowerCLI C:\> $Object | Select-Object -Property Name,VMHost
Name                                 VMHost
----                                 ------
VM1                                  ESX1
```

Another way to output the properties in the order you entered them is to use an ordered hash table. Ordered hash tables are introduced in PowerShell V3. You can create an ordered hash table by putting `[ordered]` in front of the hash table, for example:

```
PowerCLI C:\> $Hash = [ordered]@{
>> Name = "VM1"
>> VMHost = "ESX1"
>> }
>> $Object = New-Object -TypeName PSObject -Property $Hash
>>
```

Creating objects using the Select-Object cmdlet

If you use the `Select-Object` cmdlet to select only specific properties of an object, then you are creating a new object type. For example, the objects returned by the `Get-VM` cmdlet are of type `VMware.VimAutomation.ViCore.Impl.V1.VM.UniversalVirtualMachineImpl`. However, if you pipe the output of the `Get-VM` cmdlet to `Select-Object`, and pipe that output to the `Get-Member` cmdlet, you will get the following output:

```
PowerCLI C:\> Get-VM | Select-Object -Property Name | Get-Member

     TypeName:
Selected.VMware.VimAutomation.ViCore.Impl.V1.VM.Universal
VirtualMachineImpl
In the TypeName, you can see that the original type name is prefixed by
Selected. You can create a new object from scratch if you pipe an empty
string to Select-Object as in the following example:
PowerCLI C:\> $Report = "" | Select-Object -Property VM,VMHost
PowerCLI C:\> $Report.VM = "VM1"
PowerCLI C:\> $Report.VMHost = "ESX1"
```

```
PowerCLI C:\> $Report
VM                                VMHost
--                                ------
VM1                               ESX1
```

In the first line, you have created a new object $Report that has two blank properties VM and VMHost. In the second and third lines, values are assigned to these properties. In the last line, the $Report object is returned.

> This technique was used a lot in PowerShell V1 and you still see it being often used. In PowerShell V3 and above, I prefer using the method from the following section.

Creating objects using [pscustomobject]

The easiest and fastest way to create objects in PowerShell is to use the [pscustomobject] type declaration introduced in PowerShell V3. Put [pscustomobject] in front of a hash table, and the output will be a PowerShell object of type System.Management.Automation.PSCustomObject, for example:

```
PowerCLI C:\> [pscustomobject]@{
>> Name = "VM1"
>> VMHost = "ESX1"
>> }
>>
Name                              VMHost
----                              ------
VM1                               ESX1
```

PowerShell will output the properties of a PSCustomObject sorted in the order you specified them.

Adding properties to an object with Add-Member

If you want to add one or more properties to an existing object, you can use the Add-Member cmdlet.

The `Add-Member` cmdlet has the following syntax. With the first parameter set, you can specify the type of the new member:

```
Add-Member [-MemberType] {AliasProperty | CodeProperty | Property |
NoteProperty | ScriptProperty | Properties | PropertySet | Method |
CodeMethod | ScriptMethod | Methods | ParameterizedProperty | MemberSet |
Event | Dynamic | All} [-Name] <String> [[-Value] <Object>] [[-SecondValue]
<Object>] [-Force] -InputObject <PSObject> [-PassThru] [-TypeName <String>]
[<CommonParameters>]
```

The `-MemberType`, `-Name`, and `-InputObject` parameters are require.

The second parameter set can be used to add a single `NoteProperty` value:

```
Add-Member [-NotePropertyName] <String> [-NotePropertyValue] <Object> [-
Force] -InputObject <PSObject> [-PassThru] [-TypeName <String>]
[<CommonParameters>]
```

The `-NotePropertyName`, `-NotePropertyValue`, and `-InputObject` parameters are required.

You can use the third parameter set to add multiple `NoteProperty` values:

```
Add-Member [-NotePropertyMembers] <IDictionary> [-Force] -InputObject
<PSObject> [-PassThru] [-TypeName <String>] [<CommonParameters>]
```

The `-NotePropertyMembers` and `-InputObject` parameters are required.

The fourth parameter set can be used to modify the type of the input object:

```
Add-Member -InputObject <PSObject> [-PassThru] -TypeName <String>
[<CommonParameters>]
```

The `-InputObject` and `-TypeName` parameters are required.

To create a new PowerCLI object, you can use the `New-Object` cmdlet to create a new object of type `PSObject` and then use the `Add-Member` cmdlet to add properties, for example:

```
PowerCLI C:\> $Object = New-Object -TypeName PSObject
PowerCLI C:\> $Object | Add-member -NotePropertyName VM
-NotePropertyValue "VM1"
PowerCLI C:\> $Object | Add-member -NotePropertyName VMHost
-NotePropertyValue "ESX1"
PowerCLI C:\> $Object


VM                                      VMHost
```

```
--                              ------
VM1                             ESX1
```

This technique was common in PowerShell V1. Because it is the slowest method to create PowerShell objects, it is not used often anymore.

The `Add-Member` cmdlet adds properties to the input object and does not generate output unless you specify the `-PassThru` parameter. If you want to use more than one `Add-Member` commands in a pipeline, don't forget to use the `-PassThru` parameter, for example:

```
PowerCLI C:\> New-Object -TypeName PSObject |
>> Add-member -NotePropertyName VM -NotePropertyValue "VM1" -Passthru |
>> Add-member -NotePropertyName VMHost -NotePropertyValue "ESX1"
-Passthru
>>

VM                              VMHost
--                              ------
VM1                             ESX1
```

An advantage of the `Add-Member` cmdlet over the other methods to create PowerShell objects is that you can specify the type of the member to add. All other methods only create properties of type `NoteProperty`.

Using COM objects

You can also use the `New-Object` cmdlet to create an instance of a COM object. COM objects were used a lot in VBScript. In PowerShell, you can still use them to do things that you cannot do in native PowerShell. The following example will use the `SAPI.SpVoice` COM object to output a text as voice. It will say **The script is finished.** Append this piece of code at the end of your PowerCLI script, and you will hear your computer say that the script is finished so that you don't have to keep watching your computer screen. Isn't this cool?

```
PowerCLI C:\> $Voice = New-Object -ComObject SAPI.SpVoice
PowerCLI C:\> $Voice.Speak("The script is finished.") | Out-Null
```

The output of the $Voice.Speak() method is piped to the Out-Null cmdlet to suppress output to the screen. The Out-Null cmdlet sends the output to the NULL device, which is the same as deleting it.

You can get a list of all of the COM objects on your computer with the following PowerShell code:

```
Get-ChildItem -Path HKLM:\Software\Classes -ErrorAction `
SilentlyContinue |
Where-Object {$_.PSChildName -match '^\w+\.\w+$' -and `
(Get-Itemproperty "$($_.PSPath)\CLSID" -ErrorAction `
SilentlyContinue)} |
Format-Table -Property PSChildName
```

The script lists all of the subkeys in the HKEY_LOCAL_MACHINE\Software\Classes registry key. It then uses a regular expression to select only the subkeys with a PSChildName property that contains two words separated by a dot. The subkeys must have a subkey themselves named CLSID. Finally, the value of the PSChildName property is shown in a table format.

The script uses the backtick or *grave accent* (`` ` ``), the Microsoft PowerShell continuation character, to continue commands on the next line.

You cannot use all of the COM objects in a PowerShell script. Some COM objects are not compatible with PowerShell.

Summary

In this chapter, you learned how to use PowerShell objects, their properties, and methods. You saw variable and subexpression expansion in strings and here-strings. You learned about the PowerShell pipeline and parameter binding using the ByValue or ByPropertyName parameter binding types. You learned how to use the PowerShell object cmdlets: Select-Object, Where-Object, ForEach-Object, Sort-Object, Measure-Object, Group-Object, Compare-Object, Tee-Object, and New-Object. We looked at different methods to create new objects. Finally, you saw an example of how to use COM objects. In the next chapter, you will learn how to manage VMware vSphere Hosts with PowerCLI.

4
Managing vSphere Hosts with PowerCLI

In a VMware vSphere environment, the hosts are the working horses. They provide the power on which the virtual machines run. So before you can deploy your virtual machines, you first have to deploy your hosts.

In this chapter, you will learn how to manage your hosts using PowerCLI. We will focus on:

- Adding hosts to a VMware vCenter Server
- Enabling and disabling maintenance mode
- Working with host profiles
- Working with host services
- Configuring the host firewall
- Configuring vSphere Image Builder and Auto Deploy
- Using `esxcli` from PowerCLI
- Removing hosts from a VMware vCenter Server

Adding hosts to a VMware vCenter Server

VMware vCenter Server provides a centralized platform to manage your VMware vSphere environments. With vCenter Server, you can create clusters of hosts with **High Availability (HA)** and **Distributed Resource Scheduler (DRS)**. In this section, you will learn how to add hosts to a VMware vCenter Server.

Creating a data center

After deploying a new vCenter Server, you cannot add a host to a vCenter Server until you have created a data center. So we will start with creating a data center. To create a data center, you have to use the `New-Datacenter` cmdlet. This cmdlet has the following syntax:

```
New-Datacenter [-Location] <VIContainer> [-Name] <String>
[-Server <VIServer[]>] [-WhatIf] [-Confirm] [<CommonParameters>]
```

The `-Location` and `-Name` parameters are required.

When you create a data center, you have to specify a value for the location parameter. This location has to be a folder. You can create the data center in the root of your vCenter Server environment. This root is a folder named `Datacenters`. You can also create a subfolder in the `Datacenters` folder and create the data center in this subfolder. It is not possible to create a data center in a folder inside another data center. You can use the following command to find all of the folders that can be used to create data centers in:

```
PowerCLI C:\> Get-Folder -Type Datacenter

Name                          Type
----                          ----
Datacenters                   Datacenter
```

The following screenshot shows how you can create a data center in the vSphere Web Client. This is different from PowerCLI because you can specify the vCenter Server as the location in the vSphere Web Client.

In the following example, we will create a data center named `New York` in the `Datacenters` folder. First, we use the `Get-Folder` cmdlet to get the `Datacenters` folder. Then, we use the pipeline to pass the `Datacenters` folder to the `-Location` parameter of the `New-Datacenter` cmdlet. The `-Location` parameter accepts the pipeline input `ByValue`:

```
PowerCLI C:\> $Datacenter = Get-Folder -Name Datacenters |
>> New-Datacenter -Name "New York"
PowerCLI C:\> $Datacenter

Name
----
New York
```

Creating a cluster

You probably want to create a cluster in which you place your hosts so that you can take advantage of HA and DRS. In Chapter 8, *Managing High Availability and Clustering*, you will learn all about clusters. However, we will show you how to create a default cluster here, so you can make your hosts a member of the cluster.

The following screenshot shows how you can create a cluster in the vSphere Web Client:

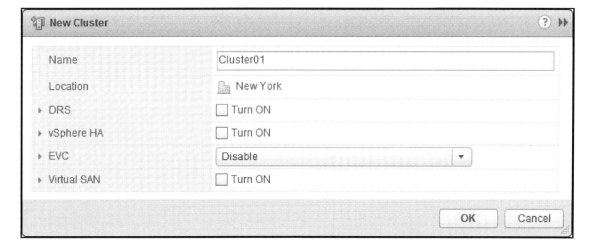

You have to use the New-Cluster cmdlet to create a cluster. The New-Cluster cmdlet has the following syntax:

```
New-Cluster [-HARestartPriority <HARestartPriority>] [-HAIsolationResponse
<HAIsolationResponse>] [-VMSwapfilePolicy <VMSwapfilePolicy>] [-Name]
<String> -Location <VIContainer> [-HAEnabled] [-HAAdmissionControlEnabled]
[-HAFailoverLevel <Int32>] [-DrsEnabled] [-DrsMode <DrsMode>] [-
DrsAutomationLevel <DrsAutomationLevel>] [-VsanDiskClaimMode
<VsanDiskClaimMode>] [-VsanEnabled] [-EVCMode <String>] [-Server
<VIServer[]>] [-WhatIf] [-Confirm] [<CommonParameters>]
```

To create a default cluster, you only have to specify the name and location. The -Name and -Location parameters are required:

```
PowerCLI C:\> $Cluster = New-Cluster -Name Cluster01 -Location
$Datacenter PowerCLI C:\> $Cluster

Name        HAEnabled HAFailoverLevel DrsEnabled DrsAutomationLevel
----        --------- --------------- ---------- ------------------
Cluster01 False       1               False      FullyAutomated
```

Adding a host

To add a host to a VMware vCenter Server, you need to use the Add-VMHost cmdlet. This cmdlet has the following syntax:

```
Add-VMHost [-Name] <String> [-Port <Int32>] [-Location] <VIContainer> [-
Credential <PSCredential>] [-User <String>] [-Password <String>] [-Force]
[-RunAsync] [-Server <VIServer[]>] [-WhatIf] [-Confirm]
[<CommonParameters>]
```

The -Name and -Location parameters are required.

The following screenshot shows how you can add a host to a cluster in the vSphere Web Client:

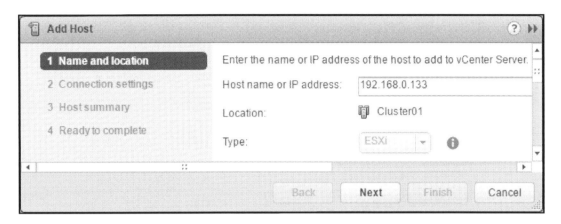

While adding a host to a vCenter Server, you have to supply the username and the password for the user you want to use, to authenticate with the host. You can specify the username and password as a string, or you can use the -Credential parameter and pass a PSCredential object created with the Get-Credential cmdlet. You also have to specify the DNS name or IP address of the host and the location where you want to add the host. Let's try to add the host to the cluster we created in the preceding section. The following screenshot will show you the output of the Add-VMHost cmdlet:

As you can see from the error message, the command failed because the host is using a self-signed SSL certificate. You have to give the host a trusted certificate or you can use the -Force parameter to skip the certificate check. Take a look at the following code:

```
PowerCLI C:\> Add-VMHost -Name 192.168.0.133 -Location $Cluster `
>> -User root -Password VMware1! -Force

Name                ConnectionState PowerState NumCpu CpuUsageMhz
----                --------------- ---------- ------ -----------
192.168.0.133       Connected       PoweredOn       2           0
```

The host is now added to the cluster. You can check this with the following command:

```
PowerCLI C:\> $Cluster | Get-VMHost

Name                ConnectionState PowerState NumCpu CpuUsageMhz
----                --------------- ---------- ------ -----------
192.168.0.133       Connected       PoweredOn       2          49
```

Enabling and disabling maintenance mode

If you want to shut down, patch, upgrade, or reconfigure a host, you do not want any virtual machines running on the host. If you put a host in **maintenance mode**, you are sure that no virtual machines will be moved to or started on the host. If the host is running on a fully automated DRS-enabled cluster, the DRS will move the running virtual machines from the host to other hosts in the cluster using vMotion.

The following screenshot of the vSphere Web Client shows the different DRS automation levels that a cluster can have:

To put a host in maintenance mode, you have to use the Set-VMHost cmdlet.

This cmdlet has the following syntax:

```
Set-VMHost [-VMHost] <VMHost[]> [[-State] <VMHostState>] [-VMSwapfilePolicy
<VMSwapfilePolicy>] [-VMSwapfileDatastore <Datastore>] [-Profile
<VMHostProfile>] [-Evacuate] [-TimeZone <VMHostTimeZone>] [-LicenseKey
<String>] [-VsanDataMigrationMode <VsanDataMigrationMode>] [-Server
<VIServer[]>] [-RunAsync] [-WhatIf] [-Confirm] [<CommonParameters>]
```

The –VMHost parameter is required.

To put a host in maintenance mode, you have to set the state to Maintenance. To disable maintenance mode, you have to set the state to Connected. The Set-VMHost –State parameter has a third possible value, which is Disconnected. You can use Disconnected to disconnect a host from the vCenter Server.

So, let's put the host in maintenance mode first:

```
PowerCLI C:\> $VMHost = Get-VMHost -Name 192.168.0.133
PowerCLI C:\> $VMHost | Set-VMHost -State Maintenance

Name              ConnectionState PowerState NumCpu CpuUsageMhz
----              --------------- ---------- ------ -----------
192.168.0.133 Maintenance        PoweredOn       2          47
```

To disable maintenance mode, you have to use the following command:

```
PowerCLI C:\> $VMHost | Set-VMHost -State Connected

Name              ConnectionState PowerState NumCpu CpuUsageMhz
----              --------------- ---------- ------ -----------
192.168.0.133 Connected          PoweredOn       2         139
```

Working with host profiles

A host profile is a collection of all of the configuration settings for an ESXi host, such as storage and networking configurations and security settings. You can create a host profile from a reference host or import an existing host profile. After attaching a host profile to a host, the host can be checked for compliance with the host profile. If the host is compliant, you know the settings of the host are the same as the settings of the host profile. If the host is not compliant, the host profile can be applied to the host to make the host compliant.

The following screenshot of the vSphere Web Client shows you some of the settings that you can configure in a host profile:

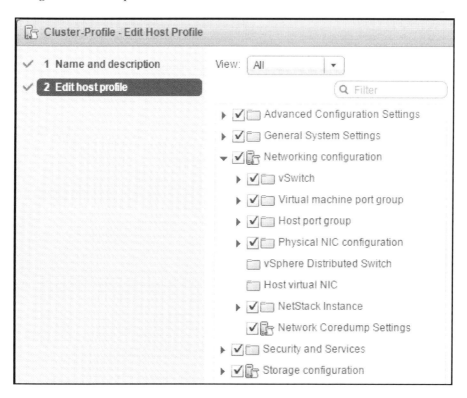

Common Information Model (**CIM**) indication subscriptions are subscriptions to notifications for hardware-related events, such as problems with the cooling, battery, processor, memory, or power of an ESXi server.

Creating a host profile

To get started, you first need to configure a reference host. You have to configure general system settings, such as date and time configuration; network configuration, such as, switches, port groups, and NICs; security and services; and storage and advanced configuration settings, such as DirectPath I/O configuration. Once you are happy with the configuration of the reference host, you create a new host profile using the configuration of the reference host as a base. You need to use `New-VMHostProfile` to create the host profile.

The `New-VMHostProfile` cmdlet has the following syntax:

```
New-VMHostProfile [-Name] <String> [-ReferenceHost] <VMHost> [-Description
<String>] [-CompatibilityMode] [-Server <VIServer[]>] [-WhatIf] [-Confirm]
[<CommonParameters>]
```

The `-Name` and `-ReferenceHost` parameters are required.

Let's create a host profile named `Cluster-Profile` using host `192.168.0.133` as a reference host, as follows:

```
PowerCLI C:\> New-VMHostProfile -Name Cluster-Profile -ReferenceHost
192.168.0.133 -Description "Host Profile for cluster"

Name                              Description
----                              -----------
Cluster-Profile                   Host Profile for cluster
```

Attaching the host profile to a cluster or a host

After creating the host profile, you have to attach the host profile to a cluster or a host. You can attach a profile using the PowerCLI `Invoke-VMHostProfile -AssociateOnly` command.

The `Invoke-VMHostProfile` cmdlet has the following syntax:

```
Invoke-VMHostProfile [-Entity] <InventoryItem[]> [-Profile <VMHostProfile>]
[-Variable <Hashtable>] [-AssociateOnly] [-ApplyOnly] [-RunAsync] [-Server
<VIServer[]>] [-WhatIf] [-Confirm] [<CommonParameters>]
```

The `-Entity` parameter is required, and it accepts pipeline input.

The following screenshot shows you how to attach a host profile in the vSphere Web Client:

Let's attach the host profile to cluster `Cluster01` we created earlier in this chapter:

```
PowerCLI C:\> Get-Cluster -Name Cluster01 |
>> Invoke-VMHostProfile -Profile Cluster-Profile -AssociateOnly
-Confirm:$false

Name       HAEnabled HAFailoverLevel DrsEnabled DrsAutomationLevel
----       --------- --------------- ---------- ------------------
Cluster01 False     1                False      FullyAutomated
```

The `-Confirm:$false` parameter suppresses the prompt for confirmation before executing the command.

Testing the host profile for compliance

After attaching a host profile to a cluster or a host, you can use the `Test-VMHostProfileCompliance` cmdlet for compliance with the profile.

The `Test-VMHostProfileCompliance` cmdlet has the following syntax. You can use the first parameter set to specify a host to test for compliance with the attached profile:

```
Test-VMHostProfileCompliance [-VMHost] <VMHost[]> [-UseCache]
[[-Server] <VIServer[]>] [<CommonParameters>]
```

The `-VMHost` parameter is required.

The second parameter set can be used to specify a host profile. All of the clusters and hosts attached to the profile will be tested for compliance against the host profile:

```
Test-VMHostProfileCompliance [-Profile] <VMHostProfile[]> [-UseCache]
[[-Server] <VIServer[]>] [<CommonParameters>]
```

The `-Profile` parameter is required.

There is no parameter set in which you can specify a cluster to check for compliance.

If you want to check a cluster for compliance against a host profile, you either have to specify the host profile or all of the hosts in the cluster.

Let's test the `Cluster-Profile` host profile for compliance against all attached clusters and hosts:

```
PowerCLI C:\> Test-VMHostProfileCompliance -Profile Cluster-Profile
```

If the command returns nothing, it means that the host profile is compliant against all attached clusters and hosts. In this case, you could expect that the `Cluster-Profile` host profile was compliant because we used the host `192.168.0.133` as a reference host and this host is the only host in the cluster.

Let's add a second host to the cluster and test it for compliance:

```
PowerCLI C:\> Add-VMHost -Name 192.168.0.134 -Location $Cluster `
>> -User root -Password VMware1! -Force

Name              ConnectionState PowerState NumCpu CpuUsageMhz
----              --------------- ---------- ------ -----------
192.168.0.134     Maintenance     PoweredOn       2           0
```

I made some changes to the configuration of the new host, so let's check whether the `Test-VMHostProfileCompliance` cmdlet finds them:

```
PowerCLI C:\> Test-VMHostProfileCompliance -Profile Cluster-Profile |
>> Select-Object -ExpandProperty IncomplianceElementList

PropertyName    Description
------------    -----------
network.ipRo... Number of IPv4 routes did not match
network-vswi... Additional vSwitch(es) vSwitch1 found
network-port... Additional portgroup(s) vMotion found
```

As you can see, the command found three things that are not compliant with the host profile.

Applying a host profile to a host or cluster

You can apply a host profile to a host or cluster so that the configuration of this host or cluster becomes compliant with the host profile. To apply a host profile, you have to use the `Invoke-VMHostProfile` cmdlet that we have used before to attach a host profile to a cluster or a host. The host or cluster must be in maintenance mode before you can apply a host profile to it.

First, we will set the host in maintenance mode, as follows:

```
PowerCLI C:\> $VMHost = Get-VMHost -Name 192.168.0.134
PowerCLI C:\> $VMHost | Set-VMHost -State Maintenance

Name              ConnectionState PowerState NumCpu CpuUsageMhz
----              --------------- ---------- ------ -----------
192.168.0.134     Maintenance     PoweredOn       2          45
```

Next, we will apply the host profile that is attached to the cluster, using the following commands:

```
PowerCLI C:\> $VMHost | Invoke-VMHostProfile -Confirm:$false

Name              ConnectionState PowerState NumCpu CpuUsageMhz
----              --------------- ---------- ------ -----------
192.168.0.134     Maintenance     PoweredOn       2         420
```

You can now test the host for compliance with the host profile, as follows:

```
PowerCLI C:\> Test-VMHostProfileCompliance -VMHost $VMHost
```

If the command returns nothing, the host is compliant.

Using host profile answer files

If you apply a host profile and the host profile requires additional information because settings are configured as `Prompt the user ...`, the `Invoke-VMHostProfile` cmdlet will return a hash table with the settings that need to be answered. For example:

```
PowerCLI C:\> $VMHost = Get-VMHost -Name 192.168.0.134
PowerCLI C:\> $VMHost | Invoke-VMHostProfile -Confirm:$false

Name                               Value
----                               -----
network.hostPortGroup["key-...     00:0c:29:4a:aa:55
network.hostPortGroup["key-...
network.hostPortGroup["key-...
network.dnsConfig.HostNameP...
```

You can save the hash table in a `$HashTable` variable:

```
PowerCLI C:\> $HashTable = $VMHost |
>> Invoke-VMHostProfile -Confirm:$false
>>
```

You can get the full key names of the hash table elements with the following command:

```
PowerCLI C:\> $HashTable.Keys
network.hostPortGroup["key-vim-profile-host-HostPortgroupProfile-Ma
nagementNetwork"].MacAddressPolicy.mac
network.hostPortGroup["key-vim-profile-host-HostPortgroupProfile-Ma
nagementNetwork"].ipConfig.IpAddressPolicy.address
network.hostPortGroup["key-vim-profile-host-HostPortgroupProfile-Ma
nagementNetwork"].ipConfig.IpAddressPolicy.subnetmask
network.dnsConfig.HostNamePolicy.hostName
```

For every empty value in the hash table, you have to specify a value:

```
PowerCLI C:\> $HashTable['network.hostPortGroup["key-vim-profile-hos
t-HostPortgroupProfile-ManagementNetwork"].ipConfig.IpAddressPolicy.
address'] = '192.168.0.134'
PowerCLI C:\> $HashTable['network.hostPortGroup["key-vim-profile-hos
t-HostPortgroupProfile-ManagementNetwork"].ipConfig.IpAddressPolicy.
subnetmask'] = '255.255.255.0'
PowerCLI C:\> $HashTable['network.dnsConfig.HostNamePolicy.hostName'
] = 'Esx001'
```

You are now ready to apply the host profile to the host with the answers you provided in the hash table using the $HashTable variable as the value of the -Variable parameter:

```
PowerCLI C:\> $HashTable = $VMHost |
>> Invoke-VMHostProfile -Variable $HashTable -Confirm:$false
>>
```

Exporting a host profile

You can use the Export-VMHostProfile cmdlet to export a host profile to a file that is in the VMware profile format (.vpf). This can be useful if you want to transfer a host profile to another vCenter Server. Just export the host profile on the first vCenter Server and then import the host profile on the second vCenter Server.

When exporting, a host profile administrator and user profile passwords are not exported for security reasons. When a host profile is imported and applied to a host, you will be prompted to enter values for the passwords.

The syntax of the Export-VMHostProfile cmdlet is as follows:

```
Export-VMHostProfile [-FilePath] <String> [-Profile] <VMHostProfile>
[-Force] [-Server <VIServer>] [<CommonParameters>]
```

The -FilePath and -Profile parameters are required.

Let's export the Cluster-Profile host profile to a .vpf file, using the following command:

```
PowerCLI C:\> Get-VMHostProfile -Name Cluster-Profile |
>> Export-VMHostProfile -FilePath ~\Cluster-Profile.vpf

Mode                LastWriteTime        Length Name
----                -------------        ------ ----
-a----              1/8/2017  10:42 AM   770559 Cluster-Profile.vpf
```

The ~ character in the file path is a PowerShell way to specify the default directory of the current user account.

The Cluster-Profile.vpf file is an XML file that contains the configuration of the reference host that was used to create the host profile. This is a huge file. If you are wondering what is in this file, take a look at the content with Notepad or another editor.

Importing a host profile

You can use the Import-VMHostProfile cmdlet to import a host profile from a file.

The Import-VMHostProfile cmdlet has the following syntax:

```
Import-VMHostProfile [-FilePath] <String> [-Name] <String>
[[-ReferenceHost] <VMHost>] [-Description <String>]
[-Server <VIServer[]>] [-WhatIf] [-Confirm] [<CommonParameters>]
```

The -FilePath and -Name parameters are required.

Let's import the Cluster-Profile.vpf file that we just created to create a new host profile named New-Profile:

```
PowerCLI C:\> Import-VMHostProfile -Name New-Profile `
>> -FilePath C:\Users\Robert\Cluster-Profile.vpf `
>> -ReferenceHost 192.168.0.133 -Description "New profile"
>>

Name                          Description
----                          -----------
New-Profile                   New profile
```

You can now attach the host profile `New-Profile` to a cluster or a host.

 When writing this book, the `Import-VMHostProfile` cmdlet does not understand the ~ character in the value of the `-FilePath` parameter. This is why I use the full path for the `Cluster-Profile.vpf` file.

Working with host services

PowerCLI has some cmdlets to work with host services. You can easily find these cmdlets using the `Get-Command` cmdlet, as follows:

```
PowerCLI C:\> Get-Command -Noun VMHostService
```

The preceding command has the following output:

```
CommandType Name                     ModuleName
----------- ----                     ----------
Cmdlet      Get-VMHostService        VMware.VimAutomation.Core
Cmdlet      Restart-VMHostService    VMware.VimAutomation.Core
Cmdlet      Set-VMHostService        VMware.VimAutomation.Core
Cmdlet      Start-VMHostService      VMware.VimAutomation.Core
Cmdlet      Stop-VMHostService       VMware.VimAutomation.Core
```

In the following sections, we will discus the `*-VMHostService` cmdlets.

Retrieving information about host services

You can use the `Get-VMHostService` cmdlet to retrieve information about the services running on a host.

The syntax of the `Get-VMHostService` cmdlet is:

```
Get-VMHostService [-VMHost] <VMHost[]> [-Refresh] [-Server
<VIServer[]>] [<CommonParameters>]
```

The `-VMHost` parameter is required.

Let's retrieve a list of all of the services of one of the hosts:

```
PowerCLI C:\> Get-VMHostService -VMHost 192.168.0.133

Key              Label                       Policy Running Required
```

```
---             -----                      ------  -------  --------
DCUI            Direct Console UI          on      True     False
TSM             ESXi Shell                 off     False    False
TSM-SSH         SSH                        off     False    False
lbtd            Load-Based Teaming Daemon  on      True     False
lwsmd           Active Directory Service   off     False    False
ntpd            NTP Daemon                 on      True     False
pcscd           PC/SC Smart Card Daemon    off     False    False
sfcbd-watchdog  CIM Server                 on      True     False
snmpd           SNMP Server                on      False    False
vmsyslogd       Syslog Server              on      True     True
vprobed         VProbe Daemon              off     False    False
vpxa            VMware vCenter Agent       on      True     False
xorg            X.Org Server               on      False    False
```

Starting a host service

Starting a host service can be useful to temporarily enable a service. For example, if you want to enable the ESXi shell to log in to an ESXi server, you need to start the TSM service. The `Start-VMHostService` cmdlet will start a host service. The syntax of this cmdlet is as follows:

```
Start-VMHostService [-HostService] <HostService[]> [-WhatIf]
[-Confirm] [<CommonParameters>]
```

The `-HostService` parameter is required.

For example, to start the TSM service, you can use the following command:

```
PowerCLI C:\> Get-VMHost -Name 192.168.0.133 | Get-VMHostService |
>> Where-Object {$_.Key -eq "TSM"} | Start-VMHostService
>>

Key             Label                      Policy  Running  Required
---             -----                      ------  -------  --------
TSM             ESXi Shell                 off     True     False
```

The command first retrieves host `192.68.0.133`. Then, it retrieves all of the services running on the host and selects only the service where the `Key` property has the value `TSM`. Finally, it starts the selected service.

Stopping a host service

After you have temporarily enabled a service, you should stop the service if you don't plan to use it anymore. Some services, such as the SSH service, produce a warning if you keep them running. To stop a service, you need to use the `Stop-VMHostService` cmdlet. The syntax is similar to the `Start-VMHostService` cmdlet's syntax:

```
Stop-VMHostService [-HostService] <HostService[]> [-WhatIf]
[-Confirm] [<CommonParameters>]
```

The `-HostService` parameter is required.

To stop the TSM service we started in the preceding section, use the following command line:

```
PowerCLI C:\> Get-VMHost -Name 192.168.0.133 | Get-VMHostService |
>> Where-Object {$_.Key -eq 'TSM'} |
>> Stop-VMHostService -Confirm:$false
>>

Key            Label                    Policy Running Required
---            -----                    ------ ------- --------
TSM            ESXi Shell               off    False   False
```

As you can see, the command to stop a host service is similar to the command to start a host service from the preceding section.

Restarting a host service

If you want to restart a host service because it is not running well or you modified the settings of the service, you can use the `Restart-VMHostService` cmdlet.

The syntax of this cmdlet is as follows:

```
Restart-VMHostService [-HostService] <HostService[]> [-WhatIf]
[-Confirm] [<CommonParameters>]
```

In the following example, we will restart the TSM service. I modified this example, in comparison with the preceding start and stop host services examples, to show you that in PowerCLI there are different ways you can use to perform a task:

```
PowerCLI C:\> $HostService = Get-VMHost -Name 192.168.0.133 |
>> Get-VMHostService | Where-Object {$_.Key -eq 'TSM'}
>> Restart-VMHostService -HostService $HostService -Confirm:$false
>>
```

```
Key              Label                      Policy Running Required
---              -----                      ------ ------- --------
TSM              ESXi Shell                 off    True    False
```

The command from the preceding example saves the host service with `Key` value `TSM` in a variable named `$HostService`. This variable is used as the value of the `-HostService` parameter in the `Restart-VMHostService` command to restart the service.

Modifying the startup policy of a host service

You can use the `Set-VMHostService` cmdlet to modify the startup policy of a host service.

The following screenshot shows you how to edit the startup policy of a host service in the **vSphere Web Client**:

The syntax of the `Set-VMHostService` cmdlet is:

```
Set-VMHostService [-HostService] <HostService[]> [-Policy]
<HostServicePolicy> [-WhatIf] [-Confirm] [<CommonParameters>]
```

The `-HostService` and `-Policy` parameters are required.

Possible values for the `-Policy` parameter are `automatic`, `on`, and `off`. These values correspond to the following values in the VMware vSphere Client:

VMware vSphere Client service startup policy	Set-VMHostService -Policy value
Start and stop with port usage	`automatic`
Start and stop with host	`on`
Start and stop manually	`off`

Let's modify the startup policy of the `TSM` service and set it to `on`. We will use the `$HostService` variable from the preceding example:

```
PowerCLI C:\> Set-VMHostService -HostService $HostService -Policy on

Key            Label                    Policy  Running  Required
---            -----                    ------  -------  --------
TSM            ESXi Shell               on      True     False
```

In the following example, the startup policy of the `TSM` service for all of your hosts will be set to `off`:

```
PowerCLI C:\> Get-VMHost | Get-VMHostService |
>> Where-Object {$_.Key -eq 'TSM'} |
>> Set-VMHostService -Policy Off
>>

Key            Label                    Policy  Running  Required
---            -----                    ------  -------  --------
TSM            ESXi Shell               off     True     False
TSM            ESXi Shell               off     False    False
```

Configuring the host firewall

A host firewall is a VMware vSphere feature to protect the host against attacks. The host firewall allows or blocks traffic to and from specific host services. You can use PowerCLI to configure the host firewall.

To get a list of all of the PowerCLI cmdlets that you can use to configure a host firewall, type the following command:

```
PowerCLI C:\> Get-Command -Noun VMHostFirewall*

CommandType Name                             ModuleName
----------- ----                             ----------
Cmdlet      Get-VMHostFirewallDefaultPolicy  VMware.VimAutomation.Core
Cmdlet      Get-VMHostFirewallException      VMware.VimAutomation.Core
Cmdlet      Set-VMHostFirewallDefaultPolicy  VMware.VimAutomation.Core
Cmdlet      Set-VMHostFirewallException      VMware.VimAutomation.Core
```

Getting the host firewall default policy

To get the host firewall default policy of a host, you have to use the Get-VMHostFirewallDefaultPolicy cmdlet.

The syntax of the Get-VMHostFirewallDefaultPolicy cmdlet is as follows:

```
Get-VMHostFirewallDefaultPolicy [-VMHost] <VMHost[]> [[-Server]
<VIServer[]>] [<CommonParameters>]
```

The -VMHost parameter is required.

Let's first get the host firewall default policy for a host:

```
PowerCLI C:\> $VMHost = Get-VMHost -Name 192.168.0.133
PowerCLI C:\> Get-VMHostFirewallDefaultPolicy -VMHost $VMHost

IncomingEnabled OutgoingEnabled
--------------- ---------------
False           False
```

In the given example, the default policy is that the incoming and outgoing traffic is disabled. This is, of course, the most secure policy, and it is recommended to keep this policy unless you have a very good reason to change it.

Modifying the host firewall default policy

You can change the host firewall default policy using the Set-VMHostFirewallDefaultPolicy cmdlet.

The `Set-VMHostFirewallDefaultPolicy` cmdlet has the following syntax:

```
Set-VMHostFirewallDefaultPolicy [[-AllowIncoming] [<Boolean>]]
[[-AllowOutgoing] [<Boolean>]] [-Policy]
<VMHostFirewallDefaultPolicy[]> [-WhatIf] [-Confirm]
[<CommonParameters>]
```

Only the `-Policy` parameter is required.

If your host firewall default policy enables incoming or outgoing traffic, you can set it to be disabled for both with the following command:

```
PowerCLI C:\> $VMHost = Get-VMHost -Name 192.168.0.133
PowerCLI C:\> $Policy = $VMHost | Get-VMHostFirewallDefaultPolicy
PowerCLI C:\> $Policy | Set-VMHostFirewallDefaultPolicy `
>> -AllowIncoming $false -AllowOutgoing $false
>>

IncomingEnabled OutgoingEnabled
--------------- ---------------
False           False
```

Getting the host firewall exceptions

You can specify exceptions from the host firewall default policy. To get a list of all of the exceptions for a specific host, you have to use the `Get-VMHostFirewallException` cmdlet.

This cmdlet has the following syntax:

```
Get-VMHostFirewallException [[-Name] <String[]>] [-VMHost]
<VMHost[]> [-Port <Int32[]>] [-Enabled [<Boolean>]]
[-Server <VIServer[]>] [<CommonParameters>]
```

The `-VMHost` parameter is required.

To get a list of all of the exceptions, you can use the following command:

```
PowerCLI C:\> $VMHost | Get-VMHostFirewallException
```

The preceding command has the following output:

```
Name               Enabled IncomingPorts OutgoingPorts Protocols
----               ------- ------------- ------------- ---------
CIM Server         True    5988                        TCP
CIM Secure Server  True    5989                        TCP
```

CIM SLP	True	427	427	UDP, TCP
DHCPv6	False	546	547	TCP, UDP
DVFilter	False	2222		TCP
DVSSync	True	8301, 8302	8302, 8301	UDP
HBR	True		31031, 44046	TCP
NFC	True	902	902	TCP
WOL	True		9	UDP
Active Directory All	False		88, 123, 13...	UDP, TCP
Virtual SAN Clust...	True	12345, 2345...	12345, 2345...	UDP
DHCP Client	True	68	68	UDP
DNS Client	True	53	53	UDP, TCP
esxupdate	False		443	TCP
Fault Tolerance	True	8100, 8200,...	80, 8100, 8...	TCP, UDP
FTP Client	False	20	21	TCP
gdbserver	False	1000-9999, ...		TCP
httpClient	False		80, 443	TCP
Software iSCSI Cl...	False		3260	TCP
iofiltervp	False	9080		TCP
NSX Distributed L...	False	6999	6999	UDP
nfs41Client	False		0-65535	TCP
NFS Client	False		0-65535	TCP
NTP Client	True		123	UDP
pvrdma	False	28250-28761	28250-28761	TCP
rabbitmqproxy	True		5671	TCP
Virtual SAN Trans...	True	2233	2233	TCP
VM serial port co...	False	23, 1024-65535	0-65535	TCP
SNMP Server	True	161		UDP
SSH Client	False		22	TCP
SSH Server	True	22		TCP
syslog	False		514, 1514	UDP, TCP
vCenter Update Ma...	True		80, 9000-9100	TCP
vMotion	True	8000	8000	TCP
VM serial port co...	False		0-65535	TCP
vSphere Web Client	True	902, 443		TCP
VMware vCenter Agent	True		902	UDP
vsanEncryption	False		0-65535	TCP
vsanhealth-multic...	False	5001	5001	UDP
vsanvp	True	8080	8080	TCP
vvold	False		0-65535	TCP
vSphere Web Access	True	80		TCP

You can use the `-Name` or `-Port` parameters to filter for a specific exception. For example, to get all of the exceptions for port number `22`, use the following command:

```
PowerCLI C:\> $VMHost | Get-VMHostFirewallException -Port 22
Name                  Enabled IncomingPorts OutgoingPorts Protocols
----                  ------- ------------- ------------- ---------
nfs41Client           False                 0-65535       TCP
```

```
NFS Client             False                        0-65535    TCP
VM serial port co... False     23, 1024-65535 0-65535    TCP
SSH Client             False                        22         TCP
SSH Server             True      22                            TCP
VM serial port co... False                        0-65535    TCP
vsanEncryption         False                        0-65535    TCP
vvold                  False                        0-65535    TCP
```

Modifying a host firewall exception

Sometimes, it is necessary to make changes to the host firewall exceptions, for example, when you want to configure an external syslog server. In this section, I will show you how to do this.

To modify the host firewall exceptions, you have to use the Set-VMHostFirewallException cmdlet. This cmdlet has the following syntax:

```
Set-VMHostFirewallException [-Enabled] [<Boolean>] [-Exception]
<VMHostFirewallException[]> [-WhatIf] [-Confirm] [<CommonParameters>]
```

The -Enabled and -Exception parameters are required.

Let's assume that we have configured a syslog server on a vCenter Server 192.168.0.132. To configure the syslog server on the host, you can use the Set-VMHostSysLogServer cmdlet. The syntax of this cmdlet is as follows:

```
Set-VMHostSysLogServer [[-SysLogServer] <NamedIPEndPoint[]>]
[-VMHost] <VMHost[]> [-SysLogServerPort <Int32>] [-Server
<VIServer[]>] [-WhatIf] [-Confirm] [<CommonParameters>]
```

The -VMHost parameter is required. The -SysLogServerPort parameter is deprecated. Specify the port through the -SyslogServer parameter.

First, you need to set the remote syslog server, using the following command:

```
PowerCLI C:\> $VMHost | Set-VMHostSysLogServer `
>> -SysLogServer 192.168.0.132:514

Host                            Port
----                            ----
192.168.0.132                   514
```

After this, you have to enable the host firewall exception for the syslog server:

```
PowerCLI C:\> $VMHost | Get-VMHostFirewallException -Name syslog | `
>> Set-VMHostFirewallException -Enabled $true

Name                 Enabled IncomingPorts  OutgoingPorts  Protocols
----                 ------- -------------  -------------  ---------
syslog               True                   514, 1514      UDP, TCP
```

Using vSphere Image Builder and Auto Deploy

VMware vSphere **Auto Deploy** is a cool feature introduced in VMware vSphere 5.0 that enables you to provide physical hosts with the ESXi software via the PXE boot instead of installing an ESXi server from a CD-ROM. Auto Deploy can be useful if you need to deploy many ESXi servers. If you only have a few ESXi servers, Auto Deploy is probably not the best solution for you because of the amount of work you have to do to set up Auto Deploy. To enable Auto Deploy, you need a vCenter Server, an Auto Deploy server, a DNS server, a DHCP server, a TFTP server, and PowerCLI. Yes, you have seen it right. PowerCLI is a core component of Auto Deploy. All of the information you need to enable and configure Auto Deploy can be found in the VMware document, *vSphere Installation and Setup Guide*. You can download this document from the VMware documentation page at
https://www.vmware.com/support/pubs/.

 Because this is a PowerCLI book, we will focus on the PowerCLI cmdlets that you can use to create and deploy a host image.

Using Image Builder

Before you can deploy an image using Auto Deploy, you first have to create the image using **Image Builder**. In PowerCLI, the Image Builder cmdlets are in a separate module named VMware.ImageBuilder. This module is loaded by default if you start PowerCLI. Let's get a list of all of the Image Builder cmdlets:

```
PowerCLI C:\> Get-Command -Module VMware.ImageBuilder

CommandType Name                         ModuleName
----------- ----                         ----------
```

```
Cmdlet          Add-EsxSoftwareDepot          VMware.ImageBuilder
Cmdlet          Add-EsxSoftwarePackage        VMware.ImageBuilder
Cmdlet          Compare-EsxImageProfile       VMware.ImageBuilder
Cmdlet          Export-EsxImageProfile        VMware.ImageBuilder
Cmdlet          Get-EsxImageProfile           VMware.ImageBuilder
Cmdlet          Get-EsxSoftwareDepot          VMware.ImageBuilder
Cmdlet          Get-EsxSoftwarePackage        VMware.ImageBuilder
Cmdlet          New-EsxImageProfile           VMware.ImageBuilder
Cmdlet          Remove-EsxImageProfile        VMware.ImageBuilder
Cmdlet          Remove-EsxSoftwareDepot       VMware.ImageBuilder
Cmdlet          Remove-EsxSoftwarePackage     VMware.ImageBuilder
Cmdlet          Set-EsxImageProfile           VMware.ImageBuilder
```

Adding ESXi software depots to your PowerCLI session

First, you have to add an ESXi software depot to your PowerCLI session. An ESXi software depot contains image profiles and **vSphere Installation Bundle** (VIB) files. An image profile is a list of VIBs. If you want to know what is in VIB, you can read this at `http://blogs.vmware.com/vsphere/2011/09/whats-in-a-vib.html`.

Use the `Add-EsxSoftwareDepot` cmdlet to add an ESXi software depot or **ESXi Offline Bundle** to your PowerCLI session. You can use an ESXi software depot provided on the VMware website, or you can download the ESXi installable from the VMware website in the `zip` format. For example, for ESXi 6.5, this file is named `VMware-ESXi-6.5.0-4564106-depot.zip`.

The `Add-EsxSoftwareDepot` cmdlet has the following syntax:

```
Add-EsxSoftwareDepot [-DepotUrl] <String[]> [-WarningAction
<ActionPreference>] [-WarningVariable <String>] [<CommonParameters>]
```

The `-DepotUrl` parameter is required.

To add the official VMware software depot to your PowerCLI session, use the following PowerCLI command:

```
PowerCLI C:\> Add-EsxSoftwareDepot -DepotUrl
https://hostupdate.vmware.com/software/VUM/PRODUCTION/
main/vmw-depot-index.xml

Depot Url
---------
https://hostupdate.vmware.com/software/VUM/PRODUCTION/main/vmw-d...
```

To add the official Hewlett Packard Enterprise software depot to your PowerCLI session, use the following command:

```
PowerCLI C:\> Add-EsxSoftwareDepot -DepotUrl
http://vibsdepot.hpe.com/index.xml

Depot Url
---------
http://vibsdepot.hpe.com/index.xml
```

To add the software depot from an ESXi software depot file that you downloaded from the VMware website, use a command similar to the following code:

```
PowerCLI C:\> Add-EsxSoftwareDepot -DepotUrl C:\users\Robert\
Downloads\VMware-ESXi-6.5.0-4564106-depot.zip'

Depot Url
---------
zip:C:\users\Robert\Downloads\VMware-ESXi-6.5.0-4564106
-depot.zip?index.xml
```

Retrieving the ESXi software depots added to your PowerCLI session

You can use the Get-EsxSoftwareDepot cmdlet to retrieve a list of the software depots you added to your PowerCLI session. The Get-EsxSoftwareDepot cmdlet has the following syntax:

```
Get-EsxSoftwareDepot [-WhatIf] [-Confirm] [<CommonParameters>]
```

The following command will retrieve a list of the software depots you added to your PowerCLI session:

```
PowerCLI C:\> Get-EsxSoftwareDepot

Depot Url
---------
https://hostupdate.vmware.com/software/VUM/PRODUCTION/main/vmw-de...
http://vibsdepot.hpe.com/index.xml
http://192.168.0.132/vSphere-HA-depot/index.xml
zip:C:\users\Robert\Downloads\VMware-ESXi-6.5.0-4564106-depot.zip...
file://custom/depot/index.xml
```

Retrieving the image profiles in your PowerCLI session

After adding ESXi software depots to your PowerCLI session, you can use the `Get-EsxImageProfile` cmdlet to see the image profiles in your PowerCLI session.

The `Get-EsxImageProfile` cmdlet has the following syntax:

```
Get-EsxImageProfile [[-Name] <String[]>] [[-Vendor] <String[]>]
[[-AcceptanceLevel] <AcceptanceLevels[]>] [-WarningAction
<ActionPreference>] [-WarningVariable <String>] [-WhatIf] [-Confirm]
[<CommonParameters>]
```

The following command will retrieve the image profiles of ESXi 6.5 in your PowerCLI session:

```
PowerCLI C:\> Get-EsxImageProfile | Where-Object {$_.Name -like 'Esxi
-6.5.0*'}
```

Name	Vendor	Last Modified	Acceptance Level
ESXi-6.5.0-4564106-standard	VMware, Inc.	10/27/2016 5:43:44 AM	Pa...
ESXi-6.5.0-4564106-no-tools	VMware, Inc.	10/27/2016 5:43:44 AM	Pa...

Creating image profiles

You can create new image profiles from scratch, or you can clone existing image profiles using the `New-EsxImageProfile` cmdlet. The newly created image profiles will exist in your PowerCLI session until you close the session. If you want to keep the image profiles for later use after you close your PowerCLI session, you will have to export the image profiles using the `Export-EsxImageProfile` cmdlet discussed later in this chapter. The syntax of the `New-EsxImageProfile` cmdlet is as follows. The first parameter set is for creating image profiles from scratch:

```
New-EsxImageProfile -NewProfile [-Name] <String> [-Vendor]
<String> -SoftwarePackage <SoftwarePackage[]> [-AcceptanceLevel
<AcceptanceLevels>] [-Description <String>] [-ReadOnly] [-WarningAction
<ActionPreference>] [-WarningVariable <String>] [-WhatIf] [-Confirm]
[<CommonParameters>]
```

The `-NewProfile`, `-Name`, `-Vendor`, and `-SoftwarePackage` parameters are required.

The second parameter set is for cloning image profiles:

```
New-EsxImageProfile -CloneProfile <ImageProfile> [-Name]
<String> [-Vendor] <String> -SoftwarePackage <SoftwarePackage[]>
[-AcceptanceLevel <AcceptanceLevels>] [-Description <String>]
[-ReadOnly] [-WarningAction <ActionPreference>] [-WarningVariable
<String>] [-WhatIf] [-Confirm] [<CommonParameters>]
```

The second parameter set is for cloning image profiles.

The `-NewProfile`, `-Name`, `-Vendor`, and `-CloneProfile` parameters are required.

In the following example, we will clone the `ESXi-6.5.0-4564106-standard` image profile and will name the new image profile `ESXi-6.5.0-cloned`. Because I made the image profile, I will use `MySelf` as the name of the vendor:

```
PowerCLI C:\> New-EsxImageProfile -CloneProfile
'ESXi-6.5.0-4564106-standard' -Name 'ESXi-6.5.0-cloned' -Vendor
'MySelf'

Name                 Vendor Last Modified        Acceptance Level
----                 ------ -------------        ----------------
ESXi-6.5.0-cloned MySelf 10/27/2016 5:43:44 AM PartnerSupported
```

Retrieving VIB objects from all of the connected depots

To retrieve a list of **SoftwarePackage (VIB) objects** from all of the connected depots, you can use the `Get-EsxSoftwarePackage` cmdlet. The `Get-EsxSoftwarePackage` cmdlet has the following syntax:

```
Get-EsxSoftwarePackage [[-Name] <String[]>] [[-Version] <String[]>]
[-Vendor <String[]>] [-Tag <String[]>] [-AcceptanceLevel
<AcceptanceLevels[]>] [-CreatedBefore <DateTime>] [-CreatedAfter
<DateTime>] [-Newest] [-WarningAction <ActionPreference>]
[-WarningVariable <String>] [-WhatIf] [-Confirm] [<CommonParameters>]
Get-EsxSoftwarePackage [-PackageUrl <String[]>] [<CommonParameters>]
```

If you use the cmdlet without any parameters, it will return all of the VIBs from all of the connected depots. You can use the parameters to filter for specific VIBs. For example, the following command will retrieve all of the VIBs with a name starting with `emulex`:

```
PowerCLI C:\> Get-EsxSoftwarePackage -Name emulex*

Name                  Version                   Vendor Creation Date
----                  -------                   ------ -------------
emulex-esx-elxnetcli  10.2.309.6v-0.0.2494585   VMware 2/6/2015 2:37...
emulex-esx-elxnetcli  11.1.28.0-0.0.4564106     VMware 10/27/2016 4:...
```

Adding VIBs to an image profile or updating existing VIBs

To add new VIBs to an image profile or update existing VIBs in an image profile, you can use the `Add-EsxSoftwarePackage` cmdlet. You may want to add a VIB because it contains a device driver for a device in your ESXi server hardware. It can be necessary to update a VIB because VMware or another vendor released a patch that solves a problem you have. The `Add-EsxSoftwarePackage` cmdlet has the following syntax:

```
Add-EsxSoftwarePackage [-ImageProfile] <ImageProfile>
[-SoftwarePackage] <SoftwarePackage[]> [-Force] [-WarningAction
<ActionPreference>] [-WarningVariable <String>] [-WhatIf] [-Confirm]
[<CommonParameters>]
```

The `-ImageProfile` and `-SoftwarePackage` parameters are required.

In the following example, we will add the `hpnmi` VIB from the Hewlett-Packard Enterprise software depot to the `ESXi-6.5.0-cloned` image profile we created in a preceding section of this chapter:

```
PowerCLI C:\> Get-EsxImageProfile -Name ESXi-6.5.0-cloned |
>> Add-EsxSoftwarePackage -SoftwarePackage hpnmi

Name              Vendor Last Modified          Acceptance Level
----              ------ -------------          ----------------
ESXi-6.5.0-cloned MySelf 1/8/2017 10:02:48 AM   PartnerSupported
```

Exporting an image profile to an ISO or ZIP file

You can export an image profile to an ESXi ISO image or an offline bundle ZIP file. An ESXi ISO image can be booted up and used as an ESXi installer.

An offline depot ZIP file can be:

- Imported into VMware Update Manager for patch remediation
- Downloaded to an ESXi host and used for installation with `esxcli`
- Imported into Image Builder using the `Add-EsxSoftwareDepot` cmdlet

To export an image profile, you have to use the `Export-EsxImageProfile` cmdlet that has the following syntax. The first parameter set is for exporting to an ISO:

```
Export-EsxImageProfile [-ImageProfile] <ImageProfile> [-FilePath]
<String> -ExportToIso [-Force] [-NoSignatureCheck] [-RunAsync]
[-WarningAction <ActionPreference>] [-WarningVariable <String>]
[<CommonParameters>]
```

The `-ImageProfile`, `-FilePath`, and `-ExportToIso` parameters are required.

The second parameter set is for creating an offline bundle ZIP file:

```
Export-EsxImageProfile [-ImageProfile] <ImageProfile> [-FilePath]
<String> -ExportToBundle [-Force] [-NoSignatureCheck] [-RunAsync]
[-WarningAction <ActionPreference>] [-WarningVariable <String>]
[<CommonParameters>]
```

The `-ImageProfile`, `-FilePath`, and `-ExportToBundle` parameters are required.

In the following example, we will export the `ESXi-6.5.0-cloned` image profile created in the preceding sections to an ISO file, so we can use it to install ESXi servers:

```
PowerCLI C:\> Get-EsxImageProfile -Name ESXi-6.5.0-cloned |
>> Export-EsxImageProfile -FilePath c:\users\Robert\
ESXi-6.5.0-cloned.iso -ExportToIso
```

The preceding command does not return any output.

Configuring Auto Deploy

The Auto Deploy cmdlets are in the PowerCLI module `VMware.DeployAutomation`. You can use the `Get-Command` cmdlet to list all of the Auto Deploy cmdlets:

```
PowerCLI C:\> Get-Command -Module VMware.DeployAutomation
```

CommandType	Name	Version	Source
Alias	Apply-ESXImageProfile	6.0.0.0	VMware.DeployA...
Function	Get-AutoDeployCommand	6.0.0.0	VMware.DeployA...

```
Cmdlet       Add-DeployRule                   6.0.0.0 VMware.DeployA...
Cmdlet       Add-ProxyServer                  6.0.0.0 VMware.DeployA...
Cmdlet       Add-ScriptBundle                 6.0.0.0 VMware.DeployA...
Cmdlet       Copy-DeployRule                  6.0.0.0 VMware.DeployA...
Cmdlet       Export-AutoDeployState           6.0.0.0 VMware.DeployA...
Cmdlet       Get-DeployOption                 6.0.0.0 VMware.DeployA...
Cmdlet       Get-DeployRule                   6.0.0.0 VMware.DeployA...
Cmdlet       Get-DeployRuleSet                6.0.0.0 VMware.DeployA...
Cmdlet       Get-ProxyServer                  6.0.0.0 VMware.DeployA...
Cmdlet       Get-ScriptBundle                 6.0.0.0 VMware.DeployA...
Cmdlet       Get-VMHostAttributes             6.0.0.0 VMware.DeployA...
Cmdlet       Get-VMHostImageProfile           6.0.0.0 VMware.DeployA...
Cmdlet       Get-VMHostMatchingRules          6.0.0.0 VMware.DeployA...
Cmdlet       Import-AutoDeployState           6.0.0.0 VMware.DeployA...
Cmdlet       New-DeployRule                   6.0.0.0 VMware.DeployA...
Cmdlet       Remove-DeployRule                6.0.0.0 VMware.DeployA...
Cmdlet       Remove-ProxyServer               6.0.0.0 VMware.DeployA...
Cmdlet       Repair-DeployImageCache          6.0.0.0 VMware.DeployA...
Cmdlet       Repair-DeployRuleSetCompliance   6.0.0.0 VMware.DeployA...
Cmdlet       Set-DeployOption                 6.0.0.0 VMware.DeployA...
Cmdlet       Set-DeployRule                   6.0.0.0 VMware.DeployA...
Cmdlet       Set-DeployRuleSet                6.0.0.0 VMware.DeployA...
Cmdlet       Set-ESXImageProfileAssociation   6.0.0.0 VMware.DeployA...
Cmdlet       Switch-ActiveDeployRuleSet       6.0.0.0 VMware.DeployA...
Cmdlet       Test-DeployRuleSetCompliance     6.0.0.0 VMware.DeployA...
```

Before you can use Auto Deploy, you have to start the VMware Auto Deploy Service. You can do this in the vSphere Web Client with the following path:

Administration | **System Configuration** | **Services** | **Auto Deploy** | **Actions** | **Start**

You also have to set the startup type of the VMware Auto Deploy Service to Automatic to start the VMware Auto Deploy Service when the vCenter Server starts, using the following path:

Administration | **System Configuration** | **Services** | **Auto Deploy** | **Actions** | **Edit Startup Type...** | **Automatic** | **OK**

Creating deploy rules

Now that we have the image profiles created with Image Builder, we need to create deploy rules to specify the image to be deployed to the hosts. You can create a deploy rule using the New-DeployRule cmdlet that has the following syntax:

```
New-DeployRule [-Name] <String> -Pattern <String[]> -Item
<VIObjectCore[]> [<CommonParameters>]
New-DeployRule [-Name] <String> -AllHosts -Item <VIObjectCore[]>
[<CommonParameters>]
```

The -Name and -Item parameters are required. If you use the -AllHosts parameter, the new rule will be applied to all of the hosts managed by Auto Deploy.

Let's create a deploy rule that will deploy the ESXi-6.5.0-4564106-standard image to all of the hosts:

```
PowerCLI C:\> New-DeployRule -Name ImageRule `
>> -Item ESXi-6.5.0-4564106-standard -AllHosts
```

The preceding command generates too many lines of output to show them all in this book. The command will download all of the VIBs in the image profile and upload them to the Auto Deploy server. For all of the VIBs it shows the status of downloading the VIB, and the status of uploading the VIB to the Auto Deploy server.

I will show only the last few lines of output for the preceding command:

```
Downloading shim-iscsi-linux-9-2-1-0 6.5.0-0.0.4564106
Download finished, uploading to AutoDeploy...
Upload finished.

Name        : ImageRule
PatternList :
ItemList    : {ESXi-6.5.0-4564106-standard}
```

You also need to create a deploy rule that specifies the location for the hosts. Let's locate the hosts in the data center New York:

```
PowerCLI C:\> New-DeployRule -Name LocationRule -Item "New York" `
>> -AllHosts

Name        : LocationRule
PatternList :
ItemList    : {New York}
```

Adding deploy rules to a ruleset

There are two rulesets in Auto Deploy, the working, and the active ruleset. The working ruleset can be used to test changes you made to the ruleset before making them active. The active ruleset specifies how new hosts unknown to the vCenter Server will be deployed.

Now, we have to add the rules created in the preceding section to the working and active rulesets using the `Add-DeployRule` cmdlet. The `Add-DeployRule` cmdlet has the following syntax:

```
Add-DeployRule [-DeployRule] <DeployRule[]> [[-At] <UInt32>]
[-NoActivate] [<CommonParameters>]
```

The `-DeployRule` parameter is required. If you use the `-NoActive` parameter, the rule is added to the working ruleset but not to the active ruleset.

You must have the `AutoDeploy.RuleSet.Edit` privilege on the root folder of the vCenter Server to use this cmdlet.

To add both rules to the working and active ruleset, use the following command:

```
PowerCLI C:\> Add-DeployRule -DeployRule ImageRule

Name        : ImageRule
PatternList :
ItemList    : {ESXi-6.5.0-4564106-standard}

PowerCLI C:\> Add-DeployRule -DeployRule LocationRule

Name        : ImageRule
PatternList :
ItemList    : {ESXi-6.5.0-4564106-standard}

Name        : LocationRule
PatternList :
ItemList    : {New York}
```

Retrieving deploy rulesets

To check which rulesets are active, you can use the `Get-DeployRuleSet` cmdlet. This cmdlet has the following syntax:

```
Get-DeployRuleSet [-Active] [-Working] [<CommonParameters>]
```

The cmdlet has two parameters `-Active` and `-Working`:

- The `-Active` parameter will retrieve the active ruleset. The active ruleset shows how new hosts are to be deployed.
- The `-Working` parameter will retrieve the working ruleset. This ruleset can be used to test changes before making them active.

Let's retrieve the active deploy ruleset:

```
PowerCLI C:\> Get-DeployRuleSet -Active

Name        : ImageRule
PatternList :
ItemList    : {ESXi-6.5.0-4564106-standard}

Name        : LocationRule
PatternList :
ItemList    : {New York}
```

Adding host profiles to a deploy ruleset

Now, you are almost ready to deploy hosts using Auto Deploy. The hosts only need a configuration, which will be done using host profiles. You have to connect the host profiles to Auto Deploy using deploy rules. Let's assume that you have a host profile named `Cluster-Profile`. You can connect this host profile to Auto Deploy using the `New-DeployRule` and `Add-DeployRule` cmdlets that you have seen before. Let's create a deploy rule named `HostProfileRule`, which connects the host profile `Cluster-Profile` to all hosts:

```
PowerCLI C:\> New-DeployRule -Name HostProfileRule `
>> -Item Cluster-Profile -AllHosts

Name        : HostProfileRule
PatternList :
ItemList    : {Cluster-Profile}
```

Next, we add the `HostProfileRule` deploy rule to the working and active deploy rulesets:

```
PowerCLI C:\> Add-DeployRule -DeployRule HostProfileRule

Name        : ImageRule
PatternList :
ItemList    : {ESXi-6.5.0-4564106-standard}

Name        : LocationRule
```

```
PatternList :
ItemList      : {New York}

Name          : HostProfileRule
PatternList :
ItemList      : {Cluster-Profile}
```

To configure the hostname and IP addresses, the preferred way is to use static DHCP entries. An alternative is to use static IP addresses in the host profile and use answer files for each host.

Using esxcli from PowerCLI

VMware offers more command-line interfaces for vSphere than PowerCLI. One of them is the vSphere **Command-Line Interface (CLI)**. The vSphere CLI has a command named esxcli. PowerCLI has built-in support for this esxcli command in the Get-EsxCli cmdlet.

 There are no New-EsxCli, Set-EsxCli and Remove-EsxCli cmdlets. The Get-EsxCli cmdlet exposes the esxcli functionality for a host. You cannot create a new one, modify, or remove it.

The syntax of the Get-EsxCli cmdlet is as follows:

```
Get-EsxCli -VMHost <VMHost[]> [-V2] [[-Server] <VIServer[]>]
[<CommonParameters>]
```

Use the Get-EsxCli cmdlet to connect to the esxcli functionality of a host and save the connection in a variable $esxcli:

```
PowerCLI C:\> $esxcli = Get-EsxCli -VMHost 192.168.0.133
```

In the vSphere CLI, the command to get information about the CPUs in your host is:

```
C:\>esxcli --server=192.168.0.133 hardware cpu list
Enter username: root
Enter password:
```

In PowerCLI, the command becomes a little different. The Get-EsxCLI cmdlet returns a PowerShell object, and you have to use the properties and methods of this object to create the commands. This is why you have to put dots between all of the words in the command. And if the last word is a method, you have to specify parentheses for a parameter list even if there are no parameters. The command from the preceding example becomes the following in PowerCLI:

```
PowerCLI C:\> $esxcli.hardware.cpu.list()
```

You can, of course, use the vSphere documentation to find the available esxcli commands. But you can also use PowerCLI for help. If you type in a partial command, you will get a list of elements and methods that are possible for this command. Let's start with $esxcli itself:

```
PowerCLI C:\> $esxcli

======================
EsxCli: 192.168.0.133

    Elements:
    ---------
    device
    elxnet
    esxcli
    fcoe
    graphics
    hardware
    iscsi
    network
    nvme
    rdma
    sched
    software
    storage
    system
    vm
    vsan
```

You can see that one of the elements is hardware. Let's try hardware as the next command:

```
PowerCLI C:\> $esxcli.hardware

=======================
EsxCliElement: hardware

    Elements:
    ---------
    bootdevice
```

```
clock
cpu
ipmi
memory
pci
platform
smartcard
trustedboot
usb

Methods:
--------
string Help()
```

You now have all of the command elements you can use after hardware. Let's try cpu:

```
PowerCLI C:\> $esxcli.hardware.cpu

==================
EsxCliElement: cpu

    Elements:
    ---------
    cpuid
    global

    Methods:
    --------
    Cpu[] list()
    string Help()
    string Help(string methodName)
```

And now you have obtained the list() method that we used in the preceding example.

A lot of the esxcli commands also provide a help() method that gives information about the command. To get help about the $esxcli.hardware.cpu command, type the following command:

```
PowerCLI C:\> $esxcli.hardware.cpu.help()

================================================================
vim.EsxCLI.hardware.cpu
----------------------------------------------------------------
CPU information.

ChildElement
----------------------------------------------------------------
- hardware.cpu.cpuid | Information from the CPUID instruction on ea
```

```
                            | ch CPU.
 - hardware.cpu.globa       | Information and configuration global to all
   l                        | CPUs.

Method
------------------------------------------------------------------
 - list                     | List all of the CPUs on this host.
```

If you want to know what the parameters for an `esxcli` method are, you can use the vSphere documentation, or you can use the `Get-Member` cmdlet:

```
PowerCLI C:\> $esxcli.hardware.cpu | Get-Member

    TypeName:
VMware.VimAutomation.ViCore.Impl.V1.EsxCli.EsxCliElementImpl

Name                       MemberType    Definition
----                       ----------    ----------
Help                       CodeMethod    string Help(); string Help(s...
list                       CodeMethod    vim.EsxCLI.hardware.cpu.list...
cpuid                      CodeProperty  VMware.VimAutomation.Sdk.Uti...
global                     CodeProperty  VMware.VimAutomation.Sdk.Uti...
ConvertToVersion           Method        T VersionedObjectInterop.Con...
Equals                     Method        bool Equals(System.Object obj)
GetHashCode                Method        int GetHashCode()
GetType                    Method        type GetType()
IsConvertableTo            Method        bool VersionedObjectInterop....
ToString                   Method        string ToString()
ChildElements              Property      System.Collections.Generic.L...
Client                     Property      VMware.VimAutomation.ViCore....
FullName                   Property      string FullName {get;}
Id                         Property      string Id {get;}
IsManagedObjectInstance    Property      bool IsManagedObjectInstance...
Methods                    Property      System.Collections.Generic.L...
Name                       Property      string Name {get;}
Uid                        Property      string Uid {get;}
```

The relevant information in the `Definition` column is abbreviated because of the limited width of a book page. You will get more information if you run this command in a PowerCLI session with a larger window width.

Removing hosts from a VMware vCenter Server

To remove a host from your vCenter Server inventory, you have to use the `Remove-VMHost` cmdlet. The `Remove-VMHost` cmdlet has the following syntax:

```
Remove-VMHost [-VMHost] <VMHost[]> [-Server <VIServer[]>]
[-WhatIf] [-Confirm] [<CommonParameters>]
```

Let's try to remove a host, as seen in the following screenshot:

The operation failed because the host must be in maintenance mode or disconnected state before you can remove it, as you can see in the following screenshot from the vSphere Web Client:

So, let's put the host in maintenance mode first and then try to remove it:

```
PowerCLI C:\> $VMHost = Get-VMHost -Name 192.168.0.133
PowerCLI C:\> $VMHost | Set-VMHost -State Maintenance

Name                 ConnectionState PowerState NumCpu CpuUsageMhz
----                 --------------- ---------- ------ -----------
192.168.0.133        Maintenance     PoweredOn       2          41

PowerCLI C:\> $VMHost | Remove-VMHost -Confirm:$false
```

The preceding command sets the host in maintenance mode and will remove it from the vCenter Server inventory and cluster.

Summary

In this chapter, we covered working with ESXi hosts using PowerCLI. You saw how to add and remove hosts to and from your vSphere vCenter Server inventory. We looked at putting a host in maintenance mode and how to exit maintenance mode. We have seen how PowerCLI commands work with host profiles and host services. You learned to use the PowerCLI commands for Image Builder and Auto Deploy, and finally, the use of the `esxcli` command from PowerCLI was discussed. The next chapter will be about managing virtual machines with PowerCLI.

5
Managing Virtual Machines with PowerCLI

As a VMware vSphere administrator, you probably spend a lot of your time creating, modifying, or removing virtual machines. In this chapter, you will learn how to manage virtual machines, templates, OS customization specifications, snapshots, VMware Tools, and tags with PowerCLI.

The topics that will be covered in this chapter are as follows:

- Creating virtual machines
- Registering virtual machines
- Using OS customization specifications
- Importing OVF or OVA packages
- Starting and stopping virtual machines
- Modifying the settings of virtual machines
- Converting virtual machines into templates
- Moving virtual machines to another folder, host, cluster, resource pool, or datastore
- Updating VMware Tools
- Upgrading virtual machine compatibility
- Using snapshots
- Running commands in the guest OS
- Configuring Fault Tolerance
- Opening the console of virtual machines
- Removing virtual machines
- Using tags

Creating virtual machines

There are several ways in which you can create a new virtual machine, such as:

- Deploying a virtual machine from a template
- Cloning another virtual machine
- Using VMware vCenter Converter to convert a physical computer to a virtual machine (P2V)
- Building a new virtual machine from scratch using traditional methods such as an installation CD-ROM or ISO file to install the operating system

To create a new virtual machine using PowerCLI, you have to use the New-VM cmdlet. The New-VM cmdlet has the following syntax, containing four parameter sets.

The default parameter set is shown in the following command line:

```
New-VM [-AdvancedOption <AdvancedOption[]>] [[-VMHost] <VMHost>]
[-Version <VMVersion>] -Name <String> [-ResourcePool <VIContainer>]
[-VApp <VApp>] [-Location <Folder>] [-Datastore <StorageResource>]
[-DiskMB <Int64[]>] [-DiskGB <Decimal[]>] [-DiskPath <String[]>]
[-DiskStorageFormat <VirtualDiskStorageFormat>] [-MemoryMB <Int64>]
[-MemoryGB <Decimal>] [-NumCpu <Int32>] [-CoresPerSocket <Int32>]
[-Floppy] [-CD] [-GuestId <String>] [-AlternateGuestName <String>]
[-NetworkName <String[]>] [-Portgroup <VirtualPortGroupBase[]>]
[-HARestartPriority <HARestartPriority>] [-HAIsolationResponse
<HAIsolationResponse>] [-DrsAutomationLevel <DrsAutomationLevel>]
[-VMSwapfilePolicy <VMSwapfilePolicy>] [-Server <VIServer[]>]
[-RunAsync] [-Notes <String>] [-WhatIf] [-Confirm] [<CommonParameters>]
```

The parameter set for cloning a virtual machine is as follows:

```
New-VM [-AdvancedOption <AdvancedOption[]>] [[-VMHost] <VMHost>]
[-Name <String>] [-ResourcePool <VIContainer>] [-VApp <VApp>]
[-Location <Folder>] [-Datastore <StorageResource>]
[-DiskStorageFormat <VirtualDiskStorageFormat>] [-OSCustomizationSpec
<OSCustomizationSpec>] [-HARestartPriority <HARestartPriority>]
[-HAIsolationResponse <HAIsolationResponse>] [-DrsAutomationLevel
<DrsAutomationLevel>] [-LinkedClone] [-ReferenceSnapshot <Snapshot>]
[-Server <VIServer[]>] [-RunAsync] [-Notes <String>] -VM
<VirtualMachine[]> [-WhatIf] [-Confirm] [<CommonParameters>]
```

The parameter set for creating a virtual machine from a template is as follows:

```
New-VM [-AdvancedOption <AdvancedOption[]>] [[-VMHost] <VMHost>]
-Name <String> [-ResourcePool <VIContainer>] [-VApp <VApp>]
[-Location <Folder>] [-Datastore <StorageResource>] [-Template]
<Template> [-DiskStorageFormat <VirtualDiskStorageFormat>]
[-OSCustomizationSpec <OSCustomizationSpec>] [-HARestartPriority
<HARestartPriority>] [-HAIsolationResponse <HAIsolationResponse>]
[-DrsAutomationLevel <DrsAutomationLevel>] [-Server <VIServer[]>]
[-RunAsync] [-Notes <String>] [-WhatIf] [-Confirm] [<CommonParameters>]
```

The parameter set for registering a virtual machine is as follows:

```
New-VM [[-VMHost] <VMHost>] [-Name <String>] [-ResourcePool
<VIContainer>] [-VApp <VApp>] [-Location <Folder>]
[-HARestartPriority <HARestartPriority>] [-HAIsolationResponse
<HAIsolationResponse>] [-DrsAutomationLevel <DrsAutomationLevel>]
-VMFilePath <String> [-Server <VIServer[]>] [-RunAsync] [-Notes
<String>] [-WhatIf] [-Confirm] [<CommonParameters>]
```

The –Name, –Template, –VM, and –VMFilePath parameters are required for registering a virtual machine.

The parameter set for creating a virtual machine from a **Content Library item** is as follows:

```
New-VM [[-VMHost] <VMHost>] [-Name <String>] [-ResourcePool
<VIContainer>] [-Location <Folder>] [-Datastore <StorageResource>]
[-DiskStorageFormat <VirtualDiskStorageFormat>] [-HARestartPriority
<HARestartPriority>] [-HAIsolationResponse <HAIsolationResponse>]
[-DrsAutomationLevel <DrsAutomationLevel>] [-ContentLibraryItem]
<ContentLibraryItem> [-Server <VIServer[]>] [-RunAsync] [-WhatIf]
[-Confirm] [<CommonParameters>]
```

The –Name and –ContentLibraryItem parameters are required for creating a virtual machine from a Content Library item.

Remember that if you use parameters, they will all have to come from the same set.

How do you find the names of the parameter sets? You can find these names using the Get-Command cmdlet, as shown in the following command:

```
PowerCLI C:\> (Get-Command New-VM).ParameterSets.Name
```

The output of the preceding command is as follows:

```
DefaultParameterSet
CloneVm
Template
RegisterVm
FromContentLibraryItem
```

The preceding command is in PowerShell V3 syntax. In PowerShell V2, the command is as follows:

```
PowerCLI C:\> (Get-Command New-VM).ParameterSets |
>> Select-Object -ExpandProperty Name
```

You can see that the PowerShell V3 syntax is shorter and more elegant. If you are still using PowerShell V2, I encourage you to upgrade to PowerShell V5, because PowerCLI 6.5 is only compatible with PowerShell V3, V4, and V5.

 You can find the PowerShell version of your session with the following command:

```
PowerCLI C:\> $PSVersionTable.PSVersion
```

 As you can see from the following output, I am using PowerShell V5.1:

```
Major   Minor   Build   Revision
-----   -----   -----   --------
5       1       14393   576
```

As you can see in the output of the preceding command, `Get-Command` shows you the names of the parameter sets, in this case, `DefaultParameterSet`, `CloneVm`, `Template`, `RegisterVm`, and `FromContentLibraryItem`.

You can see that there are different parameter sets for creating a virtual machine from a template, cloning a virtual machine, registering a virtual machine, and creating a virtual machine from a Content Library item. Registering a virtual machine is not really creating a new virtual machine. It is adding an existing virtual machine to a vSphere inventory. I will show you examples from these parameter sets in the following sections: *Creating virtual machines from scratch, Creating virtual machines from templates, Cloning virtual machines*, and *Registering virtual machines*.

Creating virtual machines from scratch

In this section, we'll start by creating a virtual machine from scratch. For this purpose, you'll need to use the `DefaultParameterSet` parameter set of the `New-VM` cmdlet. You'll need to specify values for the `-Name` parameter, which is required, and one of these parameters: `-ResourcePool`, `-VMHost`, or `-VApp`. The `-ResourcePool` parameter accepts `VMHost`, `Cluster`, `ResourcePool`, and `VApp` objects. These objects collectively act as a resource pool. We will create a virtual machine named `VM1` and add it to the cluster `Cluster01` with the following commands:

```
PowerCLI C:\> $Cluster = Get-Cluster -Name Cluster01
PowerCLI C:\> New-VM -Name VM1 -ResourcePool $Cluster
```

The output of the preceding command is as follows:

```
Name        PowerState   Num CPUs  MemoryGB
----        ----------   --------  --------
VM1         PoweredOff   1         0.250
```

You have now created your first virtual machine with PowerCLI. This virtual machine has the default settings, because you only specified the minimum required parameters. For example, the virtual machine has only 256 MB of memory and a 4 GB disk. You probably want to change these figures. To do this, you can use other parameters, such as `-Datastore`, `-DiskGB`, `-DiskStorageFormat`, `-MemoryGB`, `-NumCpu`, and `-NetworkName`, to create a virtual machine that fulfills your needs. After creating a virtual machine, you can modify it using the `Set-VM` cmdlet, which will be discussed later in this chapter, in the *Modifying the settings of virtual machines* section. However, some settings, such as the disk size, you are better off knowing right from the start. This is because increasing the disk size also requires changes to the filesystem.

Shrinking the disk size is only possible by making a backup of the disk, removing the disk, creating a smaller disk, and then restoring the backup.

Let's create a more advanced virtual machine, named VM2, with the help of the following command:

```
PowerCLI C:\> $DataStore = Get-Datastore -Name Datastore1
PowerCLI C:\> New-VM -Name VM2 -ResourcePool $Cluster -Datastore `
>> $DataStore -DiskGB 20 -DiskStorageFormat Thin `
>> -MemoryGB 4 -NumCPU 2 -NetworkName 'VM Network'
```

The output of the preceding command is as follows:

```
Name       PowerState   Num CPUs  MemoryGB
----       ----------   --------  --------
VM2        PoweredOff   2         4.000
```

While creating VM2, we specified Datastore1 as the datastore for initial placement of the virtual machine. We also specified Thin as the storage format, to **thin provision** the disk, the memory size in GB, the number of virtual CPUs, and the name of the virtual machine's network.

> The virtual machines VM1 and VM2 have no operating system installed. To install an operating system, you can start the virtual machine and connect a CD-ROM or open an ISO file containing an operating system installation disk, or you can use methods such as a **Preboot eXecution Environment (PXE)** boot.

Creating virtual machines from templates

Deploying a virtual machine from a template is much easier than installing one from scratch. When you deploy a virtual machine from a template, you create a new virtual machine that is a copy of the template.

To create the template, you first have to create a virtual machine. Install the operating system with all of the software and patches to be included for each virtual machine deployed. When the virtual machine is ready, you have to convert it into a template. You will learn how to do this with PowerCLI later in this chapter, in the *Converting virtual machines into templates* section.

If you have different operating systems that you need to deploy, you can create a template for each one, for example, Microsoft Windows Server 2016, Red Hat Enterprise Linux 7 (64-bit), and so on. After creating the template, you can deploy virtual machines from this template using the `New-VM -Template` parameter.

After installing an operating system in VM1, I have converted VM1 to a template. We will use this template to deploy virtual machine VM3 with the following commands:

```
PowerCLI C:\> $Cluster = Get-Cluster -Name Cluster01
PowerCLI C:\> New-VM -Name VM3 -Template VM1 -ResourcePool $Cluster
```

The preceding command lines will give the following output:

Name	PowerState	Num CPUs	MemoryGB
VM3	PoweredOff	1	0.250

 You can also specify other parameters to change settings.

Cloning virtual machines

If you clone a virtual machine, you will create a duplicate of the virtual machine with the same configuration and installed software as that of the original virtual machine. This can be done while the source virtual machine is powered on. You have to specify the source virtual machine in the value of the -VM parameter.

Let's clone the VM3 virtual machine into a new virtual machine called VM4:

```
PowerCLI C:\> $Cluster = Get-Cluster -Name Cluster01
PowerCLI C:\> New-VM -Name VM4 -VM VM3 -ResourcePool $Cluster
```

The output will be as follows:

Name	PowerState	Num CPUs	MemoryGB
VM4	PoweredOff	1	0.250

Registering virtual machines

To register an existing virtual machine to your vCenter inventory, you have to specify the path to a `.vmx` file. A `.vmx` file contains the configuration for an existing virtual machine. Here are a few lines from a `.vmx` file:

```
.encoding = "UTF-8"
config.version = "8"
virtualHW.version = "11"
vmci0.present = "TRUE"
displayName = "VM4"
floppy0.present = "FALSE"
numvcpus = "1"
memSize = "256"
```

You typically don't modify a `.vmx` file with an editor, because you might break the connection to the virtual machine.

 For more information about modifying a `.vmx` file, read the VMware **Knowledge Base** article *Tips for editing a .vmx file (1714)* (available at `https://kb.vmware.com/kb/1714`).

The following example will register a virtual machine named `VM4` on host `192.168.0.134`. You have to specify the location of the `.vmx` file of the virtual machine on the datastore as the value of the `New-VM -VMFilePath` parameter:

```
PowerCLI C:\> New-VM -Name VM4 -VMHost 192.168.0.134 `
>> -VMFilePath '[datastore2] VM4/VM4.vmx'
```

The output of the preceding command is as follows:

```
Name                  PowerState Num CPUs MemoryGB
----                  ---------- -------- --------
VM4                   PoweredOff 1        0.250
```

In the following screenshot of the vSphere web client, you will see all the files of virtual machine **VM4** in its datastore folder:

Name	Size	Modified	Type	Path
VM4-12b02d43.hlog	0.28 KB	8-1-2017 11:51	File	[datastore2] VM4/VM4-12b02d43....
VM4.vmdk	4.194.304,00 KB	8-1-2017 11:51	Virtual Disk	[datastore2] VM4/VM4.vmdk
VM4.vmx	1,60 KB	8-1-2017 11:51	Virtual Machine	[datastore2] VM4/VM4.vmx
VM4.vmsd	0,00 KB	8-1-2017 11:51	File	[datastore2] VM4/VM4.vmsd

Using OS customization specifications

OS customization specifications are XML files that contain guest operating system settings such as the computer name, network settings, and license settings-for virtual machines. You can use OS customization specifications to modify the configuration of the operating system during the deployment of new virtual machines.

Let's get a list of the names of all the OS customization specifications cmdlets:

```
PowerCLI C:\> Get-Command -Noun OSCustomization* |
>> Select-Object -Property Name
```

The output of the preceding command is as follows:

```
Name
----
Get-OSCustomizationNicMapping
Get-OSCustomizationSpec
New-OSCustomizationNicMapping
New-OSCustomizationSpec
Remove-OSCustomizationNicMapping
Remove-OSCustomizationSpec
Set-OSCustomizationNicMapping
Set-OSCustomizationSpec
```

To create an OS customization specification or to clone an existing one, you have to use the `New-OSCustomizationSpec` cmdlet. This cmdlet has the following syntax. The first parameter set is for Linux operating systems:

```
New-OSCustomizationSpec [-OSType <String>] [-Server <VIServer[]>]
[-Name <String>] [-Type <OSCustomizationSpecType>] [-DnsServer
<String[]>] [-DnsSuffix <String[]>] [-Domain <String>] [-NamingScheme
<String>] [-NamingPrefix <String>] [-Description <String>] [-WhatIf]
[-Confirm] [<CommonParameters>]
```

The second parameter set is for cloning OS customization specifications:

```
New-OSCustomizationSpec -OSCustomizationSpec <OSCustomizationSpec>
[-Server <VIServer[]>] [-Name <String>] [-Type
<OSCustomizationSpecType>] [-WhatIf] [-Confirm] [<CommonParameters>]
```

The `-OSCustomizationSpec` parameter is required.

The third parameter set is for Windows guest operating systems:

```
New-OSCustomizationSpec -FullName <String> -OrgName <String> [-OSType
<String>] [-ChangeSid] [-DeleteAccounts] [-Server <VIServer[]>]
[-Name <String>] [-Type <OSCustomizationSpecType>] [-DnsServer
<String[]>] [-DnsSuffix <String[]>] [-GuiRunOnce <String[]>]
[-AdminPassword <String>] [-TimeZone <String>] [-AutoLogonCount
<Int32>] [-Domain <String>] [-Workgroup <String>] [-DomainCredentials
<PSCredential>] [-DomainUsername <String>] [-DomainPassword <String>]
[-ProductKey <String>] [-NamingScheme <String>] [-NamingPrefix
<String>] [-Description <String>] [-LicenseMode <LicenseMode>]
[-LicenseMaxConnections <Int32>] [-WhatIf] [-Confirm]
[<CommonParameters>]
```

The `-FullName` and `-OrgName` parameters are required.

Let's start with creating a Linux OS customization specification called `LinuxOSSpec`, which specifies `Linux` as the type of operating system and `blackmilktea.com` as the domain name, using the following command:

```
PowerCLI C:\> New-OSCustomizationSpec -Name LinuxOSSpec `
>> -OSType Linux -Domain blackmilktea.com -Description "Linux spec"
```

The preceding command will give the following output:

```
Name                          Description Type       OSType
----                          ----------- ----       ------
LinuxOSSpec                   Linux spec Persistent  Linux
```

Now, we can clone this OS customization specification with the following command:

```
PowerCLI C:\ > New-OSCustomizationSpec -Name LinuxOSSpec2 `
>> -OSCustomizationSpec LinuxOSSpec
```

The output of the preceding command is as follows:

```
Name                                    Description Type       OSType
----                                    ----------- ----       ------
LinuxOSSpec2                            Linux spec Persistent   Linux
```

Creating a Windows OS customization specification requires some more parameters:

```
PowerCLI C:\> New-OSCustomizationSpec -Name WindowsOSSpec `
>> -OSType Windows `
>> -Domain blackmilktea.com -DomainUsername DomainAdmin `
>> -DomainPassword TopSecret -FullName "Domain administrator" `
>> -OrgName "Black Milk Tea Inc." -Description "Windows Spec"
```

The output of the preceding command is as follows:

```
Name                                    Description Type       OSType
----                                    ----------- ----       ------
WindowsOSSpec                           Windows Spec Persistent Windows
```

You can now use an OS customization specification if you create a virtual machine from a template or when you clone a virtual machine. For example, you can use the following command:

```
PowerCLI C:\> New-VM -Name VM5 -Template Windows2016Template `
>> -OSCustomizationSpec WindowsOSSpec -VMHost 192.168.0.133
```

The output of the preceding command is as follows:

```
Name              PowerState Num CPUs MemoryGB
----              ---------- -------- --------
VM5               PoweredOff 1         4.000
```

Importing OVF or OVA packages

The **Open Virtualization Format** (**OVF**) is an open standard for packaging and distributing **virtual appliances** (**vApps**). An **Open Virtual Appliance** (**OVA**) is an OVF package stored in a single file in the TAR format. VMware and other vendors distribute software in the OVA or OVF format. You can create OVF or OVA packages from vApps and virtual machines using the `Export-VApp` cmdlet.

An application packaged as an OVF or OVA can be imported to your vSphere inventory using PowerCLI. Before you can import an OVF or OVA package, you will have to configure the properties required by the package, such as the following:

- Name
- Port group
- IP address

Retrieving the required properties

Because the required properties are different for each package, you will have to retrieve them first. The Get-OvfConfiguration cmdlet will retrieve required properties from the OVF or OVA package for you.

The syntax of the Get-OvfConfiguration cmdlet is as follows:

```
Get-OvfConfiguration [-Ovf] <String> [-Server <VIServer[]>]
[<CommonParameters>]
```

The -Ovf parameter is required.

This parameter specifies the local path to the OVF or OVA package for which the user-configurable options are returned. URL paths are not supported.

In this section, we will use the VMware **vSphere Management Assistant** (**vMA**) 6.5 OVF package (https://code.vmware.com/tool/vma/6.0) as an example. The vMA is a Linux virtual machine that has the vSphere command-line interface and the vSphere SDK for Perl installed. You can download the vMA from
https://my.vmware.com/web/vmware/details?downloadGroup=VMA65&productId=614.

In the following example, we will retrieve the required configuration properties of the vMA OVF package. The output of the command is stored in the $OvfConfiguration variable for later use:

```
PowerCLI C:\> $OvfConfiguration = Get-OvfConfiguration
-Ovf C:\Users\robert\Downloads\vMA-6.5.0.0-4569350\
vMA-6.5.0.0-4569350_OVF10.ovf
```

After running the preceding command, the value of the $OvfConfiguration variable can be shown by simply typing the variable:

```
PowerCLI C:\> $OvfConfiguration
```

```
==================================================
OvfConfiguration: vMA-6.5.0.0-4569350_OVF10.ovf

    Properties:
    -----------
    IpAssignment
    NetworkMapping
    vami
```

As you can see in the preceding output, the OVF configuration is for file
`vMA-6.5.0.0-4569350_OVF10.ovf`. The required properties are as follows:

- IpAssignment
- NetworkMapping
- vami

The object in the `$OvfConfiguration` variable has a method `ToHashTable()` that shows
you the required properties in more detail. In the following command, the output of the
`ToHashTable()` method is piped to the `Format-Table -AutoSize` cmdlet to show you
the full name of the required properties:

```
PowerCLI C:\> $OvfConfiguration.ToHashTable() | Format-Table -AutoSize

Name                                            Value
----                                            -----
IpAssignment.IpAllocationPolicy
NetworkMapping.Network 1
IpAssignment.IpProtocol
vami.ip0.vSphere_Management_Assistant_(vMA)
```

Assigning values to the required properties

By examining a required property, you will get more information about the required value.
In the `OvfTypeDescription` property output of the following example, you will see that
the `IpAssignment.IpAllocationPolicy` key requires one of the following strings as a
value:

- dhcpPolicy
- transientPolicy
- fixedPolicy
- fixedAllocatedPolicy

The following command will show you the current values of the properties in the
`IpAssignment.IpAllocationPolicy` key:

```
PowerCLI C:\> $OvfConfiguration.IpAssignment.IpAllocationPolicy

Key                 : IpAssignment.IpAllocationPolicy
Value               :
DefaultValue        :
OvfTypeDescription  : string["dhcpPolicy", "transientPolicy",
                      "fixedPolicy","fixedAllocatedPolicy"]
Description         :
```

The following table will give you the description of each option:

Option	Description
dhcpPolicy	Specifies that DHCP must be used to allocate an IP address to the virtual machine.
transientPolicy	Specifies that the virtual machine will get an IP address from a range managed by the vSphere platform. There is no guarantee that the virtual machine will get the same IP address after a restart.
fixedPolicy	Specifies that the virtual machine will have a manually configured IP address.
fixedAllocatedPolicy	Specifies that the virtual machine will get an IP address from a range managed by the vSphere platform. The virtual machine will keep the same IP address during its lifetime.

In the following command, we will assign the `fixedPolicy` to the
`$OvfConfiguration.IpAssignment.IpAllocationPolicy.Value` property to specify
that the vMA virtual machine will have a manually configured IP address:

```
PowerCLI C:\> $OvfConfiguration.IpAssignment.
IpAllocationPolicy.Value = "fixedPolicy"
```

Next we have to configure the network mapping. In the following example, you can see in
the output that the `OvfTypeDescription` specifies the `Value` property must be of type
`string`:

```
PowerCLI C:\> $OvfConfiguration.NetworkMapping.Network_1

Key                 : NetworkMapping.Network 1
Value               :
```

```
DefaultValue        :
OvfTypeDescription  : string
Description         : Network 1
```

So we have to assign the name of a port group to the `NetworkMapping.Network_1.Value` property. In the following command, we will assign the `VM Network` value to the `NetworkMapping.Network_1.Value` property:

```
PowerCLI C:\> $OvfConfiguration.NetworkMapping.Network_1.Value =
"VM Network"
```

The value of the `OvfTypeDescription` property in the output of the following PowerCLI command shows us that we have to assign one of the `IPv4` or `IPv6` strings to the `IpAssignment.IpProtocol.Value` property:

```
PowerCLI C:\> $OvfConfiguration.IpAssignment.IpProtocol

Key                 : IpAssignment.IpProtocol
Value               :
DefaultValue        :
OvfTypeDescription  : string["IPv4", "IPv6"]
Description         :
```

In the following command, we will assign the value `IPv4` to the `IpAssignment.IpProtocol.Value` property:

```
PowerCLI C:\> $OvfConfiguration.IpAssignment.IpProtocol.Value = "IPv4"
```

Finally, we have to assign a value to the `vami.'vSphere_Management_Assistant_(vMA)'.ip0.Value` property. The `Description` in the output of the following command shows us that the value has to be the IP address for this interface:

```
PowerCLI C:\> $OvfConfiguration.vami.
'vSphere_Management_Assistant_(vMA)'.ip0

Key                 : vami.ip0.vSphere_Management_Assistant_(vMA)
Value               :
DefaultValue        :
OvfTypeDescription  : ip:Network 1
Description         : The IP address for this interface.
```

In the following command, we will assign the IP address `192.168.0.129` to the `vami.'vSphere_Management_Assistant_(vMA)'.ip0.Value` property:

```
PowerCLI C:\> $OvfConfiguration.vami.'vSphere_Management_
Assistant_(vMA)'.ip0.Value = "192.168.0.129"
```

After assigning values to all of the required properties, we can use the `ToHashTable()` method to list the assigned values and to make sure we have assigned a value to every required property:

```
PowerCLI C:\> $OvfConfiguration.ToHashTable() | Format-Table -AutoSize

Name                                              Value
----                                              -----
IpAssignment.IpAllocationPolicy                   fixedPolicy
NetworkMapping.Network 1                          VM Network
IpAssignment.IpProtocol                           IPv4
vami.ip0.vSphere_Management_Assistant_(vMA)       192.168.0.129
```

Importing the vMA OVF file

Now that we have assigned values to all the required properties, we can use the `Import-VApp` cmdlet to import the OVF or OVA file and create a new virtual machine. The syntax of the `Import-VApp` cmdlet is as follows:

```
Import-VApp [-Source] <String> [-OvfConfiguration <Hashtable>] [[-Name]
<String>] [-Location <VIContainer>] [-VMHost] <VMHost> [-Datastore
<StorageResource>] [-Force] [-DiskStorageFormat
<VirtualDiskStorageFormat>] [-Server <VIServer[]>] [-RunAsync]
[-WhatIf] [-Confirm] [<CommonParameters>]
```

The `-Source` and `-VMHost` parameters are required.

In the following command, we will create a hash table containing the parameter values for the `Import-VApp` command. We will assign the hash table to the `$Parameters` variable. Besides the required parameters `-Source` and `-VMHost`, we will assign values to the `-OvfConfiguration`, `-Name`, `-Datastore`, and `-DiskStorageFormat` parameters:

```
PowerCLI C:\> $Parameters = @{
>>      Source = 'C:\Users\robert\Downloads\vMA-6.5.0.0-4569350\
vMA-6.5.0.0-4569350_OVF10.ovf'
>>      OvfConfiguration = $OvfConfiguration
>>      Name = 'vMA'
>>      VMHost = '192.168.0.133'
>>      Datastore ='datastore1'
```

```
>>    DiskStorageFormat = 'Thin'
>> }
```

Finally, we will use a technique called **splatting** to pass the parameters to the `Import-VApp` cmdlet. We have to specify the name of the variable containing the hash table and use an @ character instead of the $ character in front of the variable name. In the following example, we will import the vMA OVF file using the required properties and parameter values we have specified in the preceding examples:

```
PowerCLI C:\> Import-VApp @Parameters

Name                      PowerState Num CPUs MemoryGB
----                      ---------- -------- --------
vMA                       PoweredOff 1         0.586
```

To be able to start the vMA virtual machine, you will need to create a network IP pool first. Creating a network IP pool is beyond the scope of this book.

Starting and stopping virtual machines

You have created your virtual machine, but it is still powered off. In this section, you will learn how to start, suspend, and stop a virtual machine using PowerCLI.

Starting virtual machines

To start a virtual machine, you can use the `Start-VM` cmdlet. This cmdlet has the following syntax:

```
Start-VM [-RunAsync] [-VM] <VirtualMachine[]> [-Server
<VIServer[]>] [-WhatIf] [-Confirm] [<CommonParameters>]
```

The `-VM` parameter is required to start a virtual machine.

In the first example, we will start the virtual machine VM2 using the following command:

```
PowerCLI C:\> Start-VM -VM VM2
```

The output of the preceding command is as follows:

```
Name                      PowerState Num CPUs MemoryGB
----                      ---------- -------- --------
VM2                       PoweredOn  2         4.000
```

To start all of your virtual machines that are powered off, you can pipe the output of the `Get-VM` cmdlet to the `Where-Object` cmdlet, to filter only those virtual machines that are powered off. Pipe the result to the `Start-VM` cmdlet using the following command and all of your virtual machines that are powered off will be started:

```
PowerCLI C:\> Get-VM |
>> Where-Object {$_.PowerState -eq 'PoweredOff'} | Start-VM
>>
```

The output of the preceding command is as follows:

```
Name                 PowerState Num CPUs MemoryGB
----                 ---------- -------- --------
VM5                  PoweredOn  1        0.250
VM4                  PoweredOn  1        0.250
VM3                  PoweredOn  1        0.250
```

Suspending virtual machines

If you want to put a virtual machine on hold without powering it down, you can suspend it using the `Suspend-VM` cmdlet. This cmdlet has the following syntax:

```
Suspend-VM [-RunAsync] [-VM] <VirtualMachine[]> [-Server
<VIServer[]>] [-WhatIf] [-Confirm] [<CommonParameters>]
```

The `-VM` parameter is required.

In the following example, we will suspend the `VM4` virtual machine:

```
PowerCLI C:\> Get-VM -Name VM4 | Suspend-VM -Confirm:$false
```

The output of the preceding command is as follows:

```
Name                 PowerState Num CPUs MemoryGB
----                 ---------- -------- --------
VM4                  Suspended  1        0.250
```

If you want to unsuspend a virtual machine, you have to use the `Start-VM` cmdlet.

Shutting down the virtual machine's guest operating systems

If you want to shut down the operating system of a virtual machine, you should use the `Stop-VMGuest` cmdlet. This cmdlet uses VMware Tools to ask the guest operating system to perform a graceful shutdown. If VMware Tools is not running in the virtual machine, the `Stop-VMGuest` cmdlet will not work and will return an error message. The cmdlet returns immediately and does not wait until the guest operating system has been shut down. The `Stop-VMGuest` cmdlet has the following syntax:

```
Stop-VMGuest [[-VM] <VirtualMachine[]>] [[-Server]
<VIServer[]>] [-WhatIf] [-Confirm] [<CommonParameters>]
Stop-VMGuest [[-Guest] <VMGuest[]>] [-WhatIf] [-Confirm]
[<CommonParameters>]
```

You must specify either the `-Guest` or `-VM` parameter.

In the following example, we will shut down the guest operating system of the VM4 virtual machine:

```
PowerCLI C:\> Stop-VMGuest -VM VM4 -Confirm:$false
```

The output of the preceding command is as follows:

```
State    IPAddress              OSFullName
-----    ---------              ----------
Running  {192.168.0.145, f... Microsoft Windows Server 2016 (64-bit)
```

Stopping virtual machines

If shutting down a virtual machine is not possible, because VMware Tools is not installed on the guest operating system, you can use the `Stop-VM` cmdlet to stop a virtual machine. The `Stop-VM` cmdlet works similarly to the power switch on a physical computer. This will force the virtual machine to power off without gracefully shutting down the guest operating system. The syntax of the `Stop-VM` cmdlet is as follows:

```
Stop-VM [-Kill] [-RunAsync] [-VM] <VirtualMachine[]> [-Server
<VIServer[]>] [-WhatIf] [-Confirm] [<CommonParameters>]
```

The `-VM` parameter is required.

In the following example, we will stop the `VM3` virtual machine:

```
PowerCLI C:\> Stop-VM -VM VM3 -Confirm:$False
```

The output of the preceding command is as follows:

```
Name                    PowerState Num CPUs MemoryGB
----                    ---------- -------- --------
VM3                     PoweredOff 1        0.250
```

Modifying the settings of virtual machines

To modify the settings of a virtual machine, you can use the `Set-VM` cmdlet. This cmdlet has the following syntax. The first parameter set is the default:

```
Set-VM [-VM] <VirtualMachine[]> [-Name <String>] [-Version <VMVersion>]
[-MemoryMB <Int64>] [-MemoryGB <Decimal>] [-NumCpu <Int32>]
[-CoresPerSocket <Int32>] [-GuestId <String>] [-AlternateGuestName
<String>] [-OSCustomizationSpec <OSCustomizationSpec>]
[-HARestartPriority <HARestartPriority>] [-HAIsolationResponse
<HAIsolationResponse>] [-DrsAutomationLevel <DrsAutomationLevel>]
[-Server <VIServer[]>] [-RunAsync] [-VMSwapFilePolicy
<VMSwapfilePolicy>] [-Notes <String>] [-WhatIf] [-Confirm]
[<CommonParameters>]
```

The second parameter set is for reverting a virtual machine to a snapshot:

```
Set-VM [-VM] <VirtualMachine[]> [-Name <String>] [-Snapshot
<Snapshot>] [-OSCustomizationSpec <OSCustomizationSpec>]
[-HARestartPriority <HARestartPriority>] [-HAIsolationResponse
<HAIsolationResponse>] [-DrsAutomationLevel <DrsAutomationLevel>]
[-Server <VIServer[]>] [-RunAsync] [-VMSwapFilePolicy
<VMSwapfilePolicy>] [-WhatIf] [-Confirm] [<CommonParameters>]
```

The third parameter set converts a virtual machine into a template:

```
Set-VM [-VM] <VirtualMachine[]> [-Name <String>]
[-Server <VIServer[]>] [-RunAsync] [-ToTemplate]
[-WhatIf] [-Confirm] [<CommonParameters>]
```

The `-VM` parameter is required in all of the three parameter sets.

Using the default parameter set, you can modify the name, hardware version, and amount of memory, number of virtual CPUs, guest operating system, high availability settings, DRS settings, swap-file policy, and description of the virtual machine. You can also use the `Set-VM` cmdlet to apply an OS customization specification to a virtual machine.

In the following example, we will rename the virtual machine VM5 to DNS1 and give the virtual machine 2 CPUs and 8 GB of memory. If CPU **hot plug** and memory hot plug are not enabled, you have to power off the virtual machine before executing the following command or the command will fail and generate the following message:

```
"CPU hot plug is not supported for this virtual machine."
```

To perform the renaming and memory allocation, use the following command:

```
PowerCLI C:\> Set-VM –VM VM5 –Name DNS1 –NumCpu 2 –MemoryGB 8
–Confirm:$false
```

The output of the preceding command is as follows:

```
Name                  PowerState Num CPUs MemoryGB
----                  ---------- -------- --------
DNS1                  PoweredOff 2         8.000
```

In the following screenshot of vSphere web client, you will see the **Virtual Hardware** tab in the **Edit Settings** window for the virtual machine DNS1 after running the preceding PowerCLI command:

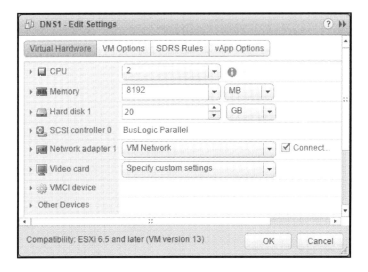

In the following example, we will configure the DNS1 virtual machine as a Microsoft Windows Server 2016 (64-bit) server using the -GuestId parameter. We will also modify the description of the virtual machine to "DNS Server":

```
PowerCLI C:\> Set-VM -VM DNS1 -GuestID windows9Server64Guest `
>> -Notes "DNS Server" -Confirm:$false
```

The output of the preceding command is as follows:

```
Name                PowerState Num CPUs MemoryGB
----                ---------- -------- --------
DNS1                PoweredOff 2          8.000
```

Go to https://www.vmware.com/support/developer/vc-sdk/ and click on **vSphere API Reference | Previous HTML interface**. You will find a list of valid GuestId values for specific ESXi versions in the description of the VirtualMachineGuestOsIdentifier enumerated type.

Using the VMware vSphere API to modify virtual machine settings

You cannot use the Set-VM cmdlet to modify all virtual machine settings. Sometimes, you have to use the VMware vSphere API, for example, if you want to enable the **Force BIOS setup** feature.

In the following screenshot of vSphere web client, you will see the **VM Options** tab in the **Edit Settings** window for the virtual machine VM2. As you can see, the **Force BIOS setup** checkbox is unchecked:

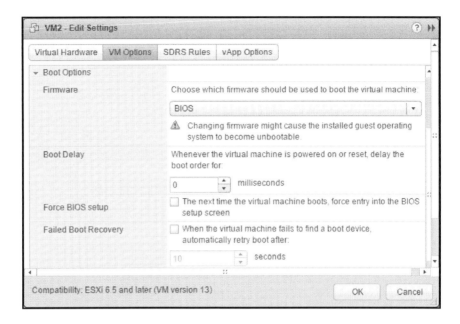

In the following example, I will show you how to enable **Force BIOS setup** for the virtual machine VM2. First, we will create an object of type Vmware.Vim.VirtualMachineConfigSpec and assign it to the variable $spec:

```
$spec = New-Object -TypeName Vmware.Vim.VirtualMachineConfigSpec
```

Next we will create an object of type Vmware.Vim.VirtualMachineBootOptions and assign it to the bootOptions property of the $spec variable:

```
$spec.bootOptions = New-Object -TypeName `
Vmware.Vim.VirtualMachineBootOptions
```

We will assign the value $true to the enterBIOSSetup property of the bootOptions property of the $spec variable, to check the **Force BIOS setup** checkbox:

```
$spec.bootOptions.enterBIOSSetup = $true
```

We will use the Get-VM cmdlet to retrieve virtual machine VM2 and assign the object to variable $vm:

```
$vm = Get-VM -Name VM2
```

Finally, we will use the `ReconfigVM_Task()` method to asynchronously modify the settings of virtual machine `VM2` according to the specifications in the `$spec` variable:

```
$vm.ExtensionData.ReconfigVM_Task($spec)
```

The preceding code returns an output similar to the following:

```
Type                              Value
----                              -----
Task                              task-212
```

If you are unsure of how to write VMware vSphere API code, take a look at VMware **Onyx Fling**. Onyx is a code generator. It can generate PowerCLI code for tasks that you perform in the VMware vSphere client.

 There is also a version of Onyx for vSphere Web Client. You can download Onyx, Onyx for the Web Client, and other VMware Flings at `https://lab s.vmware.com/flings`.

Adding devices to a virtual machine

There are several cmdlets that you can use to add devices to your virtual machines:

- `New-HardDisk`
- `New-ScsiController`
- `New-NetworkAdapter`
- `New-FloppyDrive`
- `New-CDDrive`

We will discuss these cmdlets in this section.

 While writing this book, there are no PowerCLI cmdlets to add serial ports, parallel ports, USB controllers, USB devices, or PCI devices to a virtual machine, nor to remove them. If you want to perform any of these tasks, you have to return to the VMware vSphere API.

Adding a hard disk

To add a hard disk to a virtual machine, you can use the `New-HardDisk` cmdlet. The `New-HardDisk` cmdlet has the following syntax. The first parameter set is to create a new hard disk and add it to a virtual machine:

```
New-HardDisk [-AdvancedOption <AdvancedOption[]>] [[-Persistence]
<String>] [-Controller <ScsiController>] [[-DiskType] <DiskType>]
[-CapacityKB <Int64>] [-CapacityGB <Decimal>] [-Split]
[-ThinProvisioned] [-StorageFormat <VirtualDiskStorageFormat>]
[-DeviceName <String>] [-Datastore <StorageResource>] [-VM]
<VirtualMachine[]> [-Server <VIServer[]>] [-WhatIf] [-Confirm]
[<CommonParameters>]
```

The `-VM` parameter is required.

The second parameter set is to add an existing hard disk to a virtual machine:

```
New-HardDisk [[-Persistence] <String>] [-Controller <ScsiController>]
-DiskPath <String> [-VM] <VirtualMachine[]> [-Server <VIServer[]>]
[-WhatIf] [-Confirm] [<CommonParameters>]
```

The `-VM` and `-DiskPath` parameters are required.

You can use the third parameter set to add a VDisk to a virtual machine:

```
New-HardDisk [-Controller <ScsiController>] -VDisk <VDisk> [-VM]
<VirtualMachine[]> [-Server <VIServer[]>] [-WhatIf] [-Confirm]
[<CommonParameters>]
```

The `-VM` and `-VDisk` parameters are required.

Some of the parameters are obsolete and scheduled for removal in a future PowerCLI version. These parameters are `-CapacityKB`, `-Split`, and `-ThinProvisioned`. If you want your scripts to be compatible with future PowerCLI versions, you should avoid using these parameters in your scripts. Instead of `-CapacityKB`, you should use the `-CapacityGB` parameter. Instead of `-Split`, you should use the `-StorageFormat` parameter. Instead of `-ThinProvisioned`, you should also use the `-StorageFormat` parameter.

Let's add a 20 GB, thin-provisioned hard disk drive to the virtual machine named VM2:

```
PowerCLI C:\> Get-VM -Name VM2 |
>> New-HardDisk -CapacityGB 20 -StorageFormat Thin
```

The output of the preceding command is as follows:

```
CapacityGB       Persistence                          Filename
----------       -----------                          --------
20.000           Persistent           [datastore1] VM2/VM2_1.vmdk
```

You don't have to power off a virtual machine to add a hard disk. This can be done while the virtual machine is running.

The hard disk will be created on the same datastore as the virtual machine because the -Datastore parameter is not specified.

Adding a SCSI controller

Each SCSI hard disk is connected to a SCSI controller. You can only add fifteen hard disks to one SCSI controller. If you want to add a sixteenth SCSI hard disk to a virtual machine, you have to add a new SCSI controller first and add the sixteenth SCSI hard disk to the new SCSI controller. There are four types of SCSI controllers:

- BusLogic Parallel
- LSI Logic Parallel
- LSI Logic SAS
- VMware Paravirtual

You can configure a maximum of four SCSI controllers per virtual machine. So, the maximum number of SCSI hard disks you can connect to a virtual machine is sixty.

For performance reasons, it is recommended to distributed the hard disks of a virtual machine over as many SCSI controllers as possible. If your virtual machine has a disk that does many **input/output operations per second** (**IOPS**), you should use the VMware Paravirtual SCSI controller to get the best performance.

To add a new SCSI controller to a virtual machine, you can use the New-ScsiController cmdlet. The syntax of this cmdlet is as follows:

```
New-ScsiController [-HardDisk] <HardDisk[]> [[-Type]
<ScsiControllerType>] [[-BusSharingMode] <ScsiBusSharingMode>]
[-WhatIf] [-Confirm] [<CommonParameters>]
```

The -HardDisk parameter is required. The valid values for the -Type parameter are as follows:

- ParaVirtual
- VirtualBusLogic
- VirtualLsiLogic
- VirtualLsiLogicSAS

The valid values for the -BusSharingMode parameter are as follows:

- NoSharing
- Physical
- Virtual

Did you notice that the New-ScsiController cmdlet doesn't have a -VM parameter? You have to specify a new or existing hard disk to which you want to add a new SCSI controller. Because the hard disk is connected to a virtual machine, you automatically connect the new SCSI controller to this virtual machine through the hard disk.

A virtual machine must be powered off before you add a SCSI controller to it. For example, you can use the following command to add a new SCSI controller of type VMware Paravirtual for a new, 10 GB, thin-provisioned hard disk to the VM3 virtual machine:

```
PowerCLI C:\> Get-VM -Name VM3 |
>> New-HardDisk -CapacityGB 10 -StorageFormat Thin |
>> New-ScsiController -Type ParaVirtual
```

The output of the preceding command is as follows:

```
Type                BusSharingMode      UnitNumber
----                --------------      ----------
ParaVirtual         NoSharing                    4
```

Because we didn't specify a value for the -BusSharingMode parameter, the default value of NoSharing is used.

Adding a network adapter

Most of the time, a virtual machine will have only one network adapter. However, there can be reasons to add more than one network adapter to a virtual machine. For example, if you want to use a virtual machine as a network router. You can use the New-NetworkAdapter cmdlet to add network adapters to virtual machines.

The syntax of the New-NetworkAdapter cmdlet is as follows. The first parameter set is the default:

```
New-NetworkAdapter [-MacAddress <String>] -NetworkName <String>
[- StartConnected] [-WakeOnLan] [-Type <VirtualNetworkAdapterType>]
[- VM] <VirtualMachine[]> [-Server <VIServer[]>] [-WhatIf] [-Confirm]
[<CommonParameters>]
```

The -VM, and -NetworkName parameters are required.

The second parameter set is the advanced one:

```
New-NetworkAdapter [-MacAddress <String>] [-StartConnected]
[- WakeOnLan] [-Type <VirtualNetworkAdapterType>] -PortId <String>
- DistributedSwitch <DistributedSwitch> [-VM] <VirtualMachine[]>
[- Server <VIServer[]>] [-WhatIf] [-Confirm] [<CommonParameters>]
```

The -VM, -PortId, and -DistributedSwitch parameters are required.

The third parameter set is for connecting to a port group:

```
New-NetworkAdapter [-MacAddress <String>] [-StartConnected]
[- WakeOnLan] [-Type <VirtualNetworkAdapterType>] -Portgroup
<VirtualPortGroupBase> [-VM] <VirtualMachine[]> [-Server
<VIServer[]>] [-WhatIf] [-Confirm] [<CommonParameters>]
```

The -VM and -Portgroup parameters are required.

The valid virtual network adapter types for the -Type parameter are as follows:

- e1000
- Flexible
- Vmxnet
- EnhancedVmxnet
- Vmxnet3
- Unknown

If no value is given to the `-Type` parameter, the new network adapter will be of the type recommended by VMware for the given guest OS.

The following example will add a network adapter of type `Vmxnet3` to the `VM2` virtual machine. The network adapter will be connected to port group `"VM network"` when the virtual machine is started:

```
PowerCLI C:\> Get-VM -Name VM2 |
>> New-NetworkAdapter -NetworkName "VM Network" `
>> -StartConnected -Type Vmxnet3
```

The output of the preceding command is as follows:

```
Name                     Type      NetworkName  MacAddress         WakeOnLan
                                                                    Enabled
----                     ----      -----------  ----------         ---------
Network adapter 2 Vmxnet3 VM Network  00:50:56:81:22:0b      False
```

In the following screenshot of the vSphere web client, you see the **Virtual Hardware** tab in the **Edit Settings** window for the virtual machine `VM2`. It shows the new network adapter that has just been added to the virtual machine:

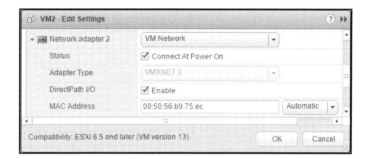

Adding a floppy drive

You can use the `New-FloppyDrive` cmdlet to connect a virtual machine to a floppy disk drive in an ESXi server or to connect a virtual machine to a floppy image file on a datastore. Modern server hardware doesn't include floppy disk drives anymore. Therefore, I will show you only how to connect to a floppy image.

The `New-FloppyDrive` cmdlet has the following syntax:

```
New-FloppyDrive [-FloppyImagePath <String>] [-NewFloppyImagePath
<String>] [-HostDevice <String>] [-StartConnected] [-VM]
<VirtualMachine[]> [-Server <VIServer[]>] [-WhatIf] [-Confirm]
[<CommonParameters>]
```

The `-VM` parameter is required.

You can use the `-FloppyImagePath` parameter to connect to an existing floppy disk drive. The `-NewFloppyImagePath` parameter can be used to create a new floppy disk drive.

The following example adds a new floppy image file to the `VM3` virtual machine, and the floppy drive starts connected when the virtual machine is powered on. You can only add a floppy drive to a virtual machine while the virtual machine is powered off. The value of the `-NewFloppyImagePath` parameter must be a path to a file on a datastore. Let's do it with the following command:

```
PowerCLI C:\> New-FloppyDrive -VM VM3 -StartConnected `
>> -NewFloppyImagePath '[datastore2] VM3/VM3.flp'
>>
```

The output of the preceding command is as follows:

```
FloppyImagePath        HostDevice              RemoteDevice
---------------        ----------              ------------
[datastore2] VM3/...
```

Adding a CD drive

Virtual CD drives can be used to connect a virtual machine to a physical CD or DVD drive on an ESXi host or a client PC or to connect to an ISO image file on a datastore.

The `New-CDDrive` cmdlet creates a new virtual CD drive. This cmdlet has the following syntax:

```
New-CDDrive [-IsoPath <String>] [-HostDevice <String>]
[- StartConnected] [-VM] <VirtualMachine[]> [-Server
<VIServer[]>] [- WhatIf] [-Confirm] [<CommonParameters>]
```

The `-VM` parameter is required.

In the following example, we will connect a new CD drive to the VM4 virtual machine. The CD drive will start connected when the virtual machine is powered on and will be connected to a Windows Server 2016 ISO file located in the ISOs folder in datastore2:

```
PowerCLI C:\> New-CDDrive -VM VM4 -StartConnected `
>> -IsoPath '[datastore2] ISOs\WindowsServer2016.iso'
>>
```

The output of the preceding command is as follows:

```
IsoPath                 HostDevice              RemoteDevice
-------                 ----------              ------------
[datastore2] ISOs...
```

You can use the PowerCLI Datastore Provider to search for files in datastores. Datastore Provider was introduced in Chapter 2, *Learning Basic PowerCLI Concepts*.

Modifying devices added to a virtual machine

After adding devices to your virtual machines, you might want to change the settings for these devices. The reason may be a hard disk that needs to grow or a network adapter that must move to another virtual network. To modify a device, you can use one of the following Set-* cmdlets:

- Set-HardDisk
- Set-ScsiController
- Set-NetworkAdapter
- Set-FloppyDrive
- Set-CDDrive

To move a hard disk to another datastore, you can use the Move-HardDisk cmdlet.

Modifying a hard disk

To modify a hard disk, you can use the Set-HardDisk cmdlet. This cmdlet has four parameter sets. The first parameter set is for changing the capacity, persistence, datastore, storage format, or SCSI controller of a hard disk:

```
Set-HardDisk [-HardDisk] <HardDisk[]> [[-CapacityKB] <Int64>]
[-CapacityGB <Decimal>] [[-Persistence] <String>] [[-Datastore]
<Datastore>] [-StorageFormat <VirtualDiskStorageFormat>]
[-Controller <ScsiController>] [-Server <VIServer[]>] [-WhatIf]
[-Confirm] [<CommonParameters>]
```

The second parameter set is for resizing a guest partition of a hard disk:

```
Set-HardDisk [-HardDisk] <HardDisk[]> [[-CapacityKB] <Int64>]
[-CapacityGB <Decimal>] [[-Persistence] <String>] [[-Datastore]
<Datastore>] [-StorageFormat <VirtualDiskStorageFormat>] [-Controller
<ScsiController>] [-Server <VIServer[]>] [-HostCredential
<PSCredential>] [-HostUser <String>] [-HostPassword <SecureString>]
[-GuestCredential <PSCredential>] [-GuestUser <String>]
[-GuestPassword <SecureString>] [-ToolsWaitSecs <Int32>] [-HelperVM
<VirtualMachine>] [-Partition <String>] [-ResizeGuestPartition]
[-WhatIf] [-Confirm] [<CommonParameters>]
```

The third parameter set is for inflating a hard disk:

```
Set-HardDisk [-HardDisk] <HardDisk[]> [-Inflate] [-WhatIf]
[-Confirm] [<CommonParameters>]
```

The fourth parameter set is for filling a hard disk with zeroes:

```
Set-HardDisk [-HardDisk] <HardDisk[]> [-ZeroOut] [-WhatIf]
[-Confirm] [<CommonParameters>]
```

The -HardDisk parameter is required in all of the parameter sets.

In the following example, we will increase the size of the hard disk for virtual machine VM6 (Hard Disk 1) to 8 GB:

```
PowerCLI C:\> Get-VM -Name VM6 | Get-HardDisk |
>> Where-Object {$_.Name -eq 'Hard Disk 1'} |
>> Set-HardDisk -CapacityGB 8 -Confirm:$false
```

The output of the preceding command is as follows:

```
CapacityGB        Persistence                                    Filename
----------        -----------                                    --------
8.000             Persistent                      [datastore1] VM6/VM6.vmdk
```

It is not possible to shrink a hard disk using the `Set-HardDisk` cmdlet. This prevents you from corrupting a guest operating filesystem after making a disk too small.

In the following example, we will modify the persistence of the hard disk for virtual machine VM6 (`Hard Disk 1`) to `IndependentPersistent` to prevent the disk from participating in virtual machine snapshots:

```
PowerCLI C:\> Get-VM -Name VM6 | Get-HardDisk |
>> Where-Object {$_.Name -eq "Hard Disk 1"} |
>> Set-HardDisk -Persistence IndependentPersistent -Confirm:$false
```

The output of the preceding command is as follows:

```
CapacityGB        Persistence                                    Filename
----------        -----------                                    --------
8.000             IndependentPersis...            [datastore1] VM6/VM6.vmdk
```

Moving a hard disk to another datastore

You can use the `Move-HardDisk` cmdlet to move a hard disk to another datastore and modify the storage format of the hard disk. This is useful if a datastore is running out of space or if a datastore has a high I/O load and you want to move a hard disk to another datastore to balance the load. If you want to move all the disks of a virtual machine to the same datastore, it is better to use the `Move-VM` cmdlet; this will be discussed later in this chapter, in the *Moving virtual machines to another folder, host, cluster, resource pool, or datastore* section. The `Move-HardDisk` cmdlet has the following syntax:

```
Move-HardDisk [-HardDisk] <HardDisk[]> [-Datastore] <Datastore>
[-StorageFormat <VirtualDiskStorageFormat>] [-Server <VIServer[]>]
[-RunAsync] [-WhatIf] [-Confirm] [<CommonParameters>]
```

The –HardDisk and –Datastore parameters are required. The possible values for the –StorageFormat parameter are as follows:

- Thin
- Thick
- EagerZeroedThick

Let's move Hard Disk 2 from the VM2 virtual machine to datastore datastore2 and change the storage format to Thick with the following command:

```
PowerCLI C:\> Get-VM -Name VM2 | Get-HardDisk |
>> Where-Object {$_.Name -eq "Hard Disk 2"} |
>> Move-HardDisk -Datastore datastore2 -StorageFormat Thick
-Confirm:$false
```

The output of the preceding command is as follows:

```
CapacityGB       Persistence                            Filename
----------       -----------                            --------
20.000           Persistent             [datastore2] VM2/VM2_1.vmdk
```

Modifying a SCSI controller

You can modify the type or the bus-sharing mode of a SCSI controller. Possible values for the type or bus-sharing mode are given in the preceding section, *Adding a SCSI controller*.

To modify a SCSI controller, you can use the Set-ScsiController cmdlet. This cmdlet has the following syntax:

```
Set-ScsiController [-ScsiController] <ScsiController[]>
[-BusSharingMode <ScsiBusSharingMode>] [-Type <ScsiControllerType>]
[-WhatIf] [-Confirm] [<CommonParameters>]
```

You cannot use the –Type and –BusSharing parameters at the same time. First, you have to run the Set-ScsiController cmdlet to set the type and then run the cmdlet again to configure the bus-sharing mode. The valid values for the –Type and –BusSharing parameters are the same as the parameters for the New-ScsiController cmdlet. To modify a SCSI controller, the virtual machine needs to be powered off.

First, we will modify the type of SCSI controller for the VM4 virtual machine to type ParaVirtual. Make sure that you have VMware Tools installed on your virtual machine because VMware Tools contains the drivers for the **paravirtual** devices:

```
PowerCLI C:\> Get-ScsiController -VM VM4 |
>> Set-ScsiController -Type ParaVirtual -Confirm:$false
```

The output of the preceding command is as follows:

```
Type                 BusSharingMode          UnitNumber
----                 --------------          ----------
ParaVirtual          NoSharing                        3
```

After this, we modify the SCSI controller's BusSharingMode parameter to Virtual. This enables virtual disks to be shared by virtual machines on the same host. If you set BusSharingMode to Physical, the virtual disks on this SCSI controller can be shared by virtual machines on any vSphere host:

```
PowerCLI C:\> Get-ScsiController -VM VM4 |
>> Set-ScsiController -BusSharingMode Virtual -Confirm:$false
```

The output of the preceding command is as follows:

```
Type                 BusSharingMode          UnitNumber
----                 --------------          ----------
ParaVirtual          Virtual                          3
```

Modifying a network adapter

The Set-NetworkAdapter cmdlet modifies the configuration of a virtual network adapter. You can change the MAC address, adapter type, and network name, and configure the Connected, StartConnected, and WakeOnLan properties of the adapter.

The Set-NetworkAdapter cmdlet has the following syntax. The first parameter set is the default:

```
Set-NetworkAdapter [-NetworkAdapter] <NetworkAdapter[]> [-MacAddress
<String>] [-NetworkName <String>] [-StartConnected [<Boolean>]]
[-Connected [<Boolean>]] [-WakeOnLan [<Boolean>]] [-Type
<VirtualNetworkAdapterType>] [-RunAsync] [-Server <VIServer[]>]
[-WhatIf] [-Confirm] [<CommonParameters>]
```

The -NetworkAdapter parameter is required.

The second parameter set is for connecting to a port by key:

```
Set-NetworkAdapter [-NetworkAdapter] <NetworkAdapter[]> [-MacAddress
<String>] [-StartConnected [<Boolean>]] [-Connected [<Boolean>]]
[-WakeOnLan [<Boolean>]] [-Type <VirtualNetworkAdapterType-]
-PortId <String> -DistributedSwitch <DistributedSwitch> [-RunAsync]
[-Server <VIServer[]>] [-WhatIf] [-Confirm] [<CommonParameters>]
```

The required parameters are `-NetworkAdapter`, `-PortId`, and `-DistributedSwitch`.

The third parameter set is for connecting to a port group:

```
Set-NetworkAdapter [-NetworkAdapter] <NetworkAdapter[]> -Portgroup
<VirtualPortGroupBase> [-RunAsync] [-Server <VIServer[]>] [-WhatIf]
[-Confirm] [<CommonParameters>]
```

The required parameters are `-NetworkAdapter` and `-Portgroup`.

If you want to give a network adapter a fixed MAC address, this address has to be in the range `00:50:56:00:00:00` to `00:50:56:3F:FF:FF`. In the following example, we'll give the network adapter of the VM4 virtual machine a fixed MAC address of `00:50:56:00:00:01`:

```
PowerCLI C:\> Get-VM -Name VM4 | Get-NetworkAdapter |
>> Set-NetworkAdapter -MacAddress 00:50:56:00:00:01 -Confirm:$false
```

The output of the preceding command is as follows:

Name	Type	NetworkName	MacAddress	WakeOnLan Enabled
Network adapter 1	Flexible	VM Network	00:50:56:00:00:01	True

We will now modify the adapter type to `e1000`, the network name to VLAN 7, and enable `StartConnected` and disable `WakeOnLan` for the same network adapter:

```
PowerCLI C:\> Get-VM -Name VM4 | Get-NetworkAdapter |
>> Set-NetworkAdapter -NetworkName "VLAN 7" -Type e1000 `
>> -StartConnected:$true -WakeOnLan:$false -Confirm:$false
```

The output of the preceding command is as follows:

Name	Type	NetworkName	MacAddress	WakeOnLan Enabled
Network adapter 1	e1000	VLAN 7	00:50:56:00:00:01	False

Modifying a floppy drive

The `Set-FloppyDrive` cmdlet can be used to modify the configuration of a floppy drive. You can set the floppy drive to point to an image, update the `StartConnected` and `Connected` properties, and remove the floppy drive's media backing and disconnect it.

The syntax of the `Set-FloppyDrive` cmdlet is as follows:

```
Set-FloppyDrive [-Floppy] <FloppyDrive[]> [-FloppyImagePath <String>]
[-HostDevice <String>] [-NoMedia] [-StartConnected [<Boolean>]]
[-Connected [<Boolean>]] [-WhatIf] [-Confirm] [<CommonParameters>]
```

The `-Floppy` parameter is required. You cannot use the `-FloppyImagePath`, `-HostDevice`, and `-NoMedia` parameters together.

To modify the floppy drive of the VM3 virtual machine to `StartConnected`, you can use the following command:

```
PowerCLI C:\> Get-VM -Name VM3 | Get-FloppyDrive |
>> Set-FloppyDrive -StartConnected:$true -Confirm:$false
```

The output of the preceding command is as follows:

```
FloppyImagePath        HostDevice              RemoteDevice
---------------        ----------              ------------
[datastore2] VM3/...
```

Modifying a CD drive

To modify the configuration of a virtual CD drive, you can use the `Set-CDDrive` cmdlet.

The `Set-CDDrive` cmdlet has the following syntax:

```
Set-CDDrive [-CD] <CDDrive[]> [-IsoPath <String>] [-HostDevice
<String>] [-NoMedia] [-StartConnected [<Boolean>]] [-Connected
[<Boolean>]] [-WhatIf] [-Confirm] [<CommonParameters>]
```

The `-CD` parameter is required.

You can use the `-IsoPath` parameter to point the CD drive to an ISO image. You can enable or disable the `StartConnected` and `Connected` flags. If the `-NoMedia` parameter is set to `$true`, it removes the CD drive's media backing and disconnects it.

A virtual CD drive can only be set to `Connected` if the virtual machine is powered on.

In the following example, we will mount an ISO image to the CD drive from the datastore of the VM4 virtual machine:

```
PowerCLI C:\> Get-VM -Name VM4 | Get-CDDrive |
>> Set-CDDrive -IsoPath '[datastore2] ISOs\ CentOS-7-
x86_64-Minimal-1511.iso' -Confirm:$false
```

The output of the preceding command is as follows:

```
IsoPath              HostDevice                RemoteDevice
-------              ----------                ------------
[datastore2] ISOs...
```

In the following example, we will remove the VM4 virtual machine's CD drive's media backing, disconnect it, and disable the `StartConnected` flag:

```
PowerCLI C:\> Get-VM -Name VM4 | Get-CDDrive |
>> Set-CDDrive -NoMedia:$true -StartConnected:$false -Confirm:$false
```

The output of the preceding command is as follows:

```
IsoPath              HostDevice                RemoteDevice
-------              ----------                ------------
```

Removing devices from a virtual machine

To remove devices from a virtual machine, you can use the following `Remove-*` cmdlets:

- `Remove-HardDisk`
- `Remove-NetworkAdapter`
- `Remove-FloppyDrive`
- `Remove-CDDrive`

There is no `Remove-ScsiController` cmdlet. When you remove the last hard disk from a SCSI controller, the SCSI controller is also removed.

Removing a hard disk

You can use the `Remove-HardDisk` cmdlet to remove a hard disk from a virtual machine. The `Remove-HardDisk` cmdlet has the following syntax:

```
Remove-HardDisk [-HardDisk] <HardDisk[]> [-DeletePermanently]
[-WhatIf] [-Confirm] [<CommonParameters>]
```

The `-HardDisk` parameter is required. To remove the hard disk not only from the inventory but also from the datastore, you have to use the `-DeletePermanently` parameter. You can remove a hard disk while the virtual machine is powered on.

The following example removes `Hard Disk 3` from the `VM2` virtual machine and deletes the hard disk from the datastore:

```
PowerCLI C:\> Get-VM -Name VM2 | Get-HardDisk |
>> Where-Object {$_.Name -eq "Hard Disk 3"} |
>> Remove-HardDisk -DeletePermanently -Confirm:$false
```

The preceding command does not return any output.

Removing a network adapter

To remove a network adapter from a virtual machine, you can use the `Remove-NetworkAdapter` cmdlet. This cmdlet has the following syntax:

```
Remove-NetworkAdapter [-NetworkAdapter] <NetworkAdapter[]>
[-WhatIf] [-Confirm] [<CommonParameters>]
```

The `-NetworkAdapter` parameter is required. You can only remove a network adapter while the virtual machine is powered off.

Let's remove `Network Adapter 2` from the `VM2` virtual machine using the following command:

```
PowerCLI C:\> Get-VM -Name VM2 | Get-NetworkAdapter |
>> Where-Object {$_.Name -eq "Network adapter 2"} |
>> Remove-NetworkAdapter -Confirm:$false
```

The preceding command does not return any output.

Removing a floppy drive

You can use the `Remove-FloppyDrive` cmdlet to remove a floppy drive from a virtual machine. The `Remove-FloppyDrive` cmdlet's syntax is similar to other `Remove-*` cmdlet syntaxes:

```
Remove-FloppyDrive [-Floppy] <FloppyDrive[]> [-WhatIf] [-Confirm]
[<CommonParameters>]
```

The `-Floppy` parameter is required. You can only remove a floppy drive while the virtual machine is powered off.

The following example removes all the floppy drives from the `VM3` virtual machine:

```
PowerCLI C:\> Get-VM -Name VM3 | Get-FloppyDrive |
>> Remove-FloppyDrive -Confirm:$false
```

The preceding command does not return any output.

Removing a CD drive

Removing a CD drive can be done with the `Remove-CDDrive` cmdlet, which has the following syntax:

```
Remove-CDDrive [-CD] <CDDrive[]> [-WhatIf] [-Confirm]
[<CommonParameters>]
```

The `-CD` parameter is required. You can only remove a CD drive while the virtual machine is powered off.

The following command will remove `'CD/DVD drive 1'` from the `VM4` virtual machine:

```
PowerCLI C:\> Get-VM -Name VM4 | Get-CDDrive |
>> Where-Object {$_.Name -eq 'CD/DVD drive 1'} |
>> Remove-CDDrive -Confirm:$false
```

The preceding command does not return any output.

Converting virtual machines into templates

You have already learned how to deploy a virtual machine from a template in the *Creating virtual machines from templates* section. You will now learn how to create a template. You begin by creating a virtual machine and installing the operating system, application software, and patches you need for all the virtual machines you want to deploy. After you have finished creating your new virtual machine, you have to convert it into a template using the `Set-VM` cmdlet, which you have already seen in the *Modifying the settings of virtual machines* section. Let's convert the `VM1` virtual machine into a template:

```
PowerCLI C:\> Get-VM -Name VM1 | Set-VM -ToTemplate -Confirm:$false
```

The output of the preceding command is as follows:

```
Name
----
VM1
```

To confirm that `VM1` is now a template, you can use the `Get-Template` cmdlet to view all the templates:

```
PowerCLI C:\> Get-Template
```

The output of the preceding command is as follows:

```
Name
----
VM1
```

The `Get-Template` cmdlet has the following syntax. The first parameter set is the default:

```
Get-Template [-Location <VIContainer[]>] [-Datastore
<StorageResource[]>] [[-Name] <String[]>] [-NoRecursion]
[-Server <VIServer[]>] [<CommonParameters>]
```

The second parameter set is for retrieving templates by ID:

```
Get-Template -Id <String[]> [-Server <VIServer[]>]
[<CommonParameters>]
```

The parameters of the `Get-Template` cmdlet are filters to retrieve only templates from a certain location or datastore, or with a specific name or ID.

Converting templates into virtual machines

Now that you have this template, you have to keep it updated with the latest software versions and patches. However, you cannot start a template to modify the installed operating system. You have to convert it into a virtual machine first, and then start the virtual machine, install the latest software versions and patches, and finally, shut the virtual machine down and convert it back into a template.

To convert a template to a virtual machine, you have to use the `Set-Template` cmdlet's `-ToVM` parameter. The `Set-Template` cmdlet has the following syntax:

```
Set-Template [-Template] <Template[]> [-Name <String>] [-ToVM]
[-Server <VIServer[]>] [-RunAsync] [-WhatIf] [-Confirm]
[<CommonParameters>]
```

Here is an example to convert a template into a virtual machine:

```
PowerCLI C:\> Set-Template -Template VM1 -ToVM
```

The output of the preceding command is as follows:

```
Name                  PowerState Num CPUs MemoryGB
----                  ---------- -------- --------
VM1                   PoweredOff 1         0.250
```

Modifying the name of a template

You can also use the `Set-Template` cmdlet to give your template a more meaningful name. You have to use the `-Name` parameter to specify the new name:

```
PowerCLI C:\> Set-Template -Template VM1 -Name Windows2016Template
```

The output of the preceding command is as follows:

```
Name
----
Windows2016Template
```

Removing templates

To remove a template, you can use the `Remove-Template` cmdlet. This cmdlet has the following syntax:

```
Remove-Template [-Template] <Template[]> [-DeletePermanently]
[-RunAsync] [-Server <VIServer[]>] [-WhatIf] [-Confirm]
[<CommonParameters>]
```

The `-Template` parameter is required. If you use the `-DeletePermanently` parameter, the template will not only be removed from the inventory, but also from the datastore.

To remove the template `Windows2016Template` from the vCenter Server inventory and also from the datastore, you can use the following command:

```
PowerCLI C:\> Remove-Template -Template Windows2016Template `
>> -DeletePermanently -Confirm:$false
```

The preceding command does not return any output.

Moving virtual machines to another folder, host, cluster, resource pool, or datastore

To move a virtual machine to another folder, host, cluster, resource pool, or datastore, you can use the `Move-VM` cmdlet. You can also use the `Move-VM` cmdlet to migrate a network adapter to a new port group. This cmdlet has the following syntax:

```
Move-VM [-AdvancedOption <AdvancedOption[]>] [[-Destination]
<VIContainer>] [-Datastore <StorageResource>] [-DiskStorageFormat
<VirtualDiskStorageFormat>] [-VMotionPriority <VMotionPriority>]
[-NetworkAdapter <NetworkAdapter[]>] [-PortGroup
<VirtualPortGroupBase[]>] [-RunAsync] [-VM] <VirtualMachine[]>
[-Server <VIServer[]>] [-WhatIf] [-Confirm] [<CommonParameters>]
```

The `-VM` parameter is required.

In the first example, we will move the VM2 virtual machine to ESXi host `192.168.0.134`:

```
PowerCLI C:\> Get-VM -Name VM2 | Move-VM -Destination 192.168.0.134
```

The output of the preceding command is as follows:

```
Name                    PowerState Num CPUs MemoryGB
----                    ---------- -------- --------
VM2                     PoweredOff 2        4.000
```

In the second example, we will move virtual machine DNS1 to the Infrastructure folder. You have learned to work with folders in Chapter 2, *Learning Basic PowerCLI Concepts*:

```
PowerCLI C:\> $Folder = Get-Folder -Name Infrastructure
PowerCLI C:\> Get-VM -Name DNS1 | Move-VM -Destination $Folder
```

The output of the preceding command is as follows:

```
Name                    PowerState Num CPUs MemoryGB
----                    ---------- -------- --------
DNS1                    PoweredOff 2        8.000
```

In the final example, we will move virtual machine DNS1 to ESXi host 192.168.0.134 and datastore datastore2:

```
PowerCLI C:\> Move-VM -VM DNS1 -Destination 192.168.0.134
-Datastore datastore2
```

The output of the preceding command is as follows:

```
Name                    PowerState Num CPUs MemoryGB
----                    ---------- -------- --------
DNS1                    PoweredOff 2        8.000
```

Updating VMware Tools

When there is a new version of the vSphere ESXi software, it normally comes with a new version of VMware Tools. There are two methods of updating VMware Tools in a guest operating system:

- Use the Update-Tools cmdlet
- Enable the **Check and upgrade VMware Tools before each power on** checkbox and reboot the virtual machine

In this section, we will discuss both options.

In the following screenshot of the vSphere web client, you will see the **VM Options** tab in the **Edit Settings** window for the VM2 virtual machine. The **Check and upgrade VMware Tools before each power on** checkbox is enabled:

Using the Update-Tools cmdlet

The Update-Tools cmdlet will update VMware Tools in a guest operating system. The syntax of this cmdlet is as follows:

```
Update-Tools [-NoReboot] [-RunAsync] [[-Guest] <VMGuest[]>]
[<CommonParameters>]
Update-Tools [-NoReboot] [-RunAsync] [[-VM] <VirtualMachine[]>]
[[-Server] <VIServer[]>] [<CommonParameters>]
```

You can use the first parameter set to specify virtual machines by the VMGuest object. The second parameter set is for specifying virtual machines by the VirtualMachine object or name.

Before you can use the Update-Tools cmdlet, you need to have an older version of VMware Tools installed.

In the following example, we will use the `Update-Tools` cmdlet to update VMware Tools in the `VM2` virtual machine. The virtual machine must be powered on:

```
PowerCLI C:\> Get-VM -Name VM2 | Update-Tools
```

The preceding command does not return any output.

Linux virtual machines require a reboot each time VMware Tools is upgraded. This is also true for Windows systems with VMware Tools version 8 or lower. The `Update-Tools` cmdlet will perform this reboot unless you specify the `-NoReboot` parameter. However, the `-NoReboot` parameter is supported only for Windows operating systems. Even if you use the `-NoReboot` parameter, the virtual machine might still reboot after updating VMware Tools. This will depend on the currently installed VMware Tools version, the VMware Tools version to which you want to upgrade, and the vCenter Server/ESXi versions.

Enabling the Check and upgrade VMware Tools before each power on checkbox

In the following example, we will enable the **Check and upgrade VMware Tools before each power on** checkbox for all the virtual machines in the inventory. Because there is no PowerCLI cmdlet to do this, we have to go back to the VMware vSphere API:

1. First, we will create an object of type `VMware.Vim.VirtualMachineConfigSpec` and assign it to the `$spec` variable:

   ```
   $spec = New-Object -Type VMware.Vim.VirtualMachineConfigSpec
   ```

2. Second, we will create an object of type `VMware.Vim.ToolsConfigInfo` and assign this object to the `Tools` property of the `$spec` variable:

   ```
   $spec.Tools = New-Object -Type VMware.Vim.ToolsConfigInfo
   ```

3. Next, we will assign the value `"UpgradeAtPowerCycle"` to the `Tools.ToolsUpgradePolicy` of the `$spec` variable:

   ```
   $spec.Tools.ToolsUpgradePolicy = "UpgradeAtPowerCycle"
   ```

4. Finally, we loop through all of our virtual machines and run the `ReconfigVM_Task()` method with the just-created `VMware.Vim.VirtualMachineConfigSpec` object as a parameter, to asynchronously reconfigure the virtual machines and enable the **Check and upgrade VMware Tools before each power on** checkbox on each virtual machine:

```
Get-VM | ForEach-Object {$_.ExtensionData.ReconfigVM_Task($spec)}
```

The preceding code returns an output similar to the following:

```
Type                                    Value
----                                    -----
Task                                    task-227
Task                                    task-228
```

To upgrade VMware Tools after enabling the **Check and upgrade VMware Tools before each power on** checkbox, you need to restart all the virtual machines with the following command:

```
PowerCLI C:\> Get-VM | Restart-VMGuest
```

Don't try the preceding command in your production environment. It will restart all your virtual machines!

Upgrading virtual machine compatibility

To upgrade virtual machine compatibility, you can use the `Set-VM` cmdlet that you have seen before in the *Modifying the settings of virtual machines* section. You have to use the `-Version` parameter and specify the new compatibility version as a parameter value. At the time of writing this book, the only valid versions are v4, v7, v8, v9, v10, and v11.

New features in virtual machines compatible with version 9 or higher can no longer be edited with the vSphere C# client. Some devices may not appear in the devices list, and the settings of some devices may appear as **Restricted**. You will have to use the vSphere web client or PowerCLI to edit the configuration for these virtual machines.

The following example will upgrade the VM7 virtual machine to compatibility version 11:

```
PowerCLI C:\ > Get-VM -Name VM7 | `
>>   Set-VM -Version V11 -Confirm:$false
>>
```

The output of the preceding command is as follows:

```
Name                  PowerState Num CPUs MemoryGB
----                  ---------- -------- --------
VM7                   PoweredOff 1          0.250
```

The virtual machine has to be powered off, or you will get the following error message:

The attempted operation cannot be performed in the current state (Powered on).

It is not possible to downgrade to an earlier compatibility version. If you specify a version lower or equal to the version the virtual machine already has, you will get the following error message:

Virtual machine compatibility is already up-to-date.

The version numbers correspond to the following virtual machine compatibilities:

PowerCLI version	Virtual machines compatible with
v4	ESX/ESXi 3.5 and later
v7	ESX/ESXi 4.0 and later
v8	ESXi 5.0 and later
v9	ESXi 5.1 and later
v10	ESXi 5.5 and later
v11	ESXi 6.0 and later
v13	ESXi 6.5 and later

In the following screenshot of the vSphere web client, you will see the **VM Hardware** window containing the status of a virtual machine, with **Compatibility** showing **ESXi 6.5 and later (VM version 13)**:

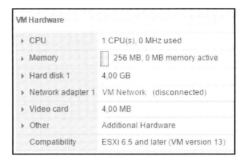

Using snapshots

Snapshots are a point in time to which you can revert a virtual machine and changes made to the virtual machine after creating the snapshot will be discarded. For example, snapshots are useful when you are installing or upgrading software on a virtual machine. If the installation or upgrade goes wrong, you can easily revert to the time the last snapshot was taken to get back to the state before you started the installation or upgrade. If you have verified that the installation or upgrade was successful, you should remove the snapshot, because snapshots use valuable space in your datastores and decrease the performance of your virtual machine.

 Snapshots are not backups!

In this section, we will discuss the PowerCLI commands to work with snapshots.

Creating snapshots

To create a new snapshot of a virtual machine, you have to use the `New-Snapshot` cmdlet. This cmdlet has the following syntax:

```
New-Snapshot [-VM] <VirtualMachine[]> [-Name] <String>
[-Description <String>] [-Memory] [-Quiesce] [-Server <VIServer[]>]
[-RunAsync] [-WhatIf] [-Confirm] [<CommonParameters>]
```

The −VM and −Name parameters are required.

In the following example, we will create a snapshot of the VM2 virtual machine before upgrading it. If something goes wrong during the upgrade, we can revert to the snapshot and will have our original virtual machine back:

```
PowerCLI C:\> New-Snapshot -VM VM2 -Name "Before Upgrade" `
>> -Description "Made before upgrading the virtual machine"
```

The output of the preceding command is as follows:

```
Name                Description                      PowerState
----                -----------                      ----------
Before Upgrade      Made before upgrading the v... PoweredOff
```

In the following screenshot of the vSphere web client, you will see the **Snapshots** tab for VM2 showing the snapshot created in the preceding PowerCLI command:

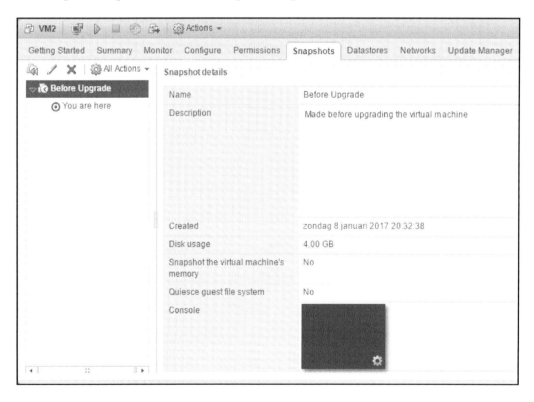

If the virtual machine is powered on, you can use the `-Memory` parameter to preserve the virtual machine's memory state with the snapshot. In the powered on state, you can also use the `-Quiesce` parameter to quiesce the filesystem of the virtual machine using VMware Tools. Quiescing ensures that a snapshot represents a consistent state of the guest filesystems.

In the following example, we will create a new snapshot of the VM2 virtual machine that includes the virtual machine's memory, and we will quiesce the virtual machine's filesystem before creating the snapshot:

```
PowerCLI C:\> New-Snapshot -VM VM2 -Name "Before patching" `
>> -Memory -Quiesce
```

The output of the preceding command is as follows:

```
Name                    Description              PowerState
----                    -----------              ----------
Before patching                                  PoweredOn
```

The value of the snapshot's `PowerState` property, `PoweredOn`, indicates that the virtual machine's memory is included in the snapshot.

Retrieving snapshots

To get a list of all the snapshots a virtual machine has or to retrieve a specific snapshot, you can use the `Get-Snapshot` cmdlet. The syntax of this cmdlet is as follows:

```
Get-Snapshot [[-Name] <String[]>] [-Id <String[]>] [-VM]
<VirtualMachine[]> [-Server <VIServer[]>] [<CommonParameters>]
```

The `-VM` parameter is required.

Let's get a list of all the snapshots of the VM2 virtual machine using the following command:

```
PowerCLI C:\> Get-VM -Name VM2 | Get-Snapshot
```

The output of the preceding command is as follows:

```
Name                    Description              PowerState
----                    -----------              ----------
Before Upgrade          Made before upgrading the v... PoweredOff
Before patching                                  PoweredOn
```

To retrieve the snapshot named `Before Upgrade`, you can use the following command:

```
PowerCLI C:\> Get-VM -Name VM2 | Get-Snapshot -Name 'Before Upgrade'
```

The output of the preceding command is as follows:

```
Name                    Description                      PowerState
----                    -----------                      ----------
Before Upgrade          Made before upgrading the v... PoweredOff
```

Snapshots can grow to the size of the original disks and can fill a datastore. The following example will show you the snapshot names, virtual machine names, snapshot size in GB, and creation data for all the snapshots that are larger than 10 GB:

```
PowerCLI C:\> Get-VM | Get-Snapshot |
>> Where-Object {$_.SizeGB -ge 10GB} |
>> Select-Object -Property Name,VM,SizeGB,Created
```

In the following example, we will retrieve a list of all the snapshots that are older than three days:

```
PowerCLI C:\> Get-VM | Get-Snapshot |
>> Where-Object {$_.Created -lt (Get-Date).AddDays(-3)} |
>> Select-Object -Property VM,Name,Description,Created
```

Reverting to a snapshot

To revert a virtual machine to an existing snapshot, you can use the `Set-VM` cmdlet that was introduced in the *Modifying the settings of a virtual machine* section. In the following example, we will revert the VM2 virtual machine to the snapshot named `Before Upgrade`:

```
PowerCLI C:\> $vm = Get-VM -Name VM2
PowerCLI C:\> $snapshot = Get-Snapshot -VM $vm -Name 'Before Upgrade'
PowerCLI C:\> Set-VM -VM $vm -Snapshot $snapshot -Confirm:$false
```

The output of the preceding command is as follows:

```
Name              PowerState Num CPUs MemoryGB
----              ---------- -------- --------
VM2               PoweredOff 2        4.000
```

Modifying snapshots

To modify the name or description of a snapshot, you can use the `Set-Snapshot` cmdlet. The `Set-Snapshot` cmdlet has the following syntax:

```
Set-Snapshot [-Snapshot] <Snapshot[]> [-Name <String>] [-Description
<String>] [-WhatIf] [-Confirm] [<CommonParameters>]
```

The `-Snapshot` parameter is required.

In the following example, we will modify the name and description of the `'Before patching'` snapshot of the VM2 virtual machine:

```
PowerCLI C:\> Get-VM -Name VM2 |
>> Get-Snapshot -Name 'Before patching' |
>> Set-Snapshot -Name 'Before Microsoft patches' `
>> -Description 'Before installing the Microsoft January patches'
```

The output of the preceding command is as follows:

```
Name                    Description                 PowerState
----                    -----------                 ----------
Before Microsoft  ...   Before installing the Micro...  PoweredOff
```

Removing snapshots

Snapshots can use a considerable amount of disk space. Therefore, it is good practice to remove snapshots on a regular basis. To remove snapshots, you can use the `Remove-Snapshot` cmdlet. This cmdlet has the following syntax:

```
Remove-Snapshot [-Snapshot] <Snapshot[]> [-RemoveChildren]
[-RunAsync] [-WhatIf] [-Confirm] [<CommonParameters>]
```

The `-Snapshot` parameter is required. You can use the `Remove-Snapshot` cmdlet to remove a single snapshot or use the `-RemoveChildren` parameter to remove a snapshot and all its children.

In the following example, we will remove the snapshot named `Before Upgrade` and its child snapshots for virtual machine `VM2`:

```
PowerCLI C:\> Get-VM -Name VM2 |
>> Get-Snapshot -Name 'Before Upgrade' |
>> Remove-Snapshot -RemoveChildren -Confirm:$false
```

The preceding command does not return any output.

Running commands in the guest OS

To run a command on the guest operating system of a virtual machine, you can use the `Invoke-VMScript` cmdlet. To use this cmdlet, the virtual machines must be powered on and must have VMware Tools installed. You also need network connectivity to the ESXi server hosting the virtual machine on port 902.

The `Invoke-VMScript` cmdlet has the following syntax:

```
Invoke-VMScript [-ScriptText] <String> [-VM] <VirtualMachine[]>
[-HostCredential <PSCredential>] [-HostUser <String>]
[-HostPassword <SecureString>] [-GuestCredential <PSCredential>]
[-GuestUser <String>] [-GuestPassword <SecureString>]
[-ToolsWaitSecs <Int32>] [-ScriptType <ScriptType>] [-RunAsync]
[-Server <VIServer[]>] [-WhatIf] [-Confirm] [<CommonParameters>]
```

The `-ScriptText` and `-VM` parameters are required. The value of the `-ScriptText` parameter is the text of the script you want to run or the path to the script. The `-ScriptType` parameter specifies the type of script. Valid values are `PowerShell`, `Bat`, and `Bash`. For Windows virtual machines, the default value is `PowerShell`, while for Linux virtual machines it is `Bash`.

The following example runs `'ipconfig /all'` on the guest operating system of the `VM2` virtual machine:

```
PowerCLI C:\> $GuestCredential = Get-Credential
PowerCLI C:\> Invoke-VMScript -VM VM2 -ScriptText 'ipconfig /all' `
>> -GuestCredential $GuestCredential
```

The output of the preceding command is as follows:

```
ScriptOutput
------------------------------------------------------------------
| Windows IP Configuration
|
|     Host Name . . . . . . . . . . . . : VM2
|     Primary Dns Suffix. . . . . . . . : blackmilktea.com
|     Node Type . . . . . . . . . . . . : Hybrid
|     IP Routing Enabled. . . . . . . . : No
|     WINS Proxy Enabled. . . . . . . . : No
|     DNS Suffix Search List. . . . . . : blackmilktea.com
|
| Ethernet adapter Local Area Connection:
|
|     Connection-specific DNS Suffix. . :
|     Description . . . . . . . . . . . : vmxnet3 Ethernet Adapter
|     Physical Address. . . . . . . . . : 00:50:56:81:1c:0c
|     DHCP Enabled. . . . . . . . . . . : No
|     Autoconfiguration Enabled . . . . : Yes
|     IPv4 Address. . . . . . . . . . . : 192.168.0.202(Preferred)
|     Subnet Mask . . . . . . . . . . . : 255.255.255.0
|     Default Gateway . . . . . . . . . : 192.168.0.1
|     DNS Servers . . . . . . . . . . . : 192.168.0.2
|                                         192.168.0.3
|     NetBIOS over Tcpip. . . . . . . . : Enabled
|
------------------------------------------------------------------
```

Configuring Fault Tolerance

VMware Fault Tolerance is a feature that allows you to run a copy of a virtual machine on another host in the same cluster. The primary virtual machine and the secondary virtual machine are synchronized and run in virtual lockstep with each other. When the primary virtual machine fails, the secondary virtual machine takes its place with the minimum possible interruption of service. Detailed instructions for configuring Fault Tolerance in your vSphere environment can be found on the *VMware vSphere 6.5 Documentation Center* page at https://pubs.vmware.com/vsphere-65/index.jsp under **ESXi and vCenter Server 6.5 Documentation | vSphere Availability | Providing Fault Tolerance for Virtual Machines**. In this section, we will discuss how to turn Fault Tolerance on and off in a virtual machine.

Turning Fault Tolerance on

There are no PowerCLI cmdlets to turn Fault Tolerance on or off in a virtual machine, so we have to use the VMware vSphere API. In the following example, we will use the CreateSecondaryVM_Task() method to create a secondary virtual machine for the VM2 virtual machine. The CreateSecondaryVM_Task() method needs one parameter, which is the Managed Object Reference of the host where the secondary virtual machine is to be created and powered on. In this case, we don't specify a host, but use $null as a placeholder. The secondary virtual machine will be created on a compatible host selected by the system:

```
PowerCLI C:\> $vm = Get-VM -Name VM2
PowerCLI C:\> $vm.ExtensionData.CreateSecondaryVM_Task($null)
```

The output of the preceding command is as follows:

```
Type                            Value
----                            -----
Task                            task-269
```

Turning Fault Tolerance off

To turn Fault Tolerance off for a virtual machine, we will use the VMware vSphere API's TurnOffFaultToleranceForVM_Task() method. In the following example, we will turn off Fault Tolerance for the VM2 virtual machine. The TurnOffFaultToleranceForVM_Task() method does not have any parameters:

```
PowerCLI C:\> $vm = Get-VM -Name VM2
PowerCLI C:\> $vm.ExtensionData.TurnOffFaultToleranceForVM_Task()
```

The output of the preceding command is as follows:

```
Type                            Value
----                            -----
Task                            task-373
```

Opening the console of virtual machines

The `Open-VMConsoleWindow` cmdlet opens the console of a virtual machine in a web browser. It will open the console in the browser configured in the `VMConsoleWindowBrowser` setting in `Set-PowerCLIConfiguration`, or in the default browser if the setting is not configured. The browser must be a 32-bit browser. You can open the console in a new window or full screen. This cmdlet uses the **VMware Remote Console** (**VMRC**) browser plugin.

The syntax of the `Open-VMConsoleWindow` cmdlet is as follows:

```
Open-VMConsoleWindow [-VM] <RemoteConsoleVM[]> [-FullScreen]
[-UrlOnly] [-Server <VIConnection[]>] [-WhatIf] [-Confirm]
[<CommonParameters>]
```

The `-VM` parameter is required. The `-FullScreen` parameter will open the console in full screen mode. The `-UrlOnly` parameter does not open the console but returns the URL needed to open the console. This URL will stay valid for 30 seconds, after which the screen authentication ticket contained in the URL expires.

The command in the following example will open the console of the `vCenter` virtual machine running in my lab environment:

```
PowerCLI C:\> Open-VMConsoleWindow -VM vcenter
```

The preceding command opens the window shown in the following screenshot:

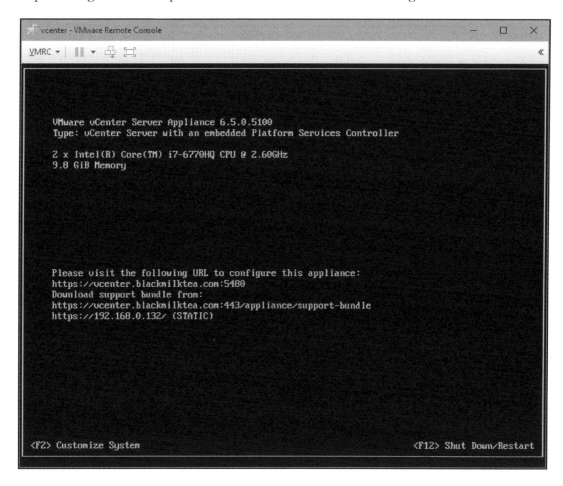

Removing virtual machines

In the lifecycle of a virtual machine, there comes a time when you may want to remove it. This may be because the application running on the virtual machine is not in use anymore, or because the operating system running on the virtual machine is obsolete and you have moved the application to a new server. To remove a virtual machine, you can use the Remove-VM cmdlet, which has the following syntax:

```
Remove-VM [-DeletePermanently] [-RunAsync] [-VM] <VirtualMachine[]>
[-Server <VIServer[]>] [-WhatIf] [-Confirm] [<CommonParameters>]
```

If you use the `-DeletePermanently` parameter, the virtual machine will be removed from your vSphere inventory and the datastores. If you omit the `-DeletePermanently` parameter, the virtual machine will only be removed from the vSphere inventory. Because the virtual machine's files remain on the datastores, you can register the virtual machine again.

In the following example, we will use the `Remove-VM` cmdlet to remove the `VM6` virtual machine from the inventory and also to remove its files from the datastore. A virtual machine must be powered off before you attempt to remove it:

```
PowerCLI C:\> Remove-VM –VM VM6 –DeletePermanently –Confirm:$false
```

The preceding command does not return any output.

Using tags

Tags are labels that you can attach to objects in the vSphere inventory. Every object can have zero, one, or many tags attached. You can use tags to group objects based on anything you want.

For example, you can create a `John Doe` tag that specifies the owner of a virtual machine is John Doe. Using the `John Doe` tag, you can easily find all of the virtual machines owned by John Doe.

Tag categories are used to group related tags together. Every tag must belong to a tag category. At the creation of a tag category, you can specify to which object types the tags in this tag category can be attached. You can also specify if only one, or more than one, tag in the tag category can be attached to an object.

Continuing the preceding example, you can create a tag category, `Owner`, which contains the tags for each owner. You can apply this tag category to the virtual machine objects. If you want your virtual machines to have only one owner, you can specify that only one tag from the `Owner` tag category can be attached to a virtual machine.

Tags and tag categories are replicated between all vCenter Servers in an Enhanced Linked Mode configuration. This allows you to search for objects on all the connected vCenter servers.

Tags replace the vSphere **custom attributes** and **annotations**. In the *Converting custom attributes and annotations to tags* section, you will learn how to convert your custom attributes and annotations to tags.

> The PowerCLI cmdlets related to tags only work with vCenter Server 5.1 or later.

Managing tag categories

Tag categories are used to group tags and define to which object types the tags in the tag category can be attached. Tag categories also specify if only one, or more than one, tag in the category can be attached to an object. Every tag must belong to one and only one tag category. So, you must create a tag category before you can create a tag. You can compare a tag category to a custom attribute name. In this section, you will learn how to create, retrieve, modify, and remove tag categories.

Creating tag categories

Before we can create tags, we have to create at least one tag category. You can use the `New-TagCategory` cmdlet to create a tag category. The syntax of this cmdlet is as follows:

```
New-TagCategory [-Name] <String> [-Description <String>]
[-Cardinality <Cardinality>] [-EntityType <String[]>]
[-Server <VIServer[]>] [-WhatIf] [-Confirm] [<CommonParameters>]
```

The `-Name` parameter is required.

If the `-Cardinality` parameter has the value `Single`, it specifies that only one tag in this tag category can be attached to an object. If the `-Cardinality` parameter has the value `Multiple`, it specifies that more than one tag in this tag category can be attached to an object. If you don't use the `-Cardinality` parameter, `Single` is used as the default value.

The -EntityType parameter specifies the types of objects to which tags in this tag category can be attached. The valid PowerCLI type names you can use as a value for this parameter are Cluster, Datacenter, Datastore, DatastoreCluster, DistributedPortGroup, DistributedSwitch, Folder, ResourcePool, VApp, VirtualPortGroup, VirtualMachine, VM, and VMHost. If you don't use the -EntityType parameter, or use All as the value, you can attach tags in this tag category to all of the valid entity types. You can also use vSphere API type names as a value of the -EntityType parameter. If you use vSphere API names that are not vCenter Server API type names, you have to use a namespace prefix in the format: <namespace>/<type>, for example vco/WorkflowItem.

To create a tag category, you need the Inventory Service.vSphere Tagging.Create vSphere Tag Category privilege.

In the following example, we will create a tag category named Owner. This tag category will only be used for VirtualMachine type objects. Each virtual machine can have only one owner:

```
PowerCLI C:\> New-TagCategory -Name Owner -Description
'Virtual machine owners' -Cardinality Single -EntityType VirtualMachine
```

The preceding command has the following output:

```
Description : Virtual machine owners
Cardinality : Single
EntityType  : {VirtualMachine}
Id          : urn:vmomi:InventoryServiceCategory:7591c2f8-9a8d-49a4-
              b9d7-ce07126d115d:GLOBAL
Name        : Owner
Uid         : /VIServer=vsphere.local\administrator@192.168.0.132:44
              3/TagCategory=urn:vmomi:InventoryServiceCategory:7591c
              2f8-9a8d-49a4-b9d7-ce07126d115d:GLOBAL/
Client      : VMware.VimAutomation.ViCore.Impl.V1.VimClient
```

Retrieving tag categories

You can retrieve the tag categories in your vSphere inventory using the Get-TagCategory cmdlet. The syntax of this cmdlet is as follows:

```
Get-TagCategory [[-Name] <String[]>] [-Server <VIServer[]>]
[<CommonParameters>]
Get-TagCategory -Id <String[]> [-Server <VIServer[]>]
[<CommonParameters>]
```

If you want to filter the tag categories by ID, the `-Id` parameter is required. You cannot use the `-Name` and `-Id` parameters in the same command because they are in a different parameter set.

In the first example, we will retrieve all of the tag categories in our vSphere inventory:

```
PowerCLI C:\> Get-TagCategory
```

The preceding command has the following output:

```
Description : Virtual machine owners
Cardinality : Single
EntityType  : {VirtualMachine}
Id          : urn:vmomi:InventoryServiceCategory:7591c2f8-9a8d-49a4-
              b9d7-ce07126d115d:GLOBAL
Name        : Owner
Uid         : /VIServer=vsphere.local\administrator@192.168.0.132:44
              3/TagCategory=urn:vmomi:InventoryServiceCategory:7591c
              2f8-9a8d-49a4-b9d7-ce07126d115d:GLOBAL/
Client      : VMware.VimAutomation.ViCore.Impl.V1.VimClient
```

In the following example, we will search for a tag category by name using the `-Name` property:

```
PowerCLI C:\> Get-TagCategory -Name Owner
```

We can also search for a tag category by ID, using the `-Id` property. In the following example, we will use the ID of the tag category named `Owner`, as retrieved in a preceding example, to retrieve the tag category by ID:

```
PowerCLI C:\> Get-TagCategory -Id urn:vmomi:InventoryServiceCategory:
7591c2f8-9a8d-49a4-b9d7-ce07126d115d:GLOBAL
```

Modifying tag categories

Using the `Set-TagCategory` cmdlet, you can modify the name, description, and cardinality of a tag category. You can also add entity types to the list of entity types to which tags in this tag category can be attached. The syntax of the `Set-TagCategory` cmdlet is as follows:

```
Set-TagCategory [-Category] <TagCategory[]> [-Name <String>]
[-Description <String>] [-Cardinality <Cardinality>]
[-AddEntityType <String[]>] [-Server <VIServer[]>] [-WhatIf]
[-Confirm] [<CommonParameters>]
```

The -Category parameter is required.

In the following example, we will modify the cardinality of the Owner tag category from Single to Multiple:

```
PowerCLI C:\> Get-TagCategory -Name Owner | Set-TagCategory
-Cardinality Multiple
```

The output of the preceding command is the following:

```
Description : Virtual machine owners
Cardinality : Multiple
EntityType  : {VirtualMachine}
Id          : urn:vmomi:InventoryServiceCategory:7591c2f8-9a8d-49a4-
              b9d7-ce07126d115d:GLOBAL
Name        : Owner
Uid         : /VIServer=vsphere.local\administrator@192.168.0.132:44
              3/TagCategory=urn:vmomi:InventoryServiceCategory:7591c
              2f8-9a8d-49a4-b9d7-ce07126d115d:GLOBAL/
Client      : VMware.VimAutomation.ViCore.Impl.V1.VimClient
```

Removing tag categories

To remove a tag category, you can use the Remove-TagCategory cmdlet. The syntax of this cmdlet is as follows:

```
Remove-TagCategory [-Category] <TagCategory[]> [-Server
<VIServer[]>] [-WhatIf] [-Confirm] [<CommonParameters>]
```

The -Category parameter is required.

In the following example, we will remove the Owner tag category created in a preceding example:

```
PowerCLI C:\> Get-TagCategory -Name Owner | Remove-TagCategory
-Confirm:$false
```

The preceding command does not return any output.

Managing tags

You can use tags to label your inventory objects. After tagging your objects, you can search your inventory using these tags. You can compare a tag to a custom attribute value. In this section, you will learn how to create, retrieve, modify, and remove tags.

Creating tags

Before you can create tags, you have to create at least one tag category. To create tags, you can use the `New-Tag` cmdlet that has the following syntax:

```
New-Tag [-Name] <String> [-Category] <TagCategory>
[-Description <String>] [-Server <VIServer[]>] [-WhatIf]
[-Confirm] [<CommonParameters>]
```

The `-Name` and `-Category` parameters are required.

In the following example, we will first recreate the `Owner` tag category and save the tag category in the variable `$TagCategory`:

```
PowerCLI C:\> $TagCategory = New-TagCategory -Name Owner
-Description 'Virtual machine owners' -Cardinality Single
-EntityType VirtualMachine
```

Then we will create two tags, named `John Doe` and `Jane Roe`, using the `$TagCategory` variable:

```
PowerCLI C:\> New-Tag -Name 'John Doe' -Category $TagCategory

Category    : Owner
Description :
Id          : urn:vmomi:InventoryServiceTag:e0dc7e28-548d-4eaf-8752-
              13c2650e20c4:GLOBAL
Name        : John Doe
Uid         : /VIServer=vsphere.local\administrator@192.168.0.132:44
              3/Tag=urn:vmomi:InventoryServiceTag:e0dc7e28-548d-4eaf
              -8752-13c2650e20c4:GLOBAL/
Client      : VMware.VimAutomation.ViCore.Impl.V1.VimClient


PowerCLI C:\> New-Tag -Name 'Jane Roe' -Category $TagCategory

Category    : Owner
Description :
Id          : urn:vmomi:InventoryServiceTag:87045222-4ac0-44b4-9867-
              8d9be3487697:GLOBAL
Name        : Jane Roe
```

```
Uid              : /VIServer=vsphere.local\administrator@192.168.0.132:44
                   3/Tag=urn:vmomi:InventoryServiceTag:87045222-4ac0-44b4
                   -9867-8d9be3487697:GLOBAL/
Client           : VMware.VimAutomation.ViCore.Impl.V1.VimClient
```

Retrieving tags

The Get-Tag cmdlet will retrieve tags for you. You can filter tags by name, tag category, or ID. The syntax of the Get-Tag cmdlet is as follows:

```
Get-Tag [[-Name] <String[]>] [-Category <TagCategory[]>]
[-Server <VIServer[]>] [<CommonParameters>]
Get-Tag -Id <String[]> [-Server <VIServer[]>]
[<CommonParameters>]
```

If you want to filter the tags by ID, the -Id parameter is required.

In the following example, we will retrieve all the tags we have created so far:

```
PowerCLI C:\> Get-Tag
```

The preceding command has the following output:

```
Category    : Owner
Description :
Id          : urn:vmomi:InventoryServiceTag:e0dc7e28-548d-4eaf-8752-
              13c2650e20c4:GLOBAL
Name        : John Doe
Uid         : /VIServer=vsphere.local\administrator@192.168.0.132:44
              3/Tag=urn:vmomi:InventoryServiceTag:e0dc7e28-548d-4eaf
              -8752-13c2650e20c4:GLOBAL/
Client      : VMware.VimAutomation.ViCore.Impl.V1.VimClient
Category    : Owner
Description :
Id          : urn:vmomi:InventoryServiceTag:87045222-4ac0-44b4-9867-
              8d9be3487697:GLOBAL
Name        : Jane Roe
Uid         : /VIServer=vsphere.local\administrator@192.168.0.132:44
              3/Tag=urn:vmomi:InventoryServiceTag:87045222-4ac0-44b4
              -9867-8d9be3487697:GLOBAL/
Client      : VMware.VimAutomation.ViCore.Impl.V1.VimClient
```

We can filter by tag category using the -Category parameter. In the following example, we will retrieve all the tags in the Owner tag category:

```
PowerCLI C:\> Get-Tag -Category Owner
```

We can also filter by ID:

```
PowerCLI C:\> Get-Tag -Id
urn:vmomi:InventoryServiceTag:87045222-4ac0-44b4-9867
-8d9be3487697:GLOBAL
```

Modifying tags

The Set-Tag cmdlet can be used to modify the name or description of a tag. The syntax of the Set-Tag cmdlet is as follows:

```
Set-Tag [-Tag] <Tag[]> [-Name <String>] [-Description
<String>] [-Server <VIServer[]>] [-WhatIf] [-Confirm]
[<CommonParameters>]
```

The -Tag parameter is required.

In the following example, we will modify the name of the tag John Doe into Michael Jackson, and modify the description into Tag for Michael Jackson:

```
PowerCLI C:\> Get-Tag -Name 'John Doe' | Set-Tag -Name
'Michael Jackson' -Description 'Tag for Michael Jackson'
The output of the preceding command is the following:
Category    : Owner
Description : Tag for Michael Jackson
Id          : urn:vmomi:InventoryServiceTag:e0dc7e28-548d-4eaf-8752-
              13c2650e20c4:GLOBAL
Name        : Michael Jackson
Uid         : /VIServer=vsphere.local\administrator@192.168.0.132:44
              3/Tag=urn:vmomi:InventoryServiceTag:e0dc7e28-548d-4eaf
              -8752-13c2650e20c4:GLOBAL/
Client      : VMware.VimAutomation.ViCore.Impl.V1.VimClient
```

Removing tags

The Remove-Tag cmdlet can be used to remove tags. This cmdlet has the following syntax:

```
Remove-Tag [-Tag] <Tag[]> [-Server <VIServer[]>]
[-WhatIf] [-Confirm] [<CommonParameters>]
```

The -Tag parameter is required.

In the following example, we will remove the tag `Michael Jackson`:

```
PowerCLI C:\> Get-Tag -Name 'Michael Jackson' |
Remove-Tag -Confirm:$false
```

The preceding command does not return any output.

Managing tag assignments

In this section, you will learn to attach tags to vSphere inventory objects, retrieve tags assigned to objects, remove tags from objects, and retrieve virtual machines by tag.

Creating tag assignments

The `New-TagAssignment` cmdlet can be used to attach or assign tags to a vSphere inventory object. The syntax of the `New-TagAssignment` cmdlet is as follows:

```
New-TagAssignment [-Tag] <Tag> [-Entity] <VIObjectCore>
[-Server <VIServer[]>] [-WhatIf] [-Confirm] [<CommonParameters>]
```

The `-Tag` and `-Entity` parameters are required.

We will use the `New-TagAssignment` cmdlet to assign the `Jane Roe` tag to virtual machine `VM2` using the following PowerCLI command:

```
PowerCLI C:\> New-TagAssignment -Tag 'Jane Roe' -Entity VM2
```

The preceding command has the following output:

```
Uid     : /VIServer=vsphere.local\administrator@192.168.0.132:443/Vir
          tualMachine=VirtualMachine-vm-97/TagAssignment=/Tag=urn:vmo
          mi:InventoryServiceTag:87045222-4ac0-44b4-9867-8d9be3487697
          :GLOBAL/
Tag     : Jane Roe
Entity  : VM2
Id      : com.vmware.cis.tagging.TagAssociationModel
Name    : com.vmware.cis.tagging.TagAssociationModel
Client  : VMware.VimAutomation.ViCore.Impl.V1.VimClient
```

Retrieving tag assignments

The `Get-TagAssignment` cmdlet can be used to retrieve tags attached to objects. The syntax of this cmdlet is as follows:

```
Get-TagAssignment [[-Entity] <VIObjectCore[]>] [-Category
<TagCategory[]>] [-Server <VIServer[]>] [<CommonParameters>]
```

If you use the `Get-TagAssignment` cmdlet without any parameters, it will return all the tag assignments in your vSphere inventory. You can use the `-Entity` parameter to filter for tags assigned to a specific object. The `-Category` parameter can be used to retrieve tags in a specific tag category that are attached to objects.

In the following example, we will retrieve all the tags attached to virtual machine `VM2`:

```
PowerCLI C:\> Get-TagAssignment -Entity VM2
```

The preceding command has the following output:

```
Uid       : /VIServer=vsphere.local\administrator@192.168.0.132:443/Vir
            tualMachine=VirtualMachine-vm-97/TagAssignment=/Tag=urn:vmo
            mi:InventoryServiceTag:87045222-4ac0-44b4-9867-8d9be3487697
            :GLOBAL/
Tag       : Jane Roe
Entity    : VM2
Id        : com.vmware.cis.tagging.TagAssociationModel
Name      : com.vmware.cis.tagging.TagAssociationModel
Client    : VMware.VimAutomation.ViCore.Impl.V1.VimClient
```

The output of the preceding command shows us that `Jane Roe` is the only tag attached to virtual machine `VM2`.

Retrieving virtual machines by tag

If you want to find virtual machine objects that have a specific tag attached, you can use the `Get-VM` cmdlet with the `-Tag` parameter. In the following example, we will retrieve all the virtual machines that have the tag `Jane Roe` attached:

```
PowerCLI C:\> Get-VM -Tag 'Jane Roe'
Name                 PowerState Num CPUs MemoryGB
----                 ---------- -------- --------
VM2                  PoweredOff 2        4.000
```

As you can see in the output of the preceding command, virtual machine VM2 is the only virtual machine with the tag Jane Roe attached.

The following PowerCLI GET-* cmdlets have a -Tag parameter, so you can use these cmdlets to find objects by tag:

- Get-Cluster
- Get-Datacenter
- Get-Datastore
- Get-DatastoreCluster
- Get-EsxSoftwarePackage
- Get-Folder
- Get-ResourcePool
- Get-SpbmStoragePolicy
- Get-VApp
- Get-VDPortgroup
- Get-VDSwitch
- Get-VirtualPortGroup
- Get-VM
- Get-VMHost

Removing tag assignments

To remove tags from a vSphere inventory object, you can use the Remove-TagAssignment cmdlet. This cmdlet has the following syntax:

```
Remove-TagAssignment [-TagAssignment] <TagAssignment[]>
[-WhatIf] [-Confirm] [<CommonParameters>]
```

The -TagAssignment parameter is required.

To retrieve the tag assignment we want to remove, we can use the `Get-TagAssignment` cmdlet, which was introduced in the *Retrieving tag assignments* section. Unfortunately, the `Get-TagAssignment` cmdlet does not have a `-Tag` parameter to specify the tag you want to retrieve. You can only specify the entity and the tag category. If the tag category of the tag that you want to remove has cardinality `Single`, this is not a problem, because the combination of entity and tag category will only return one tag. However, if the tag category has cardinality `Multiple`, you have multiple tags in this category assigned to an object, and you want to remove only one of them, you have to filter the output of the `Get-TagAssignment` cmdlet using the `Where-Object` cmdlet to return only the specific tag that you want to remove.

In the following example, we will remove the `Jane Roe` tag from the virtual machine `VM2`. Although the `Owner` tag category we created has cardinality `Single`, we will use the `Where-Object` cmdlet to filter for the `Jane Roe` tag, so you will know how to remove a tag in a tag category with cardinality `Multiple`:

```
PowerCLI C:\> Get-TagAssignment -Entity VM2 -Category Owner |
>> Where-Object {$_.Tag -eq (Get-Tag -Name 'Jane Roe')} |
>> Remove-TagAssignment -Confirm:$false
```

The preceding command does not return any output.

Converting custom attributes and annotations to tags

Tag categories are the replacement for **custom attributes**. Tags are the replacement for **annotations**. In the following sections, you will learn how to migrate your existing custom attributes to tag categories and your annotations to tags.

Creating tag categories from custom attributes

The `Get-CustomAttribute` cmdlet will be used to retrieve the existing custom attributes in your vSphere inventory. This syntax of the `Get-CustomAttribute` cmdlet is as follows:

```
Get-CustomAttribute [-Id <String[]>] [[-Name] <String[]>]
[[-TargetType] <CustomAttributeTargetType[]>] [-Global]
[-Server <VIServer[]>] [<CommonParameters>]
```

The `Get-CustomAttribute` cmdlet has no required parameters.

I have created some custom attributes and annotations in my lab environment from which to create tags. For virtual machines, I created the `Owner`, `Created by`, and `Department` custom attributes. For hosts, I created the `Enclosure` and `bay` custom attributes. The `AutoDeploy.MachineIdentity` custom attribute for hosts was already created by Auto Deploy.

The following PowerCLI commands will create a tag category for every custom attribute in your vSphere inventory if it does not already exist.

The `-ErrorAction SilentlyContinue` parameter suppresses the error message normally returned if the tag category cannot be found, and continues executing the command.

Custom attributes can have only one value, which is why I create all of my tag categories with cardinality `Single` using the following command:

```
PowerCLI C:\> foreach ($CustomAttribute in (Get-CustomAttribute)) {
>> if (-not (Get-TagCategory -Name $CustomAttribute.Name
-ErrorAction SilentlyContinue)) {
>> New-TagCategory -Name $CustomAttribute.Name -EntityType
$CustomAttribute.TargetType -Cardinality Single }}
```

Creating tags from annotations

After creating the tag categories, we can create the tags from the annotations. The `Get-Annotation` cmdlet will be used to retrieve the existing annotations. The syntax of this cmdlet is as follows:

```
Get-Annotation [[-CustomAttribute] <CustomAttribute[]>] [-Entity]
<InventoryItem> [-Server <VIServer[]>] [<CommonParameters>]
Get-Annotation [-Entity] <InventoryItem> [-Name <String[]>] [-Server
<VIServer[]>] [<CommonParameters>]
```

The `-Entity` parameter is required. Because of this, we will have to specify every object in our vSphere inventory to search for annotations. We can use the `Get-Inventory` cmdlet to retrieve all the inventory objects on a vCenter Server. The syntax of the `Get-Inventory` cmdlet is as follows:

```
Get-Inventory [-Location <VIContainer[]>] [[-Name] <String[]>]
[-NoRecursion] [-Server <VIServer[]>] [<CommonParameters>]
Get-Inventory -Id <String[]> [-Server <VIServer[]>]
[<CommonParameters>]
```

The `-Id` parameter is required if you want to specify an inventory object by ID.

The following PowerCLI command will create a tag and tag assignment for every annotation in your vCenter Server inventory. First, we will use the `Get-Inventory` cmdlet to retrieve all the objects in your vCenter Server inventory. The output of the `Get-Inventory` cmdlet will be piped to the `Get-Annotation` cmdlet, to retrieve all the annotations for every object. The `-PipelineVariable` parameter is used with the value `Annotation`, to create a variable `$Annotation` that contains the current annotation object in the pipeline. The `-PipelineVariable` parameter requires PowerShell V4 at least. The first line of the code will generate an error message if your PowerShell version is older than version 4:

```
#requires -version 4
PowerCLI C:\> Get-Inventory |
>> Get-Annotation -PipelineVariable Annotation |
```

The output of the preceding command is piped to the `Where-Object` cmdlet to select only annotations that have a value:

```
>> Where-Object {$Annotation.Value} |
```

Now we will use the `ForEach-Object` cmdlet to loop through all the annotations and create a tag if it does not already exist. The tag is saved in the variable `$Tag`:

```
>> ForEach-Object {
>> $Tag = Get-Tag -Name $Annotation.Value -Category
$Annotation.Name -ErrorAction SilentlyContinue
>> if (-not $Tag) {$Tag = New-Tag -Name
$Annotation.Value -Category $Annotation.Name}
```

Finally, we will create the tag assignments, if they don't already exist:

```
>> if (-not (Get-TagAssignment -Category $Annotation.Name -Entity
$Annotation.AnnotatedEntity | Where-Object {$_.Tag -eq $Tag}))
>> {New-TagAssignment -Tag $Tag -Entity $Annotation.AnnotatedEntity}
>> }
```

Now we have created a tag and tag assignment for every annotation in our vCenter Server inventory.

Summary

In this chapter, you learned how to create a virtual machine, use OS customization specifications, import OVF or OVA packages, start and stop virtual machines, modify the settings of virtual machines, and convert virtual machines into templates. We looked at moving virtual machines to another folder, host, cluster, resource pool, or datastore. You read how to update VMware Tools and upgrade the virtual hardware. You also learned how to use snapshots; run commands in the guest OS, configure Fault Tolerance, open the console of virtual machines, and remove virtual machines.

Finally, we discussed the use of tag categories, tags, and tag assignments. We also discussed the conversion from custom attributes to tag categories, and from annotations to tags and tag assignments.

In the following chapter, we will look at managing virtual networks with PowerCLI.

6
Managing Virtual Networks with PowerCLI

ESXi servers need network connections for management, vMotion, fault tolerance logging traffic, iSCSI, virtual SAN traffic, and NAS/NFS access. Virtual machines need network connections to communicate with other virtual or physical computers. VMware vSphere provides two types of virtual switch that you can use to configure the networks: vSphere Standard Switches and vSphere Distributed Switches. vSphere Standard Switches are specific for an ESXi server host. vSphere Distributed Switches are created and centrally managed on a vCenter Server and are copied to every host that uses the vSphere Distributed Switch.

The topics that will be covered in this chapter are as follows:

- Using vSphere Standard Switches
- Using host network adapters
- Using standard port groups
- Using vSphere Distributed Switches
- Using distributed virtual port groups
- Configuring host networking
- Configuring the network of virtual machines

Using vSphere Standard Switches

vSphere Standard Switches are created on a specific host. If you are using vSphere clusters, then normally you will create the same vSphere Standard Switches on all of your hosts in a cluster, and give the switches the same configuration on all of the hosts. You can use PowerCLI to create and configure the switches on all of your hosts.

The following figure shows two hosts, and each host has a vSphere Standard Switch:

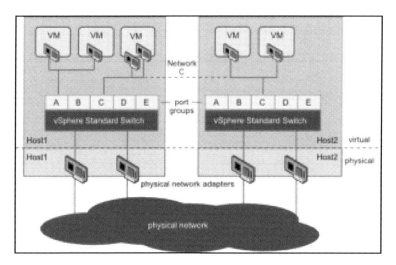

Creating vSphere Standard Switches

After deploying a new ESXi server, one vSphere Standard Switch is already created. This switch, called vSwitch0, has two port groups: **Management Network** and **VM Network**. Also, it is connected to a physical adapter, vmnic0. You can use this switch to connect the host to a vCenter Server or to connect directly to this host using the vSphere Client.

The following screenshot of vSphere Web Client shows vSphere Standard Switch vSwitch0 just after deploying the host 192.168.0.133:

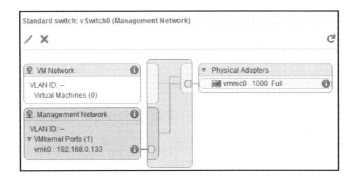

To create a new standard switch, you can use the `New-VirtualSwitch` cmdlet. This cmdlet has the following syntax:

```
New-VirtualSwitch [-VMHost] <VMHost> [-Name] <String> [[-NumPorts]
<Int32>] [[-Nic] <PhysicalNic[]>] [[-Mtu] <Int32>] [-Server
<VIServer[]>] [-WhatIf] [-Confirm] [<CommonParameters>]
```

The following is the list of parameters that are required while using the `New-VirtualSwitch` cmdlet:

- The `-VMHost` parameter is necessary, and it accepts input via the pipeline.
- The `-Name` parameter is also necessary.
- The `-Numports` parameter specifies the number of virtual switch ports. The port number displayed in the vSphere Client might differ from the value that you specified for the `-NumPorts` parameter.

 In ESXi 5.5 or later, standard virtual switches are always elastic, so the `-NumPorts` parameter is no longer applicable, and its value is ignored.

The following PowerCLI command creates a new vSphere Standard Switch named `vSwitch1` on host `192.168.0.133` and connects the switch to the network interface `vmnic2`. The **maximum transmission unit** (**MTU**) size is set to the default value of `1500`:

```
PowerCLI C:\> $VMHost = Get-VMHost -Name 192.168.0.133
PowerCLI C:\> New-VirtualSwitch -VMHost $VMHost -Name vSwitch1 `
>> -Nic vmnic2

Name                              NumPorts   Mtu   Notes
----                              --------   ---   -----
vSwitch1                          1536       1500
```

The following screenshot of the vSphere Web Client shows the Standard Switch, `vSwitch1`, that has been created with the preceding command:

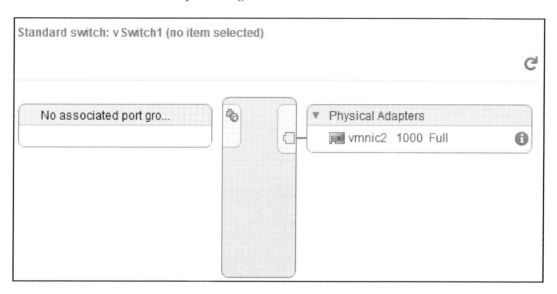

A disadvantage of vSphere Standard Switches over vSphere Distributed Switches is that you have to create a vSphere Standard Switch on every host you need it. A vSphere Distributed Switch is created in a data center or a folder, and you can add hosts to it. You don't have to create a vSphere Distributed Switch on every host. Using PowerCLI, you can easily create a vSphere Standard Switch on all of the hosts in a data center, folder, or cluster.

In the following example, we will create a vSphere Standard Switch named `vSwitch2` on all of the hosts in data center `New York`:

```
PowerCLI C:\> Get-Datacenter -Name 'New York' | Get-VMHost |
>> New-VirtualSwitch -Name vSwitch2 -Nic vmnic3

Name                            NumPorts    Mtu    Notes
----                            --------    ---    -----
vSwitch2                        1536        1500
vSwitch2                        1536        1500
```

Configuring vSphere Standard Switches

You can use the Get-VirtualSwitch cmdlet to get a list of your virtual switches. As of writing this book, the cmdlet will return vSphere Standard and Distributed Switches unless you specify the -Standard parameter to return only vSphere Standard Switches. VMware has the intention to modify this cmdlet to return only vSphere Standard Switches. To get a list of your vSphere Distributed Switches, it is better to use the Get-VDSwitch cmdlet. This cmdlet will be discussed later in this chapter, in the *Retrieving vSphere Distributed Switches* section.

The Get-VirtualSwitch cmdlet has the following syntax. The first parameter set is the default:

```
Get-VirtualSwitch [[-VMHost] <VMHost[]>] [[-VM] <VirtualMachine[]>]
[-Datacenter <Datacenter[]>] [-Name <String[]>] [-Standard]
[-Distributed] [-Server <VIServer[]>] [<CommonParameters>]
```

The second parameter set is for retrieving virtual switches by ID:

```
Get-VirtualSwitch -Id <String[]> [-Server <VIServer[]>]
[<CommonParameters>]
```

The third parameter set is for retrieving virtual switches by related object:

```
Get-VirtualSwitch -RelatedObject <VirtualSwitchRelatedObjectBase[]>
[<CommonParameters>]
```

The -Id and the -RelatedObject parameters are required.

If you use the Get-VirtualSwitch cmdlet without parameters, then you will get a list of all of your switches from your hosts. To retrieve only the switches for a specific host, you have to specify the -VMHost parameter, as shown in the following command lines:

```
PowerCLI C:\> $VMHost = Get-VMHost -Name 192.168.0.133
PowerCLI C:\> Get-VirtualSwitch -VMHost $VMHost
```

The output of the preceding commands is as follows:

```
Name                           NumPorts   Mtu   Notes
----                           --------   ---   -----
vSwitch0                       1536       1500
vSwitch1                       1536       1500
```

If you only want to retrieve a specific virtual switch, you can specify the name of the switch as follows:

```
PowerCLI C:\> Get-VirtualSwitch -VMHost $VMHost -Name vSwitch1
```

The output of the preceding command is as follows:

```
Name                         NumPorts  Mtu   Notes
----                         --------  ---   -----
vSwitch1                     1536      1500
```

To modify the settings of a vSphere Standard Switch, you can use the `Set-VirtualSwitch` cmdlet. You can use this cmdlet to change the number of ports, the MTU size, and the network interface cards for the virtual switch. The syntax of the `Set-VirtualSwitch` cmdlet is as follows:

```
Set-VirtualSwitch [-VirtualSwitch] <VirtualSwitch[]> [[-NumPorts]
<Int32>] [[-Nic] <String[]>] [[-Mtu] <Int32>] [-Server <VIServer[]>]
[-WhatIf] [-Confirm] [<CommonParameters>]
```

The `-VirtualSwitch` parameter is required.

After changing the number of switch ports using the `-NumPorts` parameter, the ESXi host must be restarted for the changes to take effect. In ESXi 5.5 or later, standard virtual switches are always elastic, so the `-NumPorts` parameter is no longer applicable, and its value is ignored.

The network interface cards specified as the value of the `-Nic` parameter will replace the old NICs. For example, you can use the following command to modify the MTU size of a switch to `9000` for Jumbo frames, and the network interface cards to `vmnic2` and `vmnic3`:

```
PowerCLI C:\> Get-VirtualSwitch -VMHost $VMHost -Name vSwitch1 |
>> Set-VirtualSwitch -Mtu 9000 -Nic vmnic2,vmnic3 -Confirm:$false
```

The output of the preceding command is as follows:

```
WARNING: Parameter 'Nic' is obsolete. This parameter is deprecated.
Use Add-VirtualSwitchPhysicalNetworkAdapter instead.
WARNING: The 'Nic' parameter of 'Set-VirtualSwitch' cmdlet is
deprecated.
Use the 'Add-VirtualSwitchPhysicalNetworkAdapter' cmdlet instead.

Name                         NumPorts  Mtu   Notes
----                         --------  ---   -----
vSwitch1                     1536      9000
```

After executing the preceding command, both `vmnic2` and `vmnic3` will be **active adapters**.

As you can see in the warning message in the output of the preceding command, the `-Nic` parameter of the `Set-VirtualSwitch` cmdlet is deprecated. In the following section, we will look at the `Add-VirtualSwitchPhysicalNetworkAdapter` cmdlet that should be used instead.

Ethernet uses a frame size of 1,500 bytes by default. **Jumbo frames** are Ethernet frames that are larger than 1,500 bytes and are often 9,000 bytes per frame. In a reliable network, Jumbo frames have less overhead than the standard Ethernet frames and a better throughput. In an unreliable network, however, the chance of losing a frame is bigger for Jumbo frames than for the standard frame size. The loss of a frame requires the retransmission of a frame. In an unreliable network, it is better to use the standard frame sizes. If you use Jumbo frames, then all of the switches and routers between two communicating computers must support the Jumbo frame size. If there are switches or routers along the transmission path that have varying frame sizes, then you can end up with fragmentation problems. If a switch or router along the path does not support Jumbo frames and it receives one, it will drop the frame. The use case for Jumbo frames is IP-based storage, iSCSI, and NFS. Upgrading your network from 1 Gigabit to 10 Gigabit might be a better solution for IP-based storage than Jumbo frames. If you use NSX, you have to set the MTU size to at least 1,550 to add space for the VXLAN headers. The default MTU size for NSX is 1,600.

Adding network adapters to a switch

To add a physical network adapter to a virtual switch, you should use the `Add-VirtualSwitchPhysicalNetworkAdapter` cmdlet. This cmdlet has the following syntax:

```
Add-VirtualSwitchPhysicalNetworkAdapter [-VMHostPhysicalNic]
<PhysicalNic[]> [-VirtualSwitch] <VirtualSwitch> [-VirtualNicPortgroup]
<VirtualPortGroup[]>] [-VMHostVirtualNic <HostVirtualNic[]>] [-Server
<VIServer[]>] [-WhatIf] [-Confirm] [<CommonParameters>]
```

The `-VMHostPhysicalNic` and `-VirtualSwitch` parameters are required.

The following example adds network adapter `vmnic3` to the virtual switch `vSwitch1` on the host `192.168.0.133`:

```
PowerCLI C:\> $VMHost = Get-VMHost -Name 192.168.0.133
PowerCLI C:\> $NetworkAdapter = Get-VMHostNetworkAdapter
-VMHost $VMHost -Physical -Name vmnic3
PowerCLI C:\> Get-VirtualSwitch -Name vSwitch1 -VMHost $VMHost |
>> Add-VirtualSwitchPhysicalNetworkAdapter -VMHostPhysicalNic
$NetworkAdapter -Confirm:$false
```

The preceding command does not return any output.

Removing vSphere Standard Switches

To remove a vSphere Standard Switch, you can use the `Remove-VirtualSwitch` cmdlet. The syntax of this cmdlet is as follows:

```
Remove-VirtualSwitch [-VirtualSwitch] <VirtualSwitch[]>
[-Server <VIServer[]>] [-WhatIf] [-Confirm] [<CommonParameters>]
```

The `-VirtualSwitch` parameter is required.

In the following example, we will remove virtual switch `vSwitch1` from the host `192.168.0.133`:

```
PowerCLI C:\> $VMHost = Get-VMHost -Name 192.168.0.133
PowerCLI C:\> Get-VirtualSwitch -VMHost $VMHost -Name vSwitch1 |
>> Remove-VirtualSwitch -Confirm:$False
```

The preceding command does not return any output.

Using host network adapters

A vSphere Standard or Distributed Switch can have virtual and physical network adapters. Physical network adapters are used to connect virtual switches to physical switches and have a name starting with `vmnic`. Virtual network adapters or VMKernel network adapters can be used to set various properties such as management traffic, vMotion, fault tolerance logging, IP address, and subnet mask. Virtual network adapters have a name starting with `vmk`. You can see virtual and physical network adapters in the screenshot given in the preceding section, *Creating vSphere Standard Switches*.

Creating host network adapters

To create a new virtual network adapter or VMkernel port, you can use the New-VMHostNetworkAdapter cmdlet. The cmdlet creates a port group if the -PortGroup parameter is used. The syntax of this cmdlet is as follows:

```
New-VMHostNetworkAdapter [[-VMHost] <VMHost>] [[-PortGroup] <String>]
[-PortId <String>] [-VirtualSwitch] <VirtualSwitchBase> [[-IP]
<String>] [[-SubnetMask] <String>] [[-Mac] <String>] [-Mtu <Int32>]
[-ConsoleNic] [-VMotionEnabled [<Boolean>]]
[-FaultToleranceLoggingEnabled [<Boolean>]] [-IPv6ThroughDhcp]
[-AutomaticIPv6] [-IPv6 <String[]>] [-ManagementTrafficEnabled
[<Boolean>]] [-VsanTrafficEnabled [<Boolean>]]
[-Server <VIServer[]>] [-WhatIf] [-Confirm] [<CommonParameters>]
```

The -VirtualSwitch parameter is required.

In the following example, we will create a new VMkernel port called vmk1 on the vSwitch1 virtual switch that is present on the host 192.168.0.133. A port group named VMKernelPortGroup1 is also created:

```
PowerCLI C:\> $VMHost = Get-VMHost -Name 192.168.0.133
PowerCLI C:\> $VirtualSwitch = $VMHost |
>> Get-VirtualSwitch -Name vSwitch1
PowerCLI C:\> New-VMHostNetworkAdapter -VMHost $VMhost -PortGroup
VMKernelPortGroup1 -VirtualSwitch $VirtualSwitch -IP 192.168.0.150
-SubnetMask 255.255.255.0

Name Mac             DhcpEnabled IP           SubnetMask     Device
                                                             Name
---- ---             ----------- --           ----------     ------
vmk1 00:50:56:6c:a8:38 False       192.168.0.150 255.255.255.0 vmk1
```

Retrieving host network adapters

The Get-VMHostNetworkAdapter cmdlet can be used to retrieve the physical and virtual host network adapters. This cmdlet will retrieve the network adapters for vSphere Standard Switches and also for vSphere Distributed Switches. The syntax of the Get-VMHostNetworkAdapter cmdlet is as follows:

```
Get-VMHostNetworkAdapter [-VMHost <VMHost[]>] [[-VirtualSwitch]
<VirtualSwitchBase[]>] [-PortGroup <VirtualPortGroupBase[]>]
[-Physical] [-VMKernel] [-Console] [[-Name] <String[]>]
[-Id <String[]>] [-Server <VIServer[]>] [<CommonParameters>]
```

In the following example, all of the host network adapters of the host 192.168.0.133 are retrieved. To fit the output of the command on a page of this book, the output of the Get-VMHostNetworkAdapter cmdlet is piped to the Select-Object cmdlet to select only the Name, Mac, DhcpEnabled, IP, and SubnetMask properties, and is then piped to the Format-Table -AutoSize command, to write the output in the table format, and to adjust the column size based on the width of the data:

```
PowerCLI C:\> $VMHost = Get-VMHost -Name 192.168.0.133
PowerCLI C:\> $VMHost | Get-VMHostNetworkAdapter | Select-Object
-Property Name,Mac,DhcpEnabled,IP,SubnetMask | Format-Table -AutoSize
```

The output of the preceding command is as follows:

```
Name    Mac               DhcpEnabled IP            SubnetMask
----    ---               ----------- --            ----------
vmnic0  00:0c:29:23:ab:67       False
vmnic1  00:0c:29:23:ab:71       False
vmnic2  00:0c:29:23:ab:7b       False
vmnic3  00:0c:29:23:ab:85       False
vmnic4  00:0c:29:23:ab:8f       False
vmnic5  00:0c:29:23:ab:99       False
vmnic6  00:0c:29:23:ab:a3       False
vmnic7  00:0c:29:23:ab:ad       False
vmk0    00:0c:29:23:ab:67       False 192.168.0.133 255.255.255.0
vmk1    00:50:56:6c:a8:38       False 192.168.0.150 255.255.255.0
```

Configuring host network adapters

To modify the settings of a host network adapter, you can use the Set-VMHostNetworkAdapter cmdlet. The syntax of this cmdlet is as follows. The first parameter set is for setting the network speed on the physical network adapters to half or full duplex or auto negotiate:

```
Set-VMHostNetworkAdapter -PhysicalNic <PhysicalNic[]>
[-Duplex <String>] [-BitRatePerSecMb <Int32>] [-AutoNegotiate]
[-WhatIf] [-Confirm] [<CommonParameters>]
```

The second parameter set is for configuring virtual network adapters:

```
Set-VMHostNetworkAdapter -VirtualNic <HostVirtualNic[]> [-Dhcp]
[-IP <String>] [-SubnetMask <String>] [-Mac <String>] [-Mtu <Int32>]
[-VMotionEnabled [<Boolean>]] [-FaultToleranceLoggingEnabled
[<Boolean>]] [-ManagementTrafficEnabled [<Boolean>]]
[-VsanTrafficEnabled [<Boolean>]] [-IPv6ThroughDhcp [<Boolean>]]
[-AutomaticIPv6 [<Boolean>]] [-IPv6 <String[]>] [-IPv6Enabled
[<Boolean>]] [-WhatIf] [-Confirm] [<CommonParameters>]
```

The third parameter set is for migrating a virtual network adapter from a Standard Port Group to a Distributed Port Group:

```
Set-VMHostNetworkAdapter -VirtualNic <HostVirtualNic[]> -PortGroup
<DistributedPortGroup> [-WhatIf] [-Confirm] [<CommonParameters>]
```

The `-PhysicalNic`, `-VirtualNic`, and `-PortGroup` parameters are required.

Configuring network speed and duplex setting

In the first example of the `Set-VMHostNetworkAdapter` cmdlet, we will set the speed of the physical network adapter `vmnic2` of the host `192.168.0.133` to 1,000 MB and full duplex:

```
PowerCLI C:\> Get-VMHostNetworkAdapter -VMHost 192.168.0.133
-Name vmnic2 |
>> Set-VMHostNetworkAdapter -BitRatePerSecMb 10000 -Duplex
Full -Confirm:$false

Name      Mac               DhcpEnabled  IP  SubnetMask  DeviceName
----      ---               -----------  --  ----------  ----------
vmnic2    00:0c:29:23:ab:7b False                        vmnic2
```

Configuring the management network

To enable a VMkernel port on an ESXi server for management traffic, you have to use the `Set-VMHostNetworkAdapter-ManagementTrafficEnabled` parameter. Using `$true` as the value for this parameter will enable management traffic, and `$false` will disable it. In the following example, we will enable management traffic for the VMkernel port `vmk1` of the host `192.168.0.133`:

```
PowerCLI C:\> Get-VMHostNetworkAdapter -VMHost 192.168.0.133
-Name vmk1 |
>> Set-VMHostNetworkAdapter -ManagementTrafficEnabled:$true
```

```
-Confirm:$false
```

Name Mac	DhcpEnabled IP	SubnetMask	Device
---- ---	----------- --	----------	------
vmk1 00:50:56:6c:a8:38 False	192.168.0.150	255.255.255.0	vmk1

Configuring vMotion

In the following example, we will enable vMotion on the VMkernel network adapter vmk2 for the host 192.168.0.133:

```
PowerCLI C:\> Get-VMHostNetworkAdapter -VMHost 192.168.0.133
-Name vmk1 |
>> Set-VMHostNetworkAdapter -VMotionEnabled:$true
-Confirm:$false
```

Name Mac	DhcpEnabled IP	SubnetMask	Device
---- ---	----------- --	----------	------
vmk1 00:50:56:6c:a8:38 False	192.168.0.150	255.255.255.0	vmk1

To disable vMotion, you have to modify $true in the preceding example to $false.

Removing host network adapters

To remove a host network adapter, you can use the Remove-VMHostNetworkAdapter cmdlet, which has the following syntax:

```
Remove-VMHostNetworkAdapter [-Nic] <HostVirtualNic[]> [-WhatIf]
[-Confirm] [<CommonParameters>]
```

The -Nic parameter is required.

In the following example, we will use the Remove-VMHostNetworkAdapter cmdlet to remove the host network adapter vmk1 from the host 192.168.0.133:

```
PowerCLI C:\> Get-VMHostNetworkAdapter -VMHost 192.168.0.133
-Name vmk1 |
>> Remove-VMHostNetworkAdapter -Confirm:$false
```

The preceding command returns no output.

Configuring NIC teaming

NIC Teaming, also known as **Load Balancing and Failover (LBFO)**, allows you to combine multiple network adapters into one virtual NIC for fault tolerance and better performance. You can configure NIC Teaming for an entire virtual switch or per virtual port group. The Get-NicTeamingPolicy and Set-NicTeamingPolicy cmdlets that we will discuss in this section have two parameter sets, one for NIC Teaming at the virtual switch level and one for NIC Teaming at the virtual port group level. The syntax of the Get-NicTeamingPolicy cmdlet is as follows. The first parameter set is for retrieving the NIC Teaming policy of a virtual switch:

```
Get-NicTeamingPolicy [-VirtualSwitch] <VirtualSwitch[]>
[-Server <VIServer[]>] [<CommonParameters>]
```

The second parameter set is for retrieving the NIC Teaming policy of a virtual port group:

```
Get-NicTeamingPolicy [-VirtualPortGroup] <VirtualPortGroup[]>
[-Server <VIServer[]>] [<CommonParameters>]
```

One of the -VirtualSwitch or -VirtualPortGroup parameter is required.

In the following example, we will retrieve the NIC Teaming policy for virtual switch vSwitch1 of host 192.168.0.133:

```
PowerCLI C:\> Get-VMHost -Name 192.168.0.133 |
>> Get-VirtualSwitch -Name vSwitch1 |
>> Get-NicTeamingPolicy

VirtualSwitch ActiveNic StandbyNic UnusedNic FailbackEnabled NotifySw
                                                             itches
------------- --------- ---------- --------- --------------- --------
vSwitch1      {vmnic2}                       True            True
```

In the following example, we will retrieve the NIC Teaming policy for the virtual port group Management Network of the host 192.168.0.133:

```
PowerCLI C:\> Get-VMHost -Name 192.168.0.133 |
>> Get-VirtualPortGroup -Name 'Management Network' |
>> Get-NicTeamingPolicy

VirtualPortGroup    ActiveNic StandbyNic UnusedNic FailbackEnabled
----------------    --------- ---------- --------- ---------------
Management Network {vmnic0}                        True
```

To configure a NIC Teaming policy by using the `Set-NicTeamingPolicy` cmdlet, you have to use a Teaming policy, which was retrieved by the `Get-NicTeamingPolicy` cmdlet, as the input. You can pass this Teaming policy via the pipeline. The syntax of the `Set-NicTeamingPolicy` cmdlet is as follows. The first parameter set is for configuring the NIC Teaming policy of a virtual switch:

```
Set-NicTeamingPolicy [-VirtualSwitchPolicy]
<NicTeamingVirtualSwitchPolicy[]> [-BeaconInterval <Int32>]
[-LoadBalancingPolicy <LoadBalancingPolicy>]
[-NetworkFailoverDetectionPolicy <NetworkFailoverDetectionPolicy>]
[-NotifySwitches [<Boolean>]] [-FailbackEnabled [<Boolean>]]
[-MakeNicActive <PhysicalNic[]>] [-MakeNicStandby <PhysicalNic[]>]
[-MakeNicUnused <PhysicalNic[]>] [-WhatIf] [-Confirm]
[<CommonParameters>]
```

The second parameter set is for configuring the NIC teaming policy of a virtual port group:

```
Set-NicTeamingPolicy [-VirtualPortGroupPolicy]
<NicTeamingVirtualPortGroupPolicy[]> [-InheritLoadBalancingPolicy
[<Boolean>]] [-InheritNetworkFailoverDetectionPolicy [<Boolean>]]
[-InheritNotifySwitches [<Boolean>]] [-InheritFailback [<Boolean>]]
[-InheritFailoverOrder [<Boolean>]] [-LoadBalancingPolicy
<LoadBalancingPolicy>] [-NetworkFailoverDetectionPolicy
<NetworkFailoverDetectionPolicy>] [-NotifySwitches [<Boolean>]]
[-FailbackEnabled [<Boolean>]] [-MakeNicActive <PhysicalNic[]>]
[-MakeNicStandby <PhysicalNic[]>] [-MakeNicUnused <PhysicalNic[]>]
[-WhatIf] [-Confirm] [<CommonParameters>]
```

One of the `-VirtualSwitchPolicy` or `-VirtualPortGroupPolicy` parameters is required.

In the following example, we will first add the physical network adapter `vmnic1` to the virtual switch `vSwitch0` on the host `192.168.0.133`, using the `Add-VirtualSwitchPhysicalNetworkAdapter` cmdlet we have already seen in the Adding network adapters to a switch section:

```
PowerCLI C:\> $VMHost = Get-VMHost -Name 192.168.0.133
PowerCLI C:\> $NetworkAdapter = Get-VMHostNetworkAdapter
-VMHost $VMHost -Physical -Name vmnic1
PowerCLI C:\> Get-VirtualSwitch -Name vSwitch0 -VMHost $VMHost |
>> Add-VirtualSwitchPhysicalNetworkAdapter -VMHostPhysicalNic
$NetworkAdapter -Confirm:$false
```

The preceding command does not return any output.

Next, we will configure NIC Teaming for the virtual port group `Management Network` and add `vmnic1` to the active NICs:

```
PowerCLI C:\> $Policy = $VMHost |
>> Get-VirtualPortGroup -Name 'Management Network' |
>> Get-NicTeamingPolicy
PowerCLI C:\> Set-NicTeamingPolicy -VirtualPortGroupPolicy $Policy
-MakeNicActive vmnic1

VirtualPortGroup    ActiveNic        StandbyNic UnusedNic FailbackEna
                                                          bled
----------------    ---------        ---------- --------- -----------
Management Network {vmnic0, vmnic1}                       True
```

In the screenshot of the vSphere Web Client, you can see the teamed **Physical Adapters** `vmnic0` and `vmnic1` after executing the commands from the preceding example:

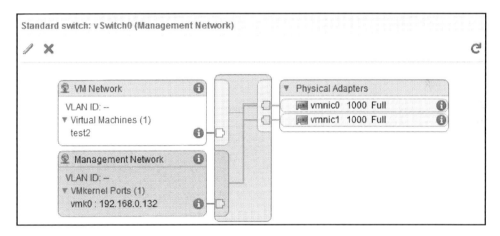

Using standard port groups

Port groups are collections of ports that have the same properties, such as the same virtual switch, VLAN ID, Teaming policy, policies for filtering, tagging, and traffic shaping. Port groups are identified by a network label name. You should give all port groups in a data center, which are connected to the same network, the same network label. This will make virtual machine configurations portable across hosts. Using the PowerCLI cmdlets, you can only specify a network label name for the port group and a VLAN ID.

A **Virtual Local Area Network** (**VLAN**) is a virtual computer network independent of physical location. All of the computers in a VLAN can receive broadcasts from the others and are usually in the same IP subnet.

Creating standard port groups

The `New-VirtualPortGroup` cmdlet will create a new port group for a vSphere Standard Switch. The syntax of this cmdlet is as follows:

```
New-VirtualPortGroup [-Name] <String> [-VirtualSwitch]
<VirtualSwitch> [-VLanId <Int32>] [-Server <VIServer[]>]
[-WhatIf] [-Confirm] [<CommonParameters>]
```

The `-Name` and `-VirtualSwitch` parameters are required.

In the following example, we will create a new standard port group named VLAN 10 Port Group for the virtual switch vSwitch1 on all of the hosts in the cluster Cluster01. The standard port group is connected to VLAN 10:

```
PowerCLI C:\> Get-Cluster -Name Cluster01 |
>> Get-VMHost |
>> Get-VirtualSwitch -Name vSwitch1 |
>> New-VirtualPortGroup -Name "VLAN 10 Port Group" -VLanId 10

Name                 Key                   VLanId PortBinding NumPorts
----                 ---                   ------ ----------- --------
VLAN 10 Port Group key-vim.host.PortGr... 10
```

Configuring standard port groups

To get a list of all of your standard port groups or to retrieve just one port group, you can use the `Get-VirtualPortGroup` cmdlet. The syntax of this cmdlet is as follows. The first parameter set is the default:

```
Get-VirtualPortGroup [[-VMHost] <VMHost[]>] [-VM <VirtualMachine[]>]
[-VirtualSwitch <VirtualSwitchBase[]>] [-Name <String[]>]
[-Datacenter <Datacenter[]>] [-Standard] [-Distributed]
[-Tag <Tag[]>] [-Server <VIServer[]>] [<CommonParameters>]
```

The second parameter set is for retrieving virtual port groups by ID:

```
Get-VirtualPortGroup -Id <String[]> [-Server <VIServer[]>]
[<CommonParameters>]
```

The third parameter set is for retrieving virtual port groups by related object:

```
Get-VirtualPortGroup -RelatedObject
<VirtualPortGroupRelatedObjectBase[]> [<CommonParameters>]
```

If you use the Get-VirtualPortGroup cmdlet without parameters, then you will get a list of all of the port groups in your environment. You can specify a data center, host, virtual machine, virtual switch, or name of a port group to filter for specific port groups.

To retrieve the VLAN 10 Port Group we just created from all of the hosts in cluster Cluster01, you can use the following command:

```
PowerCLI C:\> Get-Cluster -Name Cluster01 |
>> Get-VMHost |
>> Get-VirtualPortGroup -Name "VLAN 10 Port Group"

Name                    Key                        VLanId PortBinding NumPorts
----                    ---                        ------ ----------- --------
VLAN 10 Port Group key-vim.host.PortGr... 10
```

The Set-VirtualPortGroup cmdlet can be used to change the name and the VLAN ID of a port group.

 If you change the name of a port group, any virtual machine using this port group will not be updated. These virtual machines will continue to show the previous network label and will no longer be connected to any virtual port group.

The Set-VirtualPortGroup cmdlet has the following syntax:

```
Set-VirtualPortGroup [-Name <String>] [-VLanId <Int32>]
[-VirtualPortGroup] <VirtualPortGroup[]> [-WhatIf] [-Confirm]
[<CommonParameters>]
```

The -VirtualPortGroup parameter is required.

The following example will rename VLAN 10 Port Group to VLAN 11 Port Group and change the VLAN ID to 11 on all of the hosts in the cluster Cluster01:

```
PowerCLI C:\> Get-Cluster -Name Cluster01 |
>> Get-VMHost |
>> Get-VirtualPortGroup -Name "VLAN 10 Port Group" |
```

```
>> Set-VirtualPortGroup -Name "VLAN 11 Port Group" -VLanId 11

Name                    Key                   VLanId PortBinding NumPorts
----                    ---                   ------ ----------- --------
VLAN 11 Port Group key-vim.host.PortGr... 11
```

Removing standard port groups

The `Remove-VirtualPortGroup` cmdlet will remove a standard port group for you. The syntax of this cmdlet is as follows:

```
Remove-VirtualPortGroup [-VirtualPortGroup] <VirtualPortGroup[]>
[-WhatIf] [-Confirm] [<CommonParameters>]
```

In the following example, we will remove `VLAN 11 Port Group` from all of the hosts in cluster `Cluster01`:

```
PowerCLI C:\> Get-Cluster -Name Cluster01 |
>> Get-VMHost |
>> Get-VirtualPortGroup -Name "VLAN 11 Port Group" |
>> Remove-VirtualPortGroup -Confirm:$false
```

The preceding command does not return any output.

Using vSphere Distributed Switches

The vSphere Distributed Switches are virtual switches that span multiple hosts. This makes it easier to configure hosts that need similar network configurations. It also ensures that virtual machines will get the same network configuration when they migrate to another host. You need a vSphere Enterprise Plus license and a vCenter Server to be able to use vSphere Distributed Switches.

In PowerCLI, there are separate sets of cmdlets for working with vSphere Standard Switches and vSphere Distributed Switches. In the past, the VMware PowerCLI team tried to integrate both types of switches into one set of cmdlets. This is why, for example, the `Get-VirtualSwitch` cmdlet has a `-Distributed` parameter. However, this parameter is now obsolete, and VMware made a new set of cmdlets specific for vSphere Distributed Switches. The PowerCLI VDS snap-in that provides support for managing Distributed Switches and port groups was introduced in PowerCLI 5.1 Release 2. In this section, you will learn more about these new cmdlets.

In the following figure, you see a vSphere Distributed Switch that spans two hosts:

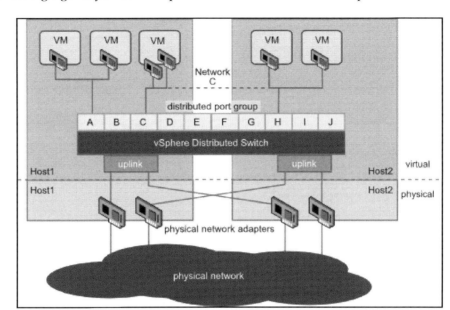

Creating vSphere Distributed Switches

The `New-VDSwitch` cmdlet creates new vSphere Distributed Switches. This cmdlet has three parameter sets in the following syntax. The first parameter set is the default:

```
New-VDSwitch [-ContactDetails <String>] [-ContactName <String>]
[-LinkDiscoveryProtocol <LinkDiscoveryProtocol>]
[-LinkDiscoveryProtocolOperation <LinkDiscoveryOperation>]
[-MaxPorts <Int32>] [-Mtu <Int32>] [-Notes <String>]
[-NumUplinkPorts <Int32>] [-Version <String>] -Name <String>
-Location <VIContainer> [-RunAsync] [-Server <VIServer[]>]
[-WhatIf] [-Confirm] [<CommonParameters>]
```

The second parameter set is for copying a vSphere Distributed Switch from a reference switch:

```
New-VDSwitch -ReferenceVDSwitch <VDSwitch> -Name <String> -Location
<VIContainer> [-WithoutPortGroups] [-RunAsync] [-Server <VIServer[]>]
[-WhatIf] [-Confirm] [<CommonParameters>]
```

The third parameter set is for creating a vSphere Distributed Switch from a backup:

```
New-VDSwitch -BackupPath <String> [-KeepIdentifiers] [-Name <String>]
-Location <VIContainer> [-WithoutPortGroups] [-RunAsync]
[-Server <VIServer[]>] [-WhatIf] [-Confirm] [<CommonParameters>]
```

The `-Name`, `-Location`, `-ReferenceVDSwitch`, and `-BackupPath` parameters are required.

If you compare the preceding syntax with the syntax of the `New-VirtualSwitch` cmdlet, then you will see that the `New-VDSwitch` cmdlet has much more scope to configure the virtual switch during creation. In vSphere 5.1 and later versions, you can even specify a reference vSphere Distributed Switch or a backup profile from where a new switch can be created.

Creating a new vSphere Distributed Switch from scratch

To create a new vSphere Distributed Switch from scratch, you have to specify at least the `-Name` and the `-Location` parameters. The location can be a data center or a folder.

In the following example we will create a new vSphere Distributed Switch named `VDSwitch1` in a data center called `New York`:

```
PowerCLI C:\> $Datacenter = Get-Datacenter -Name "New York"
PowerCLI C:\> New-VDSwitch -Name "VDSwitch1" -Location $Datacenter

Name                     NumPorts   Mtu        Version  Vendor
----                     --------   ---        -------  ------
VDSwitch1                0          1500       6.5.0    VMware, Inc.
```

Cloning a vSphere Distributed Switch

We can now clone the `VDSwitch1` to a new switch `VDSwitch2`. Of course, this is not very useful because `VDSwitch1` is not configured yet. We will clone the switch just to show you how to do it:

```
PowerCLI C:\> New-VDSwitch -Name "VDSwitch2" `
>> -ReferenceVDSwitch "VDSwitch1" -Location $Datacenter

Name                     NumPorts   Mtu        Version  Vendor
----                     --------   ---        -------  ------
VDSwitch2                0          1500       6.5.0    VMware, Inc.
```

If you want to clone a vSphere Distributed Switch without cloning the port groups, then you can use the `-WithoutPortGroups` parameter.

 Cloning a vSphere Distributed Switch and the `New-VDSwitch -ReferenceVDSwitch` parameter is only supported in VMware vSphere 5.1 and later versions.

Creating a vSphere Distributed Switch from an export

Later in this chapter, in the *Exporting the configuration of vSphere Distributed Switches* section, we will see how to create an export of the configuration of a vSphere Distributed Switch. If you have an export, you can use it to recreate a switch or to create a new one. The following example will create a new vSphere Distributed Switch named `VDSwitch3` in the `New York` data center, from an export of the configuration of `VDSwitch1`:

```
PowerCLI C:\> New-VDSwitch -BackupPath C:\VDSwitch1Config.zip `
>> -Name VDSwitch3 -Location (Get-Datacenter -Name "New York")

Importing vSphere Distributed Switch - Switch name: 'VDSwitch1',
Switch version: 6.5.0, Number of port groups: 1, Number of
resource pools: 9, Number of uplinks: 1, Notes: VDSwitch1 Configuration
```

Name	NumPorts	Mtu	Version	Vendor
VDSwitch3	0	1500	6.5.0	VMware, Inc.

You can also use the `-WithoutPortGroups` parameter for importing an export to prevent importing the port groups.

 Creating a vSphere Distributed Switch from an export and creating the `New-VDSwitch -BackupPath` parameter is only supported in VMware vSphere 5.1 and later versions.

Retrieving vSphere Distributed Switches

You can retrieve vSphere Distributed Switches with the `Get-VDSwitch` cmdlet. The syntax of this cmdlet is as follows. The first parameter set is the default:

```
Get-VDSwitch [[-Name] <String[]>] [-Location <FolderContainer[]>]
[-VMHost <VMHost[]>] [-VM <VirtualMachine[]>] [-Tag <Tag[]>]
[-Server <VIServer[]>] [<CommonParameters>]
```

The second parameter set is for retrieving vSphere Distributed Switches by ID:

```
Get-VDSwitch -Id <String[]> [-Server <VIServer[]>] [<CommonParameters>]
```

The third parameter set is for retrieving vSphere Distributed Switches by related object:

```
Get-VDSwitch -RelatedObject <VDSwitchRelatedObjectBase[]>
[<CommonParameters>]
```

If you use the Get-VDSwitch cmdlet without parameters, then it will return all of the vSphere Distributed Switches in your environment. You can use the -Location parameter to specify a data center or folder in which you want to search for vSphere Distributed Switches.

The following example will retrieve all of the vSphere Distributed Switches in the New York data center:

```
PowerCLI C:\> Get-Datacenter -Name 'New York' | Get-VDSwitch

Name                    NumPorts    Mtu      Version    Vendor
----                    --------    ---      -------    ------
VDSwitch1               0           1500     6.5.0      VMware, Inc.
VDSwitch2               0           1500     6.5.0      VMware, Inc.
VDSwitch3               0           1500     6.5.0      VMware, Inc.
```

You can specify a value for the -Name parameter to retrieve a specific vSphere Distributed Switch. In the following example, we will retrieve the vSphere Distributed Switch VDSwitch1:

```
PowerCLI C:\> Get-VDSwitch -Name VDSwitch1

Name                    NumPorts    Mtu      Version    Vendor
----                    --------    ---      -------    ------
VDSwitch1               0           1500     6.5.0      VMware, Inc.
```

Configuring vSphere Distributed Switches

The selection you make using Get-VDSwitch can be used as input of the Set-VDSwitch cmdlet to modify the configuration or version of one or more vSphere Distributed Switches, to roll back the configuration to its previous state, or import the configuration from a backup profile.

Rolling back the configuration of a vSphere Distributed Switch and importing the configuration of a vSphere Distributed Switch from a backup are available only on vSphere 5.1 and later versions.

The `Set-VDSwitch` cmdlet syntax has three parameter sets. The first parameter set is the default:

```
Set-VDSwitch [-Name <String>] [-ContactDetails <String>]
[-ContactName <String>] [-LinkDiscoveryProtocol
<LinkDiscoveryProtocol>] [-LinkDiscoveryProtocolOperation
<LinkDiscoveryOperation>] [-MaxPorts <Int32>] [-Mtu <Int32>]
[-Notes <String>] [-NumUplinkPorts <Int32>] [-Version <String>]
[-VDSwitch] <VDSwitch[]> [-RunAsync] [-Server <VIServer[]>]
[-WhatIf] [-Confirm] [<CommonParameters>]
```

The second parameter set is for importing the configuration of a vSphere Distributed Switch from a backup:

```
Set-VDSwitch -BackupPath <String> [-WithoutPortGroups] [-VDSwitch]
<VDSwitch[]> [-RunAsync] [-Server <VIServer[]>] [-WhatIf] [-Confirm]
[<CommonParameters>]
```

The third parameter set is for rolling back the configuration of the vSphere Distributed Switch to an earlier state:

```
Set-VDSwitch -RollBackConfiguration [-VDSwitch] <VDSwitch[]>
[-RunAsync] [-Server <VIServer[]>] [-WhatIf] [-Confirm]
[<CommonParameters>]
```

The `-VDSwitch`, `-BackupPath`, and `-RollBackConfiguration` parameters are required.

In the following example, we will set almost every property for `VDSwitch1` that you can set using PowerShell. We will use a PowerShell technique called **splatting** to create a parameter list for the `Set-VDSwitch` cmdlet. The parameter list will be a hash table called `$Parameters`. By using the **splat operator** `@`, you can add the parameters in the `$Parameters` hash table to the `Set-VDSwitch` cmdlet call.

 When you use splatting, you have to use the name of the variable containing the parameter's hash table without the dollar sign, that is, `@Parameters` and not `@$Parameters`.

```
PowerCLI C:\> $VDSwitch = Get-VDSwitch -Name vDSWitch1
PowerCLI C:\> $Parameters = @{
>>    NumUplinkPorts = 2
```

```
>>    MaxPorts = 1024
>>    LinkDiscoveryProtocol = 'LLDP'
>>    LinkDiscoveryProtocolOperation = 'Both'
>>    ContactName = 'vsphereadmin@blackmilktea.com'
>>    ContactDetails = 'New York office'
>>    Notes = 'VDSwitch for New York datacenter'
>> }
>> $VDSwitch | Set-VDSwitch @Parameters


Name                         NumPorts   Mtu       Version  Vendor
----                         --------   ---       -------  ------
VDSwitch1                    0          1500      6.5.0    VMware, Inc.
```

To retrieve all of the properties of vSphere Distributed Switch VDSwitch1, and format them as a list, we will pipe the output of the Get-VDSwitch cmdlet to the Format-List -Property * command:

```
PowerCLI C:\> Get-VDSwitch -Name vDSWitch1 | Format-List -Property *

LinkDiscoveryProtocol        : LLDP
LinkDiscoveryProtocolOperation : Both
VlanConfiguration            :
Name                         : VDSwitch1
ExtensionData                : VMware.Vim.VmwareDistributedVirtualS
                               witch
NumPorts                     : 0
Key                          : de 86 01 50 19 be 36 23-23 bd fa 6f
                               6c 9e ef a5
Mtu                          : 1500
Notes                        : VDSwitch for New York datacenter
Datacenter                   : New York
NumUplinkPorts               : 4
ContactName                  : vsphereadmin@blackmilktea.com
ContactDetails               : New York office
Version                      : 6.5.0
Vendor                       : VMware, Inc.
Folder                       : network
MaxPorts                     : 1024
Id                           : VmwareDistributedVirtualSwitch-dvs-
                               84
Uid                          : /VIServer=vsphere.local\administrato
                               r@192.168.0.132:443/DistributedSwitc
                               h=VmwareDistributedVirtualSwitch-dvs
                               -84/
Client                       : VMware.VimAutomation.Vds.Impl.V1.VDC
                               lientImpl
```

The following screenshot of the vSphere Web Client shows the settings of the Distributed Switch VDSwitch1 after executing the preceding commands:

```
General
    Name:                           VDSwitch1
    Manufacturer:                   VMware, Inc.
    Version:                        6.5.0
    Number of uplinks:              4
    Number of ports:                0
    Network I/O Control:            Disabled

Description:
    VDSwitch for New York datacenter

Advanced
    MTU:                            1500 Bytes
    Multicast filtering mode:       Basic

Discovery protocol
    Type:                           Link Layer Discovery Protocol
    Operation:                      Both

Administrator contact
    Name:                           vsphereadmin@blackmilktea.com
    Other details:                  New York office
```

Rolling back the configuration of a vSphere Distributed Switch

If you made a mistake in the configuration of a vSphere Distributed Switch, then you can roll back the configuration to its previous state using the Set-VDSwitch -RollbackConfiguration parameter.

In the following example, we will modify the MTU size of the switch VDSwitch1 to 9000:

```
PowerCLI C:\> Get-VDSwitch -Name VDSwitch1 | Set-VDSwitch -MTU 9000

Name                    NumPorts    Mtu        Version    Vendor
----                    --------    ---        -------    ------
VDSwitch1               0           9000       6.5.0      VMware, Inc.
```

Now we will use the `Set-VDSwitch -RollbackConfiguration` parameter to revert to the previous MTU size value of `1500`:

```
PowerCLI C:\> Get-VDSwitch -Name VDSwitch1 |
>> Set-VDSwitch -RollbackConfiguration

Name                     NumPorts   Mtu       Version  Vendor
----                     --------   ---       -------  ------
VDSwitch1                0          1500      6.5.0    VMware, Inc.
```

Importing the configuration of a vSphere Distributed Switch from a backup

In this section, we will show you how to restore the configuration of a vSphere Distributed Switch from a backup created with the `Export-VDSwitch` cmdlet. Later in this chapter, you will learn how to create a backup, in the *Exporting the configuration of vSphere Distributed Switches* section.

You have to use the `Set-VDSwitch -BackupPath` parameter to specify the path to the configuration `.zip` file. You can also use the `-WithoutPortGroups` parameter if you don't want to restore the port groups.

In the following example, we will import the configuration of `VDSwitch1` from a backup file called `c:\myVDSwitch1Config.zip`:

```
PowerCLI C:\> Get-VDSwitch -Name VDSwitch1 |
>> Set-VDSwitch -BackupPath 'c:\myVDSwitch1Config.zip'

Restoring vSphere Distributed Switch configuration - Switch name:
'VDSwitch1', Switch version: 6.5.0, Number of port groups: 1, Number
of resource pools: 9, Number of uplinks: 1, Notes: VDSwitch1
Configuration

Name                     NumPorts   Mtu       Version  Vendor
----                     --------   ---       -------  ------
VDSwitch1                0          1500      6.5.0    VMware, Inc.
```

Upgrading a vSphere Distributed Switch

In every new VMware vSphere version, VMware introduces new features to the vSphere Distributed Switch. To be able to use these new features, you have to upgrade your switches to the new version.

In the following command, we will create a new vSphere Distributed Switch named VDSwitch4 switch with version 5.5.0:

```
PowerCLI C:\> New-VDSwitch -Name VDSwitch4 -Version 5.5.0 -Location
(Get-Datacenter 'New York')

Name                    NumPorts   Mtu        Version   Vendor
----                    --------   ---        -------   ------
VDSwitch4               0          1500       5.5.0     VMware, Inc.
```

In the following command, we will upgrade the version of the VDSwitch4 switch to 6.5.0:

```
PowerCLI C:\> Get-VDSwitch -Name VDSwitch4 | Set-VDSwitch
-Version 6.5.0

Name                    NumPorts   Mtu        Version   Vendor
----                    --------   ---        -------   ------
VDSwitch4               0          1500       6.5.0     VMware, Inc.
```

Adding hosts to vSphere Distributed Switches

After creating a vSphere Distributed Switch, you have to add hosts to the switch. Normally, you add at least all of the hosts that are in the same cluster. Because a vSphere Distributed Switch is created in a datacenter or a folder, a vSphere Distributed Switch is not limited to one cluster. You can add hosts of multiple clusters to the same switch.

The Add-VDSwitchVMHost cmdlet will add hosts to a vSphere Distributed Switch. The syntax of this cmdlet is as follows:

```
Add-VDSwitchVMHost -VDSwitch <VDSwitch> -VMHost <VMHost[]>
[-Server <VIServer[]>] [-RunAsync] [-WhatIf] [-Confirm]
[<CommonParameters>]
```

The -VDSwitch, and -VMHost parameters are required.

In the following example, we will add all of the hosts of the cluster Cluster01 to the vSphere Distributed Switch VDSwitch2:

```
PowerCLI C:\> $VMHost = Get-Cluster Cluster01 | Get-VMHost
PowerCLI C:\> Add-VDSwitchVMHost -VDSwitch VDSwitch2 -VMHost $VMHost
```

The preceding commands do not return any output.

Retrieving hosts connected to vSphere Distributed Switches

There is no `Get-VDSwitchVMHost` cmdlet, to retrieve which hosts are connected to a vSphere Distributed Switch. You can use the code in the following example to retrieve the hosts connected to vSphere Distributed Switch `VDSwitch2`. The example retrieves the hosts using the `ExtensionData` property to access the vSphere API:

```
PowerCLI C:\> $VDSwitch = Get-VDSwitch -Name VDSwitch2
PowerCLI C:\> $VDSwitch.ExtensionData.Runtime.HostMemberRuntime |
ForEach-Object {Get-VMHost -Id $_.Host}

Name              ConnectionState PowerState NumCpu CpuUsageMhz CpuTotal
                                                                Mhz
----              --------------- ---------- ------ ----------- --------
192.168.0.133 Connected          PoweredOn       2          77     5386
192.168.0.134 Connected          PoweredOn       2        1754     5386
```

Adding host physical network adapters to a vSphere Distributed Switch

Adding hosts to a vSphere Distributed Switch does not add physical network adapters to the switch. For each host, you have to add network adapters to the vSphere Distributed Switch to give the switch connectivity to the external network.

The `Add-VDSwitchPhysicalNetworkAdapter` cmdlet will connect a host's physical network adapter to a vSphere Distributed Switch. The syntax of this cmdlet is as follows:

```
Add-VDSwitchPhysicalNetworkAdapter [-VMHostPhysicalNic] <PhysicalNic[]>
[-DistributedSwitch] <DistributedSwitch> [-VirtualNicPortgroup
<VDPortgroup[]>] [-VMHostVirtualNic <HostVirtualNic[]>] [-Server
<VIServer[]>] [-WhatIf] [-Confirm] [<CommonParameters>]
```

The `-VMHostPhysicalNic` and `-DistributedSwitch` parameters are required.

The following example will add the physical network adapter `vmnic4` of the host `192.168.0.133` to the vSphere Distributed Switch `VDSwitch2`:

```
PowerCLI C:\> $NetworkAdapter = Get-VMHost –Name 192.168.0.133 |
>> Get-VMHostNetworkAdapter –Name vmnic4 –Physical
PowerCLI C:\> Add-VDSwitchPhysicalNetworkAdapter `
>> –DistributedSwitch VDSwitch2 `
>> –VMHostPhysicalNic $NetworkAdapter –Confirm:$false
```

The preceding commands do not return any output.

> Before you move the last remaining uplink from a vSphere Standard Switch to a vSphere Distributed Switch, make sure you have migrated the network of all virtual machines to a port group on the vSphere Distributed Switch.

Removing host physical network adapters from a vSphere Distributed Switch

Removing a physical network adapter from a vSphere Distributed Switch can be done using the `Remove-VDSwitchPhysicalNetworkAdapter` cmdlet. The syntax of this cmdlet is as follows:

```
Remove-VDSwitchPhysicalNetworkAdapter [-VMHostNetworkAdapter]
<PhysicalNic[]> [-WhatIf] [-Confirm] [<CommonParameters>]
```

The `-VMHostNetworkAdapter` parameter is required.

In the following example, the physical network adapter `vmnic4` from the host `192.168.0.133` will be removed from the vSphere Distributed Switch `VDSwitch1`:

```
PowerCLI C:\> Get-VMhost –Name 192.168.0.133 |
>> Get-VMHostNetworkAdapter –Physical –Name vmnic4 |
>> Remove-VDSwitchPhysicalNetworkAdapter –Confirm:$false
```

The preceding command does not return any output.

Removing hosts from a vSphere Distributed Switch

You can use the `Remove-VDSwitchVMHost` cmdlet to remove a host from a vSphere Distributed Switch. This cmdlet has the following syntax:

```
Remove-VDSwitchVMHost -VDSwitch <VDSwitch> -VMHost <VMHost[]>
[-Server <VIServer[]>] [-RunAsync] [-WhatIf] [-Confirm]
[<CommonParameters>]
```

The `-VDSwitch` and `-VMHost` parameters are required.

In the following example, we will remove the host `192.168.0.134` from the vSphere Distributed Switch `VDSwitch2`:

```
PowerCLI C:\> Get-VDSwitch -Name VDSwitch2 |
>> Remove-VDSwitchVMHost -VMHost 192.168.0.134 -Confirm:$false
```

The preceding command does not return any output.

Exporting the configuration of vSphere Distributed Switches

In the case of database or upgrade failures, you can restore the configuration of vSphere Distributed Switches from an export. You can also use an export of a vSphere Distributed Switch to recreate or clone the vSphere Distributed Switch. If you export the configuration of a vSphere Distributed Switch, you create a `.zip` file that can be used as a backup for the configuration of the vSphere Distributed Switch. The `Export-VDSwitch` cmdlet that you can use to create the `.zip` file has the following syntax:

```
Export-VDSwitch [-VDSwitch] <VDSwitch[]> [-WithoutPortGroups]
[-Description <String>] [-Destination <String>] [-Force]
[-Server <VIServer[]>] [<CommonParameters>]
```

The `-VDSwitch` parameter is required.

The following PowerCLI example will export the configuration of the vSphere Distributed Switch VDSwitch1 into a file called VDSwitch1Config.zip:

```
PowerCLI C:\> Get-VDSwitch -Name VDSwitch1 |
>> Export-VDSwitch -Description "VDSwitch1 Configuration" `
>> -Destination "c:\VDSwitch1Config.zip"

Mode              LastWriteTime     Length Name
----              -------------     ------ ----
-a---       1/29/2017   5:03 PM       4606 VDSwitch1Config.zip
```

To export the vSphere Distributed Switch without port groups, use the -WithoutPortGroups parameter. If the .zip file already exists, you can use the -Force parameter to overwrite the existing file.

 Exporting the configuration of a vSphere Distributed Switch and the Export-VDSwitch cmdlet is only supported in VMware vSphere 5.1 and later versions.

Removing vSphere Distributed Switches

To remove a vSphere Distributed Switch, you can use the Remove-VDSwitch cmdlet. This cmdlet has the following syntax:

```
Remove-VDSwitch [-VDSwitch] <VDSwitch[]> [-RunAsync]
[-Server <VIServer[]>] [-WhatIf] [-Confirm] [<CommonParameters>]
```

The -VDSwitch parameter is required.

In the following example, we will remove the vSphere Distributed Switch VDSwitch1:

```
PowerCLI C:\> Get-VDSwitch -Name VDSwitch1 |
>> Remove-VDSwitch -Confirm:$false
```

The preceding command does not return any output.

Using distributed virtual port groups

A description of port groups has already been given in the *Using standard port groups* section. In this section, you will learn how to use port groups on Distributed Virtual Switches.

Creating distributed virtual port groups

You can use the New-VDPortgroup cmdlet to create distributed virtual port groups from scratch, from the reference port groups or from an export of a Distributed Virtual Switch. The syntax of the New-VDPortgroup cmdlet is as follows. The first parameter set is the default one:

```
New-VDPortgroup [-VDSwitch] <VDSwitch> -Name <String>
[-Notes <String>] [-NumPorts <Int32>] [-VlanId <Int32>]
[-VlanTrunkRange <VlanRangeList>] [-PortBinding
<DistributedPortGroupPortBinding>] [-RunAsync]
[-Server <VIServer[]>] [-WhatIf] [-Confirm] [<CommonParameters>]
```

The second parameter set can be used to create a port group from a reference port group:

```
New-VDPortgroup [-VDSwitch] <VDSwitch> [-Name <String>]
-ReferencePortgroup <VDPortgroup> [-RunAsync] [-Server <VIServer[]>]
[-WhatIf] [-Confirm] [<CommonParameters>]
```

The third parameter set can be used to create a port group from an export:

```
New-VDPortgroup [-VDSwitch] <VDSwitch> [-Name <String>] -BackupPath
<String> [-KeepIdentifiers] [-RunAsync] [-Server <VIServer[]>]
[-WhatIf] [-Confirm] [<CommonParameters>]
```

The -VDSwitch, -Name, -ReferencePortgroup, and -BackupPath parameters are required.

The following example creates a new distributed virtual port group on the vSphere Distributed Switch VDSwitch2 with 64 ports and VLAN ID 10:

```
PowerCLI C:\> Get-VDSwitch -Name VDSwitch2 |
>> New-VDPortgroup -Name "VLAN 10 Port Group" -NumPorts 64 -VLanId 10

Name                            NumPorts PortBinding
----                            -------- -----------
VLAN 10 Port Group              64       Static
```

Creating distributed virtual port groups from a reference group

In the following example, we will create a new distributed virtual port group named VLAN 10 Port group 2 using the VLAN 10 Port Group port group as a reference:

```
PowerCLI C:\> $Portgroup = Get-VDPortgroup -Name 'VLAN 10 Port Group'
PowerCLI C:\> Get-VDSwitch -Name VDSwitch2 |
>> New-VDPortgroup -Name 'VLAN 10 Port group 2' -ReferencePortgroup
$Portgroup

Name                          NumPorts PortBinding
----                          -------- -----------
VLAN 10 Port group 2          64       Static
```

 Creating distributed virtual port groups from a reference group and the New-VDPortgroup-ReferencePortgroup parameter is only supported in VMware vSphere 5.1 and later versions.

Creating distributed virtual port groups from an export

In the last example of this section, we will create a new distributed virtual port group named VLAN 10 Port group 3 using an export. Later in this chapter, in the *Exporting the configuration of distributed virtual port groups* section, we will show you how to create an export of a distributed virtual port group.

```
PowerCLI C:\> Get-VDSwitch -Name VDSwitch2 |
>> New-VDPortgroup -Name 'VLAN 10 Port group 3' -BackupPath
c:\ vlan10portgroup.zip

Restoring vSphere distributed port group configuration - Name: VLAN 10
Port Group, VLAN: 'Access: 10', Type: standard, Port binding: static,
Port allocation: elastic, Notes:

Name                          NumPorts PortBinding
----                          -------- -----------
VLAN 10 Port group 3          64       Static
```

 Creating distributed virtual port groups from an export and the New-VDPortgroup -BackupPath parameter is only supported in VMware vSphere 5.1 and later versions.

Retrieving distributed virtual port groups

You can use the Get-VDPortgroup cmdlet to retrieve all of your distributed virtual port groups or to retrieve a specific one. The syntax of this cmdlet is as follows. The first parameter set is the default:

```
Get-VDPortgroup [[-Name] <String[]>] [-NetworkAdapter
<NetworkAdapter[]>] [-VDSwitch <VDSwitch[]>]
[-VMHostNetworkAdapter <HostVirtualNic[]>] [-Server <VIServer[]>]
[-Tag <Tag[]>] [<CommonParameters>]
```

The second parameter set is for retrieving distributed virtual port groups by ID:

```
Get-VDPortgroup -Id <String[]> [-Server <VIServer[]>]
[<CommonParameters>]
```

The third parameter set is for retrieving distributed virtual port groups by related object:

```
Get-VDPortgroup -RelatedObject <VDPortgroupRelatedObjectBase[]>
[<CommonParameters>]
```

The -Id or the -RelatedObject parameter is required if you want to retrieve a distributed virtual port group by ID or related object.

In the following example, we will retrieve all of our distributed virtual port groups:

```
PowerCLI C:\> Get-VDPortGroup

Name                          NumPorts  PortBinding
----                          --------  -----------
VDSwitch2-DVUplinks-86        4         Static
VDSwitch3-DVUplinks-88        0         Static
VDSwitch4-DVUplinks-90        0         Static
VLAN 10 Port Group            64        Static
VLAN 10 Port group 2          64        Static
VLAN 10 Port group 3          64        Static
```

Modifying distributed virtual port groups

The `Set-VDPortgroup` cmdlet can be used to modify the configuration of distributed virtual port groups, to roll back distributed virtual port groups to their last valid configuration, or to import the configuration from a `.zip` file created earlier with the `Export-VDPortgroup` cmdlet. The syntax of the `Set-VDPortgroup` cmdlet is as follows. The first parameter set is the default:

```
Set-VDPortgroup [-Name <String>] [-Notes <String>] [-NumPorts
<Int32>] [-VlanId <Int32>] [-VlanTrunkRange <VlanRangeList>]
[-PrivateVlanId <Int32>] [-PortBinding
<DistributedPortGroupPortBinding>] [-DisableVlan] [-VDPortgroup]
<VDPortgroup[]> [-RunAsync] [-Server <VIServer[]>] [-WhatIf]
[-Confirm] [<CommonParameters>]
```

The second parameter set is for rolling back distributed virtual port groups to its last valid configuration:

```
Set-VDPortgroup -RollbackConfiguration [-VDPortgroup] <VDPortgroup[]>
[-RunAsync] [-Server <VIServer[]>] [-WhatIf] [-Confirm]
[<CommonParameters>]
```

The third parameter set is for importing the configuration of distributed virtual port groups from a backup:

```
Set-VDPortgroup -BackupPath <String> [-VDPortgroup] <VDPortgroup[]>
[-RunAsync] [-Server <VIServer[]>] [-WhatIf] [-Confirm]
[<CommonParameters>]
```

The `-VDPortGroup`, `-RollbackConfiguration`, and `-BackupPath` parameters are required.

Renaming a distributed virtual port group

In the following example, we will rename distributed virtual port group VLAN 10 Port Group 2 to VLAN 10 Port Group 4, and modify the number of ports to 128:

```
PowerCLI C:\> Get-VDPortgroup -Name 'VLAN 10 Port Group 2' |
>> Set-VDPortgroup -Name 'VLAN 10 Port Group 4' -NumPorts 128

Name                          NumPorts PortBinding
----                          -------- -----------
VLAN 10 Port Group 4          128      Static
```

Rolling back the configuration of a distributed virtual port group

In the following example, we will roll back the configuration of distributed virtual port group VLAN 10 Port Group 4 to its last valid configuration using the following command:

```
PowerCLI C:\> Get-VDPortgroup -Name 'VLAN 10 Port Group 4' |
>> Set-VDPortgroup -RollbackConfiguration

Name                         NumPorts PortBinding
----                         -------- -----------
VLAN 10 Port Group 2         64       Static
```

As you can see in the output of the preceding command, the port group name is returned to VLAN 10 Port Group 2, and the number of ports is set back to 64.

> Rolling back the configuration of a distributed virtual port group and the Set-VDPortgroup -RollbackConfiguration parameter is only supported in VMware vSphere 5.1 and later versions.

Restoring the configuration of a distributed virtual port group

In the following example, we will restore the configuration of distributed virtual port group VLAN 10 Port Group from a .zip file created earlier using the Export-VDPortgroup cmdlet:

```
PowerCLI C:\> Get-VDPortgroup -Name 'VLAN 10 Port Group' |
>> Set-VDPortgroup -BackupPath c:\Vlan10PortGroup.zip

Applying vSphere distributed port group configuration
- Name: VLAN 10 Port Group, VLAN: 'Access: 10', Type: standard,
Port binding: static, Port allocation: elastic, Notes:

Name                         NumPorts PortBinding
----                         -------- -----------
VLAN 10 Port Group           64       Static
```

Restoring the configuration of a distributed virtual port group and the `Set-VDPortgroup -BackupPath` parameter is only supported in VMware vSphere 5.1 and later versions.

Configuring network I/O control

The virtual Distributed Switch cmdlets don't have a method to configure **network I/O Control**. However, in PowerCLI you can use all of the VMware vSphere public APIs. It is not difficult to use them to enable or disable Network I/O Control.

Enabling network I/O control

In the following example, we will enable Network I/O Control for the `VDSwitch2` switch using the `EnableNetworkResourceManagement()` method from the API:

```
PowerCLI C:\> $VDSwitch = Get-VDSwitch -Name VDSwitch2
PowerCLI C:\> $VDSwitch.ExtensionData
.EnableNetworkResourceManagement($true)
```

The preceding command does not return any output.

Retrieving the network I/O control enabled status

You can check if Network I/O Control is enabled on vSphere Distributed Switch `VDSwitch2`, using the following PowerCLI commands:

```
PowerCLI C:\> $VDSwitch = Get-VDSwitch -Name VDSwitch2
PowerCLI C:\> $VDSwitch.ExtensionData.Config
.NetworkResourceManagementEnabled
True
```

Because the output of the preceding command is `True`, you know that Network I/O Control is enabled on vSphere Distributed Switch `VDSwitch2`.

Disabling network I/O control

Disabling Network I/O Control for `VDSwitch1` can be done by replacing `$true` in the preceding example with `$false`:

```
PowerCLI C:\> $VDSwitch = Get-VDSwitch -Name VDSwitch2
PowerCLI C:\> $VDSwitch.ExtensionData
.EnableNetworkResourceManagement($false)
```

The preceding command does not return any output.

Exporting the configuration of distributed virtual port groups

You can make an export of one or more distributed virtual port groups with the `Export-VDPortGroup` cmdlet. You can use this export to create new port groups or to restore the configuration of port groups. The syntax of the `Export-VDPortGroup` cmdlet is as follows:

```
Export-VDPortGroup [-VDPortGroup] <VDPortgroup[]> [-Description
<String>] [-Destination <String>] [-Force] [-Server <VIServer[]>]
[<CommonParameters>]
```

The `-VDPortGroup` parameter is required.

In the following example, we will create an export of `VLAN 10 Port Group`:

```
PowerCLI C:\> Get-VDPortGroup -Name 'VLAN 10 Port Group' |
>> Export-VDPortGroup -Destination C:\Vlan10PortGroup.zip

Mode              LastWriteTime       Length Name
----              -------------       ------ ----
-a--        1/29/2017  11:23 AM         1865 Vlan10PortGroup.zip
```

 The `Export-VDPortGroup` cmdlet is supported only in VMware vSphere 5.1 and later versions.

Migrating a host network adapter from a standard port group to a distributed port group

In the following example, we will use the `Set-VMHostNetworkAdapter` cmdlet, which we have seen before in the *Configuring host network adapters* section, to migrate the virtual network adapter `vmk1` to the distributed port group `VLAN 10 Port Group`:

```
PowerCLI C:\> Get-VMHostNetworkAdapter -Name vmk1 |
>> Set-VMHostNetworkAdapter -PortGroup 'VLAN 10 Port Group'
-Confirm:$false

Name   Mac                 DhcpEnabled IP              SubnetMask      Device
                                                                       Name
----   ---                 ----------- --              ----------      ------
vmk1   00:50:56:6c:a8:38 False           192.168.0.150 255.255.255.0 vmk1
```

Removing distributed virtual port groups

To remove a distributed virtual port group, you can use the `Remove-VDPortGroup` cmdlet. The syntax of this cmdlet is as follows:

```
Remove-VDPortGroup [-VDPortGroup] <VDPortgroup[]> [-RunAsync]
[-Server <VIServer[]>] [-WhatIf] [-Confirm] [<CommonParameters>]
```

The `-VDPortGroup` parameter is required.

In the following example, we will remove the port group named `VLAN 10 Port Group 3`:

```
PowerCLI C:\> Get-VDPortGroup -Name 'VLAN 10 Port Group 3' |
>> Remove-VDPortGroup -Confirm:$false
```

The preceding command does not return any output.

Configuring host networking

The `Get-VMHostNetwork` cmdlet will retrieve information about the network on a specific host. This cmdlet has the following syntax:

```
Get-VMHostNetwork [-Server <VIServer[]>] [-VMHost] <VMHost[]>
[<CommonParameters>]
```

The `-VMHost` parameter is required.

In the following example, we will retrieve the information about the network on the host `192.168.0.133`, and format the output as a list:

```
PowerCLI C:\> Get-VMHost -Name 192.168.0.133 | Get-VMHostNetwork |
>> Format-List *
```

The output of the preceding command is as follows:

```
WARNING: The 'VMKernelGatewayDevice' property of VMHostNetworkInfo
type is deprecated and will be removed in a future release.
WARNING: The 'VirtualSwitch' property of VMHostNetworkInfo type is
deprecated. Use 'Get-VirtualSwitch' cmdlet instead.
WARNING: The 'PhysicalNic' property of VMHostNetworkInfo type is
deprecated. Use 'Get-VMHostNetworkAdapter' cmdlet instead.
WARNING: The 'ConsoleNic' property of VMHostNetworkInfo type is
deprecated. Use 'Get-VMHostNetworkAdapter' cmdlet instead.
WARNING: The 'VirtualNic' property of VMHostNetworkInfo type is
deprecated. Use 'Get-VMHostNetworkAdapter' cmdlet instead.
WARNING: The value of 'ExtensionData' property of VMHostNetworkInfo
type is deprecated and will be changed to the value of 'ExtensionData2'
property in a future release. Use 'ExtensionData2' property instead.
VMHostId                  : HostSystem-host-23
VMHost                    : 192.168.0.133
VMKernelGateway           : 192.168.0.1
VMKernelGatewayDevice     :
ConsoleGateway            :
ConsoleGatewayDevice      :
DnsAddress                : {192.168.0.130}
DnsFromDhcp               : False
DnsDhcpDevice             :
DomainName                : localdomain
HostName                  : esx1
SearchDomain              : {localdomain, blackmilktea.com}
VirtualSwitch             : {vSwitch0, vSwitch1}
PhysicalNic               : {vmnic0, vmnic1, vmnic2, vmnic3...}
ConsoleNic                : {}
VirtualNic                : {vmk0, vmk1}
Uid                       : /VIServer=vsphere.local\administrator@192.1
                            68.0.132:443/VMHost=HostSystem-host-23/VMHo
                            stNetwork=/
IPv6Enabled               : True
ConsoleV6Gateway          :
ConsoleV6GatewayDevice    :
VMKernelV6Gateway         :
VMKernelV6GatewayDevice   :
ExtensionData             : VMware.Vim.HostNetworkInfo
ExtensionData2            : VMware.Vim.HostNetworkSystem
Name                      :
```

```
Id                          : HostNetworkSystem-networkSystem-23
Client                      : VMware.VimAutomation.ViCore.Impl.V1.VimClie
                              nt
```

The hosts used as examples in this book are all virtual ESXi servers running in my home lab. As you can see from the preceding output, the hostname is `esx1`, and the domain is `localdomain`. Let's try to change the hostname and domain.

The `Set-VMHostNetwork` cmdlet will modify the network settings of a host. The syntax of this cmdlet is as follows:

```
Set-VMHostNetwork [-Network] <VMHostNetworkInfo[]>
[-ConsoleGateway <String>] [-VMKernelGateway <String>]
[-VMKernelGatewayDevice <String>] [-ConsoleGatewayDevice<String>]
[-DomainName <String>] [-HostName <String>] [-DnsFromDhcp
[<Boolean>]] [-DnsDhcpDevice <Object>] [-DnsAddress <String[]>]
[-SearchDomain <String[]>] [-IPv6Enabled [<Boolean>]]
[-ConsoleV6Gateway <String>] [-ConsoleV6GatewayDevice <String>]
[-VMKernelV6Gateway <String>] [-VMKernelV6GatewayDevice <String>]
[-WhatIf][-Confirm] [<CommonParameters>]
```

The `-Network` parameter is required.

In the following example, we will change the host name of the host `192.168.0.133` into `ESX001`, and modify the domain name to `blackmilktea.com`. To be able to do this, `DnsFromDhcp` must be disabled, because the domain name and host name cannot be explicitly set if `DnsFromDhcp` is enabled:

```
PowerCLI C:\> Get-VMHost -Name 192.168.0.133 | Get-VMHostNetwork |
>> Set-VMHostNetwork -HostName ESX001 -DomainName blackmilktea.com

HostName DomainName DnsFrom ConsoleGateway ConsoleGateway DnsAddress
                    Dhcp                   Device
-------- ---------- ------ -------------- -------------- ----------
ESX001   blackmi... False                                {192.16...
```

Configuring the network of virtual machines

To configure the network of a virtual machine guest operating system, you can use the `Invoke-VMScript` cmdlet, to run scripts in the guest operating system of a virtual machine. You have already seen the `Invoke-VMScript` cmdlet in Chapter 5, *Managing Virtual Machines with PowerCLI*.

To configure the network of Microsoft Windows virtual machines with PowerShell V3 or later versions installed, you can use the cmdlets in the `netadapter` and `NetTCPIP` modules to modify network adapters and TCP/IP settings. For Microsoft Windows virtual machines with PowerShell V1 or V2 installed, you can use the **Windows Management Instrumentation** (**WMI**) `Get-WMIObject` cmdlet with the `Win32_NetworkAdapterConfiguration` class. In this section, we will focus on using the cmdlets from the `NetTCPIP` module.

Setting the IP address

The PowerShell cmdlet we will use for setting the IP address, network mask, and default gateway is `New-NetIPAddress`. This cmdlet has the following syntax. The first parameter set is for creating and configuring an IP address by using an interface alias:

```
New-NetIPAddress [-IPAddress] <String> [-AddressFamily {IPv4 |
IPv6}] [-CimSession <CimSession[]>] [-DefaultGateway <String>]
[-PolicyStore <String>] [-PreferredLifetime <TimeSpan>]
[-PrefixLength <Byte>] [-SkipAsSource <Boolean>] [-ThrottleLimit
<Int32>] [-Type {Unicast | Anycast}] [-ValidLifetime <TimeSpan>]
-InterfaceAlias <String> [-Confirm] [-WhatIf] [<CommonParameters>]
```

The second parameter set is for creating and configuring an IP address by using an interface index:

```
New-NetIPAddress [-IPAddress] <String> [-AddressFamily {IPv4 | IPv6}]
[-CimSession <CimSession[]>] [-DefaultGateway <String>] [-PolicyStore
<String>] [-PreferredLifetime <TimeSpan>] [-PrefixLength <Byte>]
[-SkipAsSource <Boolean>] [-ThrottleLimit <Int32>] [-Type {Unicast |
Anycast}] [-ValidLifetime <TimeSpan>] -InterfaceIndex <UInt32>
[-Confirm] [-WhatIf] [<CommonParameters>]
```

The `-InterfaceAlias`, `-InterfaceIndex`, and `-IPAddress` parameters are required.

To use the `Invoke-VMScript` cmdlet, we have to specify credentials for the guest operating system. We will retrieve these credentials using the `Get-Credential` cmdlet and save them in the variable `$GuestCredential`, using the following command:

```
PowerCLI C:\> $GuestCredential = Get-Credential
```

Next, we will create a string with the PowerShell command to set the IP address, network mask, and default gateway for network interface `Ethernet`. We will save the command in the variable `$ScriptText`. Notice that the `-PrefixLength` parameter specifies the number of bits of the network mask. A network mask of 255.255.255.0 is a 24-bit network mask. So we will use 24 as the value of the `-PrefixLength` parameter:

```
PowerCLI C:\> $ScriptText = 'New-NetIPAddress -InterfaceAlias
"Ethernet" -AddressFamily IPv4 -IPAddress 192.168.10.31
-PrefixLength 24 -DefaultGateway 192.168.10.1'
```

Finally, we will call the `Invoke-VMScript` cmdlet, to run the command in the `$ScriptText` variable, in the guest operating system of virtual machine VM2:

```
PowerCLI C:\> Invoke-VMScript -ScriptText $ScriptText -VM VM2
-GuestCredential $GuestCredential
```

The preceding command gives the following output:

```
ScriptOutput
----------------------------------------------------------------
|
----------------------------------------------------------------
```

Setting the DNS server addresses

We have to use the `Set-DnsClientServerAddress` cmdlet to specify the DNS servers. This cmdlet has the following syntax. The first parameter set is for setting the DNS servers by using an interface alias:

```
Set-DnsClientServerAddress [-InterfaceAlias] <String[]>
[-CimSession <CimSession[]>] [-PassThru] [-ResetServerAddresses]
[-ServerAddresses <String[]>] [-ThrottleLimit <Int32>] [-Validate]
[-Confirm] [-WhatIf] [<CommonParameters>]
```

The second parameter set is for setting the DNS servers by name:

```
Set-DnsClientServerAddress [-CimSession <CimSession[]>]
[-PassThru] [-ResetServerAddresses] [-ServerAddresses <String[]>]
[-ThrottleLimit <Int32>] [-Validate] [-Confirm] [-WhatIf]
[<CommonParameters>]
```

The third parameter set is for setting the DNS servers by using an input object:

```
Set-DnsClientServerAddress [-CimSession <CimSession[]>] [-PassThru]
[-ResetServerAddresses] [-ServerAddresses <String[]>] [-ThrottleLimit
<Int32>] [-Validate] -InterfaceIndex <UInt32[]> [-Confirm] [-WhatIf]
[<CommonParameters>]
```

The `-InterfaceAlias` or `-InterfaceIndex` parameter is required.

In the following command, we will create a string with the command to set the DNS server of the interface `Ethernet` to IP address `192.168.0.130` and save this string to a variable called `$ScriptText`:

```
PowerCLI C:\> $ScriptText = 'Set-DnsClientServerAddress
-InterfaceAlias "Ethernet0" -ServerAddresses 192.168.0.130'
```

Finally, we will call the `Invoke-VMScript` cmdlet to run the command in the `$ScriptText` variable, in the guest operating system of virtual machine VM2:

```
PowerCLI C:\> Invoke-VMScript -ScriptText $ScriptText -VM VM2
-GuestCredential $GuestCredential
```

The preceding command gives the following output:

```
ScriptOutput
-----------------------------------------------------------------------
|
-----------------------------------------------------------------------
```

Retrieving the network configurations

To retrieve the IP configuration of a Microsoft Windows virtual machine, we can either use the `ipconfig /all` command or the `Get-NetIPConfiguration` cmdlet. This cmdlet has the following syntax. The first parameter set is for retrieving the network configuration of a network adapter by interface alias:

```
Get-NetIPConfiguration [[-InterfaceAlias] <String>]
[-AllCompartments] [-CimSession <CimSession>] [-CompartmentId <Int32>]
[-Detailed] [<CommonParameters>]
```

The second parameter set is for retrieving the network configuration of all network adapters:

```
Get-NetIPConfiguration [-AllCompartments] [-CimSession <CimSession>]
[-CompartmentId <Int32>] [-Detailed] -All [<CommonParameters>]
```

The third parameter set is for retrieving the network configuration of a network adapter by interface index:

```
Get-NetIPConfiguration [-AllCompartments] [-CimSession <CimSession>]
[-CompartmentId <Int32>] [-Detailed] -InterfaceIndex <Int32>
[<CommonParameters>]
```

The `-All`, or `-InterfaceIndex` parameter is required.

First, we will save the string with the command to retrieve the network configuration for the network interface `Ethernet` in the variable `$ScriptText`:

```
PowerCLI C:\> $ScriptText = 'Get-NetIPConfiguration
-InterfaceAlias "Ethernet0"'
```

Finally, we will call the `Invoke-VMScript` cmdlet, to run the command in the `$ScriptText` variable, in the guest operating system of virtual machine VM2:

```
PowerCLI C:\> Invoke-VMScript -ScriptText $ScriptText -VM VM2
-GuestCredential $GuestCredential
```

The output of the preceding command is as follows:

```
ScriptOutput
------------------------------------------------------------------------
|
|
|  InterfaceAlias       : Ethernet0
|  InterfaceIndex       : 12
|  InterfaceDescription : Intel(R) 82574L Gigabit Network Connection
|  IPv4Address          : 192.168.10.31
|  IPv6DefaultGateway   :
|  IPv4DefaultGateway   : 192.168.10.1
|  DNSServer            : 192.168.0.130
|
|
|
|
------------------------------------------------------------------------
```

Summary

In this chapter, we covered virtual networking. We showed you how to work with vSphere Standard Switches and vSphere Distributed Switches using PowerCLI. You learned how to use port groups, how to use host network adapters, and how to configure the management network of a host and the network of a virtual machine.

In the next chapter, you will learn all about managing storage with PowerCLI.

7
Managing Storage

Your virtual machines need storage for their configuration files, disks, swap files, and snapshot files. These files can be placed on **datastores** that reside on a host's **local storage**, **Network File System (NFS)**, **Internet Small Computer System Interface (iSCSI)**, **Fibre Channel (FC)**, **Fibre Channel over Ethernet (FCoE)**, **Storage Area Networks (SANs)**, or **VMware vSAN**. Datastores can be grouped into **datastore clusters** to create pools of datastores for storage aggregation, easy initial placement of disks, and load balancing using **Storage Distributed Resource Scheduler (Storage DRS)**. vSphere storage policy-based management can be used to create virtual machines on storage that is compliant with a certain storage policy. In this chapter, we will discuss managing storage with PowerCLI.

The following topics will be covered in this chapter are:

- Rescanning for new storage devices
- Creating datastores
- Retrieving datastores
- Setting the multipathing policy
- Configuring vmhba paths to a SCSI device
- Working with Raw Device Mappings
- Configuring Storage I/O Control
- Configuring Storage DRS
- Upgrading datastores to VMFS-5
- Removing datastores
- Using VMware vSAN
- Using vSphere storage policy-based management

Rescanning for new storage devices

After creating LUN on your Fibre Channel storage system and presenting LUN to your ESXi servers, you have to rescan HBAs on the ESXi servers before you can create a datastore on LUN. An ESXi host will not see newly attached LUN before a rescan is performed. You can use the Get-VMHostStorage cmdlet to rescan the HBAs of a host. The Get-VMHostStorage cmdlet has the following syntax; the first parameter set is the default:

```
Get-VMHostStorage [-VMHost] <VMHost[]> [-Refresh] [-RescanAllHba]
[-RescanVmfs] [-Server <VIServer[]>] [<CommonParameters>]
```

The second parameter set is for retrieving host storage by ID:

```
Get-VMHostStorage -Id <String[]> [-Server <VIServer[]>]
[<CommonParameters>]
```

The -VMHost and -Id parameters are required.

In the following example, we will rescan all the HBAs of the hosts of cluster Cluster01:

```
PowerCLI C:\> Get-Cluster -Name Cluster01 |
>> Get-VMHost | Get-VMHostStorage -RescanAllHba
SoftwareIScsiEnabled
--------------------
False
False
```

Creating datastores

You can use the New-Datastore cmdlet to create a new datastore. The syntax of the New-Datastore cmdlet is as follows. The first parameter set is to create NFS datastores:

```
New-Datastore [-Server <VIServer[]>] [-VMHost] <VMHost[]> [-Name]
<String> -Path <String> [-Nfs] -NfsHost <String[]> [-ReadOnly]
[-Kerberos] [-FileSystemVersion <String>] [-WhatIf] [-Confirm]
[<CommonParameters>]
```

The second parameter set is to create VMFS datastores:

```
New-Datastore [-Server <VIServer[]>] [-VMHost] <VMHost[]> [-Name]
<String> -Path <String> [-Vmfs] [-BlockSizeMB <Int32>]
[- FileSystemVersion <String>] [-WhatIf] [-Confirm]
[<CommonParameters>]
```

The `-VMHost`, `-Name`, `-Path`, and `-NfsHost` parameters are required.

Creating NFS datastores

In the first example, we will create an NFS datastore. To indicate that we want to create an NFS datastore, we have to use the `-Nfs` parameter. The datastore will be created on host `192.168.0.133` with name `Cluster01_Nfs01`. The IP address of the NFS server is `192.168.0.157`, and the remote path of the NFS mount point is `/mnt/Cluster01_Nfs01`:

```
PowerCLI C:\> New-Datastore -Nfs -VMHost 192.168.0.133
-Name Cluster01_Nfs01 -NfsHost 192.168.0.157 -Path /mnt/Cluster01_Nfs01
WARNING: Parameter 'VMHost' is obsolete. This parameter no longer
accepts multiple values.

Name                                  FreeSpaceGB       CapacityGB
----                                  -----------       ----------
Cluster01_Nfs01                           249.314          249.314
```

Getting SCSI LUNs

Before we can create a VMFS datastore, we need to know the **canonical name** of the **SCSI logical unit** that will contain the new VMFS datastore.

The `Get-ScsiLun` cmdlet retrieves the SCSI devices available on the vCenter Server system and their canonical names. The syntax of the `Get-ScsiLun` cmdlet is as follows. The first parameter set is for retrieving SCSI LUNs by a host:

```
Get-ScsiLun [[-CanonicalName] <String[]>] [-VmHost] <VMHost[]>
[-Key <String[]>] [-LunType <String[]>] [-Server <VIServer[]>]
[<CommonParameters>]
```

The second parameter set is for retrieving SCSI LUNs by ID:

```
Get-ScsiLun -Id <String[]> [-Server <VIServer[]>]
[<CommonParameters>]
```

The third parameter set is for retrieving SCSI LUNs by datastore:

```
Get-ScsiLun [[-CanonicalName] <String[]>] [-Datastore]
<Datastore[]> [-Key <String[]>] [-LunType <String[]>]
[-Server <VIServer[]>] [<CommonParameters>]
```

The fourth parameter set is for retrieving SCSI LUNs by a **host bus adapter** (**HBA**):

```
Get-ScsiLun [[-CanonicalName] <String[]>] [-Hba] <Hba[]>
[-Key <String[]>] [-LunType <String[]>] [-Server <VIServer[]>]
[<CommonParameters>]
```

The -VmHost, -Id, -Datastore, and -Hba parameters are required.

In the following example, we will get all of the SCSI LUNs of host 192.168.0.133 and select the RuntimeName and CanonicalName properties:

```
PowerCLI C:\> Get-VMHost -Name 192.168.0.133 | Get-ScsiLun |
>> Select-Object -Property RuntimeName,CanonicalName


RuntimeName        CanonicalName
-----------        -------------
3PARdata VV        vmhba0:C0:T3:L54 naa.60002ac000000000000002f400004ca6
HP        HSVX700  vmhba0:C0:T0:L10 naa.600a0b80001111550000f4f44041944d
HP        HSVX700  vmhba0:C0:T0:L2  naa.600a0b8000111155000025315052494d
HP        HSVX700  vmhba0:C0:T0:L25 naa.600a0b8000111155000059ba3f0d204e
3PARdata VV        vmhba0:C0:T2:L51 naa.60002ac00000000000000035000004bee
```

Creating VMFS datastores

To create a VMFS datastore, we have to use the New-datastore -Vmfs parameter to indicate that we want to create a VMFS datastore. We have to specify a name for the datastore and a host on which we want to create the datastore. Finally, we have to specify the canonical name of the SCSI logical unit that will contain the new VMFS datastore:

```
PowerCLI C:\> New-Datastore -Vmfs -VMHost 192.168.0.133
-Name Cluster01_Vmfs01 -Path naa.60002ac00000000000000035000004bee


Name                               FreeSpaceGB        CapacityGB
----                               -----------        ----------
Cluster01_Vmfs01                       248.801           249.750
```

If you create the VMFS datastore on a host that is part of a cluster, the new datastore will be mounted on all hosts of the cluster.

Creating software iSCSI VMFS datastores

To create a datastore on iSCSI SAN, you can use hardware iSCSI initiators or software iSCSI initiators. Hardware iSCSI initiators are similar to Fibre Channel HBAs. In this section, we will discuss how to create VMFS datastores using software iSCSI initiators. Before you can connect your ESXi hosts to an iSCSI LUN, your storage administrators will have to create such LUN and expose it to your ESXi servers. To set up software iSCSI initiators, you have to enable software iSCSI on your hosts using the `Set-VMHostStorage` cmdlet. The syntax of this cmdlet is as follows:

```
Set-VMHostStorage -VMHostStorage <VMHostStorageInfo[]>
-SoftwareIScsiEnabled [<Boolean>] [-WhatIf] [-Confirm]
[<CommonParameters>]
```

The `-VMHostStorage` and `-SoftwareIScsiEnable` parameters are required.

Then, you can create an iSCSI HBA target. First, you have to find iSCSI HBA using the `Get-VMHostHba` cmdlet. This cmdlet has the following syntax:

```
Get-VMHostHba [[-VMHost] <VMHost[]>] [[-Device] <String[]>]
[-Type <HbaType[]>] [-Server <VIServer[]>] [<CommonParameters>]
```

This cmdlet has no required parameters.

To create the iSCSI HBA target, you can use the `New-IScsiHbaTarget` cmdlet. The syntax for the `New-IScsiHbaTarget` cmdlet is as follows:

```
New-IScsiHbaTarget -IScsiHba <IScsiHba[]> [-Address] <String[]>
[[-Port] <Int32>] [-Type <IScsiHbaTargetType>] [[-IScsiName]
<String>] [-ChapType <ChapType>] [-ChapName <String>] [-ChapPassword
<String>] [-MutualChapEnabled [<Boolean>]] [-MutualChapName
<String>] [-MutualChapPassword <String>] [-InheritChap
[<Boolean>]] [-InheritMutualChap [<Boolean>]] [-Server <VIServer[]>]
[-WhatIf] [-Confirm] [<CommonParameters>]
```

The $-$IScsiHba and $-$Address parameters are required.

After creating the iSCSI HBA target, we have to rescan HBAs.

iSCSI HBA has to be bound to a VMkernel port group. In the script given later, we will create a dedicated switch and VMkernel port group for iSCSI. There are no cmdlets to bind an iSCSI HBA to a VMkernel port group, so we have to fallback to the vSphere API IscsiManager BindVnic() method.

After the binding, we have iSCSI LUN that we can use to create a datastore.

The following script performs all of the necessary steps. The script first defines the variables we use and then it retrieves the VMHost object of the host on which the iSCSI datastore will be created. Software iSCSI will be enabled on this host. Then, an iSCSI target will be created, and a rescan of the HBAs will be performed on the host. A new virtual switch and a VMkernel port group will be created. The VMkernel port group will be bound to the iSCSI HBA. Finally, the new iSCSI datastore will be created.

First, we will define the variables we need for later use:

```
$HostName = '192.168.0.133'
$iSCSITarget = '192.168.0.157'
$VirtualSwitchName = 'vSwitch2'
$NicName = 'vmnic3'
$PortGroupName = 'iSCSI Port group 1'
$ChapType = 'Preferred'
$ChapUser = 'Cluster01User'
$ChapPassword = ' Cluster01Pwd'
$DatastoreName = 'Cluster01_iSCSI01'
```

Then, we will retrieve the host to add the iSCSI datastore to and store it in the variable $VMHost:

```
$VMHost = Get-VMHost -Name $HostName
```

We need to enable software iSCSI support on the host:

```
$VMHost | Get-VMHostStorage | Set-VMHostStorage -SoftwareIScsiEnabled:$true
```

And we have to create an iSCSI target:

```
$VMHostHba = $VMHost | Get-VMHostHba -Type iSCSI
$VMHostHba |
New-IScsiHbaTarget -Address $iSCSITarget -ChapType $ChapType -ChapName
$ChapUser -ChapPassword $ChapPassword
```

Next, we have to rescan all HBAs:

```
$VMHost | Get-VMHostStorage -RescanAllHba
```

We have to create a new virtual switch and a VMkernel port group on the host:

```
$vSwitch = New-VirtualSwitch -VMHost $VMHost -Name $VirtualSwitchName -Nic
$NicName
$NetworkAdapter = New-VMHostNetworkAdapter -VirtualSwitch $vSwitch -
PortGroup $PortGroupName
```

Now we bind the VMkernel port group to the iSCSI HBA:

```
$IscsiManager = Get-View -Id
$vmhost.ExtensionData.Configmanager.IscsiManager
$IscsiManager.BindVnic($VMHostHba.Device, $NetworkAdapter.Name)
```

Finally, we can create the iSCSI datastore:

```
$ScsiLun = $VMHost |
Get-ScsiLun |
Where-Object {$_.Model -eq 'iSCSI Disk'}
New-Datastore -Vmfs -VMHost $VMHost -Name $DatastoreName -Path
$ScsiLun.CanonicalName
```

Retrieving datastores

You can use the `Get-Datastore` cmdlet to retrieve a specific datastore or a list of all of your datastores. The syntax of the `Get-Datastore` cmdlet is as follows. The first parameter set is the default:

```
Get-Datastore [-Server <VIServer[]>] [[-Name] <String[]>]
[-Location <VIObject[]>] [-RelatedObject
<DatastoreRelatedObjectBase[]>] [-Refresh] [-Tag <Tag[]>]
[<CommonParameters>]
```

The second parameter set is for retrieving datastores by ID:

```
Get-Datastore [-Server <VIServer[]>] -Id <String[]>
[-Refresh] [<CommonParameters>]
```

The `-Id` parameter is required.

In the following example, we will retrieve the datastore with name `Cluster01_Vmfs01`:

```
PowerCLI C:\> Get-Datastore -Name Cluster01_Vmfs01

Name                              FreeSpaceGB       CapacityGB
----                              -----------       ----------
Cluster01_Vmfs01                      248.801          249.750
```

Setting the multipathing policy

If you use Fibre Channel or iSCSI storage devices, it is highly recommended to have multiple paths between your hosts and SAN and to use multipathing. Depending on the recommendations made by your storage vendor, you have to set the multipathing policy to either Fixed, Most Recently Used (MRU), or Round Robin (RR).

 More information about multipathing policies can be found in VMware Knowledge Base article 1011340: *Multipathing policies in ESXi 5.x and ESXi/ESX 4.x*, `http://kb.vmware.com/kb/1011340`.

You can use the `Get-ScsiLun` cmdlet to retrieve the current multipathing policy for your LUNs:

```
PowerCLI C:\> Get-VMHost -Name 192.168.0.133 | Get-ScsiLun |
>> Where-Object {$_.LunType -eq 'disk'} |
>> Select-Object -Property CanonicalName,LunType,MultipathPolicy

CanonicalName                      LunType   MultipathPolicy
-------------                      -------   ---------------
naa.600a0b80001111550000f35b93e19350 disk    MostRecentlyUsed
naa.600a0b80001111550000a8adc7e19350 disk    MostRecentlyUsed
naa.600a0b80001111550000893247e29350 disk    MostRecentlyUsed
naa.600a0b80001111550000b6182ca14450 disk    MostRecentlyUsed
naa.600a0b80001111550000d2c418e29350 disk    MostRecentlyUsed
```

If you want to modify the multipathing policy, you can use the `Set-ScsiLun` cmdlet `-MultipathPolicy` parameter to do so. The syntax of the `Set-ScsiLun` cmdlet is as follows:

```
Set-ScsiLun [[-MultipathPolicy] <ScsiLunMultipathPolicy>]
[[-PreferredPath] <ScsiLunPath>] [-ScsiLun] <ScsiLun[]>
[-CommandsToSwitchPath <Int32>] [-BlocksToSwitchPath <Int32>]
[-NoCommandsSwitch] [-NoBlocksSwitch] [-WhatIf] [-Confirm]
[<CommonParameters>]
```

The `-ScsiLun` parameter is required. The `-MultipathPolicy` parameter has four valid parameter values:

- `Fixed`: This uses the preferred path whenever possible
- `RoundRobin`: This uses load balancing
- `MostRecentlyUsed`: This uses the most recently used path
- `Unknown`: This is supported only when connected to vCenter Server 4.1/ESX 4.1

In the following example, we will set the multipathing policy for all the disk LUNs of host `192.168.0.133` to Round Robin:

```
PowerCLI C:\> Get-VMHost -Name 192.168.0.133 | Get-ScsiLun |
>> Where-Object {$_.LunType -eq 'disk'} |
>> Set-ScsiLun -MultipathPolicy RoundRobin |
>> Select-Object -Property CanonicalName,LunType,MultipathPolicy

CanonicalName                          LunType MultipathPolicy
-------------                          ------- ---------------
naa.600a0b80001111550000f35b93e19350 disk        RoundRobin
naa.600a0b80001111550000a8adc7e19350 disk        RoundRobin
naa.600a0b80001111550000893247e29350 disk        RoundRobin
naa.600a0b80001111550000b6182ca14450 disk        RoundRobin
naa.600a0b80001111550000d2c418e29350 disk        RoundRobin
```

Configuring vmhba paths to an SCSI device

For each vmhba path to a storage device, you can indicate that the path is active or not active and you can also indicate that the path is the preferred path to the SCSI device.

Retrieving vmhba paths to an SCSI device

You can use the `Get-ScsiLunPath` to retrieve the list of vmhba paths to a specified SCSI device. The syntax of the `Get-ScsiLunPath` cmdlet is as follows:

```
Get-ScsiLunPath [[-Name] <String[]>] [-ScsiLun] <ScsiLun[]>
[<CommonParameters>]
```

The `-ScsiLun` parameter is required, and it accepts input from the pipeline.

In the following example, we will retrieve the vmhba paths of the LUN with `Canonical Namenaa.600a0b80001111550000f35b93e19350` from the host `192.168.0.133`:

```
PowerCLI C:\> Get-VMHost -Name 192.168.0.133 | Get-ScsiLun |
>> Where-Object {$_.CanonicalName -eq
'naa.600a0b80001111550000f35b93e19350'} |
>> Get-ScsiLunPath

Name         SanID                              State      Preferred
----         -----                              -----      ---------
fc.5001...   50:01:43:81:09:CF:CD:40            Standby    False
fc.5001...   50:01:43:81:09:CF:CD:24            Active     False
fc.5001...   50:01:43:81:09:CF:CD:44            Standby    False
fc.5001...   50:01:43:81:09:CF:CD:20            Standby    False
```

Modifying vmhba paths to an SCSI device

You can use the `Set-ScsiLunPath` cmdlet to enable or disable a vmhba path and to set the preferred path. The syntax of the `Set-ScsiLunPath` cmdlet is as follows:

```
Set-ScsiLunPath [[-Active] [<Boolean>]] [-ScsiLunPath] <ScsiLunPath[]>
[-Preferred] [-WhatIf] [-Confirm] [<CommonParameters>]
```

The `-ScsiLunPath` parameter is required.

In the following example, we will set the vmhba path with `SanId` `50:01:43:81:09:CF:CD:40` to `Active` and `Preferred`:

```
PowerCLI C:\> Get-VMHost -Name 192.168.0.133 | Get-ScsiLun |
>> Where-Object {$_.CanonicalName -eq
'naa.600a0b80001111550000f35b93e19350'} |
>> Get-ScsiLunPath |
>> Where-Object {$_.SanId -eq '50:01:43:81:09:CF:CD:40'} |
>> Set-ScsiLunPath -Active:$true -Preferred

Name         SanID                              State      Preferred
----         -----                              -----      ---------
fc.5001...   50:01:43:81:09:CF:CD:40            Active     True
```

If you give the `-Active` parameter the value `$false`, you will disable the vmhba path:

```
PowerCLI C:\> Get-VMHost -Name 192.168.0.133 | Get-ScsiLun |
>> Where-Object {$_.CanonicalName -eq
'naa.600a0b80001111550000f35b93e19350'} |
>> Get-ScsiLunPath |
>> Where-Object {$_.SanId -eq '50:01:43:81:09:CF:CD:24'} |
```

```
>> Set-ScsiLunPath -Active:$false
```

Name	SanID	State	Preferred
----	-----	-----	---------
fc.5001...	50:01:43:81:09:CF:CD:24	Disabled	True

Working with Raw Device Mappings

A **Raw Device Mapping** (**RDM**) is a storage device that is presented directly to a virtual machine. RDMs are available in two compatibility modes: physical and virtual. The most important difference is that virtual compatibility mode RDMs can be a part of a VMware vSphere snapshot. Snapshots of a physical compatibility mode RDM can only be taken on the storage array.

There are some use cases for RDMs. The most common use case is the quorum disk in a Microsoft Windows cluster. A quorum disk must be in physical compatibility mode.

 For more information about using Microsoft Windows Clusters on VMware vSphere, you should read the *Setup for Failover Clustering and Microsoft Cluster Service* guide. You can find this guide on `https://www.vmware.com/support/pubs/`. VMware Knowledge base article 1037959: *Guidelines for Microsoft Clustering on vSphere* can be found at `http://kb.vmware.com/kb/1037959`.

To add RDM to a virtual machine, you can use the `New-Harddisk` cmdlet. You have already seen the syntax of this cmdlet in `Chapter 5`, *Managing Virtual Machines with PowerCLI*. The value of the `-DiskType` parameter specifies what type of disk it will be. The valid values are:

- `rawVirtual`
- `rawPhysical`
- `flat`
- `unknown`

You also need to specify a value for the `New-Harddisk -DeviceName` parameter. You can retrieve the device name with the `Get-ScsiLun` cmdlet. In the following example, we will retrieve all the LUNs of host `192.168.0.133` and display the `CanonicalName` and `ConsoleDeviceName` properties:

```
PowerCLI C:\> Get-VMHost -Name 192.168.0.133 | Get-ScsiLun |
>> Select-Object -Property CanonicalName,ConsoleDeviceName
```

```
CanonicalName    ConsoleDeviceName
-------------    -----------------
naa.50014381...  /vmfs/devices/genscsi/naa.5001438109cfcd00
naa.600a0b80...  /vmfs/devices/disks/
                 naa.600a0b80001111550000b6182ca14450
naa.600a0b80...  /vmfs/devices/disks/
                 naa.600a0b80001111550000f35b93e19350
naa.600a0b80...  /vmfs/devices/disks/
                 naa.600a0b80001111550000a8adc7e19350
naa.600a0b80...  /vmfs/devices/disks/
                 naa.600a0b80001111550000893247e29350
naa.600a0b80...  /vmfs/devices/disks/
                 naa.600a0b80001111550000d2c418e29350
```

In the following example, we will add a physical RDM to virtual machine VM2:

```
PowerCLI C:\> New-HardDisk -VM VM2 -DiskType RawPhysical
-DeviceName /vmfs/devices/disks/naa.600a0b80001111550000893247e29350

CapacityGB Persistence          Filename
---------- -----------          --------
500.000    IndependentPersis... [Cluster01_Vmfs01] VM2/VM2_1.vmdk
```

Configuring storage I/O control

Storage I/O Control (**SIOC**) is a feature of VMware vSphere Enterprise Plus that provides I/O prioritization of virtual machines running on a group of VMware vSphere hosts that have access to the same datastore. If the latencies of a datastore come above a certain threshold, Storage I/O Control will throttle the I/O bandwidth of the virtual machines that use this datastore according to their respective share value. The default value for the latency threshold is 30 milliseconds. You are better keeping this default value unless you have a good reason to change it. One good reason can be the use of SSDs where a latency threshold of 10-15 milliseconds is recommended.

You can enable or disable Storage I/O Control using the Set-Datastore cmdlet – StorageIOControlEnabled parameter. You can also specify a value for the threshold with the -CongestionThresholdMillisecond parameter. The syntax of the Set-datastore cmdlet is as follows. The first parameter set is for updating the datastore:

```
Set-Datastore [-Datastore] <Datastore[]> [[-Name] <String>]
[-CongestionThresholdMillisecond <Int32>] [-StorageIOControlEnabled
[<Boolean>]] [-Server <VIServer[]>] [-WhatIf] [-Confirm]
[<CommonParameters>]
```

The second parameter set is for enabling and disabling maintenance mode:

```
Set-Datastore [-Datastore] <Datastore[]> -MaintenanceMode [<Boolean>]
[-EvacuateAutomatically] [-RunAsync] [-Server <VIServer[]>] [-WhatIf]
[-Confirm] [<CommonParameters>]
```

The -Datastore and -MaintenanceMode parameters are required.

In the following example, we will enable Storage I/O Control for datastore Cluster01_Vmfs01:

```
PowerCLI C:\> Set-Datastore -Datastore Cluster01_Vmfs01
-StorageIOControlEnabled:$true
```

```
Name                                     FreeSpaceGB          CapacityGB
----                                     -----------          ----------
Cluster01_Vmfs01                             248.801             249.750
```

If you want to enable Storage I/O Control for all of your datastores that don't have Storage I/O Control enabled yet, you can use the following command:

```
PowerCLI C:\> Get-Datastore |
>> Where-Object {-not $_.StorageIOControlEnabled} |
>> Set-Datastore -StorageIOControlEnabled:$true
```

To disable Storage I/O Control for datastore Cluster01_Vmfs01,we have to give the -StorageIOControlEnabled parameter the value $false:

```
PowerCLI C:\> Set-Datastore -Datastore Cluster01_Vmfs01
-StorageIOControlEnabled:$false
```

```
Name                                     FreeSpaceGB          CapacityGB
----                                     -----------          ----------
Cluster01_Vmfs01                             248.801             249.750
```

Retrieving Storage I/O Control settings

StorageIOControlEnabled and CongestionThresholdMillisecond are properties of the NasDatastoreImpl and VmfsDatastoreImpl objects returned by the Get-Datastore cmdlet. It is easy to retrieve these properties by piping the output of the Get-Datastore cmdlet to the Select-Object cmdlet, as you can see in the following example:

```
PowerCLI C:\> Get-Datastore |
>> Select-Object -Property Name,StorageIOControlEnabled,
>> CongestionThresholdMillisecond
```

Name	StorageIOControlEnabled	CongestionThresholdMillisec
Cluster01_Nfs01	True	30
Cluster01_Vmfs01	False	30
Cluster01_iSCSI01	True	30

Configuring Storage DRS

vSphere Storage Distributed Resource Scheduler is a VMware vSphere Enterprise Plus feature first introduced in vSphere 5.0. It gives you the possibility to combine datastores in a datastore cluster. You can then manage the datastore cluster instead of the individual datastores. When you create a new virtual machine and put the disks on a datastore cluster, Storage DRS will place the disks on the optimal datastore based on utilized disk space and datastore performance. Storage DRS can also migrate disks to another datastore in the same datastore cluster when the utilized disk space or latency of a datastore becomes too high. You can also make **affinity rules** to separate disks and virtual machines over multiple datastores or keep them together on the same datastore. If you put a datastore in **Datastore Maintenance Mode**, Storage DRS will move all the disks on this datastore to other datastores in the same datastore cluster.

The first thing that you have to do, if you want to use Storage DRS, is to create one or more datastore clusters. If you have multiple types of datastores, such as gold, silver, and bronze, you might want to create a datastore cluster for each type.

Creating a datastore cluster

You can create a datastore cluster with the `New-DatastoreCluster` cmdlet. This cmdlet has the following syntax:

```
New-DatastoreCluster [-Name] <String> -Location <VIContainer>
[-Server <VIServer[]>] [-WhatIf] [-Confirm] [<CommonParameters>]
```

The `New-DatastoreCluster` cmdlet has two required parameters: `-Name` and `-Location`. The value of the `-Location` parameter must be a data center or a folder. The following command will create a new datastore cluster named `Gold-Datastore-Cluster` in data center `New York`:

```
PowerCLI C:\> New-DatastoreCluster -Name Gold-Datastore-Cluster
-Location (Get-Datacenter -Name 'New York')
```

Name	CapacityGB	FreeSpaceGB	SdrsAutomationLevel
Gold-Datastore-Cluster	0.000	0.000	Disabled

Retrieving datastore clusters

The `Get-DatastoreCluster` cmdlet will retrieve all of your datastore clusters or one or more specific datastore clusters. The syntax of the `Get-DatastoreCluster` cmdlet is as follows. The first parameter set is the default.

```
Get-DatastoreCluster [-Id <String[]>] [[-Name] <String[]>]
[-Location <VIContainer[]>] [-VM <VirtualMachine[]>] [-Template
<Template[]>] [-Datastore <Datastore[]>] [-Tag <Tag[]>] [-Server
<VIServer[]>] [<CommonParameters>]
```

The second parameter set is for retrieving datastore clusters by related object:

```
Get-DatastoreCluster [-RelatedObject]
<DatastoreClusterRelatedObjectBase[]> [<CommonParameters>]
```

If you don't specify a parameter, the `New-DatastoreCluster` cmdlet will retrieve all of your datastore clusters. You can use one of the parameters to retrieve datastore clusters based on ID, name, location, virtual machines, templates, datastores, tags, vCenter server, or related object. In the following example, we will retrieve all of our datastore clusters:

```
PowerCLI C:\> Get-DatastoreCluster
```

Name	CapacityGB	FreeSpaceGB	SdrsAutomationLevel
Gold-Datastore-Cluster	0.000	0.000	Disabled

Modifying datastore clusters

After creating a datastore cluster, Storage DRS is disabled. To enable Storage DRS, you have to use the `Set-DatastoreCluster` cmdlet. The syntax of this cmdlet is as follows.

```
Set-DatastoreCluster -DatastoreCluster <DatastoreCluster[]>
[-IOLatencyThresholdMillisecond <Int32>] [-IOLoadBalanceEnabled
[<Boolean>]] [-Name <String>] [-SdrsAutomationLevel
<DrsAutomationLevel>] [-SpaceUtilizationThresholdPercent <Int32>]
[-Server <VIServer[]>] [-WhatIf] [-Confirm] [<CommonParameters>]
```

The `-DatastoreCluster` parameter is required.

To enable Storage DRS, you have to use the -SdrsAutomationLevel parameter. This parameter has three possible values:

- Disabled
- Manual
- FullyAutomated

If you use Manual, Storage DRS will give you recommendations for placement of disks on datastores. You will have to apply the recommendations to move the disks. If you choose FullyAutomated, Storage DRS will automatically move disks if the utilized disk space or latency of a datastore becomes too high.

> If you want to enable load balancing based on I/O metrics, you have to use the -IOLoadBalanceEnabled parameter and pass it the value $true.

In the following example, we will enable Storage DRS and set the automation level to FullyAutomated for the Gold-Datastore-Cluster. We will also enable load balancing based on I/O metrics:

```
PowerCLI C:\> Set-DatastoreCluster -DatastoreCluster
Gold-Datastore-Cluster -SdrsAutomationLevel FullyAutomated
-IOLoadBalanceEnabled:$true
```

Name	CapacityGB	FreeSpaceGB	SdrsAutomationLevel
Gold-Datastore-Cluster	0.000	0.000	FullyAutomated

In the following screenshot of the vSphere Web Client, you will see datastore cluster Gold-datastore-Cluster after executing the preceding command:

Adding datastores to a datastore cluster

The `Move-Datastore` cmdlet will move datastores into a datastore cluster or to a folder or data center. The syntax of the `Move-Datastore` cmdlet is:

```
Move-Datastore [-Datastore] <Datastore[]> [-Destination]
<VIObject> [-Server <VIServer[]>] [-WhatIf] [-Confirm]
[<CommonParameters>]
```

The `-Datastore` and `-Destination` parameters are required.

In the following example, we will move the `Cluster01_Vmfs01` datastore into datastore cluster `Gold-Datastore-Cluster`:

```
PowerCLI C:\> Move-Datastore -Datastore Cluster01_Vmfs01
-Destination (Get-DatastoreCluster -Name Gold-Datastore-Cluster)

Name                             FreeSpaceGB     CapacityGB
----                             -----------     ----------
Cluster01_Vmfs01                     248.801        249.750
```

In the following screenshot of the vSphere Web Client, you will see datastore `Cluster01_Vmfs01` after being moved into datastore cluster `Gold-Datastore-Cluster`:

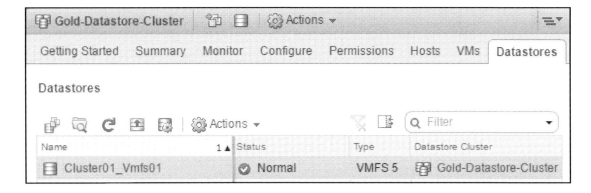

Retrieving the datastores in a datastore cluster

If you want to know which datastores are in a datastore cluster, you can use the `Get-Datastore -Location` parameter. In the following example, we will retrieve all of the datastores in the `Gold-Datastore-Cluster` datastore cluster:

```
PowerCLI C:\> Get-Datastore -Location (Get-DatastoreCluster
-Name Gold-Datastore-Cluster)
Name                            FreeSpaceGB        CapacityGB
----                            -----------        ----------
Cluster01_Vmfs01                    248.801           249.750
```

Removing datastores from a datastore cluster

To remove a datastore from a datastore cluster, you have to move the datastore to a folder or a data center. In the following example, we will move the `Cluster01_Vmfs01` datastore from the `Gold-Datastore-Cluster` datastore cluster to the `New York` data center:

```
PowerCLI C:\> Move-Datastore -Datastore Cluster01_Vmfs01
-Destination (Get-Datacenter -Name 'New York')
Name                            FreeSpaceGB        CapacityGB
----                            -----------        ----------
Cluster01_Vmfs01                    248.801           249.750
```

To check whether the `Cluster_Vmfs01` datastore was removed from the datastore cluster, we can use the `Get-Datastore` cmdlet again, as in the following example.

```
PowerCLI C:\> Get-Datastore -Location (Get-DatastoreCluster
-Name Gold-Datastore-Cluster)
PowerCLI C:\>
```

The command shows no output, so the `Gold-Datastore-Cluster` datastore cluster does not contain any datastores anymore.

Removing datastore clusters

To remove a datastore cluster, you can use the `Remove-DatastoreCluster` cmdlet. The syntax of this cmdlet is as follows:

```
Remove-DatastoreCluster [-DatastoreCluster] <DatastoreCluster[]>
[-Server <VIServer[]>] [-WhatIf] [-Confirm] [<CommonParameters>]
```

The `-DatastoreCluster` parameter is required.

In the following example, we will remove the `Gold-Datastore-Cluster` datastore cluster:

```
PowerCLI C:\> Remove-DatastoreCluster -DatastoreCluster
Gold-datastore-Cluster -Confirm:$false
```

The preceding command does not return any output.

Upgrading datastores to VMFS-5

With vSphere 5, VMware upgraded the VMFS file system to version 5. VMFS-5 came with the following new features:

- Unified 1 MB file block size
- Large single extent volumes of 64 TB
- Smaller 8 KB sub-block
- Small file support
- Increased file count limit greater than 120,000
- **VMware vSphere Storage APIs for Array Integration** (**VAAI**)
- Primitive **Atomic Test & Set** (**ATS**)
- Enhancement for file locking
- **GUID Partition Table** (**GPT**)
- A new starting sector of 2048

If you upgraded your vSphere environment from version 4 or earlier to version 5 or 6, your datastores are probably still on VMFS-3. There are two options for going to VMFS-5. The first option is to create new VMFS-5 datastores and move your virtual machines to the new datastores. When your old VMFS-3 datastores are empty, you can remove them. The advantage of this method is that the new datastores will have all of the new VMFS-5 features. However, it is a lot of work, and you need enough free space on your storage system to create at least one new datastore.

The second option is to upgrade your datastores to VMFS-5. Upgrading your datastores can be done online without downtime for your virtual machines. However, upgraded datastores will not have all of the new features. Upgraded datastores will keep the block size they had before the upgrade, still have the old Sub-Block Size of 64 KB, keep the file limit of 30,720, continue to use the **Master Boot Record** (**MBR**) partition type, and start on sector 128.

You can retrieve the VMFS version of your datastores with the following command:

```
PowerCLI C:\> Get-Datastore |
>> Where-Object {$_.GetType().Name -eq 'VmfsDatastoreImpl'} |
>> Select-Object -Property Name,FileSystemVersion

Name                                          FileSystemVersion
----                                          -----------------
Cluster01_Vmfs01                              5.81
```

In the following screenshot of the vSphere Web Client, you will see datastoreCluster01_Vmfs00 with file system version **VMFS 3.58** before being upgraded to VMFS-5:

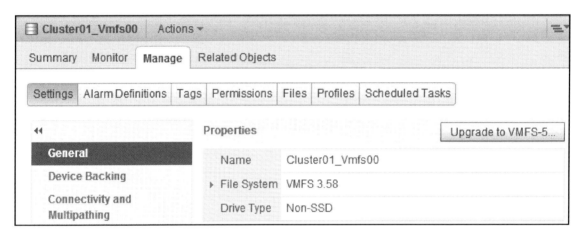

If you want to upgrade your datastores to VMFS-5, you can use the following PowerCLI script to upgrade all of your datastores. The script uses the `Get-Datastore` cmdlet to retrieve all of your datastores:

```
Get-Datastore |
```

Then, it uses the `Where-Object` cmdlet in the pipeline to filter for VMFS datastores that have a lower version than 5:

```
Where-Object {$_.GetType().Name -eq 'VmfsDatastoreImpl'
-and $_.FileSystemVersion -lt 5} |
```

The `ForEach-Object` cmdlet is used to process all of the datastores that are found:

```
ForEach-Object {
  $Datastore = $_
```

Then, the script retrieves the `HostStorageSystem` object of a host connected to the datastore:

```
$HostStorageSystem = $Datastore |
  Get-VMHost | Select-Object -First 1 |
  Get-VMHostStorage | Get-View
```

The script constructs the path to the volume to upgrade. We have the following example,

`/vmfs/volumes/4e97fa06-7fa61558-937e-984be163eb88`:

```
$Volume = '/' + $Datastore.ExtensionData.Info.Url.TrimStart
('ds:/').TrimEnd('/')
```

The `UpgradeVmfs()` method of the `HostStorageSystem` object is used to upgrade the datastore:

```
$HostStorageSystem.UpgradeVmfs($Volume)
}
```

Removing datastores

To remove a datastore, you can use the `Remove-Datastore` cmdlet. The syntax of this cmdlet is:

```
Remove-Datastore [-Datastore] <Datastore[]> [-VMHost] <VMHost>
[-Server <VIServer[]>] [-RunAsync] [-WhatIf] [-Confirm]
[<CommonParameters>]
```

The required parameters of the `Remove-Datastore` cmdlet are `-Datastore` and `-VMHost`.

In the following example, we will remove the `Cluster01_Vmfs01` datastore we created in the section, *Creating VMFS datastores*:

```
PowerCLI C:\> Remove-Datastore -Datastore Cluster01_Vmfs01
-VMHost 192.168.0.133 -Confirm:$false
```

The preceding command does not return any output.

If you try to remove a datastore, it is possible that you get an error message similar to:

```
Remove-Datastore : 1/31/2017 2:05:48 PM    Remove-Datastore
The resource 'Cluster01_Vmfs01' is in use.
```

Before you can remove a datastore, there are some requirements that must be fulfilled:

- There must be no virtual machines residing on the datastore
- The datastore must not be a part of a datastore cluster
- The datastore must not be managed by Storage DRS
- Storage I/O Control must be disabled for the datastore
- The datastore must not be used for vSphere HA heartbeat

After fulfilling all of these requirements, you will not get the **The resource is in use** error anymore when you remove a datastore.

We have not discussed the use of datastores for vSphere HA heartbeat yet. We will do this in `Chapter 8`, *Managing High Availability and Clustering*.

Using VMware vSAN

VMware vSAN is a shared storage solution for **Hyper-Converged Infrastructure (HCI)** that uses local disks in ESXi servers as the media. A vSAN cluster consists of two or more ESXi hosts. Although two hosts is the minimum number required, VMware recommends using at least four hosts in a vSAN cluster. The local disks in an ESXi server can be combined into disk groups that can be all-flash or a combination of magnetic disks and flash devices, also named **solid state drives** or SSDs. There can be a maximum of seven disks per disk group. There is also a maximum of five disk groups on a host. At least one disk in a disk group must be SSD. SSDs will be used for read-and-write cache. Magnetic disks will be used for capacity storage. In an all-flash disk group, the SSDs in the cache tier are only used for write caching. The disk groups in a cluster are combined into a vSAN datastore named `vsanDatastore`. Also, hosts without a disk group can participate in a vSAN cluster. For vSAN communication between the hosts, each host must have a VMkernel network adapter with **VMware vSAN Traffic** enabled.

 A VMware vSAN cluster can scale to 62 TB VMDK disks, 64 ESXi hosts, 35 capacity devices per host, and 200 virtual machines per host.

Configuring VMware vSAN networking

To enable vSAN communication between the hosts in a vSAN-enabled cluster, we have to enable VMware vSAN Traffic on a VMkernel network adapter on each host in the cluster.

VMware vSAN requires at least a 1 GbE network connection; however, VMware recommends having a dedicated 10 GbE network for VMware vSAN.

Because I only want to use vSAN in my laboratory environment, I will enable VMware vSAN Traffic on the vmk0 VMKernel port that is also used for Management Traffic and vMotion traffic.

In the following example, we will enable VMware vSAN Traffic on the VMKernel port vmk0 of host 192.168.0.133:

```
PowerCLI C:\> Get-VMHost -Name 192.168.0.133 |
Get-VMHostNetworkAdapter -Name vmk0 | Set-VMHostNetworkAdapter
-VsanTrafficEnabled:$true -Confirm:$false

Name        Mac                  DhcpEnabled IP               SubnetMask
----        ---                  ----------- --               ----------
vmk0        00:0c:29:23:ab:67 False          192.168.0.133 255.255.255.0
```

In the following command, VMware vSAN Traffic will be enabled on the VMKernel port vmk0 of host 192.168.0.134:

```
PowerCLI C:\> Get-VMHost -Name 192.168.0.134 |
Get-VMHostNetworkAdapter -Name vmk0 | Set-VMHostNetworkAdapter
-VsanTrafficEnabled:$true -Confirm:$false

Name        Mac                  DhcpEnabled IP               SubnetMask
----        ---                  ----------- --               ----------
vmk0        00:0c:29:d1:89:eb False          192.168.0.134 255.255.255.0
```

Enabling VMware vSAN on vSphere clusters

vSAN must be enabled on vSphere clusters using the Set-Cluster cmdlet. You will see the syntax of the Set-Cluster cmdlet in Chapter 8, *Managing High Availability and Clustering*. After enabling vSAN on a cluster, all of the hosts in the cluster can use vSAN. The Set-Cluster -VsanEnabled parameter needs to get the value $true to enable vSAN on a cluster. The parameter -VsanDiskClaimMode can have the values Automatic or Manual. If the value is Automatic, vSAN claims every empty disk on the hosts. If the value is Manual, the administrator needs to claim disks on the hosts to the vSAN storage.

In the following PowerCLI command, we will enable vSAN on the cluster `Cluster01` and set the vSAN disk claim mode to `Manual`:

```
PowerCLI C:\> Set-Cluster -Cluster Cluster01 -VsanEnabled:$true
-VsanDiskClaimMode Manual -Confirm:$false

Name        HAEnabled  HAFailoverLevel DrsEnabled DrsAutomationLevel
----        ---------  --------------- ---------- ------------------
Cluster01   False      1               False      FullyAutomated
```

After enabling VMware vSAN on a vSphere cluster, you will have a datastore named `vsanDatastore`. Initially, this datastore will have a size of `0.000` GB, as you can see in the output of the following example:

```
PowerCLI C:\> Get-Datastore -Name vsanDatastore

Name                          FreeSpaceGB     CapacityGB
----                          -----------     ----------
vsanDatastore                       0.000          0.000
```

After creating vSAN disk groups on at least two ESXi hosts in a vSAN cluster, the `vsanDatastore` datastore will grow.

Retrieving the devices available for VMware vSAN

Because we choose `Manual` as the vSAN disk claim mode for our cluster, we have to create VMware vSAN disk groups ourselves. First, we need to find the canonical names of the disk devices we want to use for our VMware vSAN disk groups. We will use the `Get-ScsiLun` cmdlet to retrieve the disk devices. The output of the `Get-ScsiLun` cmdlet will be piped to the `Select-Object` cmdlet, to select only the `CanonicalName`, and the `CapacityGB` properties. In the following example, we will retrieve the canonical name of the disk devices for host `192.168.0.133`:

```
PowerCLI C:\> Get-VMHost -Name 192.168.0.133 | Get-ScsiLun |
>> Select-Object -Property CanonicalName,CapacityGB

CanonicalName                                               CapacityGB
-------------                                               ----------
mpx.vmhba1:C0:T2:L0                                                 20
mpx.vmhba1:C0:T1:L0                                                  4
mpx.vmhba1:C0:T0:L0                                                 40
mpx.vmhba32:C0:T0:L0
mpx.vmhba1:C0:T3:L0                                                 20
```

I have created the 4 GB disk with `Canonical Namempx.vmhba1:C0:T1:L0`for caching and the 20 GB disks with `CanonicalNames, mpx.vmhba1:C0:T2:L0`, and `mpx.vmhba1:C0:T3:L0` as the capacity devices. These disk sizes are too small for production usage, but sufficient for demonstrating how to create vSAN disk groups.

Creating VMware vSAN disk groups

Disks groups are groups of local storage that an ESXi host provides to vSAN. A disk group must contain one (**solid state disk (SSD)**) for caching and up to six disk drives for capacity. At least two hosts in the cluster must provide disk groups to the cluster.

The `New-VsanDiskGroup` cmdlet can be used to create disk groups. The syntax of this cmdlet is as follows:

```
New-VsanDiskGroup -VMHost <VMHost> -SsdCanonicalName <String>
-DataDiskCanonicalName <String[]> [-Server <VIServer[]>] [-RunAsync]
[-WhatIf] [-Confirm] [<CommonParameters>]
```

The `-VMHost`, `-SsdCanonicalName`, and `-DataDiskCanonicalName` parameters are required.

In the following example, we will create a disk group for host `192.168.0.133` with device with canonical name `mpx.vmhba1:C0:T1:L0` as the caching device and device with canonical name `mpx.vmhba1:C0:T2:L0` as the capacity device:

```
PowerCLI C:\> New-VsanDiskGroup -VMHost 192.168.0.133
-SsdCanonicalName mpx.vmhba1:C0:T1:L0 -DataDiskCanonicalName
mpx.vmhba1:C0:T2:L0

Name                                              VMHost
----                                              ------
Disk group (0000000000766d686261313a313a30)      192.168.0.133
```

Retrieving VMware vSAN disk groups

The `Get-VsanDiskGroup` cmdlet can be used to retrieve VMware vSAN disk groups. The syntax of this cmdlet is as follows.

The first parameter set is the default:

```
Get-VsanDiskGroup [-Cluster <Cluster[]>] [[-Name]
<String[]>] [-Server <VIServer[]>] [<CommonParameters>]
```

The second parameter set is for retrieving disk groups by ID:

```
Get-VsanDiskGroup -Id <String[]> [-Server <VIServer[]>]
[<CommonParameters>]
```

The third parameter set is for retrieving disk groups by the ESXi host:

```
Get-VsanDiskGroup [-DiskCanonicalName <String[]>]
-VMHost <VMHost[]> [-Server <VIServer[]>] [<CommonParameters>]
```

The `-Id` and `-VMHost` parameters are required.

In the following example, we will retrieve all the VMware vSAN disk groups we have created so far:

```
PowerCLI C:\> Get-VsanDiskGroup

Name                                            VMHost
----                                            ------
Disk group (0000000000766d686261313a313a30)    192.168.0.133
```

Adding a host SCSI disk to a VMware vSAN disk group

You can use the `New-VsanDisk` cmdlet to add a disk device to a vSAN disk group. The syntax of the `New-VsanDisk` cmdlet is as follows:

```
New-VsanDisk -VsanDiskGroup <VsanDiskGroup> -CanonicalName
<String> [-RunAsync] [-WhatIf] [-Confirm] [<CommonParameters>]
```

The `-VsanDiskGroup` and `-CanonicalName` parameters are required.

In the following example, we will add a new capacity disk with the canonical name `mpx.vmhba1:C0:T3:L0` to the disk group we created in the preceding examples:

```
PowerCLI C:\> Get-VsanDiskGroup -VMHost 192.168.0.133 |
New-VsanDisk -CanonicalName mpx.vmhba1:C0:T3:L0

CanonicalName        DevicePath                                  IsSsd
-------------        ----------                                  -----
mpx.vmhba1:C0:T3:L0  /vmfs/devices/disks/mpx.vmhba1:C0:T3:L0     False
```

Retrieving the host disks that belong to a VMware vSAN disk group

The `Get-VsanDisk` cmdlet can be used to retrieve the disks in a vSAN disk group. The syntax of this cmdlet is as follows. The first parameter set is the default:

```
Get-VsanDisk [-Server <VIServer[]>] [-VsanDiskGroup
<VsanDiskGroup[]>] [[-CanonicalName] <String[]>]
[<CommonParameters>]
```

The second parameter set is for retrieving hosts disks by hosts:

```
Get-VsanDisk [-Server <VIServer[]>] [-CanonicalName <String[]>]
-VMHost <VMHost[]> [<CommonParameters>]
```

The third parameter set is for retrieving hosts disks by ID:

```
Get-VsanDisk [-Server <VIServer[]>] -Id <String[]>
[<CommonParameters>]
```

The `-VMHost` and `-Id` parameters are required.

In the following example, we will retrieve the disks in the vSAN disk group of host `192.168.0.133`:

```
PowerCLI C:\> Get-VsanDiskGroup -VMHost 192.168.0.133 | Get-VsanDisk

CanonicalName          DevicePath                                IsSsd
-------------          ----------                                -----
mpx.vmhba1:C0:T1:L0    /vmfs/devices/disks/mpx.vmhba1:C0:T1:L0   True
mpx.vmhba1:C0:T2:L0    /vmfs/devices/disks/mpx.vmhba1:C0:T2:L0   False
mpx.vmhba1:C0:T3:L0    /vmfs/devices/disks/mpx.vmhba1:C0:T3:L0   False
```

Removing disks from a VMware vSAN disk group

To remove a disk from a vSAN disk group, you can use the `Remove-VsanDisk` cmdlet that has the following syntax:

```
Remove-VsanDisk [-VsanDisk] <VsanDisk[]> [-RunAsync]
[-WhatIf][-Confirm] [<CommonParameters>]
```

The `-VsanDisk` parameter is required.

To remove the disk with canonical name `mpx.vmhba1:C0:T3:L0` from the vSAN disk group of host `192.168.0.133`, you will have to use the following command:

```
PowerCLI C:\> Get-VsanDiskGroup -VMHost 192.168.0.133 |
>> Get-VsanDisk -CanonicalName mpx.vmhba1:C0:T3:L0 |
>> Remove-VsanDisk -Confirm:$false
```

The preceding command does not return any output.

Removing VMware vSAN disk groups

If you want to remove a vSAN disk group, for example, because you want to remove an ESXi host from a vSAN cluster, you can use the `Remove-VsanDiskGroup` cmdlet. The syntax of this cmdlet is as follows:

```
Remove-VsanDiskGroup [-VsanDiskGroup] <VsanDiskGroup[]>
[-RunAsync] [-WhatIf] [-Confirm] [<CommonParameters>]
```

The `-VsanDiskGroup` parameter is required.

In the following example, we will remove the vSAN disk group of host `192.168.0.133`:

```
PowerCLI C:\> Get-VsanDiskGroup -VMHost 192.168.0.133 |
>> Remove-VsanDiskGroup -Confirm:$false
```

The preceding command does not return any output.

Using vSphere storage policy-based management

Storage policy-based management (**SPBM**) is the control plane of VMware's management layer for **Software-Defined Storage** (**SDS**). SPBM can use the **vSphere Storage APIs for Storage Awareness** (**VASA**) providers to expose storage topologies, capabilities, and state information to vCenter Server. You can also manually define storage capabilities by using tags. For example, you can create tags for replicated and nonreplicated storage. These tags will be assigned to datastores. From the capabilities or tags, you can create SPBM rules, rule sets, and storage policies. These storage policies can be used to create virtual machines on storage that is compliant with a certain storage policy. Storage policies can be exported to XML files, which can be imported later.

All the SPBM-related cmdlets will only work with vCenter Server 5.5 or higher.

Retrieving storage capabilities

If your storage has a VASA provider, you can use the `Get-SpbmCapability` cmdlet to retrieve the capabilities of your storage system. This cmdlet has the following syntax:

```
Get-SpbmCapability [[-Name] <String[]>] [-Category <String[]>]
[-Server <VIServer[]>] [<CommonParameters>]
```

The `Get-SpbmCapability` cmdlet has no required parameters. You can use the `-Name` parameter to filter for specific names. You can use the `-Category` parameter to filter for specific categories. In the following example, we will retrieve all the storage capabilities and display the `Name`, `Category`, `DefaultValue`, and `ValueType` properties:

```
PowerCLI C:\> Get-SpbmCapability | Select-Object
-Property Name,Category,DefaultValue,ValueType

Name                          Category      DefaultValue ValueType
----                          --------      ------------ ---------
VSAN.cacheReservation         Performance             0 System.Int32
VSAN.checksumDisabled         Availability        False System.Boolean
VSAN.forceProvisioning        Placement           False System.Boolean
VSAN.hostFailuresToTolerate Availability            1 System.Int32
VSAN.proportionalCapacity     Space                   0 System.Int32
VSAN.replicaPreference        Availability RAID-1 (M... System.String
VSAN.stripeWidth              Performance             1 System.Int32
```

As you can see in the output of the preceding example, the vSAN VASA provider has seven capabilities. If you want to know more about the meaning of the capabilities, each capability has the `FriendlyName` and `Description` property that gives you more information. In the following example, we will retrieve the `Name`, `FriendlyName`, and `Description` property of the `VSAN.hostFailuresToTolerate` capability. We will display the output in a list format:

```
PowerCLI C:\> Get-SpbmCapability -Name VSAN.hostFailuresToTolerate |
>> Select-Object -Property Name,FriendlyName,Description | Format-List

Name         : VSAN.hostFailuresToTolerate
FriendlyName : Number of failures to tolerate
Description  : Defines the number of host, disk, or network
```

failures a storage object can tolerate. When the
fault tolerance method is mirroring: to tolerate "n"
failures, "n+1" copies of the object are created and
"2n+1" hosts contributing storage are required (if
fault domains are configured, "2n+1" fault domains
with hosts contributing storage are required). When
the fault tolerance method is erasure coding: to
tolerate 1 failure, 4 hosts (or fault domains) are
required; and to tolerate 2 failures, 6 hosts (or
fault domains) are required. Note: A host which is
not part of a fault domain is counted as its own
single-host fault domain. Default value: 1, Maximum
value: 3.

Using tags to define storage capabilities

If your storage system does not have a VASA provider, you can use tags to manually assign
storage capabilities to datastores. You will probably have different storage tiers, such as
replicated and nonreplicated datastores or datastores with flash drives, SATA drives, or
SAS drives. You define tags for each storage tier. For example, you can create a tag named
Gold and assign it to the replicated datastores storage tier. You can create a tag named
Silver and assign it to the nonreplicated datastores storage tier. In the following example,
we will first create a tag category named StorageType for the Datastore entity type. We
will give this tag category the cardinality Single, so you can only assign one tag from the
StorageType tag category to a datastore:

```
PowerCLI C:\> New-TagCategory -Name StorageType -Description
'Type of storage' -EntityType Datastore -Cardinality Single

Name                                    Cardinality Description
----                                    ----------- -----------
StorageType                             Single      Type of storage
```

Next, we will create a tag named Gold in the StorageType tag category:

```
PowerCLI C:\> New-Tag -Name Gold -Description 'Gold storage'
-Category StorageType

Name                    Category                Description
----                    --------                -----------
Gold                    StorageType             Gold storage
```

Finally, we will assign the `Gold` tag to datastore `datastore1`:

```
PowerCLI C:\> Get-Datastore -Name datastore1 | New-TagAssignment
-Tag Gold

Tag                                    Entity
---                                    ------
StorageType/Gold                       datastore1
```

Creating SPBM rules

We can use storage capabilities retrieved by a **VASA** provider, or we can use tags to create SPBM rules. If you use storage capabilities, you can create a rule based on a capability and value. You can also create a rule based on one or more tags. To create an SPBM rule, you can use the `New-SpbmRule` cmdlet. This cmdlet has two parameter sets. The first parameter set is for creating rules based on capabilities:

```
New-SpbmRule [-Capability] <SpbmCapability> [-Value] <Object>
[-Server <VIServer>] [-WhatIf] [-Confirm] [<CommonParameters>]
```

The second parameter set is for creating rules based on tags:

```
New-SpbmRule -AnyOfTags <Tag[]> [-Server <VIServer>] [-WhatIf]
[-Confirm] [<CommonParameters>]
```

The `-Capability`, `-Value`, and `-AnyOfTags` parameters are required:

In the first example, we will create an SPBM rule based on the `VSAN.hostFailuresToTolerate` capability and give it the value `2`. We will assign the rule to the variable `$CapabilityRule`:

```
PowerCLI C:\> $CapabilityRule = New-SpbmRule -Capability
VSAN.hostFailuresToTolerate -Value 2
PowerCLI C:\> $CapabilityRule

Capability                      Value          AnyOfTags
----------                      -----          ---------
VSAN.hostFailuresToTolerate     2
```

In the following example, we will create an SPBM rule based on the tag Gold and assign the rule to the variable $TagRule:

```
PowerCLI C:\> $TagRule = New-SpbmRule -AnyOfTags (Get-Tag -Name Gold)
PowerCLI C:\> $TagRule

Capability                      Value                 AnyOfTags
----------                      -----                 ---------

{StorageType/Gold}
```

Creating SPBM rule sets

You can combine SPBM rules into SPBM rule sets. A rule set will contain one or more rules. The New-SpbmRuleSet cmdlet will do this for you. The New-SpbmRuleSet cmdlet has the following syntax:

```
New-SpbmRuleSet [-AllOfRules] <SpbmRule[]> [-Name <String>]
[-WhatIf] [-Confirm] [<CommonParameters>]
```

The -AllOfRules parameter is required.

In the following example, we will create a new SPBM rule set named GoldRuleSet from the SPBM rule in the $TagRule variable created in the preceding example:

```
PowerCLI C:\> $RuleSet = New-SpbmRuleSet -Name GoldRuleSet
-AllOfRules $TagRule
PowerCLI C:\> $RuleSet

AllOfRules
----------
{Gold}
```

Creating SPBM storage policies

To create SPBM storages policies, we can use the New-SpbmStoragePolicy cmdlet. This cmdlet will combine one or more SPBM rule sets or rules into a storage policy. The New-SpbmStoragePolicy has the following syntax:

```
New-SpbmStoragePolicy [-Name] <String> [-Description <String>]
[-AnyOfRuleSets <SpbmRuleSet[]>] [-CommonRule <SpbmRule[]>]
[-Server <VIServer>] [-WhatIf] [-Confirm] [<CommonParameters>]
```

The `-Name` parameter is required. If you use the `-CommonRule` parameter, you can only use rules from the `VAIOFilter` namespace.

> **vSphere APIs for IO Filtering (VAIO)**, introduced in ESXi 6.0 Update 1, is a framework for filters created by VMware partners, which run in ESXi and can intercept any IO requests from a guest operating system to a virtual disk. Filters are installed as a **vSphere Installation Bundle (VIB)** on the ESXi server. In ESXi 6.0 Update 1, only filters for caching and replication are supported by VMware. You can use SPBM to create storage policies that use VAIO filters. For example, you can create a storage policy that applies a caching policy to virtual machines.
>
> PowerCLI has the following four cmdlets to install, retrieve, modify, and remove VAIO filters: `New-VAIOFilter`, `Get-VAIOFilter`, `Set-VAIOFilter`, and `Remove-VAIOFilter`. While writing this book, there are no VAIO filters available. Therefore, we will not discuss the PowerCLI VAIO cmdlets in detail.

The following example will create a storage policy named `GoldPolicy` from the rule set created in the preceding example:

```
PowerCLI C:\> New-SpbmStoragePolicy -Name GoldPolicy -Description
'Policy for Gold storage' -RuleSet $RuleSet

Name                    Description                     AnyOfRuleSets
----                    -----------                     -------------
GoldPolicy              Policy for Gold storage         {(Gold)}
```

Retrieving SPBM storage policies

The `Get-SpbmStoragePolicy` cmdlet can be used to retrieve SPBM storage policies. This cmdlet has the following syntax. The first parameter set is for retrieving storage policies by requirement, name, name space, capability, or tag:

```
Get-SpbmStoragePolicy [-Requirement] [-Resource] [[-Name]
<String[]>] [-Namespace <String[]>] [-Capability <SpbmCapability[]>]
[-Tag <Tag[]>] [-Server <VIServer[]>] [<CommonParameters>]
```

The second parameter set is for retrieving storage policies by ID:

```
Get-SpbmStoragePolicy [-Id <String[]>] [-Server <VIServer[]>]
[<CommonParameters>]
```

The `Get-SpbmStoragePolicy` cmdlet has no required parameters.

In the following example, we will retrieve a list of all of the SPBM storage policies:

```
PowerCLI C:\> Get-SpbmStoragePolicy

Name                    Description                     AnyOfRuleSets
----                    -----------                     -------------
Default-VirtualDisk                                     {(VSAN.hos...
VSANStorageCapabi...                                    {(VSAN.hos...
Default-VM-Home                                         {(VSAN.hos...
Virtual SAN Defau...    Storage policy used as default ... {(VSAN.hos...
VVol No Requireme...    Allow the datastore to determi...
GoldPolicy              Policy for Gold storage         {(Gold)}
VM Encryption Policy    Sample storage policy for VMwar... {(com....
```

As you can see in the output of the preceding example, besides the `GoldPolicy` storage policy that we created, there are also policies created by vSAN and a policy for **Virtual Volumes** (**VVols**).

VMware VVols is an integration and management framework for external storage. VVols enables VM-aware storage and storage policy-based management. VVols eliminates physical containers such as LUNs. With VVols a storage administrator creates a VVols datastore. vSphere administrators create virtual disk containers (VVols) that are specific to a virtual machine. VVols becomes the unit of data management at the storage array level. All of the major storage vendors support VVols. VVols are included in all editions of vSphere 6.0 and higher.

Modifying SPBM storage policies

You can use the `Set-SpbmStoragePolicy` cmdlet to override the current name, description, and rule sets of an existing storage policy. The syntax of the `Set-SpbmStoragePolicy` cmdlet is as follows:

```
Set-SpbmStoragePolicy -StoragePolicy <SpbmStoragePolicy[]>
[-Name <String>] [-Description <String>] [-AnyOfRuleSets
<SpbmRuleSet[]>] [-CommonRule <SpbmRule[]>] [-Server <VIServer>]
[-WhatIf] [-Confirm] [<CommonParameters>]
```

The `-StoragePolicy` parameter is required.

In the following example, we will use the `Set-SpbmStoragePolicy` cmdlet to modify the description of the `GoldPolicy` storage policy:

```
PowerCLI C:\> Set-SpbmStoragePolicy -Policy GoldPolicy -Description
'Storage policy for tier-1 storage'

Name                Description                          AnyOfRuleSets
----                -----------                          -------------
GoldPolicy          Storage policy for tier-1 storage    {(Gold)}
```

Retrieving SPBM compatible storage

If you create a new virtual machine and want to store this virtual machine on storage that is compatible with a certain storage policy, you can use the `Get-SpbmCompatibleStorage` cmdlet to retrieve a list of compatible storage:

```
Get-SpbmCompatibleStorage -StoragePolicy <SpbmStoragePolicy>
[-CandidateStorage <StorageResource[]>] [-Server <VIServer[]>]
[<CommonParameters>]
```

The `-StoragePolicy` parameter is required.

You can use the `-CandidateStorage` parameter to specify a list of datastores that must be checked for compliance with the storage policy. If you don't use the `-CandidateStorage` parameter, all of your datastores will be checked for compliance with the storage policy.

In the following example, we will retrieve all the datastores that are compliant with the `GoldPolicy` storage policy:

```
PowerCLI C:\> Get-SpbmCompatibleStorage -StoragePolicy GoldPolicy

Name                         FreeSpaceGB        CapacityGB
----                         -----------        ----------
datastore1                       151.550           250.000
```

As you can see in the output of the preceding example, datastore `datastore1` is found to be compliant with the `GoldPolicy` storage policy. This was expected because we assigned the `Gold` tag to the datastore `datastore1` in the preceding section, *Using tags to define storage capabilities*.

Using SPBM to create virtual machines

Now we know how to retrieve SPBM compatible storage. We can use this to create virtual machines on datastores with a certain storage policy. In the following example, we will use the New-VM cmdlet to create a new virtual machine named VM10. We will use the Get-SpbmCompatibleStorage cmdlet to retrieve storage compatible with the GoldPolicy storage policy. Because the output of this cmdlet can be an array of datastores, we will pipe the output to the Get-Random cmdlet to randomly select a compatible datastore:

```
PowerCLI C:\> New-VM -Name VM10 -Datastore (Get-SpbmCompatibleStorage
-StoragePolicy GoldPolicy | Get-Random) -VMHost 192.168.0.133

Name                PowerState Num CPUs MemoryGB
----                ---------- -------- --------
VM10                PoweredOff 1        0.250
```

Retrieving SPBM-related configuration data of clusters, virtual machines, and hard disks

The Get-SpbmEntityConfiguration cmdlet will retrieve SPBM-related configuration data of clusters, virtual machines, and hard disks. This configuration data consists of:

- SPBM enablement status for clusters
- Associated storage policy for virtual machines or hard disks
- Compliance status for virtual machines or hard disks

The syntax of the Get-SpbmEntityConfiguration cmdlet is as follows. The first parameter set is for retrieving entity configurations by storage policy:

```
Get-SpbmEntityConfiguration [-StoragePolicy <SpbmStoragePolicy[]>]
[-VMsOnly] [-HardDisksOnly] [-CheckComplianceNow] [-Server
<VIServer[]>] [<CommonParameters>]
```

The second parameter set is for retrieving entity configurations by entity:

```
Get-SpbmEntityConfiguration [[-VM] <VIObject[]>] [-HardDisk
<HardDisk[]>] [-Cluster <Cluster[]>] [-CheckComplianceNow]
[-Server <VIServer[]>] [<CommonParameters>]
```

The `Get-SpbmEntityConfiguration` cmdlet has no required parameters. If you don't specify a storage policy, the cmdlet returns the status for all available storage policies.

In the following example we will retrieve the status for all the available storage policies:

```
PowerCLI C:\> Get-SpbmEntityConfiguration

Entity          Storage Policy              Status      Time Of Check
------          --------------              ------      -------------
VM10            GoldPolicy                  compliant   2/1/2017 4:42:39 PM
```

As you can see in the output of the preceding example, the virtual machine VM10 is compliant with the `GoldPolicy` storage policy.

In the following example, we will retrieve the SPBM-enabled status of cluster Cluster01:

```
PowerCLI C:\> Get-SpbmEntityConfiguration -Cluster Cluster01

Name                            SpbmEnabled
----                            -----------
Cluster01                       False
```

Associating storage policies with virtual machines and hard disks and enabling SPBM on clusters

You can associate SPBM storage policies with virtual machines and hard disks. You can also enable or disable SPBM for clusters. This all can be done using the `Set-SpbmEntityConfiguration` cmdlet. The syntax of this cmdlet is as follows:

```
Set-SpbmEntityConfiguration [-Configuration]
<SpbmEntityConfiguration[]> [-SpbmEnabled [<Boolean>]]
[-StoragePolicy <SpbmStoragePolicy>] [-Server <VIServer>]
[-WhatIf] [-Confirm] [<CommonParameters>]
```

The `-Configuration` parameter is required.

As you can see in the output of one of the preceding examples, virtual machine VM2 is not associated with any storage policy. In the following example, we will associate virtual machine VM2 with the GoldPolicy storage policy:

```
PowerCLI C:\> Get-VM -Name VM2 | Set-SpbmEntityConfiguration
-StoragePolicy GoldPolicy

Entity      Storage Policy      Status          Time Of Check
------      --------------      ------          -------------
VM2         GoldPolicy          nonCompliant    2/1/2017 6:08:55 PM
```

As you can see in the output of the preceding example, virtual machine VM2 is not compliant with the GoldPolicy storage policy. This is because virtual machine VM2 is not stored on a datastore associated with the GoldPolicy storage policy. To make virtual machine VM2 compliant with storage policy GoldPolicy, you have to migrate virtual machine VM2 to a datastore associated with the GoldPolicy storage policy.

In the following example, we will enable SPBM on cluster Cluster01:

```
PowerCLI C:\> Set-SpbmEntityConfiguration -Configuration
Cluster01 -SpbmEnabled $true

Name                        SpbmEnabled
----                        -----------
Cluster01                   True
```

Exporting SPBM storage policies

You can use the Export-SpbmStoragePolicy cmdlet to export a storage policy to an XML file. This can be useful for copying storage policies from one vCenter Server to another. The syntax of the Export-SpbmStoragePolicy cmdlet is as follows:

```
Export-SpbmStoragePolicy [-FilePath] <String> [-StoragePolicy]
<SpbmStoragePolicy> [-Force] [-Server <VIServer>] [-WhatIf]
[-Confirm] [<CommonParameters>]
```

The -FilePath and -StoragePolicy parameters are required.

In the following example, we will export the `GoldPolicy` storage policy to a file named `GoldPolicy.xml` in your home folder. The `-Force` parameter is used to overwrite any existing destination file:

```
PowerCLI C:\> Export-SpbmStoragePolicy -StoragePolicy GoldPolicy
-FilePath $env:HOMEPATH\GoldPolicy.xml -Force

Mode                LastWriteTime     Length Name
----                -------------     ------ ----
-a---          2/1/2017    8:26 PM      1597 GoldPolicy.xml
```

Importing SPBM storage policies

Storage policies can be imported using the `Import-SpbmStoragePolicy` cmdlet. This cmdlet has the following syntax.

```
Import-SpbmStoragePolicy [-FilePath] <String> [-Name]
<String> [-Description <String>] [-Server <VIServer>]
[-WhatIf] [-Confirm] [<CommonParameters>]
```

The `-FilePath` and `-Name` parameters are required.

We will import the `GoldPolicy.XML` file we created in the preceding example, and name the new storage policy `GoldPolicy2` using the following command:

```
PowerCLI C:\> Import-SpbmStoragePolicy -FilePath
$env:HOMEPATH\GoldPolicy.xml -Name GoldPolicy2

Name             Description                       AnyOfRuleSets
----             -----------                       -------------
GoldPolicy2      Storage policy for tier-1 storage {(Gold)}
```

Removing SPBM storage policies

To remove a storage policy you can use the `Remove-SpbmStoragePolicy` cmdlet. The syntax of this cmdlet is as follows:

```
Remove-SpbmStoragePolicy [-StoragePolicy] <SpbmStoragePolicy[]>
[-Server <VIServer[]>] [-WhatIf] [-Confirm] [<CommonParameters>]
```

The -StoragePolicy parameter is required.

In the following example, we will remove storage policy GoldPolicy2:

```
PowerCLI C:\> Remove-SpbmStoragePolicy -StoragePolicy
GoldPolicy2 -Confirm:$false
```

The preceding command does not return any output.

Summary

In this chapter, we covered managing storage. We showed you how to create and remove datastores, configure software iSCSI initiators, work with Raw Device Mappings, configure Storage I/O Control, create and remove datastore clusters, add datastores to a datastore cluster, upgrade your datastores to VMFS-5, use VMware vSAN, and use vSphere storage policy-based management.

In the next chapter, you will learn all about managing high availability and clustering with PowerCLI.

8
Managing High Availability and Clustering

The availability of the applications running in your environment is an important advantage of virtualization. In the case of a host's or operating system's failure, VMware vSphere **High Availability (HA)** will restart the affected virtual machines. This ensures that your servers are available as much as possible.

VMware vSphere **Distributed Resources Scheduler (DRS)** provides initial placement of a virtual machine on an appropriate host during power on, automated load balancing to maximize performance and distribution of virtual machines across hosts to comply with **affinity** and **anti-affinity rules**.

To save power and money, **Distributed Power Management (DPM)** will consolidate your virtual machines on fewer hosts in your cluster and power down the unused hosts when not all of the resources are needed.

To use DRS or DPM, you need a VMware vSphere Enterprise Plus or vSphere with Operations Management Enterprise Plus license.

The topics that will be covered in this chapter are:

- Creating vSphere HA and DRS clusters
- Retrieving clusters
- Modifying the cluster settings
- Moving hosts to clusters
- Moving clusters
- Using DRS rules
- Using DRS recommendations

- Using resource pools
- Using Distributed Power Management
- Removing clusters

Creating vSphere HA and DRS clusters

In Chapter 4, *Managing vSphere Hosts with PowerCLI*, you already saw how to create a vSphere cluster with the default settings using the New-Cluster cmdlet. In the default settings, HA and DRS are disabled. You will now see how to create a cluster with HA and DRS enabled. First, the syntax of the New-Cluster cmdlet will be repeated, so you don't have to look back to Chapter 4, *Managing vSphere Hosts with PowerCLI*:

```
New-Cluster [-HARestartPriority <HARestartPriority>]
[-HAIsolationResponse <HAIsolationResponse>] [-VMSwapfilePolicy
<VMSwapfilePolicy>] [-Name] <String> -Location <VIContainer>
[-HAEnabled] [-HAAdmissionControlEnabled] [-HAFailoverLevel
<Int32>] [-DrsEnabled] [-DrsMode <DrsMode>] [-DrsAutomationLevel
<DrsAutomationLevel>] [-VsanDiskClaimMode <VsanDiskClaimMode>]
[-VsanEnabled] [-EVCMode <String>] [-Server <VIServer[]>] [-WhatIf]
[-Confirm] [<CommonParameters>]
```

The -Name and -Location parameters are required.

In the following example, an HA- and DRS-enabled cluster named Cluster02 will be created in the New York datacenter. The new cluster will have the DRS migration automation level as fully automated, HA admission control will be enabled, and the cluster will have a configured failover capacity of one host. The VM restart priority will be high, and the host isolation response will be left powered on. The swap file location for virtual machines will be the virtual machine directory.

Because you will use almost every parameter of the New-Cluster cmdlet, you will use splatting to create a hash table with all the parameters and their values. Splatting was explained in Chapter 6, *Managing Virtual Networks with PowerCLI*, so I hope you still remember this great PowerShell feature. It makes your code more readable because you don't have to create a single long command. Consider the following command lines:

```
PowerCLI C:\> $Parameters = @{
>>    Name = 'Cluster02'
>>    Location = (Get-Datacenter -Name 'New York')
>>    DrsEnabled = $true
>>    DrsAutomationLevel = 'FullyAutomated'
>>    HAEnabled = $true
```

```
>>    HAAdmissionControlEnabled = $true
>>    HAFailoverLevel = 1
>>    HAIsolationResponse = 'DoNothing'
>>    HARestartPriority = 'High'
>>    VMSwapfilePolicy = 'WithVM'
>> }
>> New-Cluster @Parameters
```

Name	HAEnabled	HAFailover Level	DrsEnabled	DrsAutomationLevel
Cluster02	True	1	True	FullyAutomated

In the following image, you will see a screenshot from the vSphere Web Client showing the HA and DRS settings of `Cluster02`, after running the preceding PowerCLI commands to create the cluster:

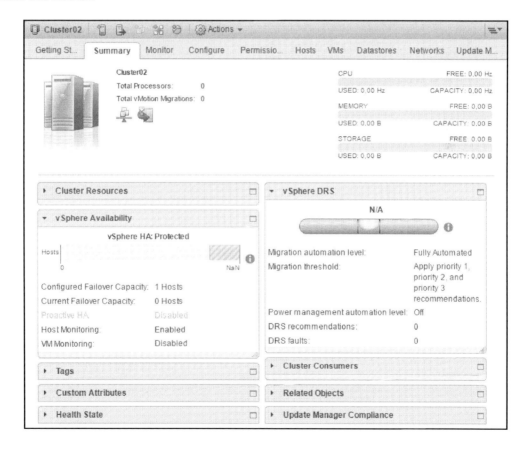

Retrieving clusters

To retrieve one or more of the clusters available on your vCenter Server system, you can use the Get-Cluster cmdlet. The syntax of the Get-Cluster cmdlet is as follows. The first parameter set is for retrieving clusters in a specific location such as a data center or a folder:

```
Get-Cluster [[-Name] <String[]>] [-Location <VIContainer[]>]
[-NoRecursion] [-Tag <Tag[]>] [-Server <VIServer[]>]
[<CommonParameters>]
```

The second parameter set is for retrieving clusters by a related object.

```
Get-Cluster [-RelatedObject] <ClusterRelatedObjectBase[]>
[<CommonParameters>]
```

The third parameter set is to retrieve clusters containing specific virtual machines or ESXi hosts:

```
Get-Cluster [[-Name] <String[]>] [-VM <VirtualMachine[]>]
[-VMHost <VMHost[]>] [-Tag <Tag[]>] [-Server <VIServer[]>]
[<CommonParameters>]
```

The fourth parameter set is to retrieve clusters by ID:

```
Get-Cluster [-Server <VIServer[]>] -Id <String[]>
[<CommonParameters>]
```

The -RelatedObject and -Id parameters are required.

In the first example, you will retrieve the cluster named Cluster02 that you created in the preceding section, *Creating vSphere HA and DRS clusters*:

```
PowerCLI C:\> Get-Cluster -Name Cluster02

Name            HAEnabled  HAFailover DrsEnabled DrsAutomationLevel
                                      Level
----            ---------  ---------- ---------- ------------------
Cluster02       True       1          True       FullyAutomated
```

In the second example, you will retrieve the cluster on which virtual machine VM2 runs:

```
PowerCLI C:\> Get-Cluster -VM VM2

Name            HAEnabled  HAFailover DrsEnabled DrsAutomationLevel
                                      Level

----            ---------  ---------- ---------- ------------------
Cluster01       True       1          False      FullyAutomated
```

Retrieving the HA master or primary hosts

In a vSphere HA cluster, one of the hosts is the master host, and all other hosts are slave hosts. The master host monitors the state of slave hosts and the power state of all protected virtual machines, manages the lists of cluster hosts and protected virtual machines, acts as vCenter Server management interface to the cluster, and reports the cluster health state. The Get-HAPrimaryVMHost cmdlet will retrieve the master host on a vCenter 5.0 or higher HA cluster, and it will also retrieve the primary HA hosts on an earlier than vCenter 5.0 cluster. The syntax of the Get-HAPrimaryVMHost cmdlet is as follows:

```
Get-HAPrimaryVMHost [[-Cluster] <Cluster[]>]
[-Server <VIServer[]>] [<CommonParameters>]
```

In the example, the master host on Cluster01 is retrieved using the following command:

```
PowerCLI C:\> Get-Cluster -Name Cluster01 | Get-HAPrimaryVMHost

Name            ConnectionState PowerState NumCpu CpuUsageMhz
----            --------------- ---------- ------ -----------
192.168.0.133   Connected       PoweredOn  2      69
```

Retrieving cluster configuration issues

If your cluster is incorrectly configured, the vSphere Web Client will show you the issues in the **Summary** tab. In the following screenshot of the vSphere Web Client, you will see two cluster configuration issues: **Insufficient capacity in cluster Cluster01 to satisfy resource configuration in New York** and **vCenter Server is unable to find a master vSphere HA agent in the cluster Cluster01 in New York**:

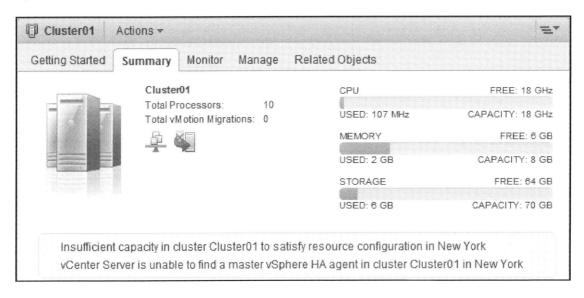

You can easily find any cluster configuration issues with PowerCLI. The following PowerCLI script displays the cluster name, creation time, and the full formatted message of all of the cluster configuration issues in your environment.

The script uses the `Get-Cluster` cmdlet to retrieve all the clusters. It pipes the output to the `Get-View` cmdlet to return the vSphere View objects of the clusters. The vSphere View objects are piped to the `Select-Object` cmdlet to expand the `ConfigIssue` property. Another `Select-Object` cmdlet is used in the pipeline to retrieve the cluster name using a calculated property, the creation time, and the full formatted message. Finally, the output is piped to `Format-Table -AutoSize` to display it in a compact table format:

```
PowerCLI C:\> Get-Cluster | Get-View |
>> Select-Object -ExpandProperty ConfigIssue |
>> Select-Object -Property@{Name="Cluster";Expression=
{$_.ComputeResource.Name}},
>> CreatedTime,FullFormattedMessage | Format-Table -AutoSize

Cluster    CreatedTime          FullFormattedMessage
```

```
-------  ----------         --------------------
Cluster01 2/1/2017 06:03:36 PM  vCenter Server is unable to
find a master vSphere HA agent in cluster Cluster01 in New York
Cluster01 2/1/2017 05:48:27 AM Insufficient capacity in cluster
Cluster01 to satisfy resource configuration in New York
```

Modifying the cluster settings

To modify the settings of a cluster, you can use the `Set-Cluster` cmdlet. This cmdlet has basically the same parameters as the `New-Cluster` cmdlet, with the addition of the `-Profile` parameter that enables you to associate a host profile with a cluster. The syntax of the `Set-Cluster` cmdlet is as follows:

```
Set-Cluster [-HARestartPriority <HARestartPriority>]
[-HAIsolationResponse <HAIsolationResponse>] [-VMSwapfilePolicy
<VMSwapfilePolicy>] [-Cluster] <Cluster[]> [[-Name] <String>]
[-HAEnabled [<Boolean>]] [-HAAdmissionControlEnabled [<Boolean>]]
[-HAFailoverLevel <Int32>] [-DrsEnabled [<Boolean>]] [-DrsMode
<DrsMode>] [-DrsAutomationLevel <DrsAutomationLevel>] [-VsanEnabled
[<Boolean>]] [-VsanDiskClaimMode <VsanDiskClaimMode>] [-Profile
<VMHostProfile>] [-EVCMode <String>] [-Server <VIServer[]>]
[-RunAsync] [-WhatIf] [-Confirm] [<CommonParameters>]
```

The `-Cluster` parameter is required.

In the following sections, you will see some use cases of the `Set-Cluster` cmdlet.

Configuring enhanced vMotion compatibility (EVC) mode

If you have a cluster of ESXi hosts using different processor types, for example, if you have an HP ProLiant DL380e Gen8 server and an HP ProLiant DL380 Gen9 server in the same cluster, you cannot vMotion a virtual machine that is started on the Gen9 server to the Gen8 server, unless you have the **enhanced vMotion compatibility** (**EVC**) mode enabled. After enabling the EVC mode, all of the hosts in the cluster will present the same CPU features to the virtual machines. This will make the hosts compatible for vMotion. vCenter Server will not allow you to add a server to a cluster that is not compatible with the EVC mode of the cluster.

You can find the EVC capability modes supported by a server, in the VMware Compatibility Guide, on `http://www.vmware.com/resources/compatibility/search.php`.

Coming back to our preceding example, the highest enhanced vMotion capability mode of the HP ProLiant DL380e Gen8 is the Intel® Sandy-Bridge generation. The highest enhanced vMotion capability mode of the HP ProLiant DL380 Gen9 is the Intel® Haswell Generation. The Gen9 server is also compatible with the Intel® Sandy-Bridge Generation. The Gen8 server is not compatible with the Intel® Haswell Generation. To be able to use both types of servers in the same cluster, we have to set the EVC mode of the cluster to an EVC mode that both types of servers in the cluster are compatible with. So in this example, we have to set the EVC mode of the cluster to the Intel® Sandy-Bridge Generation.

> For more information on the EVC Mode, you can read the VMware knowledge base article Enhanced vMotion Compatibility (EVC) processor support (1003212), which you can find at `https://kb.vmware.com/kb/1003212`.

When writing this book, the EVC modes supported by the `Set-Cluster` cmdlet are: `intel-merom`, `intel-penryn`, `intel-nehalem`, `intel-westmere`, `intel-sandybridge`, `intel-ivybridge`, `intel-haswell`, `amd-rev-e`, `amd-rev-f`, `amd-greyhound-no3dnow`, `amd-greyhound`, `amd-bulldozer`, `amd-piledriver`, and `amd-steamroller`.

In the following example, we will set the EVC mode of `Cluster02` to the Intel® Sandy-Bridge Generation:

```
PowerCLI C:\> Get-Cluster -Name Cluster02 |
>> Set-Cluster -EVCMode intel-sandybridge -Confirm:$false

Name           HAEnabled HAFailoverLevel DrsEnabled DrsAutomationLevel
----           --------- --------------- ---------- ------------------
Cluster02 True     1                    True       FullyAutomated
```

To retrieve the EVC mode of a cluster, you have to select to `EVCMode` property. In the following example, we will retrieve the EVC modes of all our clusters.

```
PowerCLI C:\> Get-Cluster | Select-Object -Property Name,EVCMode

Name                             EVCMode
----                             -------
Cluster02                        intel-sandybridge
Cluster01
```

As you can see in the output of the preceding example, `Cluster02` has the EVC mode set to `intel-sandybridge`. `Cluster01` does not have an EVC mode set.

Disabling HA

The following example will disable HA for `Cluster02`. This might be useful when you perform network maintenance that may cause isolation responses:

```
PowerCLI C:\> Get-Cluster -Name Cluster02 | Set-Cluster
-HAEnabled $false -Confirm:$false

Name              HAEnabled  HAFailover DrsEnabled DrsAutomationLevel
                                        Level

----              ---------  ---------- ---------- --------------------
Cluster02         False      1          True       FullyAutomated
```

Disabling or enabling host monitoring

To disable host monitoring, you have to use the vSphere API. The following script will disable host monitoring for `Cluster02`. In the script, a `ClusterConfigSpecEx` object is created and a `ClusterDasConfigInfo` object for the `dasConfig` property of the `ClusterConfigSpecEx` object. The `hostMonitoring` property of the `ClusterDasConfigInfo` object is set to `disabled`. Finally, the `ReconfigureComputeResource_Task()` method is called using the `ClusterConfigSpecEx` object as the first parameter.

The second parameter of the `ReconfigureComputeResource_Task()` method is named modify. If the value of the modify parameter is set to `$true`, the changes specified in the `ClusterConfigSpecEx` object will be applied incrementally to the cluster object. If the value of the modify parameter is `$false`, the configuration of the cluster will match the specification exactly. In this case, any unset properties of the specification will result in unset or default properties of the configuration of the cluster.

The `ReconfigureComputeResource_Task()` method creates a vSphere task and runs asynchronously:

```
# Disabling host monitoring
$Cluster = Get-Cluster -Name Cluster02
$spec = New-Object VMware.Vim.ClusterConfigSpecEx
$spec.dasConfig = New-Object VMware.Vim.ClusterDasConfigInfo
$spec.dasConfig.hostMonitoring = "disabled"
$Cluster.ExtensionData.ReconfigureComputeResource_Task($spec, $true)
```

If you want to enable host monitoring, you have to modify `disabled` in line 5 of the preceding script to `enabled`.

Enabling VM and application monitoring

VM and application monitoring will restart a virtual machine if **VMware tools heartbeats** are not received for a specific time frame. This time frame, named `failureInterval`, is configurable. You can also specify the minimum time the virtual machine must be up, named `minUpTime`, and the maximum number of times a virtual machine will be restarted in a certain time window, named `maxFailures`. The maximum resets time window is named `maxFailureWindow`. In the vSphere client, there are three predefined settings for the monitoring sensitivity named low, medium, and high.

The preset values for the low, medium, and high monitoring sensitivities are:

Monitoring Sensitivity	Low	Medium	High
`failureInterval` (seconds)	120	60	30
`minUpTime` (seconds)	480	240	120
`maxFailures`	3	3	3
`maxFailureWindow` (seconds)	604800	86400	3600

Of course, you can use your own custom values. If you don't want to use the **Maximum resets time window**, you have to use the value –1 for the `maxFailureWindow` property.

You cannot use the `Set-Cluster` cmdlet to enable or disable VM and application monitoring. You have to use the vSphere API again to do this. In the following script, you will create the `ClusterConfigSpecEx` and `ClusterDasConfigInfo` objects as you have seen earlier. The `vmMonitoring` property of the `ClusterDasConfigInfo` object will get the value `vmAndAppMonitoring`. You will also create a `ClusterDasVmSettings` object as the value of the `defaultVmSettings` property of the `ClusterDasConfigInfo` object. A `ClusterVmToolsMonitoringSettings` object is created as the value of the `vmToolsMonitoringSettings` property of the `ClusterDasVmSettings` object. The properties of the `ClusterVmToolsMonitoringSettings` object will get a value that corresponds with the medium monitoring sensitivity. Finally, the `ReconfigureComputeResource_Task()` method is called to reconfigure the cluster:

```
# Enabling VM and application monitoring
$Cluster = Get-Cluster -Name Cluster02
$spec = New-Object VMware.Vim.ClusterConfigSpecEx
```

```
$spec.dasConfig = New-Object VMware.Vim.ClusterDasConfigInfo
$spec.dasConfig.vmMonitoring = "vmAndAppMonitoring"
$spec.dasConfig.defaultVmSettings = New-Object
VMware.Vim.ClusterDasVmSettings
$spec.dasConfig.defaultVmSettings.vmToolsMonitoringSettings = New-Object
VMware.Vim.ClusterVmToolsMonitoringSettings
$spec.dasConfig.defaultVmSettings.vmToolsMonitoringSettings.enabled = $true
$spec.dasConfig.defaultVmSettings.vmToolsMonitoringSettings.vmMonitoring =
"vmAndAppMonitoring"
$spec.dasConfig.defaultVmSettings.vmToolsMonitoringSettings.failureInterval
= 60
$spec.dasConfig.defaultVmSettings.vmToolsMonitoringSettings.minUpTime = 240
$spec.dasConfig.defaultVmSettings.vmToolsMonitoringSettings.maxFailures = 3
$spec.dasConfig.defaultVmSettings.vmToolsMonitoringSettings.maxFailureWindo
w = 86400
$Cluster.ExtensionData.ReconfigureComputeResource_Task($spec, $true)
```

The possible values for the `vmMonitoring` property are `vmMonitoringDisabled` (the default value), `vmMonitoringOnly`, or `vmAndAppMonitoring`.

Configuring the heartbeat datastore selection policy

Datastore heartbeating is a vSphere HA feature introduced in vSphere 5.0. In the case of a lost network connection between the HA master and the slaves, datastore heartbeating is used to validate whether a host has failed or just the network between the hosts is lost. If the master concludes that a slave host has failed because there are no datastore heartbeats, the virtual machines of the failed host will be restarted on other hosts in the cluster. If a host still has datastore heartbeats, the master concludes that the slave is **isolated** or **partitioned**. Depending on the configured host isolation response for the cluster, the virtual machines on the isolated host will be left powered on, shut down, or powered off.

vCenter Server selects two datastores for each host for datastore heartbeating, according to the datastore heartbeating policy defined for the cluster. The policy can be one of the following:

- Automatically select datastores accessible from the host
- Use datastores only from the specified list
- Otherwise, use datastores from the specified list and complement automatically if needed

In the following table, you will see the three datastore heartbeating policies and the possible values for the HBDatastoreCandidatePolicy property used by the vSphere API:

HBDatastoreCandidatePolicy	Description
allFeasibleDs	Automatically, select datastores accessible from the host
userSelectedDs	Use datastores only from the list specified by the user
allFeasibleDsWithUserPreference	Use datastores from the list specified by the user and complement automatically if needed

In the first example, you will retrieve the datastore heartbeating policy for Cluster01:

```
PowerCLI C:\> $Cluster = Get-Cluster -Name Cluster01
PowerCLI C:\> $Cluster.ExtensionData.Configuration
.DasConfig.HBDatastore
CandidatePolicy allFeasibleDsWithUserPreference
```

In the following example, you will retrieve the datastores used for datastore heartbeating in Cluster01:

```
PowerCLI C:\> $cluster.ExtensionData.RetrieveDasAdvancedRuntimeInfo()
.HeartbeatDatastoreInfo |
>> Select-Object -ExpandProperty Datastore |
>> Get-VIObjectByVIView
```

There are no PowerCLI cmdlets to configure datastore heartbeating, so you have to use the vSphere API. In the following example, you will configure the automatically select datastores accessible from the host datastore heartbeating policy for Cluster01. First, you create the ClusterConfigSpecEx and ClusterDasConfigInfo objects as a value of the dasConfig property of the ClusterConfigSpecEx object. Then, you give the hBDatastoreCandidatePolicy property of the ClusterDasConfigInfo object the allFeasibleDs value. Finally, you call the ReconfigureComputeResource_Task() method to reconfigure the cluster:

```
# Automatically select datastores accessible from the host
# for datastore heartbeating
$Cluster = Get-Cluster -Name Cluster01
$spec = New-Object VMware.Vim.ClusterConfigSpecEx
$spec.dasConfig = New-Object VMware.Vim.ClusterDasConfigInfo
$spec.dasConfig.hBDatastoreCandidatePolicy = "allFeasibleDs"
$Cluster.ExtensionData.ReconfigureComputeResource_Task($spec, $true)
```

The following screenshot of the vSphere Web Client will show you the **Datastore for Heartbeating** settings of `Cluster01` set to **Automatically select datastores accessible from the host** after running the preceding PowerCLI commands:

Heartbeat Datastores

vSphere HA uses datastores to monitor hosts and virtual machines when management network has failed. vCenter Server selects two datastores for each host using the policy and datastore preferences specified below.

Heartbeat datastore selection policy:

(●) Automatically select datastores accessible from the host

(○) Use datastores only from the specified list

(○) Use datastores from the specified list and complement automatically if needed

In the following example, you will configure the used datastores only from the specified list datastore heartbeating policy for `Cluster01`. The new thing in this example is that you have to specify the Managed Object References of the datastores that you selected for the datastore heartbeating. Therefore, an array of two `ManagedObjectReference` objects is specified as the value of the `heartbeatDatastore` property of the `ClusterDasConfigInfo` object. The array is filled with MoRefs of the selected datastores. The `hBDatastoreCandidatePolicy` property of the `ClusterDasConfigInfo` object is given the value `userSelectedDs`. Finally, the `ReconfigureComputeResource_Task()` method is called to reconfigure the cluster:

```
# Use datastores only from the specified list
# for datastore heartbeating
$Cluster = Get-Cluster -Name Cluster01
$Datastore1 = Get-Datastore -Name Datastore1
$Datastore2 = Get-Datastore -Name Datastore2
$spec = New-Object VMware.Vim.ClusterConfigSpecEx
$spec.dasConfig = New-Object VMware.Vim.ClusterDasConfigInfo
$spec.dasConfig.heartbeatDatastore = New-Object
VMware.Vim.ManagedObjectReference[] (2)
$spec.dasConfig.heartbeatDatastore[0] = New-Object
VMware.Vim.ManagedObjectReference
$spec.dasConfig.heartbeatDatastore[0].type = "Datastore"
$spec.dasConfig.heartbeatDatastore[0].Value =
$Datastore1.ExtensionData.MoRef.Value
$spec.dasConfig.heartbeatDatastore[1] = New-Object
VMware.Vim.ManagedObjectReference
$spec.dasConfig.heartbeatDatastore[1].type = "Datastore"
$spec.dasConfig.heartbeatDatastore[1].Value =
$Datastore2.ExtensionData.MoRef.Value
$spec.dasConfig.hBDatastoreCandidatePolicy = "userSelectedDs"
$Cluster.ExtensionData.ReconfigureComputeResource_Task($spec, $true)
```

In the last example of configuring datastore heartbeating, you will configure the use datastores from the specified list and complement automatically if needed datastore heartbeating policy for Cluster01. The example is almost the same as the preceding example. The difference is that you now give the hBDatastoreCandidatePolicy property of the ClusterDasConfigInfo object the allFeasibleDsWithUserPreference value:

```
# Use datastores from the specified list and complement
# automatically if needed for datastore heartbeating
$Cluster = Get-Cluster -Name Cluster01
$Datastore1 = Get-Datastore -Name Datastore1
$Datastore2 = Get-Datastore -Name Datastore2
$spec = New-Object VMware.Vim.ClusterConfigSpecEx
$spec.dasConfig = New-Object VMware.Vim.ClusterDasConfigInfo
$spec.dasConfig.heartbeatDatastore = New-Object
VMware.Vim.ManagedObjectReference[] (2)
$spec.dasConfig.heartbeatDatastore[0] = New-Object
VMware.Vim.ManagedObjectReference
$spec.dasConfig.heartbeatDatastore[0].type = "Datastore"
$spec.dasConfig.heartbeatDatastore[0].Value =
$Datastore1.ExtensionData.MoRef.Value
$spec.dasConfig.heartbeatDatastore[1] = New-Object
VMware.Vim.ManagedObjectReference
$spec.dasConfig.heartbeatDatastore[1].type = "Datastore"
$spec.dasConfig.heartbeatDatastore[1].Value =
$Datastore2.ExtensionData.MoRef.Value
$spec.dasConfig.hBDatastoreCandidatePolicy =
"allFeasibleDsWithUserPreference"
$Cluster.ExtensionData.ReconfigureComputeResource_Task($spec, $true)
```

Moving hosts to clusters

You can use the Move-VMHost cmdlet to move a host to a cluster. The host has to already be added to your vSphere inventory. If it isn't, you can use the Add-VMHost cmdlet to add the host to your inventory, as shown in Chapter 4, *Managing vSphere Hosts with PowerCLI*. The host also has to be in a maintenance mode or you will get the error message: **The operation is not allowed in the current state**.

The syntax of the Move-VMHost cmdlet is as follows:

```
Move-VMHost [-VMHost] <VMHost[]> [-Destination] <VIContainer>
[-Server <VIServer[]>] [-RunAsync] [-WhatIf] [-Confirm]
[<CommonParameters>]
```

The -VMHost and -Destination parameters are required.

You can also use the `Move-VMhost` cmdlet to move a host to another **VIContainer** such as a data center or a folder.

In the following example, you will first put host `192.168.0.134` in a maintenance mode, move the host to `Cluster02,` and finally exit a maintenance mode:

```
PowerCLI C:\> $VMHost = Get-VMHost -Name 192.168.0.134
PowerCLI C:\> $VMHost | Set-VMHost -State Maintenance

Name             ConnectionState PowerState NumCpu CpuUsageMhz
----             --------------- ---------- ------ -----------
192.168.0.134 Maintenance        PoweredOn       2         226

PowerCLI C:\> $VMHost | Move-VMHost -Destination
(Get-Cluster -Name Cluster02) -Confirm:$false

Name             ConnectionState PowerState NumCpu CpuUsageMhz
----             --------------- ---------- ------ -----------
192.168.0.134 Maintenance        PoweredOn       2         226

PowerCLI C:\> $VMHost | Set-VMHost -State Connected

Name             ConnectionState PowerState NumCpu CpuUsageMhz
----             --------------- ---------- ------ -----------
192.168.0.134 Connected          PoweredOn       2         619
```

Moving clusters

You can use the `Move-Cluster` cmdlet to move a cluster to a folder. The folder must be in the same data center as the cluster. The syntax of the `Move-Cluster` cmdlet is as follows:

```
Move-Cluster [-Cluster] <Cluster[]> [-Destination] <VIContainer>
[-Server <VIServer[]>] [-RunAsync] [-WhatIf] [-Confirm]
[<CommonParameters>]
```

The `-Cluster` and `-Destination` parameters are required.

Besides a folder, you can specify the data center to which the cluster belongs as the value of the `-Destination` parameter. In this case, the cluster is moved to the `host` system folder of the data center. It is not possible to move a cluster to another data center.

In the following example, `Cluster01` is moved to the `Accounting` folder:

```
PowerCLI C:\> Move-Cluster -Cluster Cluster01 -Destination Accounting

Name            HAEnabled   HAFailover  DrsEnabled  DrsAutomationLevel
                            Level

----            ---------   ----------  ----------  ------------------
Cluster01       True        1           True        FullyAutomated
```

Using DRS rules

To control the placement of virtual machines on hosts in a cluster, you can use DRS affinity rules or anti-affinity rules. There are two types of affinity rules:

- **VM-VM affinity rules**: These rules specify affinity or anti-affinity between virtual machines. An affinity rule specifies that DRS should or must keep a group of virtual machines together on the same host. A use case of the affinity rules can be performance because virtual machines on the same hosts have the fastest network connection possible. An anti-affinity rule specifies that DRS should or must keep a group of virtual machines on separate hosts. This prevents you from losing all of the virtual machines in the group if a host crashes.
- **VM-Host affinity rules**: These rules specify affinity or anti-affinity between a group of virtual machines and a group of hosts. An affinity rule specifies that the group of virtual machines should or must run on the group of hosts. An anti-affinity rule specifies that the group of virtual machines should or must not run on the group of hosts.

In PowerCLI, there are cmdlets to use VM-VM affinity rules. To use VM-Host affinity rules, you have to, unfortunately, use the vSphere API.

Creating VM-VM DRS rules

To create a VM-VM DRS rule, you can use the `New-DrsRule` cmdlet that has the following syntax:

```
New-DrsRule [-Name] <String> [-Cluster] <Cluster[]> [-Enabled
[<Boolean>]] -KeepTogether [<Boolean>] -VM <VirtualMachine[]>
[-RunAsync] [-Server <VIServer[]>] [-WhatIf] [-Confirm]
[<CommonParameters>]
```

The `-Name`, `-Cluster`, `-KeepTogether`, and `-VM` parameters are required.

If the value of the `-KeepTogether` parameter is `$true`, the new DRS rule is an affinity rule. If the value is `$false`, the new DRS rule is an anti-affinity rule.

If the value of `-Enabled` parameter is `$true`, the new DRS rule is enabled. If the value is `$false`, it is disabled.

In the following example, you will create a new, enabled DRS VM-VM affinity rule named `Keep VM1 and VM2 together` for `Cluster01`. The DRS rule will keep the two virtual machines `VM1` and `VM2` together on the same host:

```
PowerCLI C:\> New-DrsRule -Name 'Keep VM1 and VM2 together'
-Cluster Cluster01 -VM VM1,VM2 -KeepTogether:$true -Enabled:$true

Name                          Enabled Type        VMIDs
----                          ------- ----        -----
Keep VM1 and VM2 together True       VMAffinity {VirtualMachine-vm-125,
                                                  VirtualMachine-vm-105}
```

In the following screenshot of the vSphere Web Client, you will see the window of the vSphere Web Client, which you can use to create a DRS rule filled with the same settings as in the preceding PowerCLI command:

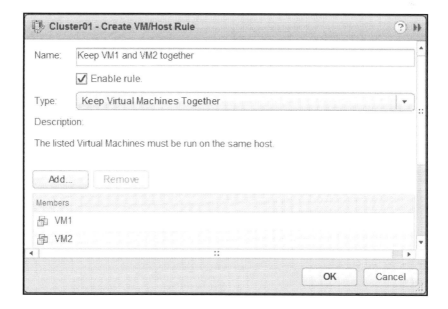

In the second example, you will create a new DRS VM-VM anti-affinity rule named `Separate VM3 and VM4` for `Cluster01`:

```
PowerCLI C:\> New-DrsRule -Name 'Separate VM3 and VM4'
-Cluster Cluster01 -VM VM3,VM4 -KeepTogether:$false -Enabled:$true

Name                     Enabled Type            VMIDs
----                     ------- ----            -----
Separate VM3 and VM4 True       VMAntiAffinity {VirtualMachine-vm-107,
                                               VirtualMachine-vm-126}
```

Creating VM-host DRS rules

Unfortunately, there are no PowerCLI cmdlets to create a VM-Host affinity rule. You have to use the vSphere API to do this. There are three steps involved in creating a VM-Host affinity rule:

1. Creating a virtual machines DRS group.
2. Creating a host's DRS group.
3. Creating a virtual machines to hosts DRS rule.

Creating virtual machines DRS groups

While creating a virtual machines DRS group, you have to add at least one virtual machine to this group. In the following example, you will create a virtual machines DRS group named `Cluster01 VMs should run on host 192.168.0.133` for `Cluster01` and add virtual machine `VM1` to this DRS group.

First, you create a `ClusterConfigSpecEx` object. Then, you add an array containing one `ClusterGroupSpec` object to the `GroupSpec` property of the `ClusterConfigSpecEx` object. The `operation` property of the `ClusterGroupSpec` object is given the value `add`. A `ClusterVmGroup` object is assigned to the `info` property of the `ClusterGroupSpec` object. The name of the DRS group is assigned to the `name` property of the `ClusterVmGroup` object. The `MoRef` of the virtual machine that will be added to the DRS group is assigned to the `vm` property of the `ClusterVmGroup` object. Finally, the cluster's `ReconfigureComputeResource_Task()` method is called to reconfigure the cluster and to add the DRS group:

```
# Creating a Virtual Machines DRS Group
$Cluster = Get-Cluster -Name Cluster01
$VM = Get-VM -Name VM1 -Location $Cluster
```

```
$DRSGroupName = 'Cluster01 VMs should run on host 192.168.0.133'
$spec = New-Object VMware.Vim.ClusterConfigSpecEx
$spec.groupSpec = New-Object VMware.Vim.ClusterGroupSpec[] (1)
$spec.groupSpec[0] = New-Object VMware.Vim.ClusterGroupSpec
$spec.groupSpec[0].operation = 'add'
$spec.groupSpec[0].info = New-Object VMware.Vim.ClusterVmGroup
$spec.groupSpec[0].info.name = $DRSGroupName
$spec.groupSpec[0].info.vm += $VM.ExtensionData.MoRef
$Cluster.ExtensionData.ReconfigureComputeResource_Task($spec, $true)
```

Creating hosts DRS groups

Creating a hosts DRS group is similar to creating a virtual machine DRS group. Instead of adding a `ClusterVmGroup` object to the `info` property of the `ClusterGroupSpec` object, you have to add a `ClusterHostGroup` object. The `host` property of the `ClusterHostGroup` will get the MoRef of the host you want to add to the DRS group assigned. You have to add at least one host to a hosts DRS group.

In the following example, you will create a hosts DRS group named `Cluster01 192.168.0.133 Hosts DRS Group`, and you will add the host `192.168.0.133` to this group:

```
# Creating a Hosts DRS Group
$Cluster = Get-Cluster -Name Cluster01
$VMHost = Get-VMHost -Name 192.168.0.133 -Location $Cluster
$DRSGroupName = 'Cluster01 192.168.0.133 Hosts DRS Group'
$spec = New-Object VMware.Vim.ClusterConfigSpecEx
$spec.groupSpec = New-Object VMware.Vim.ClusterGroupSpec[] (1)
$spec.groupSpec[0] = New-Object VMware.Vim.ClusterGroupSpec
$spec.groupSpec[0].operation = "add"
$spec.groupSpec[0].info = New-Object VMware.Vim.ClusterHostGroup
$spec.groupSpec[0].info.name = $DRSGroupName
$spec.groupSpec[0].info.host += $VMHost.ExtensionData.MoRef
$Cluster.ExtensionData.ReconfigureComputeResource_Task($spec, $true)
```

Retrieving DRS groups

There are no cmdlets to retrieve DRS groups. You will have to use the vSphere API. The DRS groups are in the `ConfigurationEx.Group` property of a vSphere `ClusterComputeResource` object.

The following example will show you how to retrieve the DRS groups of `Cluster01`:

```
PowerCLI C:\> (Get-Cluster -Name Cluster01).ExtensionData
.ConfigurationEx.Group

Vm          : {VirtualMachine-vm-125}
LinkedView  :
Name        : Cluster01 VMs should run on host 192.168.0.133
UserCreated :
UniqueID    :
Host        : {HostSystem-host-109}
LinkedView  :
Name        : Cluster01 192.168.0.133 Hosts DRS Group
UserCreated :
UniqueID    :
```

Modifying DRS groups

If you want to modify a DRS group, the only thing you can do is add or remove virtual machines or hosts to or from the DRS group. There are no PowerCLI cmdlets to do this, so you have to use the vSphere API.

Adding virtual machines to a DRS group

In the first example, you will add virtual machines VM2, VM4, and VM7 to the DRS group `Cluster01 VMs should run on host 192.168.0.133`. Because the structure of `ClusterConfigSpecEx` objects is always the same, I will explain only what is unique in this example. In this case, the operation is `edit`. The DRS group is assigned to the `info` property. All of the new group members are added to the `info.vm` property:

```
# Adding virtual machines to a DRS group
$Cluster = Get-Cluster -Name Cluster01
$GroupName = "Cluster01 VMs should run on host 192.168.0.133"
$VMs = Get-VM -Name VM2,VM4,VM7
$spec = New-Object VMware.Vim.ClusterConfigSpecEx
$spec.groupSpec = New-Object VMware.Vim.ClusterGroupSpec[] (1)
$spec.groupSpec[0] = New-Object VMware.Vim.ClusterGroupSpec
$spec.groupSpec[0].operation = "edit"
$spec.groupSpec[0].info = $Cluster.ExtensionData.ConfigurationEx.Group |
  Where-Object {$_.Name -eq $GroupName}
foreach ($VM in $VMs)
{
  $spec.groupSpec[0].info.vm += $VM.ExtensionData.MoRef
}
$Cluster.ExtensionData.ReconfigureComputeResource_Task($spec, $true)
```

Removing virtual machines from a DRS group

In the second example about modifying DRS groups, the virtual machines VM4 and VM7 will be removed from the DRS group Cluster01 VMs should run on host 192.168.0.133.

This example looks a lot like the preceding one. The difference is that virtual machines are removed from the info.vm property using the Where-Object cmdlet and the –notcontains operator. Only the virtual machines that are not in the list of virtual machines to be removed are assigned to the info.vm property:

```
# Removing virtual machines from a DRS group
$Cluster = Get-Cluster -Name Cluster01
$GroupName = "Cluster01 VMs should run on host 192.168.0.133"
$VMs = Get-VM -Name VM4,VM7
$VMsMorefs = $VMs | ForEach-Object {$_.ExtensionData.MoRef}
$spec = New-Object VMware.Vim.ClusterConfigSpecEx
$spec.groupSpec = New-Object VMware.Vim.ClusterGroupSpec[] (1)
$spec.groupSpec[0] = New-Object VMware.Vim.ClusterGroupSpec
$spec.groupSpec[0].operation = "edit"
$spec.groupSpec[0].info = New-Object VMware.Vim.ClusterVmGroup
$spec.groupSpec[0].info.name = $GroupName
$spec.groupSpec[0].info.vm = $Cluster.ExtensionData.ConfigurationEx.Group |
  Where-Object {$_.Name -eq $GroupName} |
  Select-Object -ExpandProperty vm |
  Where-Object {$VMsMorefs -notcontains $_}
$Cluster.ExtensionData.ReconfigureComputeResource_Task($spec, $true)
```

Remember that you cannot remove all of the virtual machines or hosts from a DRS group. A DRS group needs at least one group member.

Adding hosts to a DRS group and removing hosts from a DRS group is similar to adding virtual machines to a DRS group or removing virtual machines from a DRS group. I leave this to you as an exercise to solve (Hint: use Get-VMHost instead of Get-VM).

More information about the VMware.VIM.* objects used in the preceding examples can be found in *VMware vSphere API Reference Documentation*: http://pubs.vmware.com/vsphere-65/index.jsp#com.vmware.wssdk.api ref.doc/right-pane.html.

Removing DRS groups

Removing DRS groups is similar to preceding DRS groups operations. To remove a DRS group, the `operation` is `remove`, and the `removeKey` is the DRS group's name.

The following example will remove the DRS group `Cluster01 VMs should run on host 192.168.0.133`:

```
# Removing a DRS group
$Cluster = Get-Cluster -Name Cluster01
$GroupName = "Cluster01 VMs should run on host 192.168.0.133"
$spec = New-Object VMware.Vim.ClusterConfigSpecEx
$spec.groupSpec = New-Object VMware.Vim.ClusterGroupSpec[] (1)
$spec.groupSpec[0] = New-Object VMware.Vim.ClusterGroupSpec
$spec.groupSpec[0].operation = "remove"
$spec.groupSpec[0].removeKey = $GroupName
$Cluster.ExtensionData.ReconfigureComputeResource_Task($spec, $true)
```

Creating Virtual Machines to Hosts DRS rules

Finally, you have to relate the virtual machines DRS group to the hosts DRS group in a virtual machines to hosts DRS rule. There are four possible relations:

- `Must run on hosts in group`
- `Should run on hosts in group`
- `Must not run on hosts in group`
- `Should not run on hosts in group`

In the example given, you will create a `Should run on hosts in group` virtual machines to hosts DRS rule to give preference to virtual machine `VM1` to run on host `192.168.0.133`.

First, a `ClusterConfigSpecEx` object is created. An array of one `ClusterRuleSpec` object is assigned to the `rulesSpec` property of the `ClusterConfigSpecEx` object. The `operation` property of `rulesSpec` is set to `add`. A `ClusterVmHostRuleInfo` object is assigned to the info property of `rulesSpec`. The `enabled` property of the `ClusterVmHostRuleInfo` object is set to `$true`. The `name` property is given the name of the DRS rule. Because it is a `Should run on hosts in group` DRS rule, the `mandatory` property is set to `$false`. The `userCreated` property is set to `$true`. The `vmGroupName` and `affineHostGroupName` properties are assigned the names of the related DRS groups. Finally, the cluster's `ReconfigureComputeResource_Task()` method is called to create the DRS rule:

```
# Creating a Virtual Machines to Hosts DRS rule
$Cluster = Get-Cluster -Name Cluster01
$spec = New-Object VMware.Vim.ClusterConfigSpecEx
$spec.rulesSpec = New-Object VMware.Vim.ClusterRuleSpec[] (1)
$spec.rulesSpec[0] = New-Object VMware.Vim.ClusterRuleSpec
$spec.rulesSpec[0].operation = "add"
$spec.rulesSpec[0].info = New-Object VMware.Vim.ClusterVmHostRuleInfo
$spec.rulesSpec[0].info.enabled = $true
$spec.rulesSpec[0].info.name = "Cluster01 VM1 should run on host
192.168.0.133 DRS Rule"
$spec.rulesSpec[0].info.mandatory = $false
$spec.rulesSpec[0].info.userCreated = $true
$spec.rulesSpec[0].info.vmGroupName = "Cluster01 VMs should run on host
192.168.0.133"
$spec.rulesSpec[0].info.affineHostGroupName = "Cluster01 192.168.0.133
Hosts DRS Group"
$Cluster.ExtensionData.ReconfigureComputeResource_Task($spec, $true)
```

If you want to create a `Must run on hosts in group` DRS rule, you only have to change the line `$spec.rulesSpec[0].info.mandatory = $false` in the preceding code to the following:

```
$spec.rulesSpec[0].info.mandatory = $true
```

If you want to create a `Must not run on hosts in group` or `Should not run on hosts in group` DRS group, you have to assign the DRS hosts group name to `$spec.rulesSpec[0].info.antiAffineHostGroupName` instead of `$spec.rulesSpec[0].info.affineHostGroupName`.

In the following screenshot of the vSphere Web Client, you will see the virtual machines to hosts DRS rule `Cluster01 VM1 should run on host 192.168.0.133 DRS Rule` created with the preceding PowerCLI commands:

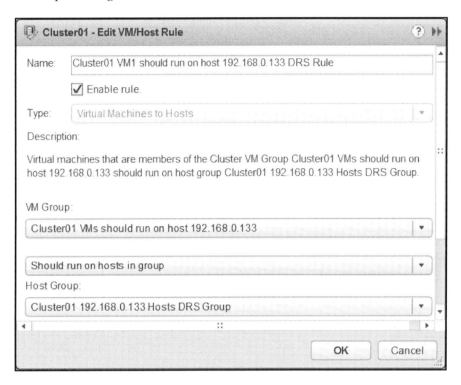

Retrieving DRS Rules

You can use the `Get-DrsRule` cmdlet to retrieve the DRS rules of the specified clusters. The syntax of this cmdlet is as follows. The first parameter set is the default:

```
Get-DrsRule [[-Name] <String[]>] [-Cluster] <Cluster[]>
[[-VM] <VirtualMachine[]>] [-Type <ResourceSchedulingRuleType[]>]
[-Server <VIServer[]>] [<CommonParameters>]
```

The second parameter set is to retrieve DRS rules that reference the specified ESXi hosts:

```
Get-DrsRule [[-Name] <String[]>] [-Cluster] <Cluster[]> [[-VM]
<VirtualMachine[]>] [-VMHost <VMHost[]>] [-Server <VIServer[]>]
[<CommonParameters>]
```

The `-Cluster` parameter is required. You cannot use the `-Type` and `-VMHost` parameters in the same command because they are in different parameter sets.

If you don't specify the `-Type` or `-VMHost` parameters, you will only retrieve VM-VM affinity or VM-VM anti-affinity rules, as in the following example:

```
PowerCLI C:\> Get-DrsRule -Cluster Cluster01

Name                          Enabled Type           VMIDs
----                          ------- ----           -----
Keep VM1 and VM2 together     True    VMAffinity     {VirtualM...
Separate VM3 and VM4          True    VMAntiAffinity {VirtualM...
```

If you also want to retrieve VM-Host DRS rules, you have to specify all of the possible types as the value of the `-Type` parameter, as we will do in the following example:

```
PowerCLI C:\> Get-DrsRule -Cluster Cluster01
-Type VMAffinity,VMAntiAffinity,VMHostAffinity

Name                          Enabled Type           VMIDs
----                          ------- ----           -----
Keep VM1 and VM2 together     True    VMAffinity     {VirtualM...
Separate VM3 and VM4          True    VMAntiAffinity {VirtualM...
Cluster01 VM1 should run on ho... True VMHostAffinity {VirtualM...
```

You can also retrieve all the DRS rules that involve certain virtual machines using the `-VM` parameter:

```
PowerCLI C:\> Get-DrsRule -Cluster Cluster01 -VM VM2

Name                          Enabled Type           VMIDs
----                          ------- ----           -----
Keep VM1 and VM2 together     True    VMAffinity     {VirtualM...
```

To retrieve all of the DRS rules that involve specific hosts, use the `-VMHost` parameter using the following command:

```
PowerCLI C:\> Get-DrsRule -Cluster Cluster01 -VMHost 192.168.0.133

Name                          Enabled Type           VMIDs
----                          ------- ----           -----
Cluster01 VM1 should run on ho... True VMHostAffinity {VirtualM...
```

Modifying DRS rules

To modify a DRS rule, you can use the `Set-DrsRule` cmdlet. The syntax of this cmdlet is as follows:

```
Set-DrsRule [[-Enabled] [<Boolean>]] [-Rule] <DrsRule[]>
[-Name <String>] [-VM <VirtualMachine[]>] [-RunAsync] [-Server
<VIServer[]>] [-WhatIf] [-Confirm] [<CommonParameters>]
```

The `-Rule` parameter is required.

In the following example, the DRS rule `Keep VM1 and VM2 together` of `Cluster01` will be disabled:

```
PowerCLI C:\> Get-DrsRule -Name 'Keep VM1 and VM2 together'
-Cluster Cluster01 | Set-DrsRule -Enabled:$false

Name                        Enabled Type        VMIDs
----                        ------- ----        -----
Keep VM1 and VM2 together   False   VMAffinity  {VirtualM...
```

Removing DRS rules

The `Remove-DrsRule` cmdlet can be used to remove a DRS rule. The syntax of the `Remove-DrsRule` cmdlet is as follows:

```
Remove-DrsRule [-Rule] <DrsRule[]> [-RunAsync] [-WhatIf]
[-Confirm] [<CommonParameters>]
```

The `-Rule` parameter is required.

In the following example, the `Keep VM1 and VM2 together` of `Cluster01` is removed:

```
PowerCLI C:\> Get-DrsRule -Cluster Cluster01 -Name 'Keep VM1
and VM2 together' | Remove-DrsRule -Confirm:$false
```

The preceding command does not return any output.

Using DRS recommendations

To retrieve the available DRS recommendations from the provided clusters, you can use the Get-DrsRecommendation cmdlet. This is useful if you configure the DrsAutomationLevel on your cluster as Manual or PartiallyAutomated. The syntax of the Get-DrsRecommendation cmdlet is as follows:

```
Get-DrsRecommendation [[-Cluster] <Cluster[]>] [-Refresh]
[-Priority <Int32[]>] [-Server <VIServer[]>] [<CommonParameters>]
```

The Get-DrsRecommendation cmdlet has no required parameters.

In the following example, you will retrieve all the DRS recommendations for all the clusters:

```
PowerCLI C:\ > Get-DrsRecommendation

Priority Recommendation                    Reason
-------- --------------                    ------
2        Migrate VM 'VM1' from host... Fix soft VM/host affinity r...
```

To apply a DRS recommendation, you can use the Invoke-DrsRecommendation cmdlet. This cmdlet has the following syntax:

```
Invoke-DrsRecommendation [-DrsRecommendation] <DrsRecommendation[]>
[-RunAsync] [-WhatIf] [-Confirm] [<CommonParameters>]
```

The -DrsRecommendation property is required.

In the following example, all the DRS recommendations will be applied:

```
PowerCLI C:\> Get-DrsRecommendation | Invoke-DrsRecommendation
```

If you have several DRS recommendations and you don't want to apply them all, you can use a filter to select the DRS recommendations you want to apply:

```
PowerCLI C:\> Get-DrsRecommendation |
>> Where-Object {$_.Recommendation -like "*VM1*" } |
>> Invoke-DrsRecommendation
```

Using resource pools

The virtual machines in a vSphere cluster share the resources of the ESXi hosts in the cluster. Resource pools are a way to divide the resources of the cluster into different pools. Virtual machines in a resource pool share the resources of their resource pool. This can be useful to always give a group of virtual machines the resources they need or to limit the number of resources for a group of virtual machines.

Each cluster has a root resource pool named `Resources`. The resource pools you create are children of the `Resources` root resource pool or other resource pools in the cluster.

Resource pools and virtual machines have settings that will be explained in the following table:

Setting	Description
Shares	A relative importance against sibling resource pools or virtual machines. Shares can have a level (`Custom`, `High`, `Low`, or `Normal`) or an amount.
Limit	The maximum allowed resources.
Reservation	The minimum available resources.
Expandable reservation (resource pool only)	If a resource pool has an expandable reservation, it can use resources of the parent resource pool, if the parent resource pool has unreserved resources.

You already saw the `Move-VM` cmdlet that can be used to move virtual machines into resource pools in `Chapter 5`, *Managing Virtual Machines with PowerCLI*.

Creating resource pools

You can use the `New-ResourcePool` cmdlet to create a resource pool. The syntax of the `New-ResourcePool` cmdlet is as follows:

```
New-ResourcePool -Location <VIContainer> -Name <String>
[-CpuExpandableReservation [<Boolean>]] [-CpuLimitMhz <Int64>]
[-CpuReservationMhz <Int64>] [-CpuSharesLevel <SharesLevel>]
[-MemExpandableReservation [<Boolean>]] [-MemLimitMB <Int64>]
[-MemLimitGB <Decimal>] [-MemReservationMB <Int64>] [-MemReservationGB
<Decimal>] [-MemSharesLevel <SharesLevel>] [-NumCpuShares <Int32>]
[-NumMemShares <Int32>] [-Server <VIServer[]>] [-WhatIf]
[-Confirm] [<CommonParameters>]
```

The `-Location` and `-Name` parameters are required. The value of the `-Location` parameter can be a resource pool, cluster, or host.

In the following example, a new resource pool named `ResourcePool2` will be created for `Cluster01`. Because the parameter list is quite long, splatting is used to make the code more readable:

```
PowerCLI C:\> $Parameters = @{
>> Location = (Get-Cluster -Name Cluster01)
>> Name = 'ResourcePool2'
>> CpuExpandableReservation = $true
>> CpuReservationMhz = 500
>> CpuSharesLevel = 'normal'
>> MemExpandableReservation = $true
>> MemReservationMB = 512
>> MemSharesLevel = 'high'
>> }
>> New-ResourcePool @Parameters
```

Name	CpuShares Level	CpuReser vationMHz	CpuLimit MHz	MemShares Level	MemReser vationGB	MemLi mitGB
ResourcePool2	Normal	500	-1	High	0.500	-1.000

Retrieving resource pools

To retrieve resource pools, you can use the `Get-ResourcePool` cmdlet. The syntax of the `Get-ResourcePool` cmdlet is as follows. The first parameter set is the default:

```
Get-ResourcePool [[-Name] <String[]>] [-Location <VIContainer[]>]
[-Server <VIServer[]>] [-Tag <Tag[]>] [-NoRecursion]
[<CommonParameters>]
```

The second parameter set to retrieve resource pools by child virtual machine:

```
Get-ResourcePool [[-Name] <String[]>] -VM <VirtualMachine[]>
[-Server <VIServer[]>] [-Tag <Tag[]>] [<CommonParameters>]
```

The third parameter set is to retrieve resource pools by ID:

```
Get-ResourcePool -Id <String[]> [-Server <VIServer[]>]
[<CommonParameters>]
```

The fourth parameter set is to retrieve resource pools by a related object:

```
Get-ResourcePool -RelatedObject
<ResourcePoolRelatedObjectBase[]> [<CommonParameters>]
```

The `-VM`, `-Id`, and `-RelatedObject` parameters are required.

If you don't specify parameters, all of the resource pools in your environment will be retrieved. You can use the different parameters to filter the resource pools. In the following example, you will retrieve all of the resource pools of `Cluster01`:

```
PowerCLI C:\> Get-Cluster -Name Cluster01 | Get-ResourcePool
```

Name	CpuShares Level	CpuReser vationMHz	CpuLimit MHz	MemShares Level	MemReser vationGB	MemLi mitGB
Resources	Normal	6560	6560	Normal	0.753	0.753
ResourcePool2	Normal	500	-1	High	0.500	-1.000

Modifying resource pools

The `Set-ResourcePool` cmdlet can be used to modify the settings of a resource pool. The syntax of this cmdlet is as follows:

```
Set-ResourcePool [-ResourcePool] <ResourcePool[]> [-Name <String>]
[-CpuExpandableReservation [<Boolean>]] [-CpuLimitMhz <Int64>]
[-CpuReservationMhz <Int64>] [-CpuSharesLevel <SharesLevel>]
[-MemExpandableReservation [<Boolean>]] [-MemLimitMB <Int64>]
[-MemLimitGB <Decimal>] [-MemReservationMB <Int64>]
[-MemReservationGB <Decimal>] [-MemSharesLevel <SharesLevel>]
[-NumCpuShares <Int32>] [-NumMemShares <Int32>] [-Server <VIServer[]>]
[-WhatIf] [-Confirm] [<CommonParameters>]
```

The `-ResourcePool` parameter is the only required parameter.

You cannot specify a new location for a resource pool using the `Set-ResourcePool` cmdlet, but the rest of the parameters of the `Set-ResourcePool` cmdlet are the same as for the `New-ResourcePool` cmdlet.

In the following example, the `ResourcePool2` memory limit and CPU limit will be modified:

```
PowerCLI C:\> Set-ResourcePool -ResourcePool Resourcepool2
-MemLimitGB 4 -CpuLimitMhz 6000
```

Name	CpuShares Level	CpuReser vationMHz	CpuLimit MHz	MemShares Level	MemReser vationGB	MemLi mitGB
ResourcePool2	Normal	500	6000	High	0.500	4.000

Moving resource pools

To move a resource pool to a new location, you can use the `Move-ResourcePool` cmdlet, which has the following syntax:

```
Move-ResourcePool [-ResourcePool] <ResourcePool[]> [-Destination]
<VIContainer> [-Server <VIServer[]>] [-WhatIf] [-Confirm]
[<CommonParameters>]
```

The `-ResourcePool` and `-Destination` parameters are required.

In the following example, a new resource pool named `ResourcePool1` is created in `Cluster01`:

```
PowerCLI C:\> New-ResourcePool -Name ResourcePool1 -Location
(Get-Cluster -Name Cluster01)
```

Name	CpuShares Level	CpuReser vationMHz	CpuLimit MHz	MemShares Level	MemReser vationGB	MemLi mitGB
ResourcePool1	Normal	0	-1	Normal	0.000	-1.000

The existing resource pool `ResourcePool2` is relocated and made a child of the `ResourcePool1` resource pool, using the following command:

```
PowerCLI C:\> Move-ResourcePool -ResourcePool ResourcePool2
-Destination (Get-ResourcePool -Name ResourcePool1)
```

Name	CpuShares Level	CpuReser vationMHz	CpuLimit MHz	MemShares Level	MemReser vationGB	MemLi mitGB
ResourcePool2	Normal	500	6000	High	0.500	4.000

If you want to see the hierarchy of the resource pools, you can look at the `Parent` property of the resource pools:

```
PowerCLI C:\> Get-ResourcePool -Location (Get-Cluster -Name
Cluster01) | Select-Object -Property Name,Parent
```

Name	Parent
Resources	Cluster01
ResourcePool1	Resources
ResourcePool2	ResourcePool1

In the output of the preceding example, you can see that the `Resources` resource pool is a child of the `Cluster01` cluster, the `ResourcePool1` resource pool is a child of the `Resources` resource pool, and the `ResourcePool2` resource pool is a child of the `ResourcePool1` resource pool.

Configuring resource allocation between virtual machines

You can also specify shares, limits, and reservations for virtual machines. You can use the `Get-VMResourceConfiguration` cmdlet to retrieve the current resource configuration of virtual machines. The syntax of the `Get-VMResourceConfiguration` cmdlet is as follows:

```
Get-VMResourceConfiguration [-Server <VIServer[]>]
[-VM] <VirtualMachine[]> [<CommonParameters>]
```

The `-VM` parameter is required.

In the following example, the resource configuration of virtual machine VM1 is retrieved and piped to the `Format-List -Property *` command to list all the property values. The output of the example is in the following screenshot:

The `Set-VMResourceConfiguration` cmdlet can be used to modify the resource configuration of a virtual machine. The syntax of the `Set-VMResourceConfiguration` is as follows:

```
Set-VMResourceConfiguration [-Configuration]
<VMResourceConfiguration[]>
[-HtCoreSharing <HTCoreSharing>] [-CpuAffinity <CpuAffinity>]
[-CpuAffinityList <Int32[]>] [-CpuReservationMhz <Int64>]
[-CpuLimitMhz <Int64>] [-CpuSharesLevel <SharesLevel>]
[-NumCpuShares <Int32>] [-MemReservationMB <Int64>]
[-MemReservationGB <Decimal>] [-MemLimitMB <Int64>]
[-MemLimitGB <Decimal>] [-MemSharesLevel <SharesLevel>]
[-NumMemShares <Int32>] [-Disk <HardDisk[]>] [-NumDiskShares <Int32>]
[-DiskSharesLevel <SharesLevel>] [-DiskLimitIOPerSecond <Int64>]
[-WhatIf] [-Confirm] [<CommonParameters>]
```

The `-Configuration` parameter is the only required parameter. Most of the parameters are similar to the parameters of the `Set-ResourcePool` cmdlet. New parameters are `-Disk`, `-NumDiskShares`, `-DiskSharesLevel`, and `-DiskLimitIOPerSecond`. These parameters allow you to set a disk I/O limit, disk shares, and a disk shares level per disk.

In the following example, the CPU and memory shares level of virtual machine `VM1` are set to `High`:

```
PowerCLI C:\> Get-VMResourceConfiguration -VM VM1 |
>> Set-VMResourceConfiguration -CpuSharesLevel High
-MemSharesLevel High
```

VM	NumCpuShares	CpuSharesLevel	NumMemShares	MemSharesLevel
VM1	2000	High	5120	High

Removing resource pools

The `Remove-ResourcePool` cmdlet will remove a resource pool for you. This cmdlet has the following syntax:

```
Remove-ResourcePool [-ResourcePool] <ResourcePool[]>
[-Server <VIServer[]>] [-WhatIf] [-Confirm] [<CommonParameters>]
```

The `-ResourcePool` parameter is required.

In the following example, the resource pool named `ResourcePool1` is removed:

```
PowerCLI C:\> Remove-ResourcePool -ResourcePool
ResourcePool1 -Confirm:$false
```

The preceding command does not return any output.

Using Distributed Power Management

The load of your virtual machines is probably not always the same. Sometimes, they need more resources, and sometimes, they need fewer resources. **Distributed Power Management (DPM)** will use DRS to consolidate virtual machines on fewer ESXi hosts during periods of low resource utilization. The unused ESXi hosts will be powered off. If more resources are needed, DPM will power on ESXi hosts, and DRS will move virtual machines to these hosts. DPM will save you or your company money in power and cooling costs.

Enabling DPM

DPM has two modes: manual and automatic. In manual mode, DPM will give recommendations to evacuate virtual machines from hosts and power off or power on the hosts. You will have to apply the recommendations manually. In automatic mode, DPM will automatically apply DPM recommendations above a certain threshold.

In the following screenshot of the vSphere Web Client, you will see the DPM settings of a cluster with **Automation Level** set to **Manual**:

DPM uses Wake-on-LAN, IPMI, or iLO to power on hosts. When using IPMI or iLO, configure IPMI or iLO separately for each participating host prior to enabling DPM. For all power-on methods, test exit standby for each participating host prior to enabling DPM.

○ Off
  vCenter Server will not provide power management recommendations. Individual host overrides may be set, but will not become active until the cluster default is either Manual or Automatic.

◉ Manual
  vCenter Server will recommend evacuating a host's virtual machines and powering off the host when the cluster's resource usage is low, and powering the host back on when necessary.

○ Automatic
  vCenter Server will automatically execute power management related recommendations.

Overrides for individual hosts can be set from the Host Options page.

There are no cmdlets to configure DPM, so you have to use the vSphere API again. You start with creating a `ClusterConfigSpecEx` object. Assign a new `ClusterDpmConfigInfo` object to the `dpmConfig` property of the `ClusterConfigSpecEx` object. Assign `$true` to the enabled property and assign `manual` or `automated` to the `defaultDpmBehavior` property. If you choose `automated`, you can assign an integer value from 1 to 5 to the `hostPowerActionRate` property, where 1 is the most aggressive threshold and 5 is the most conservative threshold:

```
# Enabling Distributed Power Management
$Cluster = Get-Cluster -Name Cluster01
$spec = New-Object VMware.Vim.ClusterConfigSpecEx
$spec.dpmConfig = New-Object VMware.Vim.ClusterDpmConfigInfo
$spec.dpmConfig.enabled = $true
$spec.dpmConfig.defaultDpmBehavior = "manual"
$spec.dpmConfig.hostPowerActionRate = 3
$Cluster.ExtensionData.ReconfigureComputeResource_Task($spec, $true)
```

Configuring hosts for DPM

For DPM to be able to power on hosts, you have to configure the **Intelligent Platform Management Interface (IPMI) / Integrated Lights-Out (iLO)** settings for power management. You have to specify the username, password, BMC IP address, and BMC MAC address of the IPMI interface in your host.

The following example will configure the IPMI information for host `192.168.0.133` using the `UpdateIpmi()` method:

```
# Updating IPMI info
$VMHost = Get-VMHost -Name 192.168.0.133
$ipmiInfo = New-Object VMware.Vim.HostIpmiInfo
$ipmiInfo.bmcIpAddress = "192.168.0.201"
$ipmiInfo.bmcMacAddress = "d4:85:64:52:1b:49"
$ipmiInfo.login = "IPMIuser"
$ipmiInfo.password = "IPMIpassword"
$VMHost.ExtensionData.UpdateIpmi($ipmiInfo)
```

Testing hosts for DPM

Before enabling DPM on a cluster or before adding a host to a DPM-enabled cluster, it is a good practice to test the IPMI settings of all the hosts. You would be in trouble if DPM stopped a host and couldn't start it, wouldn't you? You can test a host for IPMI by putting it into standby mode first and starting it afterwards.

Putting hosts into standby mode

You can use the `Suspend-VMHost` cmdlet to put a host in standby mode. The syntax of the `Suspend-VMHost` cmdlet is as follows:

```
Suspend-VMHost [-VMHost] <VMHost[]> [-TimeoutSeconds <Int32>]
[-Evacuate] [-Server <VIServer[]>] [-RunAsync] [-WhatIf]
[-Confirm] [<CommonParameters>]
```

The `-VMHost` parameter is required.

In the following example, the host `192.168.0.133` will be put into standby mode:

```
PowerCLI C:\> Get-VMHost -Name 192.168.0.133 |
>> Suspend-VMHost -Confirm:$false
```

Starting hosts

To start a host in standby mode, you can use the `Start-VMHost` cmdlet. The syntax of this cmdlet is as follows:

```
Start-VMHost [-VMHost] <VMHost[]> [-TimeoutSeconds <Int32>]
[-Server <VIServer[]>] [-RunAsync] [-WhatIf] [-Confirm]
[<CommonParameters>]
```

The `-VMHost` parameter is required.

The host `192.168.0.133` that was put into standby mode in the preceding example will be started in the next example:

```
PowerCLI C:\> Get-VMHost -Name 192.168.0.133 |
>> Start-VMHost -Confirm:$false
```

After a successful start from a standby mode, your host is ready for DPM.

Retrieving the DPM configuration of a cluster

To check whether DPM is enabled on a cluster and to see the DPM settings, you can look at the `ExtensionData.ConfigurationEx.DpmConfigInfo` property of the cluster.

In the following example, the DPM configuration of `Cluster01` is retrieved:

```
PowerCLI C:\> Get-Cluster -Name Cluster01 |
>> ForEach-Object {$_.ExtensionData.ConfigurationEx.DpmConfigInfo}

Enabled DefaultDpmBehavior HostPowerActionRate Option
------- ------------------ ------------------- ------
   True            manual                    3
```

Disabling DPM

To disable DPM, you can use almost the same script as to enable DPM. Just modify `$spec.dpmConfig.enabled = $true` into `$spec.dpmConfig.enabled = $false`.

You don't have to specify values for the `defaultDpmBehavior` or `hostPowerActionRate` properties:

```
# Disabling Distributed Power Management
$Cluster = Get-Cluster -Name Cluster01
$spec = New-Object VMware.Vim.ClusterConfigSpecEx
$spec.dpmConfig = New-Object VMware.Vim.ClusterDpmConfigInfo
$spec.dpmConfig.enabled = $false
$Cluster.ExtensionData.ReconfigureComputeResource_Task($spec, $true)
```

Removing clusters

The `Remove-Cluster` cmdlet will remove a cluster from your vSphere inventory. The `Remove-Cluster` cmdlet has the following syntax:

```
Remove-Cluster [-Cluster] <Cluster[]> [-Server <VIServer[]>]
[-RunAsync] [-WhatIf] [-Confirm] [<CommonParameters>]
```

The `-Cluster` parameter is required.

The following example will remove `Cluster02` that was created at the beginning of this chapter:

```
PowerCLI C:\> Remove-Cluster -Cluster Cluster02
-Confirm:$false
```

The preceding command does not return any output.

 Be careful. Removing a cluster will also remove all the hosts and virtual machines in the cluster!

Summary

In this chapter, you learned all about managing vSphere HA and DRS clusters. We looked at retrieving HA master or primary hosts, retrieving cluster configuration issues, and disabling HA, to perform network maintenance that may cause network isolation. You learned about disabling or enabling host monitoring, associating a host profile with a cluster, enabling VM and Application Monitoring, configuring the heartbeat datastore selection policy, moving hosts to clusters, and moving clusters.

Using DRS rules and DRS groups, we discussed how to control the placement of virtual machines on hosts in a cluster. You learned to use resource pools and to divide the resources of the cluster into different pools. We looked at configuring resource allocation between virtual machines, with shares, limits, and reservations.

Finally, you read how to use Distributed Power Management, to save money in power and cooling costs during the periods of low resource utilization.

The following chapter will be about managing vCenter Server.

9
Managing vCenter Server

If you have more than one ESXi server, a vCenter Server will make your ESXi servers much easier to manage. A vCenter Server will also add a lot of additional features, such as HA and DRS clusters, to your vSphere environment. In this chapter, we will discuss some topics that will help you manage your vSphere environment.

The following topics are covered in this chapter:

- Working with roles and permissions
- Managing licenses
- Configuring alarms
- Retrieving events

Working with roles and permissions

In a VMware vSphere environment, you might want to give certain **permissions** to users or administrators, who are not a part of the vSphere administrator's team, to perform specific tasks. For example, you might want to give the administrators of a server the permission to power on and off the server. You don't want to give these administrators all the privileges in your environment because you will lose control over it. There are many privileges you can give to somebody, and you probably want to give only a few. If you assigned privileges to users directly, it would be hard to see who has which privileges.

VMware vSphere has a nice feature named **roles**. Roles are a collection of privileges that you will need to perform a certain task. You can create a role named `Server administrator` and assign the `Power On` and `Power Off` privileges to this role. Every time you want to give an administrator the rights to power on and off a server, you can assign the `Server administrator` role to the administrator.

Permissions can be granted for every object in your vSphere environment, such as the root of your vSphere environment, data centers, folders, clusters, and virtual machines. Permissions can be propagated to the child objects of the main object to which you added a permission.

In the preceding `Server administrator` example, you might want to create a folder for all of the servers assigned to the administrator. You can grant the `Server administrator` role to the administrator in the folder and propagate this permission to all of the child objects of the folder. This will give the administrator power on and off privileges for all of the servers in the folder.

Retrieving privileges

At the time of writing this book, using vSphere 6.0, there are 310 different privilege items you can grant to somebody. These privileges are arranged in 50 privilege groups. To get a list of all of the privilege items or the privilege groups and their descriptions, you can use the `Get-VIPrivilege` cmdlet. This cmdlet has the following syntax. The first parameter set is to retrieve privileges by server:

```
Get-VIPrivilege [-PrivilegeGroup] [-PrivilegeItem] [[-Name]
<String[]>] [-Id <String[]>] [-Server <VIServer[]>]
[<CommonParameters>]
```

The second parameter set is to retrieve privileges by role:

```
Get-VIPrivilege [[-Name] <String[]>] [-Role] <Role[]>
[-Id <String[]>] [<CommonParameters>]
```

The third parameter set is to retrieve privileges by group:

```
Get-VIPrivilege [[-Name] <String[]>] [-Group] <PrivilegeGroup[]>
[-Id <String[]>] [<CommonParameters>]
```

The `-Role` and `-Group` parameters are required. Using the `Get-VIPrivilege` cmdlet without parameters will retrieve all of the privilege items and the privilege groups.

In the first example, we will retrieve all of the privilege items that have a name starting with
`Power`:

```
PowerCLI C:\> Get-VIPrivilege -PrivilegeItem -Name Power*
```

The output of the preceding command is as follows:

```
Name              Description                        Server
----              -----------                        ------
Power             Power system operations            192.168.0.132
Power On          Power On or resume a virtual machine  192.168.0.132
Power Off         Power Off a virtual machine        192.168.0.132
Power On          Power On a vApp                     192.168.0.132
Power Off         Power Off a vApp                    192.168.0.132
```

In the second example, we will use the `Get-VIPrivilege -Role` parameter to retrieve the
privileges of the `ReadOnly` role:

```
PowerCLI C:\> Get-VIPrivilege -Role ReadOnly
```

The output of the preceding command is as follows:

```
Name       Description                          Server
----       -----------                          ------
Anonymous  The only privilege held by sessions which ... 192.168.0.132
View       Visibility without read access to an entity.. 192.168.0.132
Read       Grants read access to an entity       192.168.0.132
```

In the third example, we will retrieve a list of the privilege groups using the following
command:

```
PowerCLI C:\> Get-VIPrivilege -PrivilegeGroup
```

The output of the preceding command is too long to show in this book. Try the command
yourself and see what it does.

In the fourth and last example of the `Get-VIPrivilege` cmdlet, we will use the `-Group`
parameter to retrieve all of the privilege items of the `Alarms` group:

```
PowerCLI C:\> Get-VIPrivilege -Group Alarms
```

The output of the preceding command is as follows:

```
Name                    Description                Server
----                    -----------                ------
Create alarm            Create an alarm            192.168.0.132
Remove alarm            Remove an alarm            192.168.0.132
Modify alarm            Modify an alarm            192.168.0.132
Acknowledge alarm       Acknowledge an alarm       192.168.0.132
Set alarm status        Set status for an alarm    192.168.0.132
Disable alarm action    Disable actions for an alarm 192.168.0.132
```

Using roles

Now that you know how to retrieve the vSphere privilege items and groups, you can start using the predefined roles or creating custom roles.

Creating roles

You can use the New-VIRole cmdlet to create a new role. The syntax of the New-VIRole cmdlet is as follows:

```
New-VIRole [-Name] <String> [[-Privilege] <Privilege[]>]
[-Server <VIServer[]>] [-WhatIf] [-Confirm] [<CommonParameters>]
```

The -Name parameter is required to create a new role.

In the following example, you will create the Server administrator role with the Power on and Power off privileges:

```
PowerCLI C:\> $Privileges = Get-VIPrivilege -Name 'Power On',
'Power Off'
PowerCLI C:\> New-VIRole -Name 'Server administrator'
-Privilege $Privileges
```

The output of the preceding commands is as follows:

```
Name                    IsSystem
----                    --------
Server administrator    False
```

In the following screenshot of vSphere Web Client, you will see the privileges under the **Server administrator** role under **Privileges** after executing the preceding PowerCLI commands to create the role:

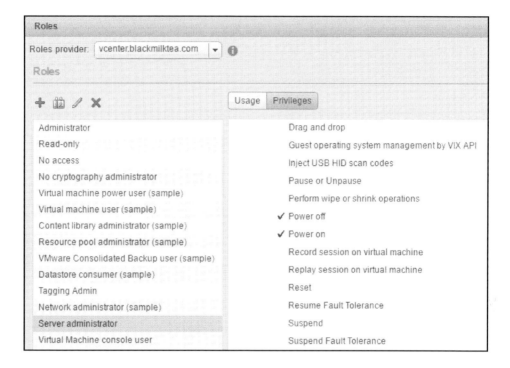

Retrieving roles

The `Get-VIRole` cmdlet retrieves all of the roles on your server. The syntax of this cmdlet is as follows:

```
Get-VIRole [[-Name] <String[]>] [-Id <String[]>]
[-Server <VIServer[]>] [<CommonParameters>]
```

The Get-VIRole cmdlet has no required parameters. The Get-VIRole cmdlet without parameters retrieves all of the roles in your environment:

```
PowerCLI C:\> Get-VIRole
```

The output of the preceding command is as follows:

```
Name                                    IsSystem
----                                    --------
com.vmware.Content.Admin                False
NoCryptoAdmin                           True
NoAccess                                True
Anonymous                               True
View                                    True
ReadOnly                                True
Admin                                   True
VirtualMachinePowerUser                 False
VirtualMachineUser                      False
ResourcePoolAdministrator               False
VMwareConsolidatedBackupUser            False
DatastoreConsumer                       False
NetworkConsumer                         False
VirtualMachineConsoleUser               False
InventoryService.Tagging.TaggingAdmin   False
Server administrator                    False
```

You can also use the -Name parameter to retrieve specific roles:

```
PowerCLI C:\> Get-VIRole -Name "Server administrator"
```

The output of the preceding command is as follows:

```
Name                    IsSystem
----                    --------
Server administrator    False
```

If you combine the Get-VIRole and Get-VIPrivilege cmdlets, you will get the privileges of a role. If you look at the privileges of the Server administrator role, you will see that it has not only the Power On and Power Off privileges, but also the Anonymous, View, and Read privileges. These three privileges are added to all of the roles you create, and they cannot be removed from the created roles:

```
PowerCLI C:\> Get-VIRole -Name 'Server administrator' | Get-VIPrivilege
```

The output of the preceding command is as follows:

```
Name        Description                                      Server
----        -----------                                      ------
Anonymous The only privilege held by sessions which ... 192.168.0.132
View        Visibility without read access to an entity.. 192.168.0.132
Read        Grants read access to an entity              192.168.0.132
Power On  Power On or resume a virtual machine         192.168.0.132
Power Off Power Off a virtual machine                  192.168.0.132
Power On  Power On a vApp                               192.168.0.132
Power Off Power Off a vApp                              192.168.0.132
```

Modifying roles

You can use the Set-VIRole cmdlet to give a new name to a role, add privileges to a role, or remove privileges from a role. The syntax of the Set-VIRole cmdlet is as follows. The first parameter set is there to add privileges or privilege groups to a role:

```
Set-VIRole [-Role] <Role[]> [-Name <String>] [-AddPrivilege
<Privilege[]>] [-Server <VIServer[]>] [-WhatIf] [-Confirm]
[<CommonParameters>]
```

The second parameter set removes privileges or privilege groups from a role:

```
Set-VIRole [-Role] <Role[]> [-Name <String>] [-RemovePrivilege
<Privilege[]>] [-Server <VIServer[]>] [-WhatIf] [-Confirm]
[<CommonParameters>]
```

The -Role parameter is required to modify a role:

In the following example, you will modify the Server administrator role into an Alarm operator role. The name will be changed, the power privileges will be removed, and the alarms privileges will be added using the following commands:

```
PowerCLI C:\> Get-VIRole -Name 'Server administrator' |
>> Set-VIRole -Name 'Alarm operator' -RemovePrivilege
(Get-VIPrivilege -Name 'Power On','Power Off') |
>> Set-VIRole -AddPrivilege (Get-VIPrivilege -Group Alarms)
```

The output of the preceding command is as follows:

```
Name                    IsSystem
----                    --------
Alarm operator          False
```

Removing roles

The `Remove-VIRole` cmdlet can be used to remove roles. This cmdlet has the following syntax:

```
Remove-VIRole [-Role] <Role[]> [-Force] [-Server <VIServer[]>]
[-WhatIf] [-Confirm] [<CommonParameters>]
```

The `-Role` parameter is required to remove a role. By default, you cannot remove a role that is associated with a permission. The `-Force` parameter indicates that you want to remove the role even if it is associated with a permission.

In the following example, we will remove the `Alarm operator` role:

```
PowerCLI C:\> Remove-VIRole -Role 'Alarm operator' -Confirm:$false
```

The preceding command does not return any output.

Using permissions

Now that you know how to create and use roles in PowerCLI, you can start creating permissions. A vSphere permission grants the privileges in a role to users or groups of users on a vSphere inventory item.

Creating permissions

The `New-VIPermission` cmdlet creates new permissions. The `New-VIPermission` cmdlet has the following syntax:

```
New-VIPermission [-Entity] <VIObject[]> [-Principal] <VIAccount[]>
[-Role] <Role> [-Propagate [<Boolean>]] [-Server <VIServer[]>]
[-WhatIf] [-Confirm] [<CommonParameters>]
```

The `-Entity`, `-Principal`, and `-Role` parameters are required to create a new permission.

By default, new permissions are propagated to child objects in the vSphere inventory. If you just want to create a permission for an inventory item and not for its child objects, you have to use the `-Propagate` parameter with the `$false` value.

It is not possible to create new permissions for the following objects:

- Direct child folders of a data center
- Root resource pools of clusters and standalone hosts

These objects always inherit the permissions of their parent.

 VMware vCenter **Single Sign-On** (**SSO**) was first introduced in vSphere 5.1. In vSphere 5.5 and 6.0, the default Single Sign-On domain is named `vsphere.local`, and the default Single Sign-On administrator account is `administrator@vsphere.local`. In vSphere 5.1, the default Single Sign-On domain is named `System-Domain`, and the default Single Sign-On administrator account is `admin@System-Domain`.

In the following example, the vCenter Single Sign-On account `VSPHERE.LOCAL\Administrator` is granted the `Admin` role for the `New York` data center:

```
PowerCLI C:\> New-VIPermission -Entity (Get-Datacenter
-Name 'New York')
-Principal VSPHERE.LOCAL\Administrator -Role Admin
```

The output of the preceding command is as follows:

```
Role            Principal        Propagate IsGroup
----            ---------        --------- -------
Admin           VSPHERE.LOCA... True      False
```

In the following screenshot of the vSphere Web Client, you will see the permissions of the `New York` data center under the **Permissions** tab after executing the preceding PowerCLI command to grant the **Admininistrator** role to the `VSPHERE.LOCAL\Administrator` account for the `New York` data center:

Retrieving permissions

The `Get-VIPermission` cmdlet retrieves the permissions defined for inventory objects. The syntax of this cmdlet is as follows:

```
Get-VIPermission [[-Entity] <VIObject[]>] [-Principal <VIAccount[]>]
[-Server <VIServer[]>] [<CommonParameters>]
```

The `Get-VIPermission` cmdlet has no required parameters. If you don't specify parameters, the cmdlet will retrieve all of the permissions in your environment. You can use the `-Entity` parameter to retrieve only the permissions for the specified inventory objects. Use the `-Principal` parameter to retrieve permissions for certain users or groups.

In the following example, we will retrieve all of the permissions of the `New York` data center:

```
PowerCLI C:\> Get-VIPermission -Entity (Get-Datacenter -Name
'New York') | Select-Object -Property Role,Principal
```

The output of the preceding command is as follows:

```
Role   Principal
----   ---------
Admin  VSPHERE.LOCAL\Administrator
Admin  VSPHERE.LOCAL\vpxd-905bbfa6-51c6-477e-b77b-8fed8fceb492
Admin  VSPHERE.LOCAL\vsphere-webclient-905bbfa6-51c6-477e-b77b-8fed...
Admin  VSPHERE.LOCAL\vpxd-extension-905bbfa6-51c6-477e-b77b-8fed8fc...
Admin  VSPHERE.LOCAL\Administrators
```

If you retrieve the permissions, the default output doesn't show you the vSphere object for the permission. You can add this object by piping the output to the `Format-Table` cmdlet. Use the `-Property` parameter and specify all of the properties you want to retrieve, as shown in the following command line. The vSphere object is in the `Entity` property:

```
PowerCLI C:\> Get-VIPermission | Format-Table -Property
Entity,Role,Propagate,IsGroup,Principal -AutoSize
```

The output of the preceding command is as follows:

```
Entity       Role   Propagate IsGroup Principal
------       ----   --------- ------- ---------
New York     Admin    True    False VSPHERE.LOCAL\Administrator
Datacenters  Admin    True    False VSPHERE.LOCAL\vpxd-905bbfa6-51...
Datacenters  Admin    True    False VSPHERE.LOCAL\vsphere-webclien...
Datacenters  Admin    True    False VSPHERE.LOCAL\vpxd-extension-9...
Datacenters  Admin    True    False VSPHERE.LOCAL\Administrator
Datacenters  Admin    True     True VSPHERE.LOCAL\Administrators
```

Modifying permissions

You can use the Set-VIPermission cmdlet to change the role of a permission or to modify a permission if it propagates to child objects or vice versa. The Set-VIPermission cmdlet has the following syntax:

```
Set-VIPermission [-Permission] <Permission[]> [-Role <Role>]
[-Propagate [<Boolean>]] [-Server <VIServer[]>] [-WhatIf]
[-Confirm] [<CommonParameters>]
```

The -Permission parameter is required to modify permissions.

In the following example, the permission of the account VSPHERE.LOCAL\Administrator on the data center New York is changed into ReadOnly, and the propagation of the permission to child objects is disabled:

```
PowerCLI C:\> Get-VIPermission -Entity (Get-Datacenter -Name 'New
York') -Principal VSPHERE.LOCAL\Administrator |
>> Set-VIPermission -Role ReadOnly -Propagate:$false
```

The output of the preceding command is as follows:

```
Role              Principal        Propagate IsGroup
----              ---------        --------- -------
ReadOnly          VSPHERE.LOCA... False     False
```

Removing permissions

The Remove-VIPermission cmdlet will remove the specified permissions from your inventory. The syntax of this cmdlet is as follows:

```
Remove-VIPermission [-Permission] <Permission[]> [-WhatIf]
[-Confirm] [<CommonParameters>]
```

The -Permission parameter is required to remove a permission.

In the following example, the permission for VSPHERE.LOCAL\Administrator is removed from the New York data center:

```
PowerCLI C:\> Get-VIPermission -Entity (Get-Datacenter -Name
'New York') -Principal VSPHERE.LOCAL\Administrator |
>> Remove-VIPermission -Confirm:$false
```

The preceding command does not return any output.

Managing licenses

While writing this book, there are no PowerCLI cmdlets to add, retrieve, update, or remove licenses. You have to use the vSphere API to manage licenses in PowerCLI. There is only one cmdlet in PowerCLI for license management, Get-LicenseDataManager, and the only thing this cmdlet does is exposes a hidden vSphere API. The syntax of the Get-LicenseDataManager cmdlet is as follows:

```
Get-LicenseDataManager [[-Server] <VIServer[]>]
[<CommonParameters>]
```

The Get-LicenseDataManager cmdlet has no required parameters.

You will use the vSphere API objects LicenseManager, LicenseAssignmentManager, and the hidden LicenseDataManager object to manage licenses.

You need to use LicenseManager to manage licenses in the license inventory on your vCenter Server. You can use LicenseAssignmentManager to manage the assignment of licenses to the ESXi servers. You use LicenseDataManager to associate licenses with containers in your vSphere environment and enable automatic license assignment to hosts that are added to a container.

The following three commands will give you hooks to the vSphere API license objects:

```
PowerCLI C:\> $LicenseManager = Get-View -Id 'LicenseManager
-LicenseManager'
PowerCLI C:\> $LicenseAssignmentManager = Get-View -Id
'LicenseAssignmentManager-LicenseAssignmentManager'
PowerCLI C:\> $LicenseDataManager = Get-LicenseDataManager
```

 You can get a list of all of the methods and properties of PowerShell objects by piping an object to the Get-Member cmdlet. Take a look at the following example:

```
PowerCLI C:\> $LicenseManager | Get-Member
```

Adding license keys to the license inventory

To add a license to your vSphere license inventory, you have to use the `Licensemanager.AddLicense()` method. This method has two parameters. The first parameter is the license key that is to be added to your license inventory. The second parameter, called labels, is a pair of key-value labels that are ignored by the ESXi servers. You can use `$null` as the second parameter.

In the following example, you will add the license `00000-00000-00000-00000-00000` to your license inventory:

```
PowerCLI C:\> $LicenseManager = Get-View -Id
'LicenseManager-LicenseManager'
PowerCLI C:\> $LicenseManager.AddLicense
('00000-00000-00000-00000-00000',$null)
```

The output of the preceding command is as follows:

```
LicenseKey : 00000-00000-00000-00000-00000
EditionKey : eval
Name       : Product Evaluation
Total      : 0
Used       : 0
CostUnit   :
Properties : {Localized}
Labels     :
```

You can also work with a real license key instead of `00000-00000-00000-00000-00000`. This is the `Product Evaluation` license key used for the 60-day evaluation period of new ESXi servers.

Retrieving license keys from the license inventory

To retrieve license keys from your license inventory, you just have to query the `Licenses` property of the `LicenseManager` object, as shown in the following commands:

```
PowerCLI C:\> $LicenseManager = Get-View -Id
'LicenseManager-LicenseManager'
PowerCLI C:\> $LicenseManager.Licenses
```

The output of the preceding commands is as follows:

```
LicenseKey  : 00000-00000-00000-00000-00000
EditionKey  : eval
Name        : Product Evaluation
Total       : 0
Used        :
CostUnit    :
Properties  : {Localized}
Labels      :
```

Removing license keys from the license inventory

You can use the `LicenseManager.RemoveLicense()` method to remove a license from your license inventory. The `RemoveLicecense()` method has only one parameter, the license key. In the following example, you will remove the license key `00000-00000-00000-00000-00000` from your inventory:

```
PowerCLI C:\> $LicenseManager = Get-View -Id
'LicenseManager-LicenseManager'
PowerCLI C:\> $LicenseManager.RemoveLicense
('00000-00000-00000-00000-00000')
```

The preceding command does not return any output.

> Removing the `Product Evaluation` license `00000-00000-00000-00000-00000` is actually not possible. You can also not remove any license that is used.

Assigning licenses to hosts

You can use `Set-VMHost -LicenseKey` parameter to assign a license key to a host using the following command:

```
PowerCLI C:\> Get-VMHost -Name '192.168.0.133' |
>> Set-VMHost -LicenseKey '00000-00000-00000-00000-00000'
```

The output of the preceding command is as follows:

```
Name                    ConnectionState PowerState NumCpu CpuUsageMhz
----                    --------------- ---------- ------ -----------
192.168.0.133           Connected       PoweredOn       2        1035
```

Retrieving assigned licenses

A VMHost object has a LicenseKey property. You can retrieve the license key of a host with the following command:

```
PowerCLI C:\> Get-VMHost -Name '192.168.0.133' |
>> Select-Object -Property Name,LicenseKey
```

The output of the preceding command is as follows:

```
Name                    LicenseKey
----                    ----------
192.168.0.133           00000-00000-00000-00000-00000
```

Using the LicenseDataManager

With the automated deployment of the ESXi hosts using Auto Deploy, you will also want to automate the assignment of vSphere license keys to hosts. PowerCLI provides an object named LicenseDataManager that you can use to associate license keys with host containers, such as clusters, data centers, and data center folders. The presence of license keys that are associated with host containers makes it possible to automatically assign a license key to a host when an unlicensed host is added to a host container or is reconnected to the vCenter Server. If a host is already licensed, the host keeps the license key it already had.

You have to use the Get-LicenseDataManager cmdlet to get an instance of the LicenseDataManager object. The Get-LicenseDataManager cmdlet is supported only by vCenter Server 5.0 or higher. The use of the Get-LicenseDataManager cmdlet is different from what you are used to in PowerCLI. You have to use this cmdlet to retrieve a LicenseDataManager object and then use the methods of this object to associate the licenses to the inventory nodes.

The syntax of the `Get-LicenseDataManager` cmdlet is as follows:

```
Get-LicenseDataManager [[-Server] <VIServer[]>]
[<CommonParameters>]
```

Be warned that the `Get-LicenseDataManager` cmdlet is defined in the `VMware.VimAutomation.License` module. If you use PowerCLI by starting PowerShell and adding the PowerCLI modules, don't forget to import the `VMware.VimAutomation.License` module if you want to use the `Get-LicenseDataManager` cmdlet.

Associating license keys with host containers

To associate license keys with host containers, you have to use the `LicenseDataManager.UpdateAssociatedLicenseData()` method. This method needs two parameters: the Managed Object Reference of the container and a `LicenseData` object. The `LicenseData` object contains a `LicenseKeyEntry` object consisting of methods named `TypeId` and `LicenseKey`. The only valid `TypeId` that I know of is `vmware-vsphere`.

In the following example, we will associate a license key to the `New York` data center:

```
$LicenseDataManager = Get-LicenseDataManager
$LicenseData = New-Object Vmware.VimAutomation.License.Types.LicenseData
$LicenseKeyEntry = New-Object
Vmware.VimAutomation.License.Types.LicenseKeyEntry
$LicenseKeyEntry.TypeId = 'vmware-vsphere'
$LicenseKeyEntry.LicenseKey = '00000-00000-00000-00000-00000'
$LicenseData.LicenseKeys += $LicenseKeyEntry
$HostContainer = Get-Datacenter -Name 'New York'
$LicenseDataManager.UpdateAssociatedLicenseData($hostContainer.Uid,
$LicenseData)
```

Applying the associated license key to all hosts

After associating a license key to a host container, the hosts that were already in the container before the license key was associated will not automatically get the associated license keys applied. You have to use the `LicenseDataManager.ApplyAssociatedLicenseData()` method to apply the license key to the hosts.

In the following example, we will apply the license key associated with the `New York` data center to all of the hosts in the data center:

```
$LicenseDataManager = Get-LicenseDataManager
foreach ($VMHost in (Get-Datacenter -Name 'New York' | Get-VMHost))
{
  $LicenseDataManager.ApplyAssociatedLicenseData($VMHost.Uid)
}
```

Retrieving license key associations

There are three possible ways to retrieve license key associations. You can do one of the following:

- Retrieve all of the license key associations to the host containers in your environment
- Retrieve the license keys associated with a specific host container
- Retrieve the effective license key of a host container.

In the following three sections, you will see examples of all the three possibilities.

Retrieving all of the license key associations to the host containers in your environment

To retrieve all of the license key associations to the host containers, you can use the `LicenseDataManager.QueryEntityLicenseData()` method. Before running the following example, I also associated a license to the cluster `Cluster01`. This cluster is in the `New York` data center. The following example retrieves all of the license key associations in your environment:

If you want to know the name of the entity `Datacenter-datacenter-2` or `ClusterComputeResource-domain-c7`, you can use the `Get-VIObjectByVIView` cmdlet to convert the `-MORef` parameter into a PowerCLI object. For example, to get the name of `Datacenter-datacenter-2`, you can use the following command:

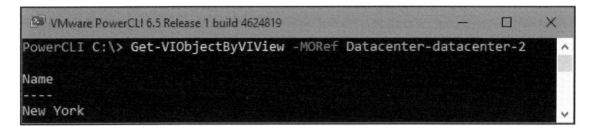

Retrieving the license keys associated with a specific host container

To retrieve the license keys associated with a specific host container, you have to use the `LicenseDataManager.QueryAssociatedLicenseData()` method. In the following example, we will retrieve the license keys associated with the `New York` data center:

```
PowerCLI C:\> $LicenseDataManager = Get-LicenseDataManager
PowerCLI C:\> $HostContainer = Get-Datacenter -Name 'New York'
PowerCLI C:\> $LicenseDataManager.QueryAssociatedLicenseData
($HostContainer.Uid)
```

The output of the preceding commands is as follows:

```
LicenseKeys
-----------
{vmware-vsphere: 00000-00000-00000-00000-00000}
```

Retrieving the effective license key of a host container

It is possible to associate a license key with a parent container and not with a child container. The license key associated with the parent container is also effective on the child container. If you want to know which is the effective license key of a host container, you have to use the `LicenseDataManager.QueryEffectiveLicenseData()` method. In the following example, we will retrieve the effective license key associated with the cluster `Cluster02`.

The cluster `Cluster02` belongs to the `New York` data center and does not have a license key associated with it:

```
PowerCLI C:\> $LicenseDataManager = Get-LicenseDataManager
PowerCLI C:\> $HostContainer = Get-Cluster -Name Cluster02
PowerCLI C:\> $LicenseDataManager.QueryEffectiveLicenseData
($HostContainer.Uid)
```

The output of the preceding commands is as follows:

```
LicenseKeys
-----------
{vmware-vsphere: 00000-00000-00000-00000-00000}
```

As you can see in the output of the preceding example, the license key associated with the `New York` data center is effective on the `Cluster02` cluster.

Modifying license key associations

To associate another license key with a host container, you just have to replace the license key associated with the host container with a new license key. The PowerCLI code that you have to use to associate a new license key is exactly the same as what we used to associate a license key with a host container, as you saw earlier in the *Associating license keys with host containers* section. After modifying a license key association, you have to apply the new license key to all of the hosts in the container, as shown in the *Applying the associated license key to all of the hosts in the container* section.

Removing license key associations

To remove the association of a license key with a host container, you have to use the `LicenseDataManager.UpdateAssociatedLicenseData()` method with `$null` as the second parameter. In the following example, we will remove the association of the license key with the data center `New York`:

```
$LicenseDataManager = Get-LicenseDataManager
$HostContainer = Get-Datacenter -Name 'New York'
$LicenseDataManager.UpdateAssociatedLicenseData($HostContainer.Uid, $null)
```

Configuring alarms

In a vSphere environment, there are conditions (such as *datastores running out of space*) that you want to know about before things run out of control. In the *datastores running out of space* example, you would want to be warned before the datastore is full, so you can move some disks to another datastore to create extra free space on the datastore that is running out of space.

VMware vSphere provides alarms that trigger warnings and alerts when certain conditions are met. There are a lot of predefined alarms for almost every condition possible in vCenter Server. For example, there is the Datastore usage on disk alarm for datastores that will, by default, give you a warning if a datastore usage is more than 75 %and give you an alert if a datastore usage is more than 85 %. It is also possible to define actions such as Send a notification email that are executed when an alarm is triggered.

In PowerCLI, there are various cmdlets to modify alarm definitions and to create and modify alarm action triggers and alarm actions.

In the following screenshot of vSphere Web Client, you will see the **Trigger states** notification of the Datastore usage on disk alarm:

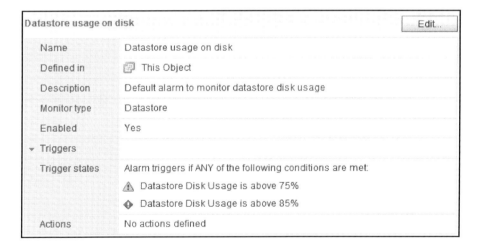

Retrieving alarm definitions

You can use the `Get-AlarmDefinition` cmdlet to retrieve the available alarm definitions. The syntax of this cmdlet is as follows:

```
Get-AlarmDefinition [-Id <String[]>] [[-Name] <String[]>] [[-Entity]
<VIObject[]>] [-Enabled [<Boolean>]] [-Server <VIServer[]>]
[<CommonParameters>]
```

The `Get-AlarmDefinition` cmdlet has no required parameters.

There are three possible ways to retrieve alarm definitions. You can do one of the following:

- Get a list of all of the available alarm definitions
- Filter the alarm definitions by name or entity
- Retrieve only the enabled alarm definitions

In the following example, we will retrieve the `Datastore usage on disk` alarm:

```
PowerCLI C:\> Get-Alarmdefinition -Name 'Datastore usage on disk'
```

The output of the preceding command is as follows:

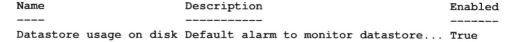

```
Name                          Description                          Enabled
----                          -----------                          -------
Datastore usage on disk Default alarm to monitor datastore... True
```

In the following screenshot of vSphere Web Client, you will see the alarm definition for the `Datastore usage on disk` alarm:

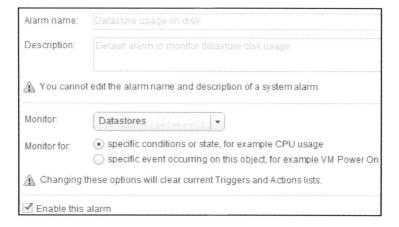

Modifying alarm definitions

To modify alarm definitions, you can use the `Set-AlarmDefinition` cmdlet that gives the ability to change the name and description of an alarm definition, specify how often the alarm actions repeat if the alarm is active, and enable or disable the alarm. The `Set-AlarmDefinition` cmdlet has the following syntax:

```
Set-AlarmDefinition [-AlarmDefinition] <AlarmDefinition[]>
[-ActionRepeatMinutes <Int32>] [-Description <String>] [-Enabled
[<Boolean>]] [-Name <String>] [-Server <VIServer[]>] [-WhatIf]
[-Confirm] [<CommonParameters>]
```

The `-AlarmDefinition` parameter is required to modify an alarm definition.

In the following example, we will disable the `Datastore usage on disk` alarm:

```
PowerCLI C:\> Get-AlarmDefinition -Name 'Datastore usage on disk' |
>> Set-AlarmDefinition -Enabled $false
```

The output of the preceding command is as follows:

```
Name                    Description                      Enabled
----                    -----------                      -------
Datastore usage on disk Default alarm to monitor datastore... False
```

Creating alarm actions

If an alarm is triggered, you can send an e-mail notification, generate an SNMP trap, or run a script. These actions can be defined with the `New-AlarmAction` cmdlet. This cmdlet has the following syntaxes. The first parameter set is required to create alarm actions that send an e-mail:

```
New-AlarmAction [-AlarmDefinition] <AlarmDefinition> -Email [-Subject
<String>] -To <String[]> [-Cc <String[]>] [-Body <String>] [-Server
<VIServer[]>] [-WhatIf] [-Confirm] [<CommonParameters>]
```

The second parameter set is to create alarm actions that run a script:

```
New-AlarmAction [-AlarmDefinition] <AlarmDefinition> -Script
-ScriptPath <String> [-Server <VIServer[]>] [-WhatIf] [-Confirm]
[<CommonParameters>]
```

The third parameter set is used to create alarm actions that generate an SNMP trap:

```
New-AlarmAction [-AlarmDefinition] <AlarmDefinition> -Snmp [-Server
<VIServer[]>] [-WhatIf] [-Confirm] [<CommonParameters>]
```

As you can see, the `New-AlarmAction` cmdlet has three parameter sets, one for each type of alarm action you can define. The `-AlarmDefinition` parameter is always required to create an alarm action. To create a `Send a notification email` alarm action, the `-Email` and `-To` parameters are also required. To create a `Send a notification trap` alarm action, the `-Snmp` parameter is required. To create a `Run a command` alarm action, the `-Script` and `-ScriptPath` parameters are required.

In the first example, we will create a `Send a notification e-mail` alarm action for the `Datastore usage on disk` alarm:

```
PowerCLI C:\> Get-AlarmDefinition -Name 'Datastore usage on disk' |
>> New-AlarmAction -Email -To user@domain.com -Subject 'Datastore
usage on disk alarm' -Body 'Datastore {targetName} usage is over its
alarm limits'
```

The output of the preceding command lines is as follows:

```
ActionType      Trigger
----------      -------
SendEmail       ...
```

The `{targetName}` variable in the preceding example will substitute the name of the datastore in the subject and body of the e-mail. The variables that you can use are shown in the following table. The table is copied from the vSphere 6.5 documentation's *Alarm Command-Line Parameters* section at http://pubs.vmware.com/vsphere-65/index.jsp#com.vmware.vsphere.monitoring.doc/G UID-B8DF4E10-89E3-409D-9111-AE405B7E5D2E_copy.html:

Variable	Description
{alarmName}	This is the name of the alarm that is triggered.
{declaringSummary}	This is a summary of the alarm declaration values.
{eventDescription}	This is the text of the `alarmStatusChange` event. The {eventDescription} variable is supported only for the condition and state alarms.
{newStatus}	This is the alarm status after the alarm is triggered.
{oldStatus}	This is the alarm status before the alarm is triggered.

{target}	This is the inventory object on which the alarm is set.
{targetName}	This is the name of the entity on which the alarm is triggered.
{triggeringSummary}	This is a summary of the alarm trigger values.

In the second example, we will create a `Send a notification trap` alarm action for the `Datastore usage on disk` alarm:

```
PowerCLI C:\> Get-AlarmDefinition -Name 'Datastore usage on disk' |
>> New-AlarmAction -Snmp
```

The output of the preceding command is as follows:

```
ActionType      Trigger
----------      -------
SendSNMP        . . .
```

In the third example, we will create a `Run a command` alarm action for the `Datastore usage on disk` alarm. The `c:\Scripts\DatastoreAlarm.cmd` script has to run when the alarm is triggered:

 `c:\scripts` is a location on the vCenter Server and not on your local PC.

Use the following command to create a `Run a command` alarm action for the `Datastore usage on disk` alarm:

```
PowerCLI C:\> Get-AlarmDefinition -Name 'Datastore usage on disk' |
>> New-AlarmAction -Script -ScriptPath c:\Scripts\DatastoreAlarm.cmd
```

The output of the preceding command is as follows:

```
ActionType        Trigger
----------        -------
ExecuteScript     ...
```

 You cannot specify a PowerShell or PowerCLI script as the value of the `ScriptPath` parameter. Rather, you have to specify a batch file. Of course, you can call PowerShell from inside the batch file. For example, you can call the script `c:\scripts\AlarmAction.ps1` from a batch file with the following command:

```
echo.| powershell -command "&{c:\scripts\AlarmAction.ps1}"
```

 You can find more information in the VMware Knowledge Base article *Unable to invoke PowerShell scripts as alarm action on vCenter Server 5.0 (2039574)* at `http://kb.vmware.com/kb/2039574`.

In the following screenshot of vSphere Web Client, you will see the alarm actions that we have created in the preceding examples:

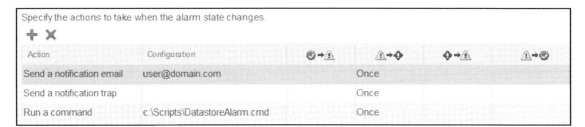

Configuring the vCenter Server mail server and sender settings

Before you can send an e-mail as an alarm action, you have to specify an SMTP server and the e-mail address that will be used as the sender's address in the e-mails sent by vCenter Server. There are no PowerCLI cmdlets to do this. You have to use the vSphere API.

In the following example, we will configure the vCenter Server with `smtpserver.blackmilktea.com` as the address of the SMTP server and `vcenter@blackmilktea.com` as the sender's e-mail address. The following script uses the `VpxSettings UpdateOptions()` method to configure the SMTP server and the sender's e-mail address:

```
$OptionValue = New-Object VMware.Vim.OptionValue[] (2)
$OptionValue[0] = New-Object VMware.Vim.OptionValue
$OptionValue[0].key = 'mail.smtp.server'
$OptionValue[0].value = 'smtpserver.blackmilktea.com'
$OptionValue[1] = New-Object VMware.Vim.OptionValue
$OptionValue[1].key = 'mail.sender'
$OptionValue[1].value = 'vcenter@blackmilktea.com'
$VpxSettings = Get-View -Id 'OptionManager-VpxSettings'
$VpxSettings.UpdateOptions($OptionValue)
```

In the following screenshot of the vCenter Server **Mail** settings (in vSphere Web Client), you will see the defined SMTP server address and sender's e-mail address in the **Mail server** and **Mail sender** text fields after executing the preceding PowerCLI script:

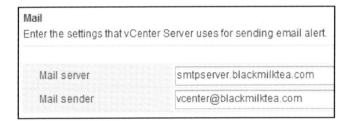

Retrieving alarm actions

The `Get-AlarmAction` cmdlet will retrieve the alarm actions of the specified alarm definitions. The syntax of the `Get-AlarmAction` cmdlet is as follows:

```
Get-AlarmAction [[-AlarmDefinition] <AlarmDefinition[]>]
[-ActionType <ActionType[]>] [-Server <VIServer[]>]
[<CommonParameters>]
```

The `Get-AlarmAction` cmdlet has no required parameters.

In the following example, we will retrieve the alarm actions of the `Datastore usage on disk` alarm definition. Because the default output shows only the `ActionType` and `Trigger` properties, the output is piped to the `Format-List -property *` command to show all of the properties:

```
PowerCLI C:\> Get-AlarmDefinition -Name 'Datastore usage on disk' |
>> Get-AlarmAction | Format-List -Property *
```

The output of the preceding command is as follows:

```
Body              : Datastore {targetName} usage is over its alarm
                    limits
Cc                : {}
To                : {user@domain.com}
Subject           : Datastore usage on disk alarm
ActionType        : SendEmail
AlarmDefinition   : Datastore usage on disk
Trigger           : {Yellow -> Red (Once)}
Uid               : /VIServer=vsphere.local\robert@192.168.0.132:443
                    /Alarm=Alarm-alarm-8/SendEmailAction=-2028157226/
AlarmVersion      : 134
Client            :
ActionType        : SendSNMP
AlarmDefinition   : Datastore usage on disk
Trigger           : {Yellow -> Red (Once)}
Uid               : /VIServer=vsphere.local\robert@192.168.0.132:443
                    /Alarm=Alarm-alarm-8/SendSNMPAction=-1381748622/
AlarmVersion      : 134
Client            :
ScriptFilePath    : c:\Scripts\DatastoreAlarm.cmd
ActionType        : ExecuteScript
AlarmDefinition   : Datastore usage on disk
Trigger           : {Yellow -> Red (Once)}
Uid               : /VIServer=vsphere.local\robert@192.168.0.132:443
                    /Alarm=Alarm-alarm-8/RunScriptAction=307617281/
AlarmVersion      : 134
Client            :
```

Removing alarm actions

You can use the `Remove-AlarmAction` cmdlet to remove an alarm action. The `Remove-AlarmAction` cmdlet has the following syntax:

```
Remove-AlarmAction [-AlarmAction] <AlarmAction[]> [-WhatIf]
[-Confirm] [<CommonParameters>]
```

The `-AlarmAction` parameter is required to remove an alarm action.

In the following example, we will remove the `SendSNMP` alarm action from the `Datastore usage on disk` alarm definition:

```
PowerCLI C:\> Get-AlarmDefinition -Name 'Datastore usage on disk' |
>> Get-AlarmAction -ActionType SendSNMP |
>> Remove-AlarmAction -Confirm:$false
```

The preceding command does not return any output.

Creating alarm action triggers

Every new alarm action will be triggered once the alarm state changes from warning (yellow) to alert (red). If you want to create additional alarm action triggers, you can use the `New-AlarmActionTrigger` cmdlet to create a new action trigger for the specified alarm action. The syntax of this cmdlet is as follows:

```
New-AlarmActionTrigger [-StartStatus] <InventoryItemStatus>
[-EndStatus] <InventoryItemStatus> -AlarmAction <AlarmAction>
[-Repeat] [-WhatIf] [-Confirm] [<CommonParameters>]
```

The `-StartStatus`, `-EndStatus`, and `-AlarmAction` parameters are required to create an alarm action trigger.

In the following example, we will create a new alarm action trigger for the `SendEmail` alarm action of the `Datastore usage on disk` alarm definition. The trigger is started when the alarm state changes from normal (green) to warning (yellow). The alarm action will be repeated once every hour until the alarm is acknowledged.

```
PowerCLI C:\> Get-AlarmDefinition -Name 'Datastore usage on disk' |
>> Get-AlarmAction -ActionType SendEmail |
>> New-AlarmActionTrigger -StartStatus 'Green' -EndStatus 'Yellow'
-Repeat
```

The output of the preceding command lines is as follows:

```
StartStatus        EndStatus          Repeat
-----------        ---------          ------
Green              Yellow             True
```

Now, use the following command to set the time intervals between the occurrences of the alarms:

```
PowerCLI C:\> Set-AlarmDefinition 'Datastore usage on disk'
-ActionRepeatMinutes 60 -Enabled:$true
```

The output of the preceding command is as follows:

```
Name                           Description                               Enabled
----                           -----------                               -------
Datastore usage on disk Default alarm to monitor datastore... True
```

Retrieving alarm action triggers

To retrieve alarm action triggers, you can use the Get-AlarmActionTrigger cmdlet. This cmdlet has the following syntax:

```
Get-AlarmActionTrigger [[-AlarmAction] <AlarmAction[]>]
[<CommonParameters>]
```

The Get-AlarmActionTrigger cmdlet has no required parameters.

In the following example, we will retrieve the alarm action triggers of the SendEmail alarm action of the Datastore usage on disk alarm definition:

```
PowerCLI C:\> Get-AlarmDefinition -Name 'Datastore usage on disk' |
>> Get-AlarmAction -ActionType SendEmail |
>> Get-AlarmActionTrigger
```

The output of the preceding command is as follows:

```
StartStatus        EndStatus          Repeat
-----------        ---------          ------
Yellow             Red                False
Green              Yellow             True
```

In the following screenshot of the vSphere Web Client, you will see the **Trigger states** and **Alarm actions** notifications for the `Datastore usage on disk` alarm:

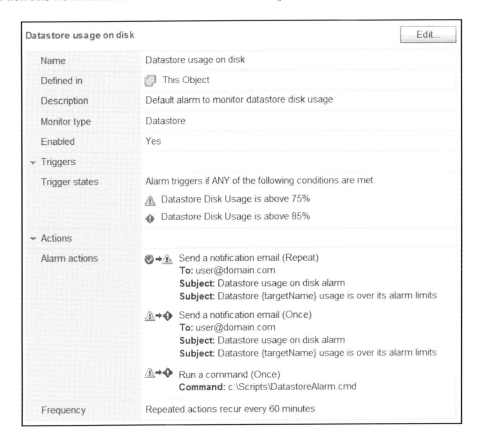

Removing alarm action triggers

We can remove alarm action triggers using the `Remove-AlarmActionTrigger` cmdlet. The syntax of the `Remove-AlarmActionTrigger` cmdlet is as follows:

```
Remove-AlarmActionTrigger [-AlarmActionTrigger]
<AlarmActionTrigger[]> [-WhatIf] [-Confirm] [<CommonParameters>]
```

The `-AlarmActionTrigger` parameter is required to remove an alarm action trigger.

In the following example, the alarm action trigger with the start status Green will be removed from the SendEmail alarm action of the Datastore usage on disk alarm definition:

```
PowerCLI C:\> Get-AlarmDefinition -Name 'Datastore usage on disk' |
>> Get-AlarmAction -ActionType SendEmail |
>> Get-AlarmActionTrigger |
>> Where-Object {$_.StartStatus -eq 'Green'} |
>> Remove-AlarmActionTrigger -Confirm:$false
```

The preceding command does not return any output.

An alarm action must have at least one alarm action trigger. You cannot remove the last one. If you try to remove the last alarm action trigger, you will get the following error message:

You cannot remove this AlarmActionTrigger. The AlarmAction must have at least one AlarmActionTrigger.

Retrieving events

The Get-VIEvent cmdlet can be used to retrieve information about the events on a vCenter Server system. The syntax of the Get-VIEvent cmdlet is as follows:

```
Get-VIEvent [[-Entity] <VIObject[]>] [-Start <DateTime>] [-Finish
<DateTime>] [-Username <String>] [-MaxSamples <Int32>] [-Types
<EventCategory[]>] [-Server <VIServer[]>] [<CommonParameters>]
```

The Get-VIEvent cmdlet has no required parameters.

If you don't specify a value for the -Start, -End, and -MaxSamples parameters, the default maximum number of objects returned will be 100. If you want to specify the maximum value possible for the -MaxSamples parameter, you can use -MaxSamples ([int]::MaxValue). This is a .NET notation, and it is the equivalent of 2,147,483,647.

You can specify `Error`, `Info`, or `Warning` as the value of the `-Types` parameter in order to retrieve the events of the specified types only. For example, to retrieve a maximum of 50 error events from the error events of the last 24 hours, you can use the following command:

```
PowerCLI C:\> $StartDate = (Get-Date).AddDays(-1)
PowerCLI C:\> Get-VIEvent -Start $StartDate -Types
Error -MaxSamples 50 |
>> Select-Object -Property CreatedTime,FullFormattedMessage
```

The output of the preceding command lines is as follows:

```
CreatedTime            FullFormattedMessage
-----------            --------------------
2/1/2017 8:45:54 PM    Host 192.168.0.133 in New York is not responding
2/1/2017 9:39:40 PM    Cannot login root@192.168.0.133
```

The events returned by the `Get-VIEvent` cmdlet are of different types, depending on the type of the event. To get a sorted list of some of the names of the event types in your environment, you can use the following command lines:

```
PowerCLI C:\> Get-VIEvent -MaxSamples 500 |
>> Select-Object -Property @{
>>    Name = "TypeName"
>>    Expression = {$_.GetType().Name}
>> }|
>> Sort-Object -Property TypeName -Unique |
>> Format-Wide -Property TypeName -Column 2
```

The output of the preceding command is as follows:

```
AlarmAcknowledgedEvent                        AlarmStatusChangedEvent
DatastoreFileDeletedEvent                     DatastoreIORMReconfiguredEvent
DrsVmMigratedEvent                            DrsVmPoweredOnEvent
DvsPortLinkDownEvent                          DvsPortLinkUpEvent
EventEx                                       NoAccessUserEvent
NonVIWorkloadDetectedOnDatastoreEvent         ScheduledTaskCompletedEvent
ScheduledTaskStartedEvent                     TaskEvent
UserLoginSessionEvent                         UserLogoutSessionEvent
VmAcquiredTicketEvent                         VmBeingHotMigratedEvent
VmDasResetFailedEvent                         VmEmigratingEvent
VmMessageEvent                                VmPoweredOnEvent
VmReconfiguredEvent                           VmRemoteConsoleConnectedEvent
VmResettingEvent                              VmResourceReallocatedEvent
VmStartingEvent
```

Play with the value of the -MaxSamples parameter to get a large or small number of event type names.

You can use the names of the event types to filter for certain events. For example, to retrieve events related to the creation of a virtual machine, you can filter for the VmBeingDeployedEvent, VmCreatedEvent, VmRegisteredEvent, or VmClonedEvent event type names.

You can use these event type names to find the person who created the virtual machine. In this case, you have to specify the virtual machine as the value of the -Entity parameter. You have to use the -MaxSamples parameter with a large value; otherwise, you might not find the event if the virtual machine was not created recently. The output of the Get-VIEvent cmdlet must be piped to the Where-Object cmdlet to filter for the events related to the creation of the virtual machine. In the following example, the event related to the creation of the virtual machine VM1 will be retrieved:

```
PowerCLI C:\> Get-VIEvent -Types Info -Entity $VM -MaxSamples
([int]::MaxValue) |
>> Where-Object {
>> @('VmBeingDeployedEvent','VmCreatedEvent','VmRegisteredEvent',
'VmClonedEvent') -contains $_.Gettype().Name
>> }
```

The output of the preceding command is as follows:

```
Template             : False
Key                  : 28367
ChainId              : 28360
CreatedTime          : 2/1/2017 9:54:51 AM
UserName             : VSPHERE.LOCAL\Administrator
Datacenter           : VMware.Vim.DatacenterEventArgument
ComputeResource      : VMware.Vim.ComputeResourceEventArgument
Host                 : VMware.Vim.HostEventArgument
Vm                   : VMware.Vim.VmEventArgument
Ds                   :
Net                  :
Dvs                  :
FullFormattedMessage : Created virtual machine VM1 on 192.168.0.134
                       in New York
ChangeTag            :
```

Now, you know that the virtual machine VM1 was created by the user VSPHERE.LOCAL\Administrator on February 1st, 2017, at 9:54:51 A.M.

Summary

In this chapter, you learned how to use PowerCLI to manage your vSphere environment with vCenter Server. Topics such as retrieving privileges, using roles, using permissions, managing licenses, using the LicenseDataManager object, modifying alarm definitions, creating alarm actions, creating alarm action triggers, retrieving events, and configuring the vCenter Server mail server and sender settings were discussed.

In the following chapter, we will learn about managing VMware vCloud Director and vCloud Air.

10
Patching ESXi Hosts and Upgrading Virtual Machines

You have to keep your ESXi hosts up to date with the latest patches to keep them secure and to solve bugs. The hardware compatibility of the virtual machines and the version of the VMware Tools in your virtual machines have to be updated as well to be able to use the newest features. All of these updates can be done and managed using the **VMware vSphere Update Manager** (**VUM**). This powerful piece of software is included in the VMware vCenter Server license.

vSphere Update Manager uses a local repository in which it stores patches downloaded from VMware and VMware partners, such as Dell and **Hewlett Packard Enterprise** (**HPE**). You can create **baselines**, in which you define the patches that have to be installed on your hosts. Then, you can scan your hosts for **compliance** with the baselines. If a host has missing patches, you can **stage** the missing patches to the host. Finally, you can **remediate** your hosts to install the missing patches. vSphere Update Manager works together with **Distributed Resource Scheduler** (**DRS**) to put hosts in the maintenance mode and migrate virtual machines to other hosts before remediation.

The following topics are covered in this chapter:

- Downloading new patches into the Update Manager repository
- Retrieving patches in the Update Manager repository
- Using baselines and baseline groups
- Testing inventory objects for compliance with baselines
- Retrieving baseline compliance data
- Initializing staging of patches
- Remediating inventory objects

Downloading new patches into the Update Manager repository

Before you can upgrade your ESXi hosts with the latest patches and upgrade the VMware Tools in your virtual machines, you have to download the patches from the enabled patch download sources to the local patch repository on your vSphere Update Manager server.

After installation of vSphere Update Manager, the download sources of VMware are already configured. Other vendors that have download sources are DELL and Hewlett-Packard Enterprise. The download sources of the companies are:

- `http://vmwaredepot.dell.com/index.xml`
- `http://vibsdepot.hpe.com/index.xml`
- `http://vibsdepot.hpe.com/index-drv.xml`

Unfortunately, you cannot use PowerCLI to add download sources to vSphere Update Manager. You have to use the vSphere Web Client to do this. Go to **Home** | **Update Manager** | Select your vSphere Update Manager in the left pane | **Manage** | **Settings** | **Download Settings** | **Edit...** to edit the download sources.

In the following screenshot of the vSphere Web Client, you will see the vSphere Update Manager download settings page:

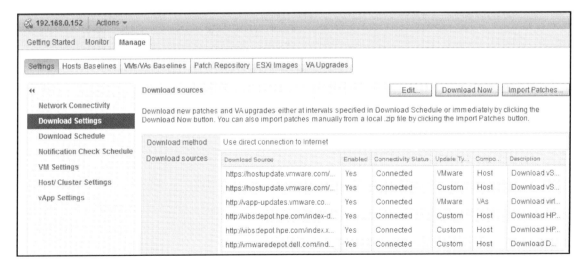

The `Sync-Patch` cmdlet downloads patches into the Update Manager repository.

The syntax of the `Sync-Patch` cmdlet is as follows:

```
Sync-Patch [-Server <VIServer[]>] [-RunAsync] [<CommonParameters>]
```

The `Sync-Patch` cmdlet has no required parameters.

In the following example, we will download patches from the configured download sources into the local vSphere Update Manager patch repository:

```
PowerCLI C:\> Sync-Patch
```

The output of the preceding command is as follows. Because of the length of the output, we have truncated the output after a few lines:

```
Name                    Product           Release Date     Severity    Vendor
                                                                       Id
----                    -------           ------------     --------    -----
Updates esx-base        {embeddedEsx...   9/13/2011 10...  Important   ES...
Updates tools-light     {embeddedEsx...   9/13/2011 10...  Moderate    ES...
Updates esx-base        {embeddedEsx...   11/3/2011 9:...  Important   ES...
Updates esx-base        {embeddedEsx...   12/15/2011 9...  Important   ES...
Updates tools-light     {embeddedEsx...   12/15/2011 9...  Important   ES...
Updates net-e1000...    {embeddedEsx...   12/15/2011 9...  Important   ES...
Updates misc-drivers    {embeddedEsx...   12/15/2011 9...  Low         ES...
Updates net-be2net      {embeddedEsx...   12/15/2011 9...  Low         ES...
Updates the ESXi ...    {embeddedEsx...   3/15/2012 9:...  Important   ES...
```

Retrieving patches in the Update Manager repository

To list the content of your vSphere Update Manager repository, you can use the `Get-Patch` cmdlet. The syntax of the `Get-Patch` cmdlet is as follows. The first parameter set is to retrieve patches by a baseline.

```
Get-Patch [[-SearchPhrase] <String[]>] [-Id <Int32[]>] [-Baseline
<Baseline[]>] [-Severity <PatchSeverity[]>] [-Product <String[]>] [-After
<DateTime>] [-Before <DateTime>] [-TargetType <PatchTargetType[]>] [-Vendor
<String[]>] [-InstallationImpact <PatchInstallationImpact[]>] [-BundleType
<PatchBundleType[]>] [-Category <UpdateCategory[]>] [<CommonParameters>]
```

The second parameter set is to retrieve patches by server:

```
Get-Patch [-Server <VIServer[]>] [[-SearchPhrase] <String[]>] [-Id
<Int32[]>] [-Severity <PatchSeverity[]>] [-Product <String[]>] [-After
<DateTime>] [-Before <DateTime>] [-TargetType <PatchTargetType[]>] [-Vendor
<String[]>] [-InstallationImpact <PatchInstallationImpact[]>] [-BundleType
<PatchBundleType[]>] [-Category <UpdateCategory[]>] [<CommonParameters>]
```

The `Get-Patch` cmdlet has no required parameters. If you use the `Get-Patch` cmdlet without parameters, it will retrieve all of the patches in your vSphere Update Manager repository.

You can use the parameters to filter patches by ID, baseline, severity, vendor, product, date, target type, and so on. In the following example, we will retrieve the patches of vendor HPE for ESXi 6.0:

```
PowerCLI C:\> Get-Patch -Vendor 'Hewlett-*' -Product
'embeddedEsx 6.0.0'
```

The output of the preceding command is the following:

```
Name                  Product         Release Date    Severity    Vendor
                                                                  Id

----                  -------         ------------    --------    -----
Device Drivers fo...  {embeddedEsx... 3/12/2015 6:... Moderate    hp...
Device Drivers fo...  {embeddedEsx... 3/30/2015 7:... Moderate    hp...
Device Drivers fo...  {embeddedEsx... 6/15/2015 7:... Moderate    hp...
Device Drivers fo...  {embeddedEsx... 7/30/2015 7:... Moderate    hp...
Device Drivers fo...  {embeddedEsx... 11/16/2015 6... Moderate    hp...
Device Drivers fo...  {embeddedEsx... 10/28/2015 6... Moderate    hp...
hpnmi: HP NMI Sou...  {embeddedEsx... 3/12/2015 8:... Important   HP...
HP ESXi 6.0 Compl...  {embeddedEsx... 3/12/2015 6:... Moderate    hp...
HP ESXi 6.0 Compl...  {embeddedEsx... 3/30/2015 7:... Moderate    hp...
HP ESXi 6.0 Compl...  {embeddedEsx... 6/15/2015 7:... Moderate    hp...
HP ESXi 6.0 Compl...  {embeddedEsx... 10/28/2015 6... Moderate    hp...
HP ESXi 6.0 Compl...  {embeddedEsx... 11/16/2015 6... Moderate    hp...
HP ESXi 6.0 Manag...  {embeddedEsx... 3/12/2015 1:... Moderate    hp...
HP ESXi 6.0 Manag...  {embeddedEsx... 3/30/2015 2:... Moderate    hp...
HP ESXi 6.0 Manag...  {embeddedEsx... 6/15/2015 2:... Moderate    hp...
HP ESXi 6.0 Manag...  {embeddedEsx... 10/15/2015 2... Moderate    hp...
HP ESXi 6.0 Manag...  {embeddedEsx... 10/1/2015 2:... Moderate    hp...
HP Utility Bundle...  {embeddedEsx... 3/12/2015 1:... Moderate    hp...
HP Utility Bundle...  {embeddedEsx... 3/30/2015 2:... Moderate    hp...
HP Utility Bundle...  {embeddedEsx... 6/15/2015 2:... Moderate    hp...
HP Utility Bundle...  {embeddedEsx... 10/1/2015 2:... Moderate    hp...
```

Using baselines and baseline groups

Baselines are a collection of patches, service packs, bug fixes, extensions, or upgrades that you want to be installed on your ESXi hosts. Baselines can be of one of the following types:

- Host patch
- Host extension
- Host upgrade
- VA upgrade

The VA upgrade type is for the upgrade of virtual appliances.

Baselines can be fixed or dynamic. A fixed baseline remains the same, even if new patches are added to the repository. Dynamic baselines are automatically updated when new patches are added to the repository.

During the installation of vSphere Update Manager, some baselines are already created:

- **Critical Host Patches (Predefined)**
- **Non-Critical Host Patches (Predefined)**
- **VA Upgrade to Latest (Predefined)**
- **VM Hardware Upgrade to Match Host (Predefined)**
- **VMware Tools Upgrade to Match Host (Predefined)**

All of the predefined baselines are dynamic.

You can create additional baselines to specify which patches must be installed. You can create fixed or dynamic baselines. You can specify the patch vendor, severity, category, product, and to include only patches released on or after a certain date and on or before another date.

Baseline groups are collections of baselines. There are two types of baseline groups:

- Host baseline group
- Virtual machines and virtual appliances baseline group

Host baseline groups can contain upgrade baselines, patch baselines, and extension baselines. Virtual machines and virtual appliances baseline groups can contain one or more of the VA upgrade baselines, **VM Hardware Upgrade to Match Host (Predefined)** baseline and the **VMware Tools Upgrade to Match Host (Predefined)** baseline.

Unfortunately, the current release of PowerCLI does not have any cmdlets to use baseline groups.

Retrieving baselines

The `Get-Baseline` cmdlet will retrieve the baselines on your vSphere Update Manager server. The syntax of the `Get-Baseline` cmdlet is as follows:

```
Get-Baseline [-TargetType <BaselineTargetType[]>] [-BaselineType
<BaselineType[]>] [-BaselineContentType <BaselineContentType[]>] [-Server
<VIServer[]>] [[-Name] <String[]>] [-Id <Int32[]>] [-Entity
<InventoryItem[]>] [-Inherit] [-Recurse] [<CommonParameters>]
```

The `Get-Baseline` cmdlet has no required parameters. If you don't specify a parameter, the `Get-Baseline` cmdlet will retrieve all of the baselines on your vSphere Update Manager server. You can use the parameters to filter baselines by name, ID, target type, baseline type, baseline content type, and vCenter Server. The `-Entity` parameter can be used to find baselines attached to specific data centers, clusters, hosts, folders, virtual machines, templates, or virtual appliances.

In the following example, we will retrieve the **Critical Host Patches (Predefined)** baseline.

```
PowerCLI C:\> Get-Baseline -Name 'Critical Host Patches (Predefined)'
```

The output of the preceding command is:

Name	Description	Id	Type	Targe tType	LastUpdat eTime
----	-----------	--	----	-----	---------
Critical Host Pat...	A predefined base...	1	Patch	Host	4/19/2...

Retrieving patch baselines

To retrieve only patch baselines, you can use the `Get-PatchBaseline` cmdlet. The `Get-PatchBaseline` cmdlet has the following syntax. The first parameter set is to retrieve patch baselines by patch.

```
Get-PatchBaseline [[-TargetType] <BaselineTargetType>] [-Patch <Patch>] [-
BaselineContentType <BaselineContentType[]>] [-Extension] [[-Name]
<String[]>] [-Id <Int32[]>] [<CommonParameters>]
```

The second parameter set is for retrieving patch baselines by server.

```
Get-PatchBaseline [[-TargetType] <BaselineTargetType>] [-
BaselineContentType <BaselineContentType[]>] [-Extension] [-Server
<VIServer[]>] [[-Name] <String[]>] [-Id <Int32[]>] [-Entity
<InventoryItem[]>] [-Inherit] [-Recurse] [<CommonParameters>]
```

The `Get-PatchBaseline` cmdlet has no required parameters.

In the first example, we will retrieve all the patch baselines.

```
PowerCLI C:\> Get-PatchBaseline
```

The output of the preceding command is the following:

Name	Description	Id	Type	Targe tType	LastUpdat eTime
----	-----------	--	----	-----	---------
Critical Host Pat...	A predefined base...	1	Patch	Host	4/19/2...
Non-Critical Host...	A predefined base...	2	Patch	Host	4/19/2...

In the second example, we will retrieve the baseline containing the patch with ID as 303.

```
PowerCLI C:\> Get-PatchBaseline -Patch (Get-Patch -Id 303)
```

The output of the preceding command is as follows.

Name	Description	Id	Type	Targe tType	LastUpdat eTime
----	-----------	--	----	-----	---------
Critical Host Pat...	A predefined base...	1	Patch	Host	4/19/2...

Creating patch baselines

The `New-PatchBaseline` cmdlet creates a new patch baseline. The syntax of the `New-PatchBaseline` cmdlet is as follows. The first parameter set is for creating fixed (static) patch baselines.

```
New-PatchBaseline [-Server <VIServer>] [-Name] <String> [-TargetType
<BaselineTargetType>] [-Description <String>] -Static -IncludePatch
<Patch[]> [-Extension] [<CommonParameters>]
```

The `-Name`, `-Static`, and `-IncludePatch` parameters are required.

The second parameter set is to create dynamic patch baselines.

```
New-PatchBaseline [-Server <VIServer>] [-Name] <String> [-TargetType
<BaselineTargetType>] [-Description <String>] -Dynamic [-IncludePatch
<Patch[]>] [-ExcludePatch <Patch[]>] [-SearchPatchStartDate <DateTime>] [-
SearchPatchEndDate <DateTime>] [-SearchPatchProduct <String[]>] [-
SearchPatchSeverity <PatchSeverity[]>] [-SearchPatchVendor <String[]>] [-
SearchPatchCategory <UpdateCategory[]>] [<CommonParameters>]
```

The -Name and -Dynamic parameters are required.

In the following example, we will first retrieve all the ESXi 6.0 patches released before April 1, 2016 and save them in the variable $Patches:

```
PowerCLI C:\> $Patches = Get-Patch -Product 'embeddedesx 6.0.*'
-Before '4/1/2016'
```

Then, we will create a fixed patch baseline named Patches before April 2016. This baseline will contain the patches retrieved in the preceding command. The output is formatted in a list view:

```
PowerCLI C:\> New-PatchBaseline -Name 'Patches before April
2016' -IncludePatch $Patches -Static | Format-List
```

The output of the preceding command is as follows:

```
Name                  : Patches before April 2016
Id                    : 1008
Description           :
BaselineType          : Patch
BaselineContentType   : Static
TargetType            : Host
IsSystemDefined       : False
IsExtension           : False
CurrentPatches        : 75
ExclPatches           : 0
InclPatches           : 0
SearchPatchPhrase     :
SearchPatchStartDate  :
SearchPatchEndDate    :
SearchPatchVendor     :
SearchPatchProduct    :
SearchPatchSeverity   :
SearchPatchCategory   :
LastUpdateTime        : 4/22/2016 7:36:53 PM
```

In the second example, we will create a dynamic patch baseline named `HPE patches`. This baseline contains all the patches released by the vendor Hewlett Packard Enterprise. The output is formatted in a list view.

```
PowerCLI C:\> New-PatchBaseline -Name 'HPE patches' -Dynamic -
SearchPatchVendor 'Hewlett Packard Enterprise' | Format-List
```

The output of the preceding command is:

```
Name                    : HPE patches
Id                      : 1011
Description             :
BaselineType            : Patch
BaselineContentType     : Dynamic
TargetType              : Host
IsSystemDefined         : False
IsExtension             : False
CurrentPatches          : 14
ExclPatches             : 0
InclPatches             : 0
SearchPatchPhrase       :
SearchPatchStartDate    :
SearchPatchEndDate      :
SearchPatchVendor       : {Hewlett Packard Enterprise}
SearchPatchProduct      :
SearchPatchSeverity     :
SearchPatchCategory     :
LastUpdateTime          : 4/22/2016 8:10:39 PM
```

Modifying patch baselines

The properties of patch baselines can be modified using the `Set-PatchBaseline` cmdlet. You cannot change the type of a baseline from fixed to dynamic or from dynamic to fixed using the `Set-PatchBaseline` cmdlet. The syntax of the `Set-PatchBaseline` cmdlet is as follows:

```
Set-PatchBaseline [-Baseline] <PatchBaseline> [-Name <String>] [-
Description <String>] [-IncludePatch <Patch[]>] [-ExcludePatch <Patch[]>]
[-SearchPatchStartDate <DateTime>] [-SearchPatchEndDate <DateTime>] [-
SearchPatchProduct <String[]>] [-SearchPatchSeverity <PatchSeverity[]>] [-
SearchPatchVendor <String[]>] [-SearchPatchCategory <UpdateCategory[]>] [-
WhatIf] [-Confirm] [<CommonParameters>]
```

The `-Baseline` parameter is required.

In the following example, we will modify the `HPE patches` baseline to include all the patches released by Hewlett Packard and Hewlett Packard Enterprise. The name of the baseline will be changed into `HP patches`. The output will be formatted in a list view.

```
PowerCLI C:\> Get-PatchBaseline 'HPE patches' | Set-PatchBaseline
-Name 'HP patches' -SearchPatchVendor 'Hewlett*' | Format-List
```

The output of the preceding command is the following:

```
Name                   : HP patches
Id                     : 1011
Description            :
BaselineType           : Patch
BaselineContentType    : Dynamic
TargetType             : Host
IsSystemDefined        : False
IsExtension            : False
CurrentPatches         : 151
ExclPatches            : 0
InclPatches            : 0
SearchPatchPhrase      :
SearchPatchStartDate   :
SearchPatchEndDate     :
SearchPatchVendor      : {Hewlett Packard Enterprise, Hewlett-Packard,
                         Hewlett-Packard Company}
SearchPatchProduct     :
SearchPatchSeverity    :
SearchPatchCategory    :
LastUpdateTime         : 4/22/2016 10:33:26 PM
```

Attaching baselines to inventory objects

Before you can use baselines to patch hosts, virtual machines, or virtual appliances, you have to attach the baselines to these inventory objects. You can use the `Add-EntityBaseline` cmdlet to attach baselines to template, virtual machine, vmhost, cluster, data center, folder, and vApp objects. If you attach a baseline to a container object, such as a data center, cluster, or folder, the baseline will be attached to all the objects in the container.

The syntax of the `Add-EntityBaseline` cmdlet is as follows:

```
Add-EntityBaseline [-Server <VIServer[]>] [-Entity] <InventoryItem[]>
-Baseline <Baseline[]> [-WhatIf] [-Confirm] [<CommonParameters>]
```

The -Entity and -Baseline parameters are required.

In the following example, we will attach all the predefined baselines to the New York data center:

```
PowerCLI C:\> $Baselines = Get-Baseline '*(Predefined)'
PowerCLI C:\> Add-EntityBaseline -Entity (Get-Datacenter -Name
'New York') -Baseline $Baselines
```

The preceding example does not return any output.

Detaching baselines from inventory objects

The Remove-EntityBaseline cmdlet can be used to detach baselines from inventory objects. The syntax of the Remove-EntityBaseline cmdlet is as follows:

```
Remove-EntityBaseline [-Server <VIServer[]>] [-Entity]
<InventoryItem[]> -Baseline <Baseline[]> [-WhatIf] [-Confirm]
[<CommonParameters>]
```

The -Entity and -Baseline parameters are required.

In the following example, we will detach the Non-Critical Host Patches (Predefined) baseline from the New York data center:

```
PowerCLI C:\> $Baseline = Get-Baseline -Name 'Non-Critical Host
Patches (Predefined)'
PowerCLI C:\> Remove-EntityBaseline -Entity (Get-Datacenter -Name
'New York') -Baseline $Baseline
```

The preceding example does not return any output.

Removing baselines

To remove baselines, you can use the Remove-Baseline cmdlet. The syntax of the Remove-Baseline cmdlet is as follows:

```
Remove-Baseline [-Baseline] <Baseline[]> [-WhatIf] [-Confirm]
[<CommonParameters>]
```

The -Baseline parameter is required.

In the following example, we will remove the `Patches before April 2016` baseline, which we created in the preceding section, *Creating patch baselines*.

```
PowerCLI C:\> $Baseline = Get-Baseline 'Patches before April 2016'
PowerCLI C:\> Remove-Baseline -Baseline $Baseline -Confirm:$false
```

The preceding example does not return any output.

Testing inventory objects for compliance with baselines

If you want to know whether your inventory objects are up to date or have missing patches, you can use the `Test-Compliance` cmdlet to test inventory objects for compliance with baselines attached to them. The syntax of the `Test-Compliance` cmdlet is as follows:

```
Test-Compliance [-Server <VIServer[]>] [-Entity] <InventoryItem[]>
[[-UpdateType] <UpdateType[]>] [-RunAsync] [-WhatIf] [-Confirm]
[<CommonParameters>]
```

The `-Entity` parameter is required. You can use the `-UpdateType` parameter to specify the type of the patches and upgrades you want to scan. The valid values are: `HostPatch`, `HostUpgrade`, `HostThirdParty`, `VmPatch`, `VmHardwareUpgrade`, `VmToolsUpgrade`, and `VaUpgrade`. The `VmPatch` value is deprecated and will be removed in a following release of PowerCLI.

In the first example, we will scan all the hosts in the `New York` data center for missing patches:

```
PowerCLI C:\> Test-Compliance -UpdateType HostPatch -Entity
(Get-Datacenter -Name 'New York')
```

The preceding command does not return any output. In the section, *Retrieving baseline compliance data*, you will learn how to retrieve the baseline compliance status of your inventory objects.

In the second example, we will scan all of the virtual machines in the `New York` data center for missing hardware upgrades or VMware Tools upgrades:

```
PowerCLI C:\> Test-Compliance -UpdateType 'VmHardwareUpgrade',
'VmToolsUpgrade' -Entity (Get-datacenter -Name 'New York')
```

The preceding command does not return any output.

Retrieving baseline compliance data

After scanning your inventory objects against one or more baselines for missing patches or upgrades, you can use the Get-Compliance cmdlet to retrieve the compliance data. The syntax of the Get-Compliance cmdlet is as follows:

```
Get-Compliance [-Server <VIServer[]>] [-Entity] <InventoryItem> [-
ComplianceStatus <ComplianceStatus>] [-Baseline <Baseline[]>] [-Detailed]
[<CommonParameters>]
```

The -Entity parameter is required.

In the following example, we will retrieve the compliance status for the hosts in the cluster Cluster01 against the Critical Host Patches (Predefined) baseline:

```
PowerCLI C:\> $Baseline = Get-Baseline -Name 'Critical Host
Patches (Predefined)'
PowerCLI C:\> Get-Compliance -Entity (Get-Cluster -Name
'Cluster01') -Baseline $Baseline
```

The output of the preceding commands is as follows:

```
Entity          Baseline                               Status
------          --------                               ------
192.168.0.133 Critical Host Patches (Predefined) Unknown
192.168.0.134 Critical Host Patches (Predefined) NotCompliant
192.168.0.135 Critical Host Patches (Predefined) Compliant
```

In the preceding output, the status of host 192.168.0.133 is Unknown because the host is powered off. vSphere Update Manager cannot determine the status of hosts that are powered off. Host 192.168.0.134 has the status NotCompliant and is missing some critical host patches. Host 192.168.0.135 has status Compliant and has all the critical host patches installed.

In the second example of the Get-Compliance cmdlet, we will retrieve the compliance of the virtual machines in the New York data center against the VM Hardware Upgrade to Match Host (Predefined) baseline.

```
PowerCLI C:\> $Baseline = Get-Baseline -Name 'VM Hardware
Upgrade to Match Host (Predefined)'
PowerCLI C:\> Get-Compliance -Entity (Get-datacenter -Name
'New York') -Baseline $Baseline
```

The preceding command returns the following output:

```
Entity   Baseline                                        Status
------   --------                                        ------
VM2      VM Hardware Upgrade to Match Host (Predefined)  Compliant
VM7      VM Hardware Upgrade to Match Host (Predefined)  Compliant
VM4      VM Hardware Upgrade to Match Host (Predefined)  Compliant
VM1      VM Hardware Upgrade to Match Host (Predefined)  Compliant
VM10     VM Hardware Upgrade to Match Host (Predefined)  Compliant
VM3      VM Hardware Upgrade to Match Host (Predefined)  Compliant
vcenter  VM Hardware Upgrade to Match Host (Predefined)  Incompatible
```

As you can see in the preceding output, only the `vcenter` virtual machine is not compliant. It has status **Incompatible**. This is because the vCenter Server is a **vCenter Server Virtual Appliance (vCSA)**.

Initializing staging of patches

Staging is the copying of patches to ESXi hosts without applying the to the hosts. This can reduce the time hosts that are in the maintenance mode during the remediation. Staging is optional. You can remediate hosts without staging the patches to the host in advance. The `Copy-Patch` cmdlet initializes staging of patchespatches to the hosts. This can reduce the time hosts that are in the maintenance mode during the remediation. Staging is optional. You can remediate hosts without staging the patches to the host in advance. The Copy-Patch cmdlet initializes staging of patches. The syntax of the `Copy-Patch` cmdlet is as follows:

```
Copy-Patch [-Server <VIServer[]>] [-Entity] <InventoryItem[]> [-Baseline
<PatchBaseline[]>] [-ExcludePatch <Patch[]>] [-RunAsync] [-WhatIf] [-
Confirm] [<CommonParameters>]
```

The `-Entity` parameter is required.

In the following example, we will stage patches to host `192.168.0.133`:

```
PowerCLI C:\> Copy-Patch -Entity (Get-VMHost -Name 192.168.0.133)
```

The preceding command does not return any output.

Remediating inventory objects

To remediate inventory objects against specified baselines, you can use the `Update-Entity` cmdlet. The syntax of the `Update-Entity` cmdlet is as follows:

```
Update-Entity [-Server <VIServer[]>] -Entity <InventoryItem> -Baseline
<Baseline[]> [-ExcludePatch <Patch[]>] [-GuestCreateSnapshot [<Boolean>]]
[-GuestKeepSnapshotHours <Int32>] [-GuestTakeMemoryDump [<Boolean>]] [-
GuestSnapshotName <String>] [-GuestSnapshotDescription <String>] [-
HostRetryDelaySeconds <Int32>] [-HostNumberOfRetries <Int32>] [-
HostFailureAction <HostRemediationFailureAction>] [-
HostPreRemediationPowerAction <HostPreRemediationPowerAction>] [-
HostDisableMediaDevices [<Boolean>]] [-HostIgnoreThirdPartyDrivers
[<Boolean>]] [-HostEnablePXEbootHostPatching [<Boolean>]] [-
ClusterDisableDistributedPowerManagement [<Boolean>]] [-
ClusterDisableHighAvailability [<Boolean>]] [-ClusterDisableFaultTolerance
[<Boolean>]] [-ClusterEnableParallelRemediation [<Boolean>]] [-RunAsync] [-
WhatIf] [-Confirm] [<CommonParameters>]
```

The `-Entity`, and `-Baseline` parameters are required. The other parameters are to specify options for the remediation, such as patches to exclude from the remediation, options for the creation of snapshots during the remediation of virtual machines, the number of retries, and running the command in asynchronous mode, so it will return immediately without waiting for the task to complete.

 You can specify multiple baselines as the value of the `-Baseline` parameter. However, you can specify only one entity as the value of the `-Entity` parameter.

In the upcoming sections *Upgrading or patching ESXi hosts*, *Updating VMware Tools*, and *Upgrading virtual machine hardware*, we will demonstrate the `Update-Entity` cmdlet in different use cases.

Upgrading or patching ESXi hosts

Before you can upgrade your ESXi hosts to a new version or install patches to ESXi hosts, you have to attach the baselines you want to use, to the hosts. In the preceding section, *Attaching baselines to inventory objects*, you learned how to do this.

In the following example, we will install the critical and noncritical host patches from the baselines `Critical Host Patches (Predefined)` and `Non-Critical Host Patches (Predefined)` on all of the ESXi hosts in `Cluster01`. During the remediation process, Distributed Power Management, Fault Tolerance, and High Availability will be disabled on the cluster. The remediation process will update hosts in parallel mode. Hosts with preinstalled third-party drivers will also be remediated.

```
PowerCLI C:\> $Cluster = Get-Cluster -Name Cluster01
PowerCLI C:\> $Baseline = Get-Baseline -Name 'Critical Host
Patches (Predefined)','Non-Critical Host Patches (Predefined)'
PowerCLI C:\> Update-Entity -Entity $Cluster -Baseline $Baseline
-Confirm:$false -ClusterDisableDistributedPowerManagement:$true
-ClusterDisableFaultTolerance:$true -ClusterDisableHighAvailability:
$true -ClusterEnableParallelRemediation:$true -
HostIgnoreThirdPartyDrivers:$true
```

The preceding commands do not return any output.

> You might receive an error message: **The underlying connection was closed: A connection that was expected to be kept alive was closed by the server**. This will not mean that the upgrade or patching was unsuccessful. The upgrade or patching just took too long to keep the connection open.

Toolspdating VMware Tools

In `Chapter 5`, *Managing Virtual Machines with PowerCLI*, you already learned how to update the VMware Tools using the `Update-Tools` cmdlet. In PowerCLI there are more ways to perform a VMware Tools update. In this section, we will use the `Update-Entity` cmdlet to do this. To update one or more virtual machines, you have to use the **VMware Tools Upgrade to Match Host (Predefined)** baseline. As the value of the `-Entity` parameter, you have to specify the virtual machine or template that you want to update, or a container object such as a folder or data center, containing the virtual machines or templates, you want to update.

In the following example, we will update the VMware Tools on all virtual machines in the data center `New York`. Before the update, we will create a snapshot of the virtual machines. In case something goes wrong during the update, you can go back to the snapshot.

> Remember to remove the snapshots after successful remediation.

If you want the snapshots to be deleted automatically, you can use the –GuestKeepSnapshotHours parameter and specify the number of hours you want to keep the snapshots, as a value. We have the following code:

```
PowerCLI C:\> $Datacenter = Get-Datacenter –Name 'New York'
PowerCLI C:\> $Baseline = Get-Baseline –Name 'VMware Tools
Upgrade to Match Host (Predefined)'
PowerCLI C:\> Update-Entity –Entity $Datacenter –Baseline
$Baseline –Confirm:$false –GuestCreateSnapshot:$true
```

The preceding commands do not return any output.

Upgrading virtual machine hardware

To upgrade virtual machine hardware, you have to use the **VM Hardware Upgrade to Match Host (Predefined)** baseline. Before you can upgrade the hardware version of a virtual machine, the VMware Tools installed on the virtual machine, must be the latest version.

In the following example, we will upgrade the version of the virtual hardware on all virtual machines in the data center New York that have the latest version of the VMware Tools installed. During the upgrade, the virtual machine will be shutdown, upgraded to the hardware version that matches the vSphere version of the host, and finally the virtual machine will be powered on.

```
PowerCLI C:\> $Datacenter = Get-Datacenter –Name 'New York'
PowerCLI C:\> $Baseline = Get-Baseline –Name 'VM Hardware
Upgrade to Match Host (Predefined)'
PowerCLI C:\> Update-Entity –Entity $Datacenter –Baseline
$Baseline –Confirm:$false
```

The preceding commands do not return any output.

Summary

In this chapter, we discussed the downloading of patches into the Update Manager repository and retrieving the patches in this repository. You saw how to use baselines and test inventory objects for compliance with these baselines. You also learned to retrieve baseline compliance data and initialize the staging of patches to ESXi hosts for faster remediation. We used the vSphere Update Manager to upgrade or update your ESXi hosts with the latest patches. You also saw how to update the VMware Tools inside your virtual machines and upgrade the hardware version of your virtual machines.

11
Managing VMware vCloud Director and vCloud Air

VMware vCloud Director (**vCD**) is VMware's product for cloud service providers to build multitenant cloud services. **VMware vCloud Air** is VMware's public cloud platform built on vCD. Virtual machines managed by vCloud Director should not be modified in VMware vSphere. Both products can be managed using PowerCLI. The PowerCLI modules `VMware.VimAutomation.Cloud` and `VMware.VimAutomation.PCloud` provides cmdlets to use vCD and vCloud Air. In this chapter, you will learn to how to manage vCD and vCloud Air virtual appliances as well as virtual machines using PowerCLI.

This chapter covers the following topics:

- Connecting to vCloud Air servers and vCloud Director servers
- Retrieving organizations
- Retrieving organization virtual data centers
- Retrieving organization networks
- Retrieving vCloud users
- Using vCloud virtual appliances
- Managing vCloud virtual machines
- Using the vCloud Director API with `Get-CIView`
- Disconnecting from vCloud Director servers

Connecting to vCloud Air servers and vCloud Director servers

Before you can start to use PowerCLI cmdlets to manage a vCloud Air or a vCD environment, you have to establish a connection to a vCloud Air or vCD server.

 You can start any of the VMware **Hands-on Labs** for vCloud Air, to get a temporary vCloud Air account. Such a temporary vCloud Air account can be used to try the examples in this chapter. The temporary account will be reset after exiting the lab. You can find the VMware Hands-on Labs at http://labs.hol.vmware.com/.
While writing this chapter, I used *HOL-1782-HBD-1 – VMware vCloud Air – Data Center Extension* for testing. After starting the lab, you have to go to http://checkin.vcahol.com and enter your e-mail address to get your student account.

In the following image, you will see the temporary credentials we received from the Hands-on Lab.

Lab	Username	Password
HOL-1782-HBD-1-HOL	student501@vcahol.com	PLGAI79hA
Cloud URL:	**Organization:**	**vRealize Operations MP:**
https://p13v37-vcd.vchs.vmware.com/cloud/org/student501	student501	student501@vcahol.com@student501
		vCloud Director Server:
		p13v37-vcd.vchs.vmware.com

The `Connect-CIServer` cmdlet establishes a connection to the specified vCD servers.

The syntax of the `Connect-CIServer` cmdlet is as follows, and the first parameter set is the default:

```
Connect-CIServer [-Server] <String[]> [-Org <String>] [-Credential
<PSCredential>] [-User <String>] [-Password <String>] [-Port <Int32>] [-
NotDefault] [-SaveCredentials][-WhatIf] [-Confirm] [<CommonParameters>]
```

The `-Server` parameter is required.

The second parameter set is to re-establish a connection to an existing vCloud server session:

```
Connect-CIServer [-Server] <String[]> [-SessionId] <String> [-Port <Int32>]
[-NotDefault] [-WhatIf] [-Confirm] [<CommonParameters>]
```

The -Server and -SessionId parameters are required.

The third parameter set is required to connect to a specific vCloud Air data center:

```
Connect-CIServer [-NotDefault] [-PIDatacenter] <CIServerRelatedObject> [-
WhatIf] [-Confirm] [<CommonParameters>]
```

The -PIDatacenter parameter is required.

The fourth parameter set is for the selection of a cloud server from a list of recently connected servers:

```
Connect-CIServer -Menu [-WhatIf] [-Confirm] [<CommonParameters>]
```

The -Menu parameter is required.

In the following example, we will connect to the vCloud Director server we received from the Hands-on Lab:

```
PowerCLI C:\> Connect-CIServer -Server p13v37-vcd.vchs.
vmware.com -Org student501 -User student501@vcahol.com
-Password PLGA179hA

Name                           User                    Org
----                           ----                    ---
p13v37-vcd.vchs.vmware.com student501@vcahol.com student501
```

After connecting to a vCloud Director server in vCloud Air, we are attached to a tenant environment. This means that we can only use tenant-related PowerCLI cmdlets. To use PowerCLI cmdlets to manage a vCloud Director from the system level, you need your own vCloud Director environment.

In the following image, you will see a screenshot of the vCloud Air portal after the login:

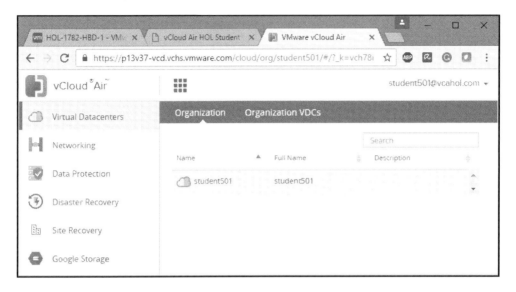

Retrieving organizations

An organization in vCloud Director is a container that contains users, vApps, **Organization Virtual Data Centers** (**Org vDCs**), and **Catalog** entities. For every tenant in vCloud Director, there is an organization.

To retrieve organizations, you can use the `Get-Org` cmdlet. This cmdlet has the following syntax. The first parameter set is the default:

```
Get-Org [[-Name] <String[]>] [-Server <CIServer[]>]
[<CommonParameters>]
```

The second parameter set is to retrieve organizations by ID:

```
Get-Org -Id <String[]> [-Server <CIServer[]>] [<CommonParameters>]
```

The `-Id` parameter is required.

If you use the `Get-Org` cmdlet without parameters, it will retrieve all of the organizations in your cloud. In the following example, we will retrieve the organization we are connected to in vCloud Air:

```
PowerCLI C:\> Get-Org

Name       FullName    Enabled Description
----       --------    ------- -----------
student501 student501  True
```

As you can see in the output of the preceding example, every vCloud Air Hands-on Labs student gets its own organization.

Retrieving organization virtual datacenters

An organization virtual data center or organization vDC is a group of computing, memory, and storage resources from one vCenter Server allocated to an organization. The `Get-OrgVdc` cmdlet retrieves organization vDCs. The syntax of the `Get-OrgVdc` cmdlet is as follows. The first parameter set is the default.

```
Get-OrgVdc [[-Name] <String[]>] [-Org <Org[]>] [-ProviderVdc
<ProviderVdc[]>] [-Server <CIServer[]>] [<CommonParameters>]
```

The second parameter set is to retrieve organization virtual data centers by ID:

```
Get-OrgVdc -Id <String[]> [-Server <CIServer[]>] [<CommonParameters>]
```

The `-Id` parameter is required.

In the following example, we will retrieve the organization vDC for our vCloud Air connection:

```
PowerCLI C:\> Get-OrgVdc

Name       Enabled CpuUsedGHz MemoryUsedGB StorageUsedGB Allocation
                                                         Model
----       ------- ---------- ------------ ------------- ----------
student501 True    1.00       1.000        9.000         PayAsYouGo
```

Retrieving organization networks

If you create virtual appliances or virtual machines, you probably want to connect them to a network. The `Get-OrgVdcNetwork` cmdlet will retrieve available organization vDC networks. The syntax of the `Get-OrgVdcNetwork` cmdlet is given here. The first parameter set is the default:

```
Get-OrgVdcNetwork [[-Name] <String[]>] [-OrgVdc <OrgVdc[]>]
[-Server <CIServer[]>] [<CommonParameters>]
```

The second parameter set is to retrieve organization vDC networks by ID:

```
Get-OrgVdcNetwork -Id <String[]> [-Server <CIServer[]>]
[<CommonParameters>]
```

The `-Id` parameter is required.

The `Get-OrgVdcNetwork` cmdlet without parameters will retrieve all of the organization vDC networks, as shown in the following example:

```
PowerCLI C:\> Get-OrgVdcNetwork

Name                       OrgVdc      DefaultGateway NetworkType
----                       ------      -------------- -----------
student501-IsolatedNetwork student501  192.16.50.1    Isolated
student501-RoutedNetwork   student501  193.1.100.1    Routed
```

Retrieving vCloud users

You can use the `Get-CIUser` cmdlet to retrieve vCloud users. The `Get-CIUser` cmdlet has an alias `Get-PIUser`.

The syntax of the `Get-CIUser` cmdlet is as follows and the first parameter set is the default:

```
Get-CIUser [[-Name] <String[]>] [-Org <Org[]>] [-Role <CIRole[]>]
[-Server <CIServer[]>] [<CommonParameters>]
```

The second parameter set is to retrieve vCloud users by ID:

```
Get-CIUser -Id <String[]> [-Server <CIServer[]>] [<CommonParameters>]
```

The `-Id` parameter is required.

In the following example, we will retrieve the user `student501@vcahol.com` and format the output in a list view:

```
PowerCLI C:\> Get-CIUser -Name student501@vcahol.com | Format-List

WARNING: PowerCLI scripts should not use the 'Client' property. The
property will be removed in a future release.
WARNING: PowerCLI scripts should not use the 'Uid' property. The
property will be removed in a future release.
Href              : https://p13v37-vcd.vchs.vmware.com/api/admin/user/
                    3445d4e0-652d-43a8-a68a-378de56d9236
StoredVMQuota     :
StoredVMCount     : 0
IM                :
DeployedVMQuota   :
DeployedVMCount   : 0
Phone             :
Org               : student501
LdapName          :
Locked            : False
IsLDapUser        : False
HasGroupRole      : False
External          : False
Enabled           : False
FullName          :
Email             :
ExtensionData     : VMware.VimAutomation.Cloud.Views.User
Name              : student501@vcahol.com
Id                : urn:vcloud:user:3445d4e0-652d-43a8-a68a-378de56d92
                    36
Description       :
Client            : /CIServer=student501@vcahol.com:student501@p13v37-
                    vcd.vchs.vmware.com:443/
Uid               : /CIServer=student501@vcahol.com:student501@p13v37-
                    vcd.vchs.vmware.com:443/CIUser=urn:vcloud:user:344
                    5d4e0-652d-43a8-a68a-378de56d9236/
```

Using vCloud virtual appliances

A **virtual appliance** (**vApp**) is a container that contains one or more virtual machines. These virtual machines together make an application. For example, if you have a three-tier application, you can have a vApp that contains the database server, the application server, and the web server. In vCloud Director every virtual machine has to be part of a vApp.

In the following sections *Retrieving vApp templates*, *Creating vCloud vApps*, *Retrieving vCloud vApps*, *Starting vCloud vApps*, and *Stopping vCloud vApps*, we will show you how to use the PowerCLI cmdlets to retrieve vApp templates, create vApps, retrieve vApps, start vApps, and stop vApps.

Retrieving vApp templates

In vCloud Air, there are some predefined vApp templates available for use in your tenant environment. You can use the vApp templates to create your vApps. The Get-CIVAppTemplate cmdlet retrieves these vApp templates. The syntax of this cmdlet is as follows, and the first parameter set is the default:

```
Get-CIVAppTemplate [[-Name] <String[]>] [-Catalog <Catalog[]>]
[-Owner <CIUser[]>] [-Server <CIServer[]>] [<CommonParameters>]
```

The second parameter set is to retrieve vApp templates by ID:

```
Get-CIVAppTemplate -Id <String[]> [-Server <CIServer[]>]
[<CommonParameters>]
```

The -Id parameter is required.

In the following example, we will retrieve the vApp templates available by default in a vCloud Air tenant of the VMware Hands-on Labs:

```
PowerCLI C:\> Get-CIVAppTemplate

Name                                          Status    Owner  StorageUsed
                                                                GB

----                                          ------    -----  -----------
CentOS63-32BIT                                Resolved  system 20.000
CentOS63-64BIT                                Resolved  system 20.000
CentOS64-32BIT                                Resolved  system 20.000
CentOS64-64BIT                                Resolved  system 20.000
CentOs-Mini                                   Resolved  system 8.000
Ubuntu Server 12.04 LTS (amd64 20150127)      Resolved  system 10.000
Ubuntu Server 12.04 LTS (i386 20150127)       Resolved  system 10.000
W2K12-STD-64BIT                               Resolved  system 40.000
W2K12-STD-64BIT-SQL2K12-STD-SP1               Resolved  system 40.000
W2K12-STD-64BIT-SQL2K12-WEB-SP1               Resolved  system 40.000
W2K12-STD-R2-64BIT                            Resolved  system 40.000
W2K12-STD-R2-SQL2K14-STD                       Resolved  system 40.000
W2K12-STD-R2-SQL2K14-WEB                       Resolved  system 40.000
W2K8-STD-R2-64BIT                             Resolved  system 40.000
W2K8-STD-R2-64BIT-SQL2K8-STD-R2-SP2           Resolved  system 40.000
```

```
W2K8-STD-R2-64BIT-SQL2K8-WEB-R2-SP2        Resolved system 40.000
```

We will use one of these vApp templates in the following section, *Creating vCloud vApps*, to create a new vApp.

Creating vCloud vApps

To create a new vApp, you can use the `New-CIVApp` cmdlet. The syntax of the `New-CIVApp` cmdlet is given here, the first parameter set is to create empty vApps:

```
New-CIVApp [-Name] <String> [-Description <String>] [-OrgVdc
<OrgVdc>] [-RunAsync] [-RuntimeLease <TimeSpan>] [-Server
<CIServer[]>] [-StorageLease <TimeSpan>] [-WhatIf] [-Confirm]
[<CommonParameters>]
```

The `-Name` and `-OrgVdc` parameters are required.

The second parameter set is to create vApps from a template:

```
New-CIVApp [-Name] <String> [-Description <String>] [-OrgVdc
<OrgVdc>] [-RunAsync] [-RuntimeLease <TimeSpan>] [-Server
<CIServer[]>] [-StorageLease <TimeSpan>] -VAppTemplate
<CIVAppTemplate> [-WhatIf] [-Confirm] [<CommonParameters>]
```

The `-Name` and `-VAppTemplate` parameters are required.

The third parameter set is for cloning a vApp:

```
New-CIVApp [-Name] <String> [-Description <String>] [-OrgVdc
<OrgVdc>] [-RunAsync] [-RuntimeLease <TimeSpan>] [-Server
<CIServer[]>] [-StorageLease <TimeSpan>] -VApp <CIVApp>
[-WhatIf] [-Confirm] [<CommonParameters>]
```

The `-Name` and `-VApp` parameters are required.

In the first example, we will create an empty vApp named `vApp001`:

```
PowerCLI C:\> New-CIVApp -Name vApp001 -Description 'Empty
vApp for later use' -OrgVdc student501

Name     Enabled InMaintenanceMode Owner
----     ------- ----------------- -----
vApp001 True     False             student501@vcahol.com
```

In the second example, we will create a vApp, named `vApp002`, from the `CentOS64-64BIT` template available in vCloud Air, containing a CentOS 6.4 64-bit virtual machine:

```
PowerCLI C:\> New-CIVApp -Name vApp002 -Description 'CentOS
6.4 64-bit Server' -OrgVdc student501 -VAppTemplate CentOS64-64BIT

Name      Enabled InMaintenanceMode Owner
----      ------- ----------------- -----
vApp002 True      False             student501@vcahol.com
```

In the following screenshot of VMware vCloud Director, you will see the vApps we have just created, plus the *student501-Cent-OS-Mini* vApp already created by the Hands-on Lab.

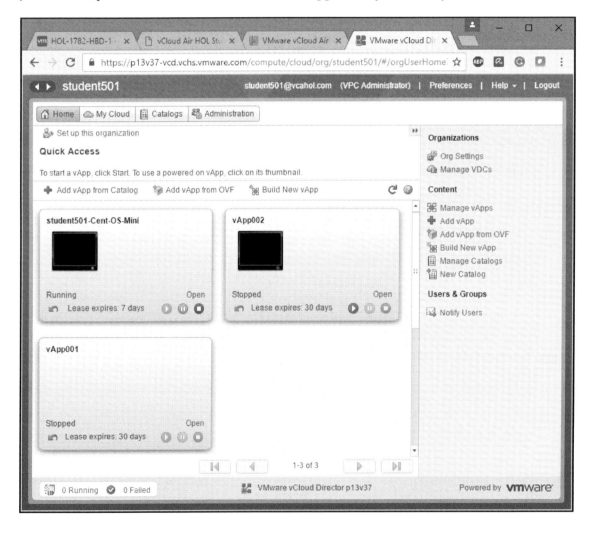

Retrieving vCloud vApps

The `Get-CIVApp` cmdlet retrieves virtual appliances in the cloud. The syntax of the `Get-CIVApp` cmdlet is as follows, and the first parameter set is the default:

```
Get-CIVApp [[-Name] <String[]>] [-Server <CIServer[]>]
[-Org <Org[]>] [-OrgVdcNetwork <OrgNetworkBase[]>] [-OrgVdc
<OrgVdc[]>] [-Owner <CIUser[]>] [-Status <CIVAppStatus[]>]
[<CommonParameters>]
```

The second parameter set is for retrieving vApps by ID.

```
Get-CIVApp -Id <String[]> [-Server <CIServer[]>] [<CommonParameters>]
```

The `-Id` parameter is required.

In the first example, we will retrieve all of the vApps.

```
PowerCLI C:\> Get-CIVApp

Name                     Enabled InMaintenanceMode Owner
----                     ------- ----------------- -----
student501-Cent-OS-Mini  True    False             system
vApp001                  True    False             student501@vcah...
vApp002                  True    False             student501@vcah...
```

In the second example, we will retrieve some other properties of the vApps, such as `Status`, `SizeGB`, `CpuCount`, `MemoryAllocationGB`, and `Shared`. A shared vApp is shared with other users or groups in your organization:

```
PowerCLI C:\> Get-CIVApp |
>> Select-Object -Property Name,Status,SizeGB,CpuCount,
MemoryAllocationGB |
>> Format-Table -AutoSize
Name                          Status SizeGB CpuCount MemoryAllocation
                                                     GB
----                          ------ ------ -------- ----------------
student501-Cent-OS-Mini   PoweredOn       8        1                1
vApp001                    Resolved       0        0                0
vApp002                   PoweredOff      20        1                1
```

Starting vCloud vApps

If you start a vApp, you will power on all of the virtual machines in the vApp. The Start-CIVApp cmdlet will start vApps for you. Unfortunately, you cannot specify the start order of the virtual machines in the vApp using the Start-CIVApp cmdlet. If you want to start the virtual machines of a vApp in a specific order, you have to use the Start-CIVM cmdlet that we will discuss in the section *Starting vCloud virtual machines*.

The syntax of the Start-CIVApp cmdlet is as follows:

```
Start-CIVApp [-VApp] <CIVApp[]> [-RunAsync] [-Server
<CIServer[]>] [-WhatIf] [-Confirm] [<CommonParameters>]
```

The -VApp parameter is required.

In the following example, we will start vApp002:

```
PowerCLI C:\> Start-CIVApp –VApp vApp002

Name                Enabled InMaintenanceMode   Owner
----                ------- -----------------   -----
vApp002             True    False               student501@vcahol.com
```

Stopping vCloud vApps

The Stop-CIVApp cmdlet stops the specified vApp. Stopping a vApp will power off all of the virtual machines in the vApp. You cannot use the Stop-CIVApp cmdlet to specify the stop order of the virtual machines in the vApp. If you want to stop the virtual machines of a vApp in a specific order, you have to use the Stop-CIVM cmdlet that we will discuss in the section *Stopping vCloud virtual machines*.

The syntax of the Stop-CIVApp cmdlet is as follows:

```
Stop-CIVApp [-VApp] <CIVApp[]> [-RunAsync] [-Server
<CIServer[]>] [-WhatIf] [-Confirm] [<CommonParameters>]
```

The -VApp parameter is required.

In the following example, we will stop vApp002:

```
PowerCLI C:\> Stop-CIVApp -VApp vApp002 -Confirm:$false

Name            Enabled InMaintenanceMode  Owner
----            ------- -----------------  -----
vApp002            True     False          student501@vcahol.com
```

Managing vCloud virtual machines

In the following sections *Creating vCloud virtual machines*, *Retrieving vCloud virtual machines*, *Starting vCloud virtual machines*, and *Stopping vCloud virtual machines*, we will show you how to use PowerCLI to create VMware vCloud Director or VMware vCloud Air virtual machines, retrieve vCloud virtual machines, start vCloud virtual machines, and stop vCloud virtual machines.

Creating vCloud virtual machines

The New-CIVM cmdlet can be used to create new cloud virtual machines. The syntax of the New-CIVM cmdlet is as follows:

```
New-CIVM -VApp <CIVApp> -VMTemplate <CIVMTemplate> [[-Name]
<String>] [-ComputerName <String>] [-RunAsync] [-Server
<CIServer[]>] [-WhatIf] [-Confirm] [<CommonParameters>]
```

The -VApp and -VMTemplate parameters are required.

In the following example, we will create a new Windows Server 2012 R2 virtual machine named Server001 in vApp001:

```
PowerCLI C:\> New-CIVM -Name Server001 -VApp vApp001
-VMTemplate W2K12-STD-R2-64BIT

Name       Status      GuestOSFullName              CpuCount MemoryGB
----       ------      ---------------              -------- --------
Server001  PoweredOff  Microsoft Windows Server 20... 1       4.000
```

Retrieving vCloud virtual machines

Retrieving all of your virtual machines or specific virtual machines in your VMware vCloud Director or VMware vCloud Air environment can be done using the `Get-CIVM` cmdlet. The syntax of the `Get-CIVM` cmdlet is as follows, and the first parameter set is the default:

```
Get-CIVM [[-Name] <String[]>] [-Org <Org[]>] [-OrgVdcNetwork
<OrgNetworkBase[]>] [-OrgVdc <OrgVdc[]>] [-VApp <CIVApp[]>]
[-Status <CIVAppStatus[]>] [-Server <CIServer[]>]
[<CommonParameters>]
```

The second parameter set is to retrieve vCloud virtual machines by ID:

```
Get-CIVM -Id <String[]> [-Server <CIServer[]>] [<CommonParameters>]
```

The `-Id` parameter is required.

In the following example, we will retrieve all of the virtual machines in our VMware vCloud Air environment:

```
PowerCLI C:\> Get-CIVM

Name            Status       GuestOSFullName         CpuCount MemoryGB
----            ------       ---------------         -------- --------
CentOS64-64BIT  PoweredOff   CentOS 4/5/6/7 (64-bit) 1        1.000
CentOs-Mini     PoweredOn    CentOS 4/5/6/7 (64-bit) 1        1.000
Server001       PoweredOff   Microsoft Windows Serv... 1      4.000
```

Starting vCloud virtual machines

You can start vCloud Air or vCloud Director virtual machines using the `Start-CIVM` cmdlet. The syntax of the `Start-CIVM` cmdlet is as follows:

```
Start-CIVM [-VM] <CIVM[]> [-RunAsync] [-Server <CIServer[]>]
[-WhatIf] [-Confirm] [<CommonParameters>]
```

The `-VM` parameter is required.

In the following example, we will power on `Server001` in `vApp001`:

```
PowerCLI C:\> Start-CIVM -VM Server001

Name            Status       GuestOSFullName         CpuCount MemoryGB
----            ------       ---------------         -------- --------
Server001       PoweredOn    Microsoft Windows Serv... 1      4.000
```

Stopping vCloud virtual machines

vCloud Air or vCloud Director virtual machines can be stopped using the `Stop-CIVM` cmdlet. The syntax of the `Stop-CIVM` cmdlet is as follows:

```
Stop-CIVM [-VM] <CIVM[]> [-RunAsync] [-Server <CIServer[]>]
[-WhatIf] [-Confirm] [<CommonParameters>]
```

The `-VM` parameter is required.

In the following example, we will stop Server001:

```
PowerCLI C:\> Stop-CIVM -VM Server001 -Confirm:$false

Name            Status      GuestOSFullName          CpuCount MemoryGB
----            ------      ---------------          -------- --------
Server001       PoweredOff  Microsoft Windows Serv... 1        4.000
```

Using the vCloud Director API with Get-CIView

While writing this book, there is no `Remove-CIVM` cmdlet available in PowerCLI. To remove a vCloud Director or a vCloud Air virtual machine, or do anything else in vCloud Director or vCloud Air for which there is no PowerCLI cmdlet, you will have to use the vCloud API. PowerCLI provides us the `Get-CIView` cmdlet that gives access to the cloud view objects of the vCloud API. You can also use the `ExtensionData` property of the vCloud objects, to access the vCloud API, just like you can do with vSphere objects to access the vSphere API. The syntax of the `Get-CIView` cmdlet is as follows. The first parameter set is to retrieve cloud view objects from a cloud object:

```
Get-CIView [-CIObject] <CIObject[]> [-Server <CIServer[]>]
[<CommonParameters>]
```

The `-CIObject` parameter is required.

The second parameter set is to retrieve cloud view objects by ID:

```
Get-CIView -Id <String[]> [-ViewLevel <CIViewLevel>]
[-Server <CIServer[]>] [<CommonParameters>]
```

The `-Id` parameter is required.

The third parameter is to retrieve cloud view objects from `CISearchResult` objects returned by the `Search-Cloud` cmdlet:

```
Get-CIView [-ViewLevel <CIViewLevel>] -SearchResult
<CISearchResult[]> [<CommonParameters>]
```

The `-SearchResult` parameter is required.

In the following sections *Removing vCloud virtual machines, Removing vCloud virtual appliances, Creating snapshots, Retrieving snapshots, Reverting to snapshots,* and *Removing snapshots,* we will give some examples of using the vCloud API.

Removing vCloud virtual machines

In this section, we will use the vCloud API to remove the `Server001` virtual machine. First, we will retrieve the vCloud virtual machine `Server001` and save it in the variable `$CIVM`:

```
PowerCLI C:\> $CIVM = Get-CIVM -Name Server001
```

We will now use the `Get-CIView` cmdlet to retrieve the cloud view object for `Server001` and save it in the variable `$CIVMView`:

```
PowerCLI C:\> $CIVMView = Get-CIView -CIObject $CIVM
```

If you pipe the `$CIVMView` variable to the `Get-Member` cmdlet, you will get a list of all of the methods available. Because there are too many methods to show them in this book, we will filter for methods with a name starting with `Delete`:

```
PowerCLI C:\> $CIVMView | Get-Member |
>> Where-Object Name -like 'Delete*'

   TypeName: VMware.VimAutomation.Cloud.Views.Vm

Name         MemberType Definition
----         ---------- ----------
Delete       Method     void Delete()
Delete_Task  Method     VMware.VimAutomation.Cloud.Views.Task
                        Delete_Task()
```

The `Delete()` method will remove a cloud virtual machine on a synchronous way. It will return after finishing the delete. The `Delete_Task()` method will remove a cloud virtual machine in an asynchronous way. It creates a delete task and will return without waiting for the task to complete. In the following command, we will use the `Delete()` method to remove `Server001`:

```
PowerCLI C:\> $CIVMView.Delete()
```

The preceding command does not return any output.

Finally, we will retrieve all of the virtual machines to show that `Server001` has been removed:

```
PowerCLI C:\> Get-CIVM

Name              Status       GuestOSFullName            CpuCount MemoryGB
----              ------       ---------------            -------- --------
CentOS64-64BIT PoweredOff CentOS 4/5/6/7 (64-bit) 1          1.000
CentOs-Mini    PoweredOn  CentOS 4/5/6/7 (64-bit) 1          1.000
```

As you can see in the preceding output, `Server001` has been deleted.

The deletion of `Server001` could have been done in a PowerCLI one-liner with the following command:

```
PowerCLI C:\> (Get-CIVM -Name Server001 | Get-
CIView).Delete()
```

An alternative to the preceding command would use the `ExtensionData` property, as shown in the following command:

```
PowerCLI C:\> (Get-CIVM -Name
Server001).ExtensionData.Delete()
```

Removing vCloud virtual appliances

After removing `Server001` in the preceding section, *Removing vCloud virtual machines*, we will remove the empty virtual appliance `vApp001` in this section. The way we do this is similar to deleting a vCloud virtual machine. First, we will retrieve `vApp001` and save it in the variable `$CIVApp`:

```
PowerCLI C:\> $CIVApp = Get-CIVApp -Name vApp001
```

Next, we will retrieve the CIView of `vApp001` and save it in the variable `$CIVAppView`:

```
PowerCLI C:\> $CIVAppView = $CIVApp | Get-CIView
```

The `Get-Member` cmdlet will be used to find methods that start with `Delete`.

```
PowerCLI C:\> $CIVAppView | Get-Member |
>> Where-Object Name -like 'Delete*'


   TypeName: VMware.VimAutomation.Cloud.Views.VApp

Name        MemberType Definition
----        ---------- ----------
Delete      Method     void Delete()
Delete_Task Method     VMware.VimAutomation.Cloud.Views.Task Dele...
```

The preceding output shows us two method names starting with `Delete`. The `Delete()` method works in a synchronous way. The `Delete_Task()` method creates a vSphere task to delete the vApp and returns right after creating the task. It does not wait until the deletion completes. In the following command, we will use the `Delete()` method to delete `vApp001`:

```
PowerCLI C:\> $CIVAppView.Delete()
```

The preceding command does not return any output.

We will now use the `Get-CIVApp` command to retrieve all of the vApps:

```
PowerCLI C:\> Get-CIVApp

Name                    Enabled InMaintenanceMode Owner
----                    ------- ----------------- -----
student501-Cent-OS-Mini True    False             system
vApp002                 True    False             student501@vcaho...
```

As you can see in the preceding output, `vApp001` has been deleted.

Creating snapshots

Just like there is no native PowerCLI cmdlet to remove cloud virtual machines, there are also no cmdlets to create and remove cloud virtual machine snapshots. So, we have to use the vCloud API also to manage snapshots. In this section, we will create a snapshot for cloud virtual machine CentOS64-64BIT. First, we will retrieve the vCloud virtual machine CentOS64-64BIT and save it in the variable $CIVM:

```
PowerCLI C:\> $CIVM = Get-CIVM -Name CentOS64-64BIT
```

We will now use the Get-CIView cmdlet to retrieve the cloud view object for CentOS64-64BIT and save it in the variable $CIVMView:

```
PowerCLI C:\> $CIVMView = Get-CIView -CIObject $CIVM
```

The Get-Member cmdlet will be used to retrieve the methods for working with snapshots:

```
PowerCLI C:\> $CIVMView | Get-Member |
>> Where-Object Name -like '*Snapshot*'


   TypeName: VMware.VimAutomation.Cloud.Views.Vm

Name                          MemberType Definition
----                          ---------- ----------
CreateSnapshot                Method     void CreateSnapshot(System...
CreateSnapshot_Task           Method     VMware.VimAutomation.Cloud...
GetSnapshotSection            Method     VMware.VimAutomation.Cloud...
RemoveAllSnapshots            Method     void RemoveAllSnapshots()
RemoveAllSnapshots_Task       Method     VMware.VimAutomation.Cloud...
RevertToCurrentSnapshot       Method     void RevertToCurrentSnapsh...
RevertToCurrentSnapshot_Task  Method     VMware.VimAutomation.Cloud...
```

As you can see in the preceding output, there are two methods to create snapshots. The CreateSnapshot() method will create a snapshot and waits until the snapshot is created before it returns. The CreateSnapshot_Task() method will create a task that creates the snapshot and will return right after creating the task. The method does not wait until the snapshot is created. Both methods have the following parameters:

- System.Nullable[bool] memory
- System.Nullable[bool] quiesce
- string name
- string description

We will now create a snapshot named `Before patching`, and description `Snapshot created before patching`. We will not snapshot the memory or quiesce the virtual machine:

```
PowerCLI C:\> $CIVMView.CreateSnapshot($false,$false,
'Before patching','Snapshot created before patching')
```

The preceding command does not return any output.

Retrieving snapshots

In the output of the `Get-Member` cmdlet in the preceding section, Creating Snapshots, you will see the only method related to snapshots with `Get` in its name is `GetSnapshotSection()`. We will use this method and see what it returns:

```
PowerCLI C:\> $CIVMView.GetSnapshotSection()

Href             : https://p13v37-vcd.vchs.vmware.com/api/vApp/vm-fe0
                   d4f43-cb41-40f9-a068-9d7d9aec9e3f/snapshotSection
Type             : application/vnd.vmware.vcloud.snapshotSection+xml
Link             :
Snapshot         : VMware.VimAutomation.Cloud.Views.Snapshot
Any              :
Required         : False
AnyAttr          : {xsi:schemaLocation}
Info             : VMware.VimAutomation.Cloud.Views.OvfMsg
Client           : VMware.VimAutomation.Cloud.Views.CloudClient
VCloudExtension  :
```

The `Snapshot` property looks like a candidate for further investigation:

```
PowerCLI C:\> $CIVMView.GetSnapshotSection().Snapshot

PoweredOn        : False
Created          : 10/10/2016 5:24:28 PM
Size             : 21474836480
AnyAttr          :
VCloudExtension  :
```

As you can see in the output of the preceding example, we can retrieve the powered on state, the creation date and time, and the size of the snapshot.

In the following example, we will list all snapshots and display the name of the vCloud virtual machine, if the machine was powered on while creating the snapshot and the memory of the virtual machine was included in the snapshot, the creation date and time of the snapshot, and the size of the snapshot. We use the `-PipelineVariable` parameter to save the vCloud virtual machine object in the `$CIVM` parameter. A calculated property is used to display the virtual machine name:

```
PowerCLI C:\> (Get-CIVM -PipelineVariable $CIVM |
>> Get-CIView).GetSnapshotSection().Snapshot |
>> Select-Object -Property @{Name='VM';Expression={$CIVM.Name}},
>> PoweredOn,Created,Size

VM              PoweredOn Created                    Size
--              --------- -------                    ----
CentOS64-64BIT     False 10/10/2016 5:24:28 PM 21474836480
```

Reverting to snapshots

If you want to discard the changes made in a virtual machine and revert to the current snapshot, you can use the following command:

```
PowerCLI C:\> $CIVMView.RevertToCurrentSnapshot()
```

The preceding command does not return any output.

Removing snapshots

If you want to keep the changes made in a virtual machine and want to remove the snapshots, you can use the following command:

```
PowerCLI C:\> $CIVMView.RemoveAllSnapshots()
```

The preceding command does not return any output.

To check whether the snapshots are removed, we can use the following command, used before in the Retrieving snapshots section:

```
PowerCLI C:\> $CIVMView.GetSnapshotSection().Snapshot
```

If the preceding command does not return any output, you are sure that all snapshots of the cloud virtual machine are removed.

Disconnecting from vCloud Director servers

To disconnect your session from the specified cloud servers, you can use the `Disconnect-CIServer` cmdlet. The syntax of the `Disconnect-CIServer` cmdlet is as follows:

```
Disconnect-CIServer [[-Server] <CIServer[]>] [-Force]
[-WhatIf] [-Confirm] [<CommonParameters>]
```

The `Disconnect-CIServer` cmdlet has no required parameters.

In the following example, we will disconnect from all default cloud servers without asking for confirmation:

```
PowerCLI C:\> Disconnect-CIServer * -Confirm:$false
```

The preceding command does not return any output.

Summary

In this chapter, you have seen how you can manage VMware vCloud Air and VMware vCloud Director servers from PowerCLI. We have used the VMware Hands-on Labs to get a temporary account to use VMware vCloud Air and connected to the vCloud Director servers used for vCloud Air.

You have learned how to retrieve organizations, organization virtual data centers, organization networks, and vCloud users. We showed how to create, retrieve, start, stop, and remove vCloud virtual machines and virtual appliances. Creating, retrieving, reverting to, and removing snapshots was discussed. Finally, we disconnected from the vCloud Director servers.

In the next chapter, you will learn how to use Site Recovery Manager from PowerCLI.

12
Using Site Recovery Manager

VMware Site Recovery Manager is VMware's product for disaster recovery. With **Site Recovery Manager (SRM)**, you can create recovery plans to migrate or failover virtual machines from protected sites to recovery sites. Virtual machines can be copied from protected sites to recovery sites using array-based replication or host-based replication.

The coverage in PowerCLI for SRM is limited. There are only two cmdlets in PowerCLI for SRM: `Connect-SrmServer` and `Disconnect-SrmServer`. After connecting to an SRM server, you have to use the SRM API to manage SRM. Fortunately, Ben Meadowcroft, a former VMware SRM product manager, has created a PowerShell module containing advanced functions to work with SRM via PowerCLI. The module is named `Meadowcroft.SRM`.

In this chapter, you will learn to use the `Meadowcroft.SRM` module and the SRM API to manage SRM.

This chapter covers the following topics:

- Installing SRM
- Connecting to SRMservers
- Downloading and installing the Meadowcroft.SRM module
- Pairing SRM sites
- Retrieving the SRM user info
- Managing protection groups
- Protecting virtual machines
- Retrieving protected virtual machines
- Unprotecting virtual machines
- Managing recovery plans
- Disconnecting from SRM servers

Installing SRM

SRM will be used to create recovery plans to migrate or failover virtual machines from protected sites to recovery sites. Because you want your virtual environment to run at the recovery site in the case your protected site is unavailable, both sites need a vCenter Server and an SRM server. The SRM application must be installed on a Windows Server computer. For supported Windows Server versions, you should check the *VMware Compatibility Guide*. You can find the VMware Compatibility Guide for SRM at

`http://www.vmware.com/resources/compatibility/search.php?deviceCategory=sra`.

Virtual machines that you want to protect using SRM have to be replicated from the protected site to the recovery site. There are two ways to replicate the virtual machines:

- Array-based replication
- Host-based replication

For array-based replication, you have to configure the replication of virtual machines from the protected site to the recovery site on your storage array.

If you don't have an array that supports replication from one site to another, you can use host-based replication. **VMware vSphere Replication** is VMware's product for host-based replication. It is a virtual appliance that can be installed by deploying an OVF template. You have to install a vSphere Replication virtual appliance on both the vCenter Server in the protected site as the vCenter Server in the recovery site.

For vSphere Replication to work, you have to enable `vSphere Replication traffic` on a VMkernel Adapter of all of the hosts that you want to use for replication traffic. On hosts that are used for outgoing replication traffic, you have to enable the `vSphere Replication traffic` service. On hosts that are used for incoming replication traffic, you have to enable the `vSphere Replication NFC traffic` service. Unfortunately, while writing this book, the `Set-VMHostNetworkAdapter` cmdlet does not support enabling `vSphere Replication traffic`.

Connecting to SRM servers

Before you can manage SRM from PowerCLI, you have to connect to the SRM servers you want to manage. Because SRM fails over virtual machines from a protected site to a recovery site, both sites need a vCenter Server and an SRM server. So, if you want to manage both SRM servers, you will have to connect to each of them. After connecting to an SRM server, you can use the `ExtensionData` property of the output of the `Connect-SrmServer` cmdlet to access the SRM API.

The `Connect-SrmServer` cmdlet establishes a connection to an SRM server. The syntax of the `Connect-SrmServer` cmdlet is given here. The first parameter set is the default. You can use this parameter set if you have a connection to a vCenter Server that has an SRM server associated with it:

```
Connect-SrmServer [-User <String>] [-Password <SecureString>]
[-Port <Int32>] [-Protocol <String>] [-Credential <PSCredential>]
[-RemoteCredential <PSCredential>] [-RemoteUser <String>]
[-RemotePassword <SecureString>] [-NotDefault]
[-IgnoreCertificateErrors] [-Server <VIServer[]>] [<CommonParameters>]
```

This parameter set has no required parameters.

The second parameter set is for manually connecting to an SRM server:

```
Connect-SrmServer [-User <String>] [-Password <SecureString>]
[-SrmServerAddress] <String> [-Port <Int32>] [-Protocol <String>]
[-Credential <PSCredential>] [-RemoteCredential <PSCredential>]
[-RemoteUser <String>] [-RemotePassword <SecureString>]
[-NotDefault] [-Locale <String>] [-IgnoreCertificateErrors]
[<CommonParameters>]
```

The `-SrmServerAddress` parameter is required.

In the following example, we will connect to an SRM server named `srmserver` and save the output in the variable `$srm` for later use:

```
PowerCLI C:\> $srm = Connect-SrmServer -SrmServerAddress
srmserver -User Administrator@vsphere.local -Password TopSecret
```

After executing the preceding command, the variable $srm has the following value:

```
PowerCLI C:\> $srm

Name                            Port  User
----                            ----  ----
srmserver                       9086  Administrator@vsphere.local
```

If you have not saved the output of the Connect-SrmServer cmdlet in a variable, you can use the $DefaultSrmServers variable. The value of this variable is an array containing all of the connected SRM servers.

The ExtensionData property of the $srm variable is our entry to the SRM API. In the following command, we will create a variable $srmApi as a shortcut to the $srm.ExtensionData property. In the rest of this chapter, we will use the variable $srmApi as our connection to the SRM API:

```
PowerCLI C:\> $srmApi = $srm.ExtensionData
```

In the following command, we will use the Get-member cmdlet to retrieve the methods and properties of the object in the $srmApi variable, as follows:

```
PowerCLI C:\> $srmApi | Get-Member
```

The output of the preceding command is as follows:

```
   TypeName: VMware.VimAutomation.Srm.Views.SrmServiceInstance

Name                            MemberType Definition
----                            ---------- ----------
Equals                          Method     bool Equals(System.Objec...
GetHashCode                     Method     int GetHashCode()
GetPairedSite                   Method     VMware.VimAutomation.Srm...
GetPairedSiteSolutionUserInfo   Method     VMware.VimAutomation.Srm...
GetSiteName                     Method     string GetSiteName()
GetSolutionUserInfo             Method     VMware.VimAutomation.Srm...
GetType                         Method     type GetType()
LoginLocale                     Method     void LoginLocale(string ...
LoginRemoteSite                 Method     void LoginRemoteSite(str...
LoginRemoteSiteByToken          Method     void LoginRemoteSiteByTo...
LogoutLocale                    Method     void LogoutLocale()
RetrieveContent                 Method     VMware.VimAutomation.Srm...
SrmLoginByTokenLocale           Method     void SrmLoginByTokenLoca...
SrmLoginSites                   Method     void SrmLoginSites(strin...
SrmLoginSitesByToken            Method     void SrmLoginSitesByToke...
ToString                        Method     string ToString()
Content                         Property   VMware.VimAutomation.Srm...
```

MoRef	Property	VMware.Vim.ManagedObject...
Protection	Property	VMware.VimAutomation.Srm...
Recovery	Property	VMware.VimAutomation.Srm...

In the rest of this chapter, you will see some examples of using the methods and properties in the preceding output.

Downloading and installing the Meadowcroft.SRM module

In this section, you will learn how to download and install the PowerShell module created by Ben Meadowcroft to manage SRM via PowerCLI. You can download this module from `http://www.benmeadowcroft.com/projects/srm-cmdlets-for-powercli/`. After opening the web page, you have to click on `SRM-Cmdlets.zip` to download the module.

After downloading the `SRM-Cmdlets.zip` file, unblock the file with the PowerShell `Unblock-File` cmdlet, using the following command:

```
PowerCLI C:\> Unblock-File -Path SRM-Cmdlets.zip
```

The preceding command does not return any output.

To import a module in your PowerSell session, you have to install the module in a folder in your PowerShell module path. The environment variable `PSModulePath` contains a list of folders where PowerShell will look for modules. You can inspect the value of the `PSModulePath` environment variable using the following PowerShell command:

```
PowerCLI C:\> $env:PSModulePath
```

On my PC, the preceding command gives the following output:

```
C:\Users\robert\Documents\WindowsPowerShell\Modules;
C:\Program Files\WindowsPowerShell\Modules;C:\WINDOWS\system32\
WindowsPowerShell\v1.0\Modules;C:\Program Files
(x86)\VMware\Infrastructure\vSphere PowerCLI\Modules
```

If you are the only user of the `Meadowcroft.SRM` module on the computer, you can install the module in the `Modules` subfolder of your `Documents` folder. If other users of the computer will also use the `Meadowcroft.SRM` module, you should install the module in one of the other `Modules` folders in the `PSModulePath`.

You can install the module, by opening the downloaded `SRM-Cmdlets.zip` file and copying the `Meadowcroft.SRM` folder from the zip file to the `Modules` folder.

After installing the module, you can import the module in your PowerCLI session with the following command:

```
PowerCLI C:\> Import-Module -Name Meadowcroft.SRM
```

The preceding command does not give any output.

The `Meadowcroft.SRM` module contains two files. The first file, `Meadowcroft.Srm.psd1` is a PowerShell module manifest source file. The second file, `Meadowcroft.Srm.psm1`, is a PowerShell module source file. This second file contains the actual PowerShell code of the module. If you want to know how the advanced functions in the module are written, this is the place to look.

Using the `Get-Command` cmdlet, we can get a list of all of the advanced functions in the module with the following command:

```
PowerCLI C:\> Get-Command -Module Meadowcroft.SRM
```

The preceding command has the following output:

CommandType	Name	Version	Source
Function	Add-SrmPostRecoveryCommand	0.1	Meadowcroft...
Function	Add-SrmPreRecoveryCommand	0.1	Meadowcroft...
Function	Add-SrmProtectionGroup	0.1	Meadowcroft...
Function	Export-SrmRecoveryPlanResultAsXml	0.1	Meadowcroft...
Function	Get-SrmPlaceholderVM	0.1	Meadowcroft...
Function	Get-SrmProtectedDatastore	0.1	Meadowcroft...
Function	Get-SrmProtectedVM	0.1	Meadowcroft...
Function	Get-SrmProtectionGroup	0.1	Meadowcroft...
Function	Get-SrmRecoveryPlan	0.1	Meadowcroft...
Function	Get-SrmRecoveryPlanResult	0.1	Meadowcroft...
Function	Get-SrmRecoverySettings	0.1	Meadowcroft...
Function	Get-SrmServer	0.1	Meadowcroft...
Function	Get-SrmServerVersion	0.1	Meadowcroft...
Function	Get-SrmTestVM	0.1	Meadowcroft...
Function	Get-SrmUnProtectedVM	0.1	Meadowcroft...
Function	New-SrmCommand	0.1	Meadowcroft...
Function	Protect-SrmVM	0.1	Meadowcroft...
Function	Remove-SrmPostRecoveryCommand	0.1	Meadowcroft...
Function	Remove-SrmPreRecoveryCommand	0.1	Meadowcroft...
Function	Set-SrmRecoverySettings	0.1	Meadowcroft...
Function	Start-SrmRecoveryPlan	0.1	Meadowcroft...

| Function | Stop-SrmRecoveryPlan | 0.1 | Meadowcroft... |
| Function | Unprotect-SrmVM | 0.1 | Meadowcroft... |

The advanced functions in the `Meadowcroft.SRM` module are not feature complete. The functions in this module do not expose all the features of the SRM API. In the rest of this chapter, we will use the functions in the `Meadowcroft.SRM` module or the SRM API, whatever is most convenient.

Pairing SRM sites

In SRM, you have to make a connection between the protected site and the recovery site. This process is named *pairing*. Unfortunately, pairing SRM sites cannot be done using the SRM API. You have to use the vSphere Web Client to pair the protected site and the recovery site. In the vSphere Web Client, you have to do the following to pair two SRM sites:

Select **Home** | select **Site Recovery** under **Inventories** | expand **Sites** | select **Sites** | select the site you want to pair | expand **Actions** | select **Pair Site** | type the address of the **Platform Services Controller** (**PSC**) in the **PSC address** field | keep 443 for the port number | click on **Next** | provide the **Single Sign On** (**SSO**) administrative credentials required to perform administrative operations in the PSC in the **Username** and **Password** fields | click on **Finish**.

If the pairing succeeds, you will see two sites in the vSphere Web Client under **Site Recovery** | **Sites**. The following screenshot of the vSphere Web Client shows the two SRM sites in my home lab:

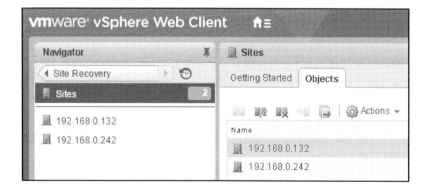

Retrieving the name of the local vCenter Server

To retrieve the name of the vCenter Server of the local SRM site, you can use the
`GetSiteName()` method of the SRM API, as shown in the following PowerCLI command:

```
PowerCLI C:\> $SrmApi.GetSiteName()
```

The output of the preceding command is as follows:

```
192.168.0.132
```

Retrieving the remote vCenter Server

To retrieve the name of the vCenter Server of the remote SRM site, you can use the
`GetPairedSite()` method of the SRM API, as shown in the following example:

```
PowerCLI C:\> $SrmApi.GetPairedSite()
```

The preceding command has the following output:

```
Name            : 192.168.0.242
Uuid            : 1977d562-cd6c-476f-b467-7d4169a1fe8d
VcHost          : 192.168.0.242
VcPort          : 443
VcInstanceUuid  : 8a88cb2a-cae5-4412-b8b0-ad077775bc78
LkpUrl          : https://192.168.0.242:443/lookupservice/sdk
```

The value of the `VcHost` property is the name of the vCenter Server of the remote SRM site.

Retrieving the SRM user info

During installation, SRM creates user accounts at the protected site and the recovery site.
You can retrieve the user account of the local site using the `GetSolutionUserInfo()`
method, as shown in the following example. The `Format-List` cmdlet displays the output
in a list view:

```
PowerCLI C:\> $srmApi.GetSolutionUserInfo() | Format-List
```

The output of the preceding command is as follows:

```
SiteUuid : b0fba581-dab6-4e92-add6-6a59589059f9
UserName : SRM-b0fba581-dab6-4e92-add6-6a59589059f9
```

In the output of the preceding example, `SiteUuid` identifies the SRM server. `UserName` is the name of the SRM user.

The following example shows you the use of the `GetPairedSiteSolutionUserInfo()` method to retrieve the user account of the paired SRM site:

```
PowerCLI C:\> $srmApi.GetPairedSiteSolutionUserInfo() | Format-List
```

The preceding command has the following output:

```
SiteUuid : 1977d562-cd6c-476f-b467-7d4169a1fe8d
UserName : SRM-remote-b0fba581-dab6-4e92-add6-6a59589059f9
```

Managing protection groups

SRM protection groups are groups of virtual machines that SRM protects together. One or more protection groups can be included in a recovery plan. Recovery plans will be discussed in more detail in the section *Managing recovery plans* in this chapter.

There are three types of protection groups:

- Array-based replication protection groups
- vSphere replication protection groups
- Storage policy protection groups

You cannot combine virtual machines replicated by array-based replication and vSphere replication in the same protection group. You cannot protect virtual machines with SRM for which you did not configure array-based or vSphere replication.

The `Protection` property of the $SrmApi variable contains methods to create and retrieve protection groups. By piping the output of the `$SrmApi.Protection` property to the `Get-Member` cmdlet, we will get a list of the available methods, as shown in the following example.

```
PowerCLI C:\> $srmApi.Protection | Get-Member
```

The preceding command has the following output:

```
    TypeName: VMware.VimAutomation.Srm.Views.SrmProtection

Name                          MemberType Definition
----                          ---------- ----------
CreateAbrProtectionGroup      Method     VMware.VimAutomatio...
CreateHbrProtectionGroup      Method     VMware.VimAutomatio...
```

Equals	Method	bool Equals(System....
GetHashCode	Method	int GetHashCode()
GetProtectionGroupRootFolder	Method	VMware.VimAutomatio...
GetType	Method	type GetType()
ListInventoryMappings	Method	VMware.VimAutomatio...
ListProtectedDatastores	Method	System.Collections....
ListProtectedVms	Method	System.Collections....
ListProtectionGroups	Method	System.Collections....
ListReplicatedDatastores	Method	System.Collections....
ListUnassignedReplicatedDatastores	Method	System.Collections....
ListUnassignedReplicatedVms	Method	System.Collections....
ToString	Method	string ToString()
MoRef	Property	VMware.Vim.ManagedO...

The `CreateAbrProtectionGroup()` method is there to create array-based replication protection groups. The `CreateHbrProtectionGroup()` is there to create host-based replication protection groups.

Creating protection groups

In the following example, we will use the `CreateHbrProtectionGroup()` method to create a host-based replication protection group named `Protected VMs Protection Group`. The `CreateHbrProtectionGroup()` method has the following parameters:

- `[vMware.Vim.ManagedObjectReference] location`: The folder in which to create the protection group
- `[string] name`: The name of the protection group
- `[string] description`: An optional description of the protection group
- `[VMware.Vim.ManagedObjectReference[]] vms`: Virtual machines to associate with the new protection group

The `CreateHbrProtectionGroup()` method does not automatically protect VMs in the protection group. The `ProtectVms()` method must be called to protect VMs.

First, we will retrieve the `MoRef` of the protection group root folder and save it in the variable `$Folder`:

```
PowerCLI C:\> $Folder = $srmApi.Protection.GetProtectionGroup
RootFolder().MoRef
```

Next, we will retrieve the `MoRef` of virtual machine `VM1` and save it in the variable `$VM`:

```
PowerCLI C:\> $VM = (Get-VM -Name VM1).ExtensionData.MoRef
```

Finally, we will call the `CreateHbrProtectionGroup()` method to create the protection group:

```
PowerCLI C:\> $srmApi.Protection.CreateHbrProtectionGroup
($Folder, 'Protected VMs Protection Group','SRM Protection
group for protected VMs',$VM)
```

The output of the preceding command is as follows:

```
MoRef
-----
SrmCreateProtectionGroupTask-srm-dr.replication.ReplicationManage...
```

Retrieving protection groups

You can retrieve SRM protection groups using the `Get-SrmProtectionGroup` function in the `Meadowcroft.SRM` module. The `Get-SrmProtectionGroup` function has the following syntax:

```
Get-SrmProtectionGroup [[-Name] <String>] [-Type <String>]
[-RecoveryPlan <SrmRecoveryPlan[]>] [-SrmServer <SrmServer>]
[<CommonParameters>]
```

The `Get-SrmProtectionGroup` function has no required parameters. You can use the -Name, -Type, -RecoveryPlan, and -SrmServer parameters to filter for specific protection groups.

In the first example, we will use the `Get-SrmProtectionGroup` function to retrieve all of the SRM protection groups:

```
PowerCLI C:\> Get-SrmProtectionGroup
```

The output of the preceding command is the following:

```
MoRef
-----
SrmProtectionGroup-srm-vm-protection-group-3027
```

The preceding output is only a managed object reference.

In the second example, we will pipe the output of the `Get-ProtectionGroup` function to the `Get-Member` cmdlet to see which methods and properties to object in the output has:

```
PowerCLI C:\> Get-SrmProtectionGroup | Get-Member
```

The preceding command gives the following output:

```
      TypeName: VMware.VimAutomation.Srm.Views.SrmProtectionGroup

   Name                        MemberType  Definition
   ----                        ----------  ----------
   AssociateVms                Method      void AssociateVms(VMware.Vim.M...
   Equals                      Method      bool Equals(System.Object obj)
   GetHashCode                 Method      int GetHashCode()
   GetInfo                     Method      VMware.VimAutomation.Srm.Views...
   GetParentFolder             Method      VMware.VimAutomation.Srm.Views...
   GetPeer                     Method      VMware.VimAutomation.Srm.Views...
   GetProtectionState          Method      VMware.VimAutomation.Srm.Views...
   GetType                     Method      type GetType()
   ListAssociatedVms           Method      System.Collections.Generic.Lis...
   ListProtectedDatastores     Method      System.Collections.Generic.Lis...
   ListProtectedVms            Method      System.Collections.Generic.Lis...
   ListRecoveryPlans           Method      System.Collections.Generic.Lis...
   ProtectVms                  Method      VMware.VimAutomation.Srm.Views...
   QueryVmProtection           Method      System.Collections.Generic.Lis...
   ToString                    Method      string ToString()
   UnassociateVms              Method      void UnassociateVms(VMware.Vim...
   UnprotectVms                Method      VMware.VimAutomation.Srm.Views...
   MoRef                       Property    VMware.Vim.ManagedObjectRefere...
```

As you can see in the preceding output, the `MoRef` property is the only property. However, the `GetInfo()` method seems to give us more information about the SRM protection groups. In the third example, we will use the `GetInfo()` method with the following command:

```
PowerCLI C:\> (Get-SrmProtectionGroup).GetInfo()
```

The output of the preceding command is as follows:

```
   Name                            Description                        Type
   ----                            -----------                        ----
   Protected VMs Protection Group  SRM Protection group for prot...   vr
```

As you can see in the preceding output, the `GetInfo()` method returns the `Name`, `Description`, and `Type` of the protection group.

The value of the `Type` property can be:

- `san`, for array-based replication
- `vr`, for vSphere replication

You can also use the SRM API to get the same output as in the preceding example using the following command:

```
PowerCLI C:\ > $srmApi.Protection.ListProtectionGroups().GetInfo()
```

The output of the preceding command is as follows:

```
Name                            Description                Type
----                            -----------                ----
Protected VMs Protection Group  SRM Protection group for prot... vr
```

The following screenshot of the vSphere Web Client shows Protected VMs Protection Group:

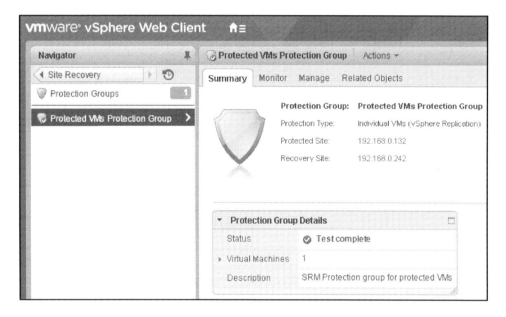

Protecting virtual machines

The Protect-SrmVm function of the Meadowcroft.SRM module will protect a virtual machine and put the virtual machine in an SRM protection group. The syntax of the Protect-SrmVm function is as follows:

```
Protect-SrmVM [-ProtectionGroup] <SrmProtectionGroup>
[[-Vm] <VirtualMachineImpl>] [[-VmView] <VirtualMachine>]
[<CommonParameters>]
```

The -ProtectionGroup parameter is required.

In the following example, we will add virtual machine VM1 to the protection group Protected VMs Protection Group. First, we will retrieve the Protected VMs Protection Group and save it in the variable $SrmProtectionGroup:

```
PowerCLI C:\> $SrmProtectionGroup = Get-SrmProtectionGroup
-Name 'Protected VMs Protection Group'
```

Next, we will retrieve the view of virtual machine VM1 and save it in variable $VMView:

```
PowerCLI C:\> $VMView = (Get-VM -Name VM1).ExtensionData
```

Finally, VM1 is added to the Protected VMs Protection Group with the following command:

```
PowerCLI C:\> Protect-SrmVM -ProtectionGroup
$SrmProtectionGroup -VmView $VMView
```

The preceding command has the following output:

```
PowerCLI C:\> Protect-SrmVM -ProtectionGroup $SrmProtectionGroup
-VmView $VMView
Key           : dr.replication.VmProtectionGroup.protectVms
TaskMoRef     : Task-dr.replication.VmProtectionGroup.protectVms77
Description   :
Name          : ProtectVms
DescriptionId : com.vmware.vcDr.dr.replication.VmProtectionGroup
                .protectVms
EntityMoRef   : VirtualMachine-vm-233
EntityName    :
Locked        :
State         : succes
Cancelled     : False
Cancelable    : False
Error         : VMware.Vim.LocalizedMethodFault
Result        :
Progress      : 0
Reason        : VMware.Vim.TaskReason
QueueTime     : 11/28/2016 6:45:42 PM
StartTime     : 11/28/2016 6:45:43 PM
CompleteTime  : 11/28/2016 6:45:49 PM
EventChainId  : 0
ChangeTag     :
ParentTaskKey :
RootTaskKey   :
```

Retrieving protected virtual machines

You can use the `Get-SrmProtectedVM` function in the `Meadowcroft.SRM` module to retrieve the virtual machines protected by SRM. The syntax of the `Get-SrmProtectedVM` function is as follows:

```
Get-SrmProtectedVM [[-Name] <String>] [-State {Ready |
FailedOver | PartiallyRecovered | Recovering | Recovered |
Testing | Shadowing}] [-PeerState {Ready | FailedOver |
PartiallyRecovered | Recovering | Recovered | Testing |
Shadowing}] [-ConfiguredOnly] [-UnconfiguredOnly]
[-ProtectionGroup <SrmProtectionGroup[]>] [-RecoveryPlan
<SrmRecoveryPlan[]>] [-ProtectionGroupName <String>]
[-SrmServer <SrmServer>] [<CommonParameters>]
```

The `Get-SrmProtectedVM` function has no required parameters. You can use the parameters of the `Get-SrmProtectedVM` function to filter for specific virtual machines by name, state, configuration, protection group, recovery plan, or SRM server.

In the following example, we will retrieve all of the protected virtual machines using the `Get-SrmProtectedVM` function:

```
PowerCLI C:\> Get-SrmProtectedVM
```

The output of the preceding command is as follows:

```
Vm                  : VMware.Vim.VirtualMachine
ProtectedVm         : protected-vm-3240
PeerProtectedVm     : protected-vm-3358
State               : Ready
PeerState           : Shadowing
NeedsConfiguration  : True
Faults              : {VMware.Vim.LocalizedMethodFault}
```

The preceding output does not give you the names of the protected virtual machines. You can use the following command to retrieve these names:

```
PowerCLI C:\> Get-SrmProtectedVM | Select-Object
-Property @{Name='VM';Expression={$_.VM.Name}}
```

The output of the preceding command is as follows:

```
VM
--
VM1
```

Unprotecting virtual machines

You can remove a virtual machine from a protection group using the `Unprotect-SrmVM` function in the `Meadowcroft.SRM` module. The syntax of the `Unprotect-SrmVM` function is as follows:

```
Unprotect-SrmVM [-ProtectionGroup] <SrmProtectionGroup> [[-Vm]
<VirtualMachineImpl>] [[-VmView] <VirtualMachine>] [[-ProtectedVm]
<SrmProtectionGroupProtectedVm>] [<CommonParameters>]
```

The `-ProtectionGroup` parameter is required.

In the following example, we will unprotect VM1 and remove it from the `Protected VMs Protection Group` using the `Unprotect-SrmVM` function from the `Meadowcroft.SRM` module, with the following command:

```
PowerCLI C:\> Unprotect-SrmVM -ProtectionGroup $Srm
ProtectionGroup -VmView $VmView
```

The output of the preceding command is as follows:

```
Key            : dr.replication.VmProtectionGroup.unprotectVms
TaskMoRef      : Task-dr.replication.VmProtectionGroup.unprotectVms59
Description    :
Name           : UnprotectVms
DescriptionId  : com.vmware.vcDr.dr.replication.VmProtectionGroup
                 .unprotectVms
EntityMoRef    : VirtualMachine-vm-233
EntityName     :
Locked         :
State          : success
Cancelled      : False
Cancelable     : False
Error          :
Result         :
Progress       : 0
Reason         : VMware.Vim.TaskReason
QueueTime      : 11/28/2016 6:50:03 PM
StartTime      : 11/28/2016 6:50:05 PM
CompleteTime   : 11/28/2016 6:50:09 PM
EventChainId   : 0
ChangeTag      :
ParentTaskKey  :
RootTaskKey    :
```

Managing recovery plans

Recovery plans are plans that describe the steps to be performed during the execution of a recovery. You can use a recovery plan for a planned migration or a disaster recovery. A recovery plan contains the following information:

- The name of the recovery plan
- The location (paired sites) of the recovery plan
- A protected site
- The site to which virtual machines in the plan will recover
- The protection groups to use for the recovery plan
- The networks to use while running tests of the plan
- The description of the recovery plan
- Steps to perform during the execution of the recovery plan

A recovery plan can include one or more protection groups. A protection group can be included in more than one recovery plan.

The steps of the recovery plan can be divided into the following:

- Test steps
- Recovery steps
- Cleanup steps
- Reprotect steps

In the following sections, *Retrieving recovery plans* and *Running recovery plans*, you will learn how to retrieve and run recovery plans. You will also see how to retrieve historical results of recovery plans in the section *Retrieving the historical results of recovery plans*.

Retrieving recovery plans

To retrieve recovery plans, we can use the `Get-SrmRecoveryPlan` function of the `Meadowcroft.SRM` module. The syntax of the `Get-SrmRecoveryPlan` function is as follows:

```
Get-SrmRecoveryPlan [[-Name] <String>] [-ProtectionGroup
<SrmProtectionGroup[]>] [-SrmServer <SrmServer>]
[<CommonParameters>]
```

The `Get-SrmRecoveryPlan` function has no required parameters.

If you call the `Get-SrmRecoveryPlan` function without parameters, it will give a list of managed object references of the available recovery plans, as shown in the following example:

```
PowerCLI C:\> Get-SrmRecoveryPlan
```

The preceding command gives the following output:

```
MoRef
-----
SrmRecoveryPlan-srm-5de18aad-2176-4acd-80c1-dca363833805
```

If we pipe the output of the `Get-SrmRecoveryPlan` function to the `Get-Member` cmdlet, we will get a list of the available methods and properties of the `SrmRecoveryPlan` object, using the following command:

```
PowerCLI C:\> Get-SrmRecoveryPlan | Get-Member
```

The output of the preceding command is as follows:

```
   TypeName: VMware.VimAutomation.Srm.Views.SrmRecoveryPlan

Name                   MemberType Definition
----                   ---------- ----------
AddProtectionGroup     Method     void AddProtectionGroup(VMware.Vim...
AnswerPrompt           Method     void AnswerPrompt(string key, bool...
Cancel                 Method     void Cancel()
Equals                 Method     bool Equals(System.Object obj)
GetHashCode            Method     int GetHashCode()
GetInfo                Method     VMware.VimAutomation.Srm.Views.Srm...
GetParentFolder        Method     VMware.VimAutomation.Srm.Views.Srm...
GetPeer                Method     VMware.VimAutomation.Srm.Views.Srm...
GetRecoverySettings    Method     VMware.VimAutomation.Srm.Views.Srm...
GetType                Method     type GetType()
ListPrompts            Method     System.Collections.Generic.List[VM...
SetRecoverySettings    Method     void SetRecoverySettings(VMware.Vi...
Start                  Method     void Start(VMware.VimAutomation.Sr...
ToString               Method     string ToString()
MoRef                  Property   VMware.Vim.ManagedObjectReference ...
```

The `GetInfo()` method seems a way to get more information about the recovery plans. Let's try the `GetInfo()` method, using the following command:

```
PowerCLI C:\> (Get-SrmRecoveryPlan).GetInfo() | Format-List
```

The preceding command gives the following output:

```
Name            : Management Servers Recovery Plan
Description     : Recovery Plan for management servers
State           : Protecting
ProtectionGroups : {VMware.VimAutomation.Srm.Views.SrmProtectionGrou
                  p}
```

The preceding output is much more useful than the managed object references.

You can retrieve the same output as in the preceding example using the SRM API with the following command:

```
PowerCLI C:\> $srmApi.Recovery.ListPlans().GetInfo() | Format-List
```

The output of the preceding command is not shown in this book because it is the same output as in the preceding example.

In the following screenshot of the vSphere Web Client, you will see the Management Servers Recovery Plan:

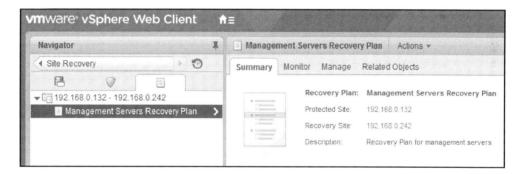

Running recovery plans

You can use the Start-SrmRecoveryPlan function in the Meadowcroft.SRM module to start a recovery plan. The Start-SrmRecoveryPlan function has the following syntax:

```
Start-SrmRecoveryPlan [-RecoveryPlan] <SrmRecoveryPlan>
[-RecoveryMode {Failover | Test | CleanupTest | Reprotect
| Revert | Migrate}] [-WhatIf] [-Confirm] [<CommonParameters>]
```

The -RecoveryPlan parameter is required.

With the following command, we will first retrieve the recovery plan Management Servers Recovery Plan and save it in the variable $RecoveryPlan:

```
PowerCLI C:\> $RecoveryPlan = Get-SrmRecoveryPlan -Name
'Management Servers Recovery Plan'
```

After creating a recovery plan, it is good practice to test the recovery plan. We will start the recovery plan in Test mode, using the following command:

```
PowerCLI C:\> Start-SrmRecoveryPlan -RecoveryPlan
$RecoveryPlan -RecoveryMode Test -Confirm:$false
```

The preceding command does not return any output.

Retrieving the historical results of recovery plans

To retrieve the historical results of a recovery plan, you can use the Get-SrmRecoveryPlanResult function of the Meadowcroft.SRM module. The syntax of the Get-SrmRecoveryPlanResult function is as follows:

```
Get-SrmRecoveryPlanResult [-RecoveryPlan] <SrmRecoveryPlan>
[-RecoveryMode {Failover | Test | CleanupTest | Reprotect |
Revert | Migrate}] [-ResultState {Success | Warnings | Errors |
Cancelled}] [-StartedAfter <DateTime>] [-startedBefore
<DateTime>] [-SrmServer <SrmServer>] [<CommonParameters>]
```

The -RecoveryPlan parameter is required.

In the following example, we will first retrieve the recovery plan Management Servers Recovery Plan, using the Get-SrmRecoveryPlan function, and save it in the variable $RecoveryPlan:

```
PowerCLI C:\> $RecoveryPlan = Get-SrmRecoveryPlan -Name
'Management Servers Recovery Plan'
```

Next, we will retrieve the historical results of the Management Servers Recovery Plan, using the following command:

```
PowerCLI C:\> Get-SrmRecoveryPlanResult -RecoveryPlan $RecoveryPlan
```

The output of the preceding command is as follows:

```
Plan                    : VMware.VimAutomation.Srm.Views
                          .SrmRecoveryPlan
Name                    : Management Servers Recovery Plan
```

```
Description                 : Recovery Plan for management servers
StartTime                   : 11/28/2016 7:51:19 PM
StopTime                    : 11/28/2016 7:52:39 PM
ExecutionTimeInSeconds      : 3
TotalPausedTimeInSeconds : 0
ResultState                 : Success
RunMode                     : Test
WarningCount                : 0
ErrorCount                  : 0
```

Disconnecting from SRM servers

To disconnect your PowerCLI session from one or more SRM servers, you can use the `Disconnect-SrmServer` cmdlet. The syntax of the `Disconnect-SrmServer` cmdlet is as follows:

```
Disconnect-SrmServer [[-Server] <SrmServer[]>] [-Force]
[-WhatIf] [-Confirm] [<CommonParameters>]
```

The `Disconnect-SrmServer` cmdlet has no required parameters.

In the following example, we will disconnect from all of the connected SRM servers:

```
PowerCLI C:\> Disconnect-SrmServer * -Confirm:$False
```

The preceding command does not return any output.

Summary

In this chapter, you learned to use SRM from PowerCLI using the Meadowcroft.SRM module and the SRM API. You saw how to install SRM and to connect to SRM servers from your PowerCLI session. We discussed downloading and installing the Meadowcroft.SRM module that provides cmdlets to use SRM. You learned to pair two SRM sites using the vSphere Web Client to make a connection between the protected site and the recovery site. SRM protection groups are groups of virtual machines that SRM protects together. You saw how to manage these protection groups. We discussed protecting virtual machines with SRM and running recovery plans to migrate or fail over virtual machines from the protected site to the recovery site. Finally, you saw how to disconnect your PowerCLI session from SRM servers.

In the following chapter, you will learn how to use VMware vRealize Operations Manager from PowerCLI.

13
Using vRealize Operations Manager

vRealize Operations Manager (**vROPs**) is VMware's product for performance monitoring, capacity planning, and alerting. In vROPs, you can install management packs to connect vRealize Operations Manager with products such as vCloud Director, Log Insight, NSX, storage devices, Cisco UCS Manager, and Amazon Web Services. These management packs make it a powerful tool to manage your entire environment. In this chapter, we will discuss the available PowerCLI cmdlets for working with vRealize Operations Manager. Because the cmdlets only scratch the surface of what you can do with vROPs, we will also give some examples of using the API to perform other tasks.

This chapter covers the following topics:

- Connecting to vRealize Operations Manager servers
- Retrieving vRealize Operations Manager resource objects
- Using alerts
- Retrieving recommendations
- Retrieving statistic keys
- Retrieving statistical data
- Retrieving local user accounts
- Using the vRealize Operations Manager API
- Disconnecting from vRealize Operations Manager servers

Connecting to vRealize Operations Manager servers

Analog to the `Connect-VIServer` cmdlet that creates a connection to a vCenter or ESXi server, the `Connect-OMServer` cmdlet establishes a connection to the specified vRealize Operations Manager server. The syntax of the `Connect-OMServer` cmdlet is as follows, and the first parameter set is the default:

```
Connect-OMServer [-Server] <String[]> [-User <String>] [-Password
<SecureString>] [-AuthSource <String>] [-Port <Int32>] [-NotDefault]
[-Force] [-SaveCredentials] [<CommonParameters>]
```

The `-Server` parameter is required. The second parameter set is required to connect an Operations Manager Server using a session secret of an existing vRealize Operations Manager session you want to re-establish:

```
Connect-OMServer [-Server] <String[]> [-Port <Int32>]
[-NotDefault] [-Force] -SessionSecret <String> [<CommonParameters>]
```

The `-Server` and `-SessionSecret` parameters are required. The third parameter set is required to connect an Operations Manager Server using a `PSCredential` object:

```
Connect-OMServer [-Server] <String[]> [-AuthSource <String>]
[-Port <Int32>] -Credential <PSCredential> [-NotDefault]
[-Force] [-SaveCredentials] [<CommonParameters>]
```

The `-Server` and `-Credential` parameters are required. The fourth parameter set is required to connect an Operations Manager Server from a menu of recently connected servers:

```
Connect-OMServer -Menu [<CommonParameters>]
```

The `-Menu` parameter is required.

In the following example, we will connect to an Operations Manager Server specifying a username and password. Because we don't specify the `-AuthSource` parameter, the value of the default authentication source type is `LocalUser`. Valid values for the `-AuthSource` parameter are:

- `LocalUser`
- `ActiveDirectory`
- `OpenLDAP`
- `VC`

The following command connects to Operations Manager Server with the IP address
`192.168.0.62`:

```
PowerCLI C:\> Connect-OMServer -Server 192.168.0.62
-User admin -Password Secret
```

The output of the preceding command is as follows:

```
WARNING: There were one or more problems with the server certificate:
* A certification chain processed correctly, but terminated in a root
certificate which isn't trusted by the trust provider.

* The certificate's CN name does not match the passed value.

Certificate: [Subject]
  OU=MBU, O="VMware, Inc.", CN=vc-ops-slice-1

[Issuer]
  OU=MBU, O="VMware, Inc.", CN=vc-ops-cluster-ca_c3e63f89
  -f5d1-4a76-89b1-19f5bfbab8db

[Serial Number]
  01

[Not Before]
  1/27/2017 20:31:33

[Not After]
  1/27/2022 20:31:33

[Thumbprint]
  101CCFE6BE33AF51EBF3A5DA8EC0FD39F9F2B4D9

WARNING:
The server certificate is not valid.

Name                User        AuthSource
----                ----        ----------
192.168.0.62        admin
```

After connecting to one or more vRealize Operations Manager servers, you can find the
connected servers in the variable `$global:DefaultOMServers`, as shown in the following
example:

```
PowerCLI C:\> $global:DefaultOMServers
```

The output of the preceding command is as follows:

```
Name              User      AuthSource
----              ----      ----------
192.168.0.62      admin
```

Retrieving vRealize Operations Manager resource objects

Resource objects are data centers, folders, clusters, ESXi hosts, datastores, virtual machines, resource pools, and so on. The Get-OMResource cmdlet retrieves vRealize Operations Manager resource objects. The syntax of Get-OMResource cmdlet is as follows. The first parameter set is the default:

```
Get-OMResource [[-Name] <String[]>] [-ResourceKind <String[]>]
[-AdapterKind <String[]>] [-Orphaned] [-Server <OMServer[]>]
[<CommonParameters>]
```

The second parameter set is there to retrieve vROPs resource objects by ID:

```
Get-OMResource -Id <String[]> [-Server <OMServer[]>]
[<CommonParameters>]
```

The -Id parameter is required.

The third parameter set is required to retrieve vROPs resource objects by specifying objects from vSphere:

```
Get-OMResource [-Entity] <VIObjectCore[]> [<CommonParameters>]
```

The -Entity parameter is required.

If you use the Get-OMResource cmdlet without parameters, it will retrieve all of the vROPs objects. The list of objects is long. In the following example, we will pipe the output of the Get-OMResource cmdlet to the Select-Object cmdlet to retrieve only the first five objects:

```
PowerCLI C:\> Get-OMResource | Select-Object -First 5
```

The output of the preceding command is as follows:

```
Name                      Health  ResourceKind   Description
----                      ------  ------------   -----------
Cluster01                 Green   ClusterCompu...
```

```
vApp01                        Green    ResourcePool
vCenter Server 192.168.0....  Green    PythonRemedi...
vSphere World                 Green    vSphere World
Container                     Green    ContainerAda...
```

Using alerts

Alerts are alarms that warn you about situations that need attention. The `Get-OMAlert` cmdlet retrieves alerts from the specified vRealize Operations Manager server. The syntax of the `Get-OMAlert` cmdlet is given here. The first parameter set is the default:

```
Get-OMAlert [-Status <OMAlertStatus[]>] [-Impact <OMImpact[]>]
[-Criticality <OMCriticality[]>] [-Resource <OMResource[]>]
[-Subtype <OMAlertSubtype[]>] [-AssignedUser <OMUser[]>]
[-Type <OMAlertType[]>] [-ControlState <OMAlertControlState[]>]
[-AlertDefinition <OMAlertDefinition[]>] [[-Name] <String[]>]
[-Server <OMServer[]>] [<CommonParameters>]
```

The second parameter set is required to retrieve alerts by ID:

```
Get-OMAlert -Id <String[]> [-Server <OMServer[]>] [<CommonParameters>]
```

The `-Id` parameter is required.

If you use the `Get-OMalert` cmdlet without parameters, it will retrieve all of the available alerts as shown in the following example:

```
PowerCLI C:\> Get-OMAlert
```

The output of the preceding command can be very long. This is why I have omitted the output. It might be better to filter the output to receive only the most important alerts. In the following example, we will retrieve only the `Critical` alerts. For this book, we select only the first alert and format the output in a list view:

```
PowerCLI C:\> Get-OMAlert -Criticality 'Critical' |
Select-Object -First 1 | Format-List
```

The output of the preceding command is as follows:

```
WARNING: PowerCLI scripts should not use the 'Client' property.
The property will be removed in a future release.
WARNING: PowerCLI scripts should not use the 'Uid' property.
The property will be removed in a future release.
ExtensionData   : VMware.VimAutomation.VROps.Views.Alert
Resource        : VM1
```

```
Subtype          : Performance
AssignedUser     :
ControlState     : Open
Type             : Virtualization/Hypervisor Alerts
Status           : Active
Impact           : Risk
Criticality      : Critical
StartTime        : 2/2/2017 8:41:28 AM
UpdateTime       : 2/2/2017 8:46:28 AM
CancelTime       :
AlertDefinition  : Virtual machine has continuous high CPU
                   usage causing stress
SuspendedUntil   :
Id               : 48dfb8ed-b95d-4c24-a39d-b5e398fcd57f
Name             : Virtual machine has continuous high CPU
                   usage causing stress
Client           : VMware.VimAutomation.vROps.Impl.V1.OMClientImpl
Uid              : /OMServer=admin@vROPs:443/OMAlert=48dfb8ed
                   -b95d-4c24-a39d-b5e398fcd57f/
```

As you can see in the preceding output, virtual machine VM1 has `continuous high CPU usage causing stress`. This might be an alert that needs action to be taken. We can solve this alert by increasing the amount of virtual CPUs of the virtual machine.

Retrieving alert definitions

Alert definitions are templates that contain a set of symptoms, recommendations, and actions. When a symptom is breached, an alert with the same name of the definition is raised. The `Get-OMAlertDefinition` cmdlet retrieves alert definitions from the specified vRealize Operations Manager server. The syntax of the `Get-OMAlertDefinition` cmdlet is as follows. The first parameter set is the default:

```
Get-OMAlertDefinition [-Impact <OMImpact[]>] [-Criticality
<OMCriticality[]>] [-ResourceKind <String[]>] [-AdapterKind
<String[]>] [-Type <OMAlertType[]>] [-SubType <OMAlertSubtype[]>]
[[-Name] <String[]>] [-Server <OMServer[]>] [<CommonParameters>]
```

The second parameter set is required to retrieve alert definitions by ID:

```
Get-OMAlertDefinition -Id <String[]> [-Server <OMServer[]>]
[<CommonParameters>]
```

The `-Id` parameter is required.

Without parameters, the `Get-OMAlertDefinition` cmdlet returns 177 alert definitions in my lab environment. To show you how an alert definition object looks, we will retrieve only the first alert definition and format the output in a list view, using the following command:

```
PowerCLI C:\> Get-OMAlertDefinition | Select-Object -First 1 |
Format-List
```

The output of the preceding command is as follows:

```
WARNING: PowerCLI scripts should not use the 'Client' property.
The property will be removed in a future release.
WARNING: PowerCLI scripts should not use the 'Uid' property.
The property will be removed in a future release.
ExtensionData : VMware.VimAutomation.VROps.Views.AlertDefinition
Description   : No data received for Windows platform
AdapterKind   : EP Ops Adapter
ResourceKind  : Windows
Type          : Application Alerts
SubType       : Performance
Criticality   : Critical
Impact        : Health
WaitCycle     : 1
CancelCycle   : 1
Id            : AlertDefinition-EP Ops Adapter-Alert
                -system-availability-Windows
Name          : No data received for Windows platform
Client        : VMware.VimAutomation.vROps.Impl.V1.OMClientImpl
Uid           : /OMServer=admin@192.168.0.62:443/
                OMAlertDefinition=AlertDefinition-EP
                Ops Adapter-Alert-system-availability-Windows/
```

As you can see in the preceding output, the type of the alert is `Application Alerts`, and the subtype is `Performance`. In the following section, *Retrieving alert types*, you will learn how to retrieve the available alert types. In the section, *Retrieving alert subtypes*, you will learn how to retrieve the available alert subtypes.

You can use the parameters of the `Get-OMAlertDefinition` cmdlet to filter the output by impact, criticality, resource kind, adapter kind, type, subtype, name, and Operations Manager server. The possible values for impact are:

- Health
- Risk
- Efficiency
- Unknown

The possible values for criticality are:

- None
- Information
- Warning
- Immediate
- Critical
- SymptomBased
- Unknown

Retrieving alert types

Alert types are categories in which alerts can be divided. You can assign alerts of a certain type to a specific administrator. The Get-OMAlertType cmdlet retrieves alert types from the specified vRealize Operations Manager server. The syntax of the Get-OMAlertType cmdlet is as follows:

The first parameter set is the default. You can use this parameter set to retrieve all of the alert types or to retrieve alert types by name:

```
Get-OMAlertType [[-Name] <String[]>] [-Server <OMServer[]>]
[<CommonParameters>]
```

The second parameter set is to retrieve alert types by ID:

```
Get-OMAlertType -Id <String[]> [-Server <OMServer[]>]
[<CommonParameters>]
```

The -Id parameter is required.

In the following example, we will retrieve all of the alert types, select only the name and description properties, and format the output in a list:

```
PowerCLI C:\> Get-OMAlertType | Select-Object -Property
Name,Description | Format-List
```

The output of the preceding command is as follows:

```
Name        : Application Alerts
Description : Alerts that indicate problems in application layer
Name        : Virtualization/Hypervisor Alerts
Description : Alerts that indicate problems in
              virtualization/hypervisor layer
```

```
Name         : Hardware (OSI) Alerts
Description : Alerts that indicate problems in hardware/operating
               system interface layer
Name         : Storage Alerts
Description : Alerts that indicate storage problems
Name         : Network Alerts
Description : Alerts that indicate network problems
```

As you can see in the preceding output, there are only five alert types.

Retrieving alert subtypes

Alert subtypes are subcategories in which alerts can be divided. You can assign alerts of a certain subtype to a particular administrator. The `Get-OMAlertSubType` cmdlet retrieves alert subtypes from the specified vRealize Operations Manager server. The syntax of the `Get-OMAlertSubType` cmdlet is as follows:

The first parameter set is the default. You can use this parameter set to retrieve all of the alert subtypes, alert subtypes by name, or by alert type:

```
Get-OMAlertSubType [[-Name] <String[]>] [-AlertType
<OMAlertType[]>] [-Server <OMServer[]>] [<CommonParameters>]
```

The second parameter set is to retrieve alert subtypes by ID:

```
Get-OMAlertSubType -Id <String[]> [-Server <OMServer[]>]
[<CommonParameters>]
```

The `-Id` parameter is required.

Every alert type, from the preceding section, *Retrieving alert types*, has the same alert subtypes. However, every combination of alert type and alert subtype has a unique ID.

In the following example, we will retrieve all of the alert subtypes available for every alert type. We will show only the `Name` and `Description` properties. The `Sort-Object -Unique` command is used to remove duplicates from the output. The output is displayed in a list format:

```
PowerCLI C:\> Get-OMAlertSubType | Select-Object
-Property Name,Description | Sort-Object -Property
Name,Description -Unique | Format-List
```

The output of the preceding command is as follows:

```
Name        : Availability
Description : Alerts that indicate the problems with resource
              availability
Name        : Capacity
Description : Alerts that indicate capacity planning problems
Name        : Compliance
Description : Alerts that indicate compliance problems
Name        : Configuration
Description : Alerts that indicate configuration problems
Name        : Performance
Description : Alerts that indicate performance problems
```

In the second example, we will retrieve all of the available subtypes and show the `Name`, `Id`, and `AlertType` properties using the following command:

```
PowerCLI C:\> Get-OMAlertSubType | Select-Object
-Property Name,Id,AlertType
```

The preceding command has the following output:

```
Name          Id                  AlertType
----          --                  ---------
Availability  Type:15 Subtype:18  Application Alerts
Performance   Type:15 Subtype:19  Application Alerts
Capacity      Type:15 Subtype:20  Application Alerts
Compliance    Type:15 Subtype:21  Application Alerts
Configuration Type:15 Subtype:22  Application Alerts
Availability  Type:16 Subtype:18  Virtualization/Hypervisor Alerts
Performance   Type:16 Subtype:19  Virtualization/Hypervisor Alerts
Capacity      Type:16 Subtype:20  Virtualization/Hypervisor Alerts
Compliance    Type:16 Subtype:21  Virtualization/Hypervisor Alerts
Configuration Type:16 Subtype:22  Virtualization/Hypervisor Alerts
Availability  Type:17 Subtype:18  Hardware (OSI) Alerts
Performance   Type:17 Subtype:19  Hardware (OSI) Alerts
Capacity      Type:17 Subtype:20  Hardware (OSI) Alerts
Compliance    Type:17 Subtype:21  Hardware (OSI) Alerts
Configuration Type:17 Subtype:22  Hardware (OSI) Alerts
Availability  Type:18 Subtype:18  Storage Alerts
Performance   Type:18 Subtype:19  Storage Alerts
Capacity      Type:18 Subtype:20  Storage Alerts
Compliance    Type:18 Subtype:21  Storage Alerts
Configuration Type:18 Subtype:22  Storage Alerts
Availability  Type:19 Subtype:18  Network Alerts
Performance   Type:19 Subtype:19  Network Alerts
Capacity      Type:19 Subtype:20  Network Alerts
Compliance    Type:19 Subtype:21  Network Alerts
```

```
Configuration Type:19 Subtype:22 Network Alerts
```

Modifying alerts

You can use the `Set-OMAlert` cmdlet to take or release ownership of an alert, suspend the alert by the time specified in minutes, or cancel an alert. The syntax of the `Set-OMAlert` cmdlet is as follows:

The first parameter set is required to take ownership of alerts:

```
Set-OMAlert -TakeOwnership [-Alert] <OMAlert[]> [-Server
<OMServer[]>] [-WhatIf] [-Confirm] [<CommonParameters>]
```

The `-TakeOwnership` parameter is required.

The second parameter set is to release ownership of alerts:

```
Set-OMAlert -ReleaseOwnership [-Alert] <OMAlert[]>
[-Server <OMServer[]>] [-WhatIf] [-Confirm] [<CommonParameters>]
```

The `-ReleaseOwnership` parameter is required.

The third parameter set is required to suspend alerts by the specified time in minutes:

```
Set-OMAlert -SuspendMinutes <Int32> [-Alert] <OMAlert[]>
[-Server <OMServer[]>] [-WhatIf] [-Confirm] [<CommonParameters>]
```

The `-SuspendMinutes` parameter is required.

The fourth parameter set is required to cancel alerts:

```
Set-OMAlert -Cancel [-Alert] <OMAlert[]> [-Server
<OMServer[]>] [-WhatIf] [-Confirm] [<CommonParameters>]
```

The `-Cancel` parameter is required.

In the first example, we will first retrieve all of the critical alerts, take ownership of them, display the `Name`, and `AssignedUser` property of the output objects:

```
PowerCLI C:\> Get-OMAlert -Criticality Critical |
Set-OMAlert -TakeOwnership | Select-Object -Property AssignedUser
```

The output of the preceding command is as follows:

```
Name                                        AssignedUser
----                                        ------------
Adapter instance Object is down             admin
Adapter instance Object is down             admin
Host has lost connection to vCenter Server  admin
Adapter instance Object is down             admin
```

You can see in the preceding output, that the admin account took ownership of four alerts.

In the second example, we will release the ownership from the alerts we took ownership from in the preceding example:

```
PowerCLI C:\> Get-OMAlert -Criticality Critical | Set-OMAlert
-ReleaseOwnership | Select-Object -Property Name,AssignedUser
```

The preceding command has the following output:

```
Name                                        AssignedUser
----                                        ------------
Adapter instance Object is down
Adapter instance Object is down
Host has lost connection to vCenter Server
Adapter instance Object is down
```

As you can see in the preceding output, `AssignedUser` property is now empty.

In the third example, we will retrieve the alerts for the host with IP address `192.168.0.201` and suspend these alerts for `30` minutes. The command only outputs the time until the alert is suspended:

```
PowerCLI C:\> Get-OMAlert -Resource 192.168.0.201 | Set-OMAlert
-SuspendMinutes 30 | Select-Object -Property SuspendedUntil
```

The preceding command has the following output:

```
SuspendedUntil
--------------
2/2/2017 5:58:15 PM
```

If you want to cancel the suspension, you cannot use `0` as the value for the `-SuspendMinutes` parameter. The minimum value is `1`.

Retrieving recommendations

The Get-OMRecommendation cmdlet retrieves recommendations from the specified vRealize Operations Manager server. The syntax of the Get-OMRecommendation cmdlet is as follows:

The first parameter set is required to retrieve recommendations by ID:

```
Get-OMRecommendation [-Id <String[]>] [-Server <OMServer[]>]
[<CommonParameters>]
```

The second parameter set is required to retrieve recommendations by alert:

```
Get-OMRecommendation -Alert <OMAlert[]> [-Server <OMServer[]>]
[<CommonParameters>]
```

The third parameter set is required to retrieve recommendations by alert definition:

```
Get-OMRecommendation -AlertDefinition <OMAlertDefinition[]>
[-Server <OMServer[]>] [<CommonParameters>]
```

The Get-OMRecommendation cmdlet has no required parameters.

If you use the Get-OMRecommendation cmdlet without parameters, it retrieves all of the recommendation definitions. The following example retrieves the recommendations, selects only the first one, and displays the output in a list view:

```
PowerCLI C:\> Get-OMRecommendation | Select-Object -First 1
| Format-List
```

The output of the preceding example is as follows:

```
AlertDefinition :
ExtensionData   : VMware.VimAutomation.VROps.Views.Recommendation
Id              : Recommendation-df-VMWARE-CheckStorageIOControl
Description     : Check whether you have enabled Storage IO Control
                  on the datastores connected to the virtual machine
Alert           :
Client          : VMware.VimAutomation.vROps.Impl.V1.OMClientImpl
Uid             : /OMServer=admin@192.168.0.62:443/OMAlertRecommenda
                  tion=Recommendation-df-VMWARE-
                  CheckStorageIOControl/
```

It is more interesting to retrieve the recommendations for the current alerts. This will give you recommendations about how to solve the alert. In the following example, we will retrieve the current alerts, pipe the output to the `Get-OMRecommendation` cmdlet to retrieve the recommendations for the alerts, select only the `Alert` and `Description` properties, and format the output in a list view:

```
PowerCLI C:\> Get-OMAlert | Get-OMRecommendation |
Select-Object -Property Alert,Description | Format-List
```

The preceding command has the following output:

```
Alert       : NTP Servers are not reachable
Description : Examine connectivity to the defined NTP server from th
              e affected machine

Alert       : Adapter instance Object is down
Description : Verify that the adapter configuration and credentials
              are correct. Ensure that the remote endpoint of the da
              ta source is available and can be reached from the Col
              lector where this adapter instance is running

Alert       : Host has lost connection to vCenter Server
Description : Click "Open Host in vSphere Web Client" in the Actions
               menu at the top of Alert details page to connect to t
              he vCenter managing this host and manually reconnect t
              he host to vCenter Server. After the connection to the
               host is restored by vCenter Server, the alert will be
              canceled.

Alert       : License will soon expire
Description : Contact VMware or solution vendor to renew the license
```

You can see in the preceding output that I have some problems to fix in my home lab.

Retrieving statistic keys

A statistic key identifies a vRealize Operations Manager metric. The `Get-OMStatKey` cmdlet retrieves vRealize Operations Manager statistic keys. The syntax of the `Get-OMStatKey` cmdlet is given here. The first parameter set is the default:

```
Get-OMStatKey [[-Name] <String[]>] [-ResourceKind
<String[]>] [-AdapterKind <String[]>] [-Server <OMServer[]>]
[<CommonParameters>]
```

The second parameter set is required to retrieve statistic keys by resource:

```
Get-OMStatKey [[-Name] <String[]>] -Resource
<OMResource[]> [-Server <OMServer[]>] [<CommonParameters>]
```

The `-Resource` parameter is required.

The `Get-OMStatKey` cmdlet without parameters returns all of the statistic keys. There are too many statistic keys to shows in this book. Piping the output of the `Get-OMStatKey` cmdlet to the `Measure-Object` cmdlet and displaying the `Count` property shows us the number of statistic keys, as in the following command:

```
PowerCLI C:\> (Get-OMStatKey | Measure-Object).Count
```

In my lab environment, the output of the preceding command is as follows:

```
24078
```

To show you the properties of a statistics key object, we will retrieve the statistic keys, select only the first one, and format the output in a list view using the following command:

```
PowerCLI C:\> Get-OMStatKey | Select-Object -First 1 | Format-List
```

The preceding command has the following output:

```
ExtensionData : VMware.VimAutomation.VROps.Views.ResourceTypeAttribu
                te
Name          : badge|stress_whatif
Unit          : %
Description   : Stress with committed projects
ResourceKind  : BusinessService
AdapterKind   : Container
Client        : VMware.VimAutomation.vROps.Impl.V1.OMClientImpl
Uid           : /OMServer=admin@192.168.0.62:443/AdapterKind=Contain
                er/ResourceKind=BusinessService/OMStatKey=badge|stre
                ss_whatif/
```

Retrieving statistical data

The `Get-OMStat` cmdlet retrieves statistical data from the specified vRealize Operations Manager server. The syntax of the `Get-OMStat` cmdlet is as follows:

```
Get-OMStat [-Resource] <OMResource[]> [-Key <OMStatKey[]>]
[-From <DateTime>] [-To <DateTime>] [-IntervalType
<OMStatIntervalType>] [-IntervalCount <Int32>] [-RollupType
<OMStatRollupType>] [-Server <OMServer[]>] [<CommonParameters>]
```

The `-Resource` parameter is required.

In the first example, we will retrieve all of the statistical data for virtual machine `DC001` and display the first five objects found, using the following command:

```
PowerCLI C:\> Get-OMStat -Resource DC001 | Select-Object -First 5
```

The output of the preceding command is as follows:

```
Resource Key                                    Value Time
-------- ---                                    ----- ----
DC001    System Attributes|alert_count_... 0         2/2/2017 9:00:44 PM
DC001    System Attributes|alert_count_... 0         2/2/2017 9:05:44 PM
DC001    System Attributes|alert_count_... 0         2/2/2017 9:10:44 PM
DC001    System Attributes|alert_count_... 0         2/2/2017 9:15:44 PM
DC001    System Attributes|alert_count_... 0         2/2/2017 9:20:44 PM
```

You can see in the output of the preceding command that the time interval between the samples is 5 seconds.

In the second example, we will the retrieve the usage of the `C:` drive of virtual machine `DC001`, using the following command:

```
PowerCLI C:\> Get-OMStat -Resource DC001 -Key
'guestfilesystem:C:\|usage' | Select-Object -Last 1
```

The preceding command has the following output:

```
Resource Key                      Value            Time
-------- ---                      -----            ----
DC001    guestfilesystem:C:\|u... 9.93389129638672 2/2/2017 21:25:44
```

The output of the preceding command tells us that the `C:` drive of virtual machine `DC001` has 9.9 GB used space.

Retrieving local user accounts

In vRealize Operations Manager, you can authenticate users using local accounts, SSO SAML, Open LDAP, Active Directory, and vCenter Server accounts. The `Get-OMUser` cmdlet retrieves local user accounts from the specified vRealize Operations Manager server. The syntax of the `Get-OMUser` cmdlet is given here. The first parameter set is the default:

```
Get-OMUser [-Enabled <Boolean>] [[-Name] <String[]>]
[-Email <String[]>] [-Server <OMServer[]>] [<CommonParameters>]
```

The second parameter set is required to retrieve local users by ID:

```
Get-OMUser -Id <String[]> [-Server <OMServer[]>] [<CommonParameters>]
```

The `-Id` parameter is required.

Using the `Get-OMUser` cmdlet without parameters will return all of the local user accounts, as follows:

```
PowerCLI C:\> Get-OMUser
```

The output of the preceding command is as follows:

```
Name                 FirstName LastName Enabled
----                 --------- -------- -------
maintenanceAdmin                        True
migrationAdmin                          True
admin                                   True
automationAdmin                         True
```

Before running the `Get-OMUser` cmdlet in the preceding example, I did not create a local user account myself. The accounts you see in the preceding output are all accounts created during installation of vRealize Operations Manager.

In the following screenshot of the vRealize Operations Manager console, you see all of the user accounts including the local user accounts:

Using the vRealize Operations Manager API

Until now, you have seen the cmdlets available in PowerCLI for vRealize Operations Manager. These cmdlets only explore a small set of things you can do with vRealize Operations Manager. vRealize Operations Manager has a **REpresentational State Transfer Application Programming Interface** (**REST API**) that you can easily use from PowerCLI. The `$global:DefaultOMServers` variable has an `ExtensionData` property that opens the gate to the API for you. First, we will create a variable `$omApi` that contains the connection to the vRealize Operations Manager API, using the following command:

```
PowerCLI C:\> $omApi = $global:DefaultOMServers[0].ExtensionData
```

The `$global:DefaultOMServers` variable can be an array containing connections to multiple vRealize Operations Manager Servers. This is why we used `[0]` to select the first vROPs server.

By piping the output of the `$omApi` variable to the `Get-Member` cmdlet, you will see the available properties and methods, as follows:

```
PowerCLI C:\> $omApi | Get-Member | Select-Object -First 20
```

In total, the `Get-Member` cmdlet returns 243 lines of output. Therefore, we only display the first 20 lines. The output of the preceding cmdlet is as follows:

```
    TypeName: VMware.VimAutomation.VROps.Views.ServerApi

    Name                           MemberType  Definition
    ----                           ----------  ----------
    AcquireToken                   Method      VMware.VimAutomation.VROps...
    AcquireTokenAsync              Method      System.Threading.Tasks.Tas...
    AddAuthSource                  Method      VMware.VimAutomation.VROps...
    AddAuthSourceAsync             Method      System.Threading.Tasks.Tas...
    AddLicenseKeyToProduct         Method      VMware.VimAutomation.VROps...
    AddLicenseKeyToProductAsync    Method      System.Threading.Tasks.Tas...
    ChangePassword                 Method      void ChangePassword(VMware...
    ChangePasswordAsync            Method      System.Threading.Tasks.Tas...
    CreateAdapterInstance          Method      VMware.VimAutomation.VROps...
    CreateAdapterInstanceAsync     Method      System.Threading.Tasks.Tas...
    CreateAlertDefinition          Method      VMware.VimAutomation.VROps...
    CreateAlertDefinitionAsync     Method      System.Threading.Tasks.Tas...
    CreateAlertPlugin              Method      VMware.VimAutomation.VROps...
    CreateAlertPluginAsync         Method      System.Threading.Tasks.Tas...
    CreateCollectorGroup           Method      VMware.VimAutomation.VROps...
    CreateCollectorGroupAsync      Method      System.Threading.Tasks.Tas...
    CreateCredential               Method      VMware.VimAutomation.VROps...
    CreateCredentialAsync          Method      System.Threading.Tasks.Tas...
    CreateEmailTemplate            Method      VMware.VimAutomation.VROps...
    CreateEmailTemplateAsync       Method      System.Threading.Tasks.Tas...
```

You can run the preceding command for yourself to see all of the available methods.

Another way to explore the vRealize Operations Manager API is via a web browser. If you go to `https://<your-vROPs-server>/suite-api`, you will open the vRealize Operations Manager API home page.

In the following sections, *Getting the user roles*, *Creating users*, *Removing users*, *Retrieving solutions*, *Creating reports*, and *Retrieving reports*, we will use the vROPs API to retrieve the user roles, create users, remove users, retrieve solutions, create reports, and retrieve reports.

Getting the user roles

User roles define what a user can do in vRealize Operations Manager. For example, the `Administrator` user role has all the rights. The `ReadOnly` user role has only read access and cannot modify anything. The following command retrieves the name and description of the existing user roles:

```
PowerCLI C:\> $omApi.GetRoles().Userrole |
Select-Object -Property Name,Description
```

The output of the preceding command is as follows:

```
Name                        Description
----                        -----------
GeneralUser-1               Configurable out of the box role
GeneralUser-2               Configurable out of the box role
Administrator               System administrator
GeneralUser-3               Configurable out of the box role
GeneralUser-4               Configurable out of the box role
ReadOnly                    Read Only access for the product
AgentManager                Deploy and configure EP Ops Management ...
PowerUserMinusRemediation   All the Privileges except the ones rela...
PowerUser                   All the Privileges except the ones rela...
ContentAdmin                Manage all the contents in the product
```

The user rules in the preceding output are the user roles available after installing vRealize Operations Manager.

Creating users

You can create new users with the `CreateUser()` method of the vRealize Operations Manager API. The following PowerCLI command retrieves the definition of the `CreateUser` method:

```
PowerCLI C:\> $omApi.CreateUser.OverloadDefinitions
```

The output of the preceding command is as follows:

```
VMware.VimAutomation.VROps.Views.User
CreateUser(VMware.VimAutomation.VROps.Views.User input)
```

The definition shows us that the `CreateUser()` method needs one parameter named the `input` of type `VMware.VimAutomation.VROps.Views.User`. The output of the `CreateUser` method is also an object of type `VMware.VimAutomation.VROps.Views.User`.

A method definition has the following layout:

```
<Output object type> <Method name>(<Input parameter type>
<Input parameter name>)
```

A method can have zero, one, or more input parameters. If the method does not return any output, `void` is used as the output object type.

To create a new user, we will first create an object of the type `VMware.VimAutomation.VROps.Views.User` and save it in the variable `$User`, with the following command:

```
PowerCLI C:\> $User = New-Object -TypeName
VMware.VimAutomation.VROps.Views.User
```

Evaluating the `$User` variable will give us the properties of the object, as follows:

```
PowerCLI C:\> $User
```

The preceding command has the following output:

```
Id               :
Username         :
FirstName        :
LastName         :
Password         :
EmailAddress     :
GroupIds         :
RoleNames        :
Rolepermissions  :
Links            :
Any              :
Enabled          : False
AnyAttr          :
```

Now, we need to assign values to the properties of the $User variable. The API documentation tells us that the Username and Password are required. Besides these, we will give the new user the Administrator role, and we will enable the account, using the following commands:

```
PowerCLI C:\> $User.UserName = 'rvdnieuwendijk'
PowerCLI C:\> $User.Password = 'VMware1!'
PowerCLI C:\> $User.RoleNames = 'Administrator'
PowerCLI C:\> $User.Enabled = $true
```

Finally, we will execute the CreateUser() method with the $User variable as an input to create the new user with the following command:

```
PowerCLI C:\> $omApi.CreateUser($User)
```

The preceding command has the following output:

```
Id               : ac6a6816-e026-46a2-be48-3c1ae1f5691d
Username         : rvdnieuwendijk
FirstName        :
LastName         :
Password         :
EmailAddress     :
GroupIds         :
RoleNames        : {Administrator}
Rolepermissions  : {Administrator}
Links            : {linkToSelf, userPermissions}
Any              :
Enabled          : True
AnyAttr          :
```

The preceding output shows us that the new user was created successfully.

Removing users

To remove a user, you can use the DeleteUsers() method of the vRealize Operations Manager API. The following command retrieves the definition of the DeleteUsers() method:

```
PowerCLI C:\> $omApi.DeleteUsers.OverloadDefinitions
```

The output of the preceding command is as follows:

```
void DeleteUsers(string[] id)
```

The preceding output teaches us that the `DeleteUsers()` method requires one or more strings containing the IDs of the users that must be deleted. The `DeleteUsers()` method does not return any output.

The following command deletes the user rvdnieuwendijk created in the preceding section, *Creating users*. `(Get-OMUser -Name rvdnieuwendijk).id` retrieves the ID of the user rvdnieuwendijk:

```
PowerCLI C:\> $omApi.DeleteUsers((Get-OMUser -Name rvdnieuwendijk).id)
```

The preceding command returns no output.

Retrieving solutions

Solutions in vRealize Operations Manager are the connections between vROPs and products such as VMware vSphere, VMware vCloud Director, and VMware Log Insight. Solutions are distributed as management packs. The `GetSolutions()` method of the API will retrieve all of the solutions available in your vRealize Operations Manager server. The following command retrieves all of the solutions:

```
PowerCLI C:\> $omApi.GetSolutions().Solution
```

In my lab environment, the preceding command has the following output:

```
Name             : VMware vRealize Operations Management Pack for Log
                   Insight
Version          : 6.0.3171089
Description      : VMware vRealize Operations Management Pack for Log
                   Insight which defines the Launch-in-context rules
                   for vSphere objects.
Vendor           : VMware Inc.
AdapterKindKeys  : LogInsightAdapter
Links            :
Any              :
Id               : MPforLogInsight
AnyAttr          :
Name             : Operating Systems / Remote Service Monitoring
Version          : 1.0.4126536
Description      : The End Point Operations Management Solution for
                   Operating Systems / Remote Service Monitoring
                   provides insight into what is happening in your OS.
```

```
                          It provides key metrics for the OS, the processes,
                          services, disk and network. It also provides a
                          solution to monitor availability of, and connectivity
                          to, platforms and services such as VMs, Web servers
                          and other applications with network listeners.
        Vendor          : VMware Inc.
        AdapterKindKeys : ep-ops-os-and-availability-kind
        Links           :
        Any             :
        Id              : ep-ops-os-and-availability
        AnyAttr         :
        Name            : VMware vSphere
        Version         : 6.0.4276420
        Description     : Manages vSphere objects such as Clusters, Hosts...
        Vendor          : VMware Inc.
        AdapterKindKeys : VMWARE PythonRemediationVcenterAdapter
        Links           :
        Any             :
        Id              : VMware vSphere
        AnyAttr         :
```

You can see in the preceding output that we have three solutions installed:

- VMware vRealize Operations Management Pack for Log Insight
- Operating Systems/Remote Service Monitoring
- VMware vSphere

Retrieving traversalSpecs

In vRealize Operations Manager, you might want to perform an operation on a subset of all of the objects. A **traversalSpec** is like a filter that you use to specify on which objects the operation must be performed. There are several predefined traversalSpecs in vROPs. The following command will retrieve the names of the traversalSpecs:

```
PowerCLI C:\> $omApi.GetTraversalSpecs().Traversalspec.Name
```

The output of the preceding command is as follows:

```
        Custom Groups
        Adapters
        Operating Systems TS
        vSphere Networking
        Custom Datacenters
        Remote Checks
        vC Ops Clusters
```

```
Applications
vSphere Hosts and Clusters
AdaptersInternal
vSphere Storage
```

To show you the properties of a traversalSpec object, we will retrieve the vSphere Hosts and Clusters traversalSpec, using the following command:

```
PowerCLI C:\> $omApi.GetTraversalSpecs().Traversalspec |
>> Where-Object {$_.Name -eq 'vSphere Hosts and Clusters'}
```

The preceding command has the following output:

```
Name                          : vSphere Hosts and Clusters
Description                   : Enables view of resources imported
                                 from vCenter like Clusters, Hosts,
                                 VMs and ResourcePools
RootAdapterKindKey            : VMWARE
RootResourceKindKey           : vSphere World
Any                           :
AdapterInstanceAssociation    : False
AnyAttr                       :
```

In the preceding output, the RootAdapterKindKey property value, VMWARE, matches the AdapterKindKeys property of the VMware vSphere solution in the output of the example in the preceding section, *Retrieving solutions*. This way, vROPs knows which solution should be used to perform the operation. The RootResourceKindKey value, vSphere World, tells us to search for objects in the entire vSphere environment.

In the following section, *Creating reports*, we will use the vSphere Hosts and Clusters traversalSpec to create a report.

Creating reports

As an advanced example of using the vRealize Operations Manager API, we will create a report in this section. There are many predefined reports available in vRealize Operations Manager. The following command will give you a list of the names of the available reports. Because the list is too long to show in this book, we will retrieve only the first 20 lines of output:

```
PowerCLI C:\> $omApi.GetReportDefinitions().Reportdefinition.Name
| Select-Object -First 20
```

The output of the preceding command is as follows:

```
Cluster Average Latency (ms) Trend View Report
Cluster Capacity Risk Forecast Report
Cluster Configuration Summary
Cluster CPU Demand (%) Trend View Report
Cluster IOPs Trend View Report
Cluster Memory Usage and Demand (%) Trend View Report
Cluster Networking Usage (KBps) Trend View Report
Cluster VM Growth Trend View Report
Datacenter CPU Usage (MHz) Trend View Report
Datacenter Host Growth Trend View Report
Datacenter Networking Usage (KBps) Trend View Report
Datacenter VM Growth Trend View Report
Datastore Average Latency (ms) Trend View Report
Datastore Capacity Risk Forecast Report
Datastore Inventory - Disk Space Report
Datastore Inventory - I/O Report
Datastore IOPs Trend View Report
Datastore Min/Max/Avg IOPs 30 Days List View Report
Datastore Used Space (%) Distribution Report
Datastore Waste List View Report
```

We will create a `Datastore Inventory - I/O Report` in the rest of this section.

The `CreateReport()` method of the API will create a report. This following command will retrieve the definition of the method:

```
PowerCLI C:\> $omApi.CreateReport.OverloadDefinitions
```

The preceding command has the following output:

```
VMware.VimAutomation.VROps.Views.Report
CreateReport(VMware.VimAutomation.VROps.Views.Report input)
```

The preceding output shows us that the `CreateReport` methods need one parameter named `input` of type `VMware.VimAutomation.VROps.Views.Report`. The method also returns an object of the type `VMware.VimAutomation.VROps.Views.Report`.

First, we will create an object of the type `VMware.VimAutomation.VROps.Views.Report`, using the following command:

```
PowerCLI C:\> $Report = New-Object -TypeName
VMware.VimAutomation.VROps.Views.Report
```

We will use the `Get-Member` cmdlet to retrieve the properties of the object in the `$Report` variable, as follows:

```
PowerCLI C:\> Get-Member -InputObject $Report
```

The output of the preceding command is as follows:

```
    TypeName: VMware.VimAutomation.VROps.Views.Report

Name                    MemberType Definition
----                    ---------- ----------
Equals                  Method     bool Equals(System.Object obj)
GetHashCode             Method     int GetHashCode()
GetType                 Method     type GetType()
ToString                Method     string ToString()
Any                     Property   System.Xml.XmlElement[] Any {get;set;}
AnyAttr                 Property   System.Xml.XmlAttribute[] AnyAttr {...
CompletionTime          Property   string CompletionTime {get;set;}
Description             Property   string Description {get;set;}
Id                      Property   string Id {get;set;}
Links                   Property   VMware.VimAutomation.VROps.Views.Li...
Name                    Property   string Name {get;set;}
Owner                   Property   string Owner {get;set;}
ReportDefinitionId      Property   string ReportDefinitionId {get;set;}
ResourceId              Property   string ResourceId {get;set;}
Status                  Property   string Status {get;set;}
Subject                 Property   string Subject {get;set;}
TraversalSpec           Property   VMware.VimAutomation.VROps.Views.Tr...
```

According to the API documentation, the `ResourceId`, `ReportDefinitionId`, and `TraversalSpec` properties are required to create a report.

Next, we will give values to the required properties using the following commands. To retrieve the `ResourceId` value, we will use the `Get-OMResource` cmdlet. The following screenshot of the vRealize Operations Manager console shows us which resources we can choose from:

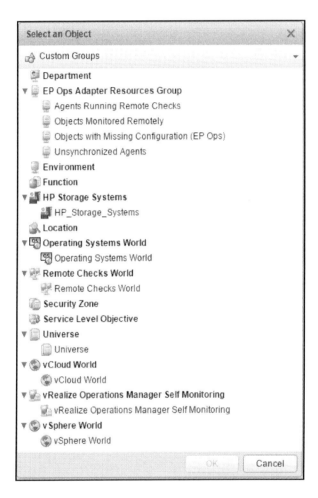

For our report, we use the `vSphere World` resource and add its ID to the `$Report.ResourceId` property, as follows:

```
PowerCLI C:\> $Report.ResourceId = (Get-OMResource -Name
'vSphere World').Id
```

We will use the `GetReportDefinitions()` method to retrieve the ID of the `Datastore Inventory – I/O Report` report. We add the ID to the `$Report.ReportDefinitionId` property, as follows:

```
PowerCLI C:\> $Report.ReportDefinitionId =
($omApi.GetReportDefinitions().Reportdefinition |
Where-Object Name -eq 'Datastore Inventory - I/O Report').Id
```

We will use the `vSphere Hosts and Clusters` traversalSpec, as follows:

```
$Report.TraversalSpec = $omApi.GetTraversalSpecs().
Traversalspec | Where-Object {$_.Name -eq 'vSphere Hosts
and Clusters'}
```

Finally, we will create the report with the following command:

```
PowerCLI C:\> $omApi.CreateReport($Report)
```

The preceding command gives the following output:

```
ResourceId           : 080067c8-5f18-474f-b69c-314ae3dac253
ReportDefinitionId   : a2c43c18-38ce-4c5a-82f6-08df9fdcfe11
TraversalSpec        :
Name                 :
Description          : Datastore Inventory - I/O Report
Subject              : Datastore
Owner                : 770d4820-81b9-4b87-b463-b42c938c4e1a
CompletionTime       : null
Status               : QUEUED
Links                : {linkToSelf}
Any                  :
Id                   : e14bffa6-0491-456d-aeb3-5cecff0710e4
AnyAttr              :
```

You can see in the preceding output that the status of the report creation is **QUEUED**.

In the following section, *Retrieving reports*, you will learn how to retrieve reports.

Refer to the blog post Using the entire API for vRealize Operations via PowerCLI at
`http://blogs.vmware.com/PowerCLI/2016/05/using-entire-api-vreali ze-operations-via-powercli.html`, which gives a good explanation of how to use the vRealize Operations Manager API documentation.

Retrieving reports

To retrieve the available reports on your vRealize Operations Manager server, you can use the `GetReports()` method of the API. You can retrieve the definition of the `GetReports()` method using the following command:

```
PowerCLI C:\> $omApi.GetReports.OverloadDefinitions
```

The output of the preceding command is as follows:

```
VMware.VimAutomation.VROps.Views.Reports GetReports
(string[] name, string[] owner, string[] status, string[] subject)
```

You can use the `name`, `owner`, `status`, or `subject` parameters to filter for specific reports. If you use the `GetReports()` method without parameters, it will return all of the available reports, as in the following command:

```
PowerCLI C:\> $omApi.GetReports().Report
```

The preceding command has the following output:

```
ResourceId        : 080067c8-5f18-474f-b69c-314ae3dac253
ReportDefinitionId : a2c43c18-38ce-4c5a-82f6-08df9fdcfe11
TraversalSpec     :
Name              :
Description       : Datastore Inventory - I/O Report
Subject           : Datastore
Owner             : admin
CompletionTime    :
Status            : COMPLETED
Links             : {linkToSelf}
Any               :
Id                : e14bffa6-0491-456d-aeb3-5cecff0710e4
AnyAttr           :
```

You can see that in the preceding output, the report we created in the preceding section, *Creating reports*, now has the status **COMPLETED**.

Disconnecting from vRealize Operations Manager servers

The `Disconnect-OMServer` cmdlet closes the connection to one or more vRealize Operations Manager servers. The syntax of the `Disconnect-OMServer` cmdlet is as follows:

```
Disconnect-OMServer [[-Server] <OMServer[]>] [-Force]
[-WhatIf] [-Confirm] [<CommonParameters>]
```

The `Disconnect-OMServer` cmdlet has no required parameters.

In the following example, we will disconnect from vRealize Operations Manager `192.168.0.62`, as follows:

```
PowerCLI C:\> Disconnect-OMServer -Server 192.168.0.62 -Confirm:$false
```

The preceding command does not return any output.

Summary

vRealize Operations Manager is VMware's product for performance monitoring, capacity planning, and alerting. PowerCLI contains a limited set of cmdlets to work with vRealize Operations Manager. You have learned to use the cmdlets to connect to and disconnect from vRealize Operations Manager servers, use alerts, retrieve recommendations, retrieve statistical data, and retrieve local user accounts.

Using the vRealize Operations Manager API, you can use all of the capabilities of vROPs. Many examples of using the API were given to retrieve user roles, create and remove users, retrieve solutions and traversalSpecs, and create and retrieve reports.

In the following chapter, Using REST API to manage NSX and vRealize Automation, we will show you how to use VMware NSX and vRealize Automation Center with PowerCLI using REST APIs.

14

Using REST API to manage NSX and vRealize Automation

Not all of the VMware products have native support in PowerCLI. Luckily, most VMware products have a **representational state transfer** (**REST**) API. PowerShell has the `Invoke-RestMethod` cmdlet that makes it the easy-to-use REST APIs. In this chapter, we will focus on using REST APIs from PowerCLI. We will use examples from VMware NSX and VMware vRealize Automation to show you the power of the `REST APIs`.

Just like VMware vSphere is VMware's product for compute virtualization, **VMware NSX** is VMware's product for network virtualization. It offers distributed switching and routing, distributed firewalling, load balancing, **Network Address Translation** (**NAT**), **Virtual Private Network** (**VPN**), and many more features. VMware NSX is one of the products you can use to build a **Software Defined Data center** (**SDDC**).

vRealize Automation (**vRA**) is VMware's product to create a self-service portal for an **Infrastructure as a Service** (**IaaS**) solution. In vRA, you can define **blueprints** for the deployment of one or more virtual machines. Through the integration with **vRealize Orchestrator**, you can automate anything you want in vRA.

In PowerCLI, there are no native cmdlets yet to manage NSX or vRealize Automation. To manage NSX, you can use the **PowerNSX** module available at `https://github.com/vmware/powernsx`. To manage vRA, you can use the PowervRA module available at `https://github.com/jakkulabs/PowervRA`. Because this chapter focuses on using REST APIs, we won't discuss the PowerNSX and PowervRA modules. Both these modules use the REST APIs themselves, and they are an excellent source of REST API example code.

This chapter covers the following topics:

- Connecting to REST API servers
- Managing NSX logical switches
- Managing NSX logical (distributed) routers
- Managing NSX Edge services gateways
- Connecting to vRA servers
- Managing vRA tenants
- Retrieving vRA business groups
- Managing vRA reservations
- Managing vRA machines and applications

Connecting to REST API servers

REST APIs provide a way to connect to servers by making requests in the **Hypertext Transfer Protocol (HTTP)** or the **Hypertext Transfer Protocol Secure (HTTPS)**. The requests you send to the servers are in the form of a **Uniform Resource Identifier (URI)**. The responses to the requests may be in **Extensible Markup Language (XML)**, **HyperText Markup Language (HTML)**, or **JavaScript Object Notation (JSON)**. REST APIs use a stateless protocol. This means that the servers don't know what your previous request was. You have to send all the necessary information, such as credentials, in every request you make.

> To connect your PowerCLI session to an NSX Manager, access to port 443/TCP is required for REST API requests.

The `Invoke-RestMethod` cmdlet sends an HTTP or HTTPS request to a RESTful web service. The syntax of the `Invoke-RestMethod` cmdlet is as follows:

```
Invoke-RestMethod [-Uri] <Uri> [-Body <Object>] [-Certificate
<X509Certificate>] [-CertificateThumbprint <String>] [-ContentType
<String>] [-Credential <PSCredential>] [-DisableKeepAlive] [-Headers
<IDictionary>] [-InFile <String>] [-MaximumRedirection <Int32>]
[-Method {Default | Get | Head | Post | Put | Delete | Trace |
Options | Merge | Patch}] [-OutFile <String>] [-PassThru] [-Proxy
<Uri>] [-ProxyCredential <PSCredential>] [-ProxyUseDefaultCredentials]
[-SessionVariable <String>] [-TimeoutSec <Int32>] [-TransferEncoding
{chunked | compress | deflate | gzip | identity}] [-UseBasicParsing]
[-UseDefaultCredentials] [-UserAgent <String>] [-WebSession
<WebRequestSession>] [<CommonParameters>]
```

The `-Uri` parameter is required.

In the following example, we will retrieve information about the connection between the NSX Manager and the vCenter Server.

 To test the examples about NSX in this chapter, you can use the VMware Hands-On Lab *HOL-1703-SDC-1 – VMware NSX: Introduction and Feature Tour* or any other NSX Hands-On lab available on `http://labs.hol.vmware.com/`. You can use the **SEND TEXT** button in the Hands-On Lab to send a text to the console. The button is on the upper left-hand side of your window.

Before we can connect to an NSX Manager, we have to connect to the vCenter Server, as follows:

```
PowerCLI C:\> Connect-VIServer -Server vcsa-01a.corp.local
```

Next, we will define variables for the NSX Manager DNS name or IP address, the username, and the password in the VMware Hands-On Lab:

```
PowerCLI C:\> $NSXManager = '192.168.110.15'
PowerCLI C:\> $Username = 'admin'
PowerCLI C:\> $Password = 'VMware1!'
```

The username and password must be converted to a **Base64** string and saved in the variable `$base64AuthInfo` using the .NET `ToBase64String()` method of the `Convert` class, using the following command:

```
PowerCLI C:\> $base64AuthInfo = [Convert]::
ToBase64String([Text.Encoding]::ASCII.GetBytes("$Username`:$Password"))
```

Base64 is a way to convert binary code to plain ASCII characters. It uses characters from the following character set:
ABCDEFGHIJKLMNOPQRSTUVWXYZabcdefghijklmnopqrstuvwxyz0123456789+/= For every 6 bits of the binary code, a character from the character set is used.

We will use the `$base64AuthInfo` variable to create the headers of the web request. The headers are a hash table and are saved in the variable `$Headers`:

```
PowerCLI C:\> $Headers = @{Authorization = "Basic $base64AuthInfo"}
```

The Uniform Resource Identifier for the API call will be saved in the variable `$Uri`, as follows:

```
PowerCLI C:\> $Uri = "https://$NSXManager/api/2.0/services/vcconfig"
```

> The information you need to create the URI can be found in the NSX vSphere API Guide. The URL of the version used in order to write this book is
> `https://pubs.vmware.com/NSX-62/topic/com.vmware.ICbase/PDF/nsx_62_api.pdf`.

Now we can use the `Invoke-RestMethod` cmdlet to retrieve the information about the connection between the NSX Manager and the vCenter Server and save it in the variable `$xml`, with the following command:

```
PowerCLI C:\> $xml = Invoke-RestMethod -Uri $Uri -Method Get
-Headers $Headers
```

If you look at the content of the object in the `$xml` variable, you will see two properties: `xml` and `vcInfo`, as follows:

```
PowerCLI C:\> $xml

xml                                 vcInfo
---                                 ------
version="1.0" encoding="UTF-8" vcInfo
```

The information we are looking for is in the `vcInfo` property, and it can be retrieved using the following command:

```
PowerCLI C:\> $xml.vcInfo
```

The output of the preceding command is the following:

```
ipAddress                 : vcsa-01a.corp.local
userName                  : administrator@vsphere.local
certificateThumbprint     : 25:CE:76:57:A1:C4:3B:56:06:68:2D:7D:
                            9C:E1:5B:1E:E0:8E:53:74
assignRoleToUser          : true
vcInventoryLastUpdateTime : 1481218425355
```

In the preceding output, you can see the IP address of the vCenter Server connected to the NSX Manager, the username used for the connection, a thumbprint of the certificate used, and the time of the last inventory update.

If you get the following error message, you should make a connection to the vCenter Server first, using the `Connect-VIServer` cmdlet:

```
Invoke-RestMethod : The underlying connection was closed: Could not
establish trust relationship for the SSL/TLS secure channel.
At line:1 char:8
+ $xml = Invoke-RestMethod -Uri $Uri -Method Get -Headers $Headers
+        ~~~~~~~~~~~~~~~~~~~~~~~~~~~~~~~~~~~~~~~~~~~~~~~~~~~~~~~~~~~~~~
    + CategoryInfo          : InvalidOperation: (System.Net.HttpWeb
                              Request:HttpWebRequest)
                              [Invoke-RestMethod], WebException
    + FullyQualifiedErrorId : WebCmdletWebResponseException,
                              Microsoft.PowerShell.Commands.
                              InvokeRestMethodCommand
```

In the following screenshot of the NSX Manager, you will see the information about the connected vCenter Server we just retrieved using the REST API:

Managing NSX logical switches

NSX logical switches are distributed switches just like vSphere distributed switches. Each logical switch is mapped to a unique **Virtual eXtensible LAN** (**VXLAN**). The VXLAN carries the virtual machine traffic over the physical network. The physical network can be a routed OSI layer three network. All the ESXi hosts in a vSphere cluster can share one or more NSX logical switches.

In the following sections, *Creating NSX logical Switches*, *Retrieving NSX logical switches*, and *Removing NSX logical switches*, you will learn to create, retrieve, and remove NSX logical switches using the NSX REST API.

Creating NSX logical switches

In the following screenshot of the vSphere Web Client, you can see that in order to create a new NSX logical switch you have to specify a name, transport zone, and the replication mode. Optionally, you can specify a description, enable IP discovery, and enable MAC learning.

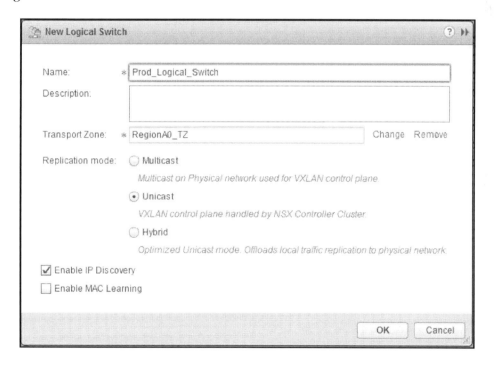

In the NSX vSphere API Guide, NSX 6.2 for vSphere, example 7-23. Create a logical switch. (`http://pubs.vmware.com/NSX-62/topic/com.vmware.ICbase/PDF/nsx_62_api.pdf`), you can read that to create a new NSX logical switch using the REST API in PowerCLI you have to use a `POST` request with the following URI:

```
https://NSX-Manager-IP-Address/api/2.0/vdn/scopes/scopeId/virtualwires
```

The `NSX-Manager-IP-Address` and the `scopeId` are variables that must be replaced by the actual values.

> In the NSX API, `POST` requests must be in XML format. Be careful, XML is case sensitive.

The request body of the `POST` request must be in the following format:

```
<virtualWireCreateSpec>
  <name>LS_vlan_tagging</name>
  <description>For guest VLAN tagging</description>
  <tenantId>virtual wire tenant</tenantId>
  <controlPlaneMode>UNICAST_MODE</controlPlaneMode> <!-- Optional.
    Default is the value specified for the transport zone. -->
  <guestVlanAllowed>true</guestVlanAllowed>
</virtualWireCreateSpec>
```

In the following example, we will create a logical switch named `Prod_Logical_Switch` with `controlPlaneMode` `UNICAST_MODE` and `guestVlanAllowed` disabled.

First, we have to retrieve the available scope IDs using the following commands:

```
PowerCLI C:\> $Uri = "https://$NSXManager/api/2.0/vdn/scopes"
PowerCLI C:\> $xml = Invoke-RestMethod -Uri $Uri -Method Get
-Headers $Headers
PowerCLI C:\> $xml.vdnScopes.vdnScope.objectId
```

The preceding command has the following output:

```
vdnscope-1
```

We will use the `vdnscope-1` scope ID in the URI, as follows:

```
PowerCLI C:\> $Uri = "https://$NSXManager/api/2.0/vdn/scopes/
vdnscope-1/virtualwires"
```

Now, we will create the body in XML format according to the example in the NSX vSphere API Guide and save it into the variable `$Body` using the following command:

```
$Body = @'
<virtualWireCreateSpec>
  <name>Prod_Logical_Switch</name>
  <tenantId>virtual wire tenant</tenantId>
  <controlPlaneMode>UNICAST_MODE</controlPlaneMode>
  <guestVlanAllowed>false</guestVlanAllowed>
```

```
</virtualWireCreateSpec>
'@
```

Finally, we will use the `Invoke-RestMethod` cmdlet using the `POST` method with the `$Body`, `$Uri` and `$Headers` variables. We will use the `-ContentType 'application/xml'` parameter to specify the type of the body as XML, as follows:

```
PowerCLI C:\> Invoke-RestMethod -Uri $Uri -Method Post -Body $Body
-ContentType 'application/xml' -Headers $Headers
```

The output of the preceding command is as follows:

```
virtualwire-14
```

Retrieving NSX logical switches

In this section, we will retrieve the logical switch `Prod_Logical_Switch` created in the preceding section Creating NSX logical switches. We will use the same URI used to create the logical switch and save it in the variable `$Uri` with the following command:

```
PowerCLI C:\> $Uri = "https://$NSXManager/api/2.0/vdn/scopes/
vdnscope-1/virtualwires"
```

The `Invoke-RestMethod` command we use is the same as for the preceding `GET` method commands, as follows:

```
PowerCLI C:\> $xml = Invoke-RestMethod -Uri $Uri -Method Get
-Headers $Headers
```

The output of the preceding command is saved in the variable `$xml`. The property `$xml.virtualWires.dataPage.virtualWire` contains all the logical switches. We will use the `Where-Object` cmdlet to filter for the `Prod_Logical_Switch` logical switch, using the following command:

```
PowerCLI C:\> $xml.virtualWires.dataPage.virtualWire |
Where-Object {$_.name -eq 'Prod_Logical_Switch'}
```

The output of the preceding example is in the following screenshot of the PowerCLI console in the VMware Hands-On Labs:

In the preceding screenshot, you can see the properties of the `Prod_Logical_Switch`.

Removing NSX logical switches

To remove a logical switch, you have to specify the `virtualwireId` in the URI and use `Delete` as the method in the `Invoke-RestMethod` call. In the following example, we will remove the logical switch `Prod_Logical_Switch` that has `virtualwireId` `virtualwire-14`. First, we create the URI and save it in the variable `$Uri`, as follows:

```
PowerCLI C:\> $Uri = "https://$NSXManager/api/2.0/vdn/
virtualwires/virtualwire-14"
```

Finally, we call the `Invoke-RestMethod` cmdlet with the `$Uri` variable and the `Delete` method, using the following command:

```
PowerCLI C:\> Invoke-RestMethod -Uri $Uri -Method Delete
-Headers $Headers
```

The preceding command does not return any output.

Managing NSX logical (distributed) routers

Before NSX, if you created a router in your network, it would be a physical or virtual machine connecting two or more networks. All of the traffic from one of the networks to another network connected to the router had to go through the router. Even if two virtual machines connected to different networks were on the same host, if the router were physical or virtual on another host, the traffic would go from the virtual machine off the host to the router and then back to the host and the other virtual machine. In NSX, routing is distributed over the hosts. Every host does a part of the routing. Traffic from one virtual machine to another virtual machine on the same host on a different network connected to the same router does not leave the host in NSX. This is a huge advantage of routing in NSX over traditional routing. NSX Edge logical routers are used for **East-West network traffic**. This means network traffic within a data center. In the following sections, *Creating NSX Edge logical routers* and *Retrieving NSX Edge logical routers*, you will learn to create and retrieve NSX logical routers in PowerCLI.

Creating NSX logical (distributed) routers

To create an NSX Distributed logical router, we will use example 8-1 of the NSX vSphere API Guide, NSX 6.2 for vSphere. I have modified the `datacenterMoid` and the `datacenterName` to match the datacenter in the VMware Hands-On Lab. You have to specify at least two `vnics`. Otherwise, you are not able to route between different networks. The XML code for the `Invoke-RestMethod` call is too big to include in this chapter. Please download the code from the Packt website `https://www.packtpub.com/`.

In the XML code, the line `<type>distributedRouter</type>` specifies that the new router will be an NSX logical (distributed) router.

The URI is saved in the variable $Uri, as follows:

```
PowerCLI C:\> $Uri = "https://$NSXManager/api/4.0/edges"
```

Now, we can use the Invoke-RestMethod command we have seen before in the section *Creating NSX logical switches* to create the logical (distributed) router:

```
PowerCLI C:\> Invoke-RestMethod -Uri $Uri -Method Post -Body $Body
-ContentType 'application/xml' -Headers $Headers
```

The preceding command does not return any output.

> To check whether your XML code is valid XML, you can use the XML validator at http://www.xmlvalidation.com/.

Retrieving NSX logical (distributed) routers

To retrieve NSX logical (distributed) routers, we can use the same URI as in the preceding section, *Creating NSX logical (distributed) routers*, as follows:

```
PowerCLI C:\> $Uri = "https://$NSXManager/api/4.0/edges"
```

The Invoke-RestMethod call with the Get method is the same as for all the retrieval commands we used before in this chapter, as follows:

```
PowerCLI C:\> $xml = Invoke-RestMethod -Uri $Uri -Method Get
-Headers $Headers
```

The output of the preceding command is saved in the variable $xml. The property $xml.pagedEdgeList.edgePage.edgeSummary contains all the NSX logical (distributed) routers and the NSX edge routers. We will use the Where-Object cmdlet in the pipeline to filter for only the NSX logical (distributed) routers, as follows:

```
PowerCLI C:\> $xml.pagedEdgeList.edgePage.edgeSummary | Where-Object
{$_.edgeType -eq 'distributedRouter'}
```

With the following command, we will retrieve all the NSX routers and pipe them to the Where-Object cmdlet to filter for only the Distributed-Router-02 created in the preceding section *Creating NSX logical (distributed) routers*:

```
PowerCLI C:\> $xml.pagedEdgeList.edgePage.edgeSummary | Where-Object
{$_.name -eq 'Distributed-Router-02'}
```

The output of the preceding command is shown in the following screenshot of the PowerCLI console in the VMware Hands-On Labs:

```
VMware vSphere PowerCLI 6.3 Release 1
PowerCLI C:\> $Uri = "https://$NSXManager/api/4.0/edges"
PowerCLI C:\> $xml = Invoke-RestMethod -Uri $Uri -Method Get -Headers
 $Headers
PowerCLI C:\> $xml.pagedEdgeList.edgePage.edgeSummary | Where-Object
{$_.name -eq 'Distributed-Router-02'}


objectId                  : edge-7
objectTypeName            : Edge
vsmUuid                   : 423A67CA-D784-ACBC-530F-F905701C3AAF
nodeId                    : 9078632b-0e49-46fb-812e-29a19676f999
revision                  : 2
type                      : type
name                      : Distributed-Router-02
clientHandle              :
extendedAttributes        :
isUniversal               : false
universalRevision         : 0
id                        : edge-7
state                     : undeployed
edgeType                  : distributedRouter
datacenterMoid            : datacenter-21
datacenterName            : RegionA01
tenantId                  : default
apiVersion                : 4.0
recentJobInfo             : recentJobInfo
edgeStatus                : GREY
numberOfConnectedVnics    : 0
appliancesSummary         : appliancesSummary
hypervisorAssist          : false
allowedActions            : allowedActions
edgeAssistId              : 5001
edgeAssistInstanceName    : default+edge-7
lrouterUuid               : 04321745-6d83-475f-bc95-5ab4e227c345

PowerCLI C:\>
```

In the preceding screenshot, you will see the properties of Distributed-Router-02. In the value of the edgeType, you will see distributedRouter. NSX has another type of router **NSX Edge services gateways** for **North-South network traffic**. NSX Edge Services Gateways will be discussed in the upcoming section, *Managing NSX Edge services gateways*.

Removing NSX logical (distributed) routers

To remove a logical (distributed) router, we have to specify the `objectId` of the router in the URI, as follows:

```
PowerCLI C:\> $Uri = "https://$NSXManager/api/4.0/edges/edge-7"
```

The `Invoke-RestMethod` call to remove the router is the same as we have seen before in the section, *Removing NSX logical switches*, as follows:

```
PowerCLI C:\> Invoke-RestMethod -Uri $Uri -Method Delete
-Headers $Headers
```

The preceding command does not return any output.

Managing NSX Edge services gateways

NSX Edge services gateways are for the connection between your data center and external networks. This is what we also call North-South network traffic. NSX Edge services gateways are deployed as a virtual appliance and provide services, such as VPN, NAT, load balancing, DHCP, and firewall.

Retrieving NSX Edge services gateways

To retrieve NSX edge services gateways, we use the same URI as in the preceding section, *Creating NSX Edge services gateways*, and save it in the variable $Uri, as follows:

```
PowerCLI C:\> $Uri = "https://$NSXManager/api/4.0/edges"
```

We use the `Invoke-RestMethod` cmdlet with the GET method to retrieve the edges and save the result in the variable $xml, using the following command:

```
PowerCLI C:\> $xml = Invoke-RestMethod -Uri $Uri -Method Get
-Headers $Headers
```

Because the `Invoke-RestMethod` call returns the NSX edge services gateways and the NSX logical (distributed) routers, we pipe the output of `$xml.pagedEdgeList.edgePage.edgeSummary` to the `Where-Object` cmdlet to return only the NSX edge services gateways, as follows:

```
PowerCLI C:\> $xml.pagedEdgeList.edgePage.edgeSummary | Where-Object
{$_.edgeType -eq 'gatewayServices'}
```

You can see the output of the preceding command in the following screenshot.

Removing NSX Edge services gateways

Removing NSX edge services gateways uses the same commands as we have used before to remove NSX logical (distributed) routers in the section, *Removing NSX logical (distributed) routers*. Please refer to that section if you want to remove NSX Edge services gateways.

Connecting to vRA servers

Using VMware vRealize Automation, you can create a web portal to automate the deployment and management of applications on multicloud environments, such as vSphere, vCloud Director, and Amazon Web Services. The **service catalog** provides items that users can request.

There are some differences between using the REST API of NSX and the REST API of vRA. The REST API of vRA uses **JavaScript Object Notation (JSON)** instead of XML. Instead of basic authentication, the REST API of vRA uses a **bearer token**. You get a bearer token by authenticating to the vRA identity service.

> To test the examples about vRealize Automation in this chapter, you can use the VMware Hands-On Lab *HOL-1721-USE-1 – vRealize Automation 7 Basics* or any other vRealize Automation Hands-On lab available on http://labs.hol.vmware.com/. You can use the **SEND TEXT** button in the Hands-On Lab to send a text to the console. The button is on the upper left-hand side of your window.

In the following example, we will retrieve a bearer token for the administrator@vsphere.local account in the vsphere.local tenant of the vra-01a.corp.local vRA server. First, we will save the server name, username, password, and tenant name in variables, using the following commands:

```
PowerCLI C:\> $vRAServer = 'vra-01a.corp.local'
PowerCLI C:\> $Username = 'administrator@vsphere.local'
PowerCLI C:\> $Password = 'VMware1!'
PowerCLI C:\> $Tenant = 'vsphere.local'
```

We will create a JSON here-string to store the username, password, and tenant name in the variable $Body, as follows:

```
$Body = @"
{
  "username":"$Username",
  "password":"$Password",
  "tenant":"$Tenant"
}
"@
```

The URI is saved in the variable $Uri, using the following command:

```
PowerCLI C:\> $Uri = "https://$vRAServer/identity/api/tokens"
```

The Invoke-RestMethod cmdlet is called with the POST method, and the output is saved in the variable $Response, as follows:

```
PowerCLI C:\> $Response = Invoke-RestMethod –Uri $Uri –Method POST
–Body $Body –ContentType 'application/json'
```

The bearer token is in the $Response.Id property. The bearer token is only valid for a specific time frame. The time the bearer token expires is in the $Response.Expires property. For convenience and later use, we create a pscustomobject containing the server name, token, token expiration time, tenant name, and username. The pscustomobject is saved in the variable $DefaultvRAServer, as follows:

```
$DefaultvRAServer = [pscustomobject]@{
  Server = $vRAServer
  Token = $Response.id
  Expires = $Response.Expires
  Tenant = $Response.tenant
  Username = $Username
}
```

Finally, we create a new hash table containing the bearer token and save the hash table in the variable $Headers for later use, using the following command:

```
$Headers = @{
  Accept = "application/json"
  'Content-Type' = "application/json"
  Authorization = "Bearer $($Global:DefaultvRAServer.Token)"
}
```

The line `Accept = "application/json"` specifies that the output of the `Invoke-RestMethod` call must be JSON. The line `'Content-Type' = "application/json"` specifies that the body of the `Invoke-RestMethod` call is JSON.

Managing vRA tenants

A tenant is an organizational unit in vRA that can be a company or a business unit in an enterprise. After deploying vRA, you will only have a **default tenant** named `vsphere.local`. To create a new tenant, you have to connect to vRA using the `administrator@vsphere.local` account that has the **system administrator** role in the `vsphere.local` tenant. In the preceding section, *Connecting to vRA servers*, we have already retrieved a bearer token for the `administrator@vsphere.local` account. In the following section, *Creating vRA tenants*, we will create a new tenant named `Research`.

Creating vRA tenants

To create a new tenant, we save the tenant name in the variable `$Tenant`, as follows:

```
PowerCLI C:\> $Tenant = 'research'
```

We will save the URI specifying the identity service and the name of the new tenant in the variable `$Uri`, using the following command:

```
PowerCLI C:\> $Uri = "https://$vRAServer/identity/api/tenants/$Tenant"
```

Next, we create a JSON here-string containing `id`, `urlName`, `name`, `description`, `contactEmail`, and `defaultTenant` to specify if the new tenant must become the default tenant. We save the here-string in the variable `$Body`, as follows:

```
$Body = @"
{ "@type" : "Tenant",
  "id" : "research",
  "urlName" : "research",
  "name" : "Research",
  "description" : "Tenant for all researchers",
  "contactEmail" : "admin@blackmilktea.com",
  "defaultTenant" : false
}
"@
```

We have to call the `Invoke-RestMethod` cmdlet with the `PUT` method to create the new tenant and save the output in the variable `$Tenant`, using the following command:

```
PowerCLI C:\> $Tenant = Invoke-RestMethod -Uri $Uri -Method PUT
-Body $Body -Headers $Headers
```

We can evaluate the `$Tenant` variable, as follows:

```
PowerCLI C:\> $Tenant
```

The output of the preceding commands is in the following screenshot:

Retrieving vRA tenants

To retrieve a list of all of the tenants, we have to use the identity service. We will save the URI in the variable `$Uri`, as follows:

```
PowerCLI C:\> $Uri = "https://$vRAServer/identity/api/tenants"
```

The `Invoke-RestMethod` cmdlet is called using the `GET` method, the URI, and the headers. The output is saved in the variable `$Tenants` with the following command:

```
PowerCLI C:\> $Tenants = Invoke-RestMethod -Uri $Uri -Method GET
-Headers $Headers
```

The tenants are available in the `$Tenants.Content` property. We will select only the `Name`, `urlName`, `Description`, and `defaultTenant` properties and format the output in a table view, as follows:

```
PowerCLI C:\> $Tenants.Content | Select-Object -Property
Name,urlName,Description,defaultTenant | Format-Table -AutoSize
```

You can see the output of the preceding command in the following screenshot:

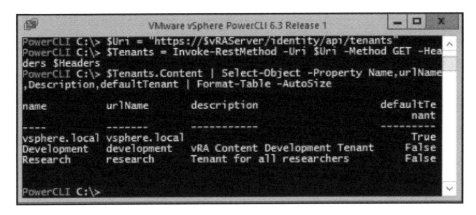

In the screenshot, you can see that there are three tenants on the vRA server named: `vsphere.local`, **Development**, and **Research**.

Removing vRA tenants

In this section, we will remove the research tenant we created in the preceding section *Creating vRA tenants*. The URI is the same as in order to create the tenant. First, we save the name of the tenant in the variable `$Tenant`, as follows:

```
PowerCLI C:\> $Tenant = 'research'
```

Next, we create the URI string using the identity service and save the string in the variable `$Uri`, using the following command:

```
PowerCLI C:\> $Uri = "https://$vRAServer/identity/api/tenants/$Tenant"
```

Finally, we call the `Invoke-RestMethod` cmdlet with the URI, the `DELETE` method, and the headers, as follows:

```
PowerCLI C:\> Invoke-RestMethod -Uri $Uri -Method DELETE
-Headers $Headers
```

The preceding command does not return any output.

Retrieving vRA business groups

A business group in vRA is a subdivision of the users in a tenant. A business group is also named a subtenant in the vRealize Automation API. Each business group must have a reservation of servers, storage, and networks.

To retrieve the vRA business groups of the `vsphere.local` tenant, we connect to the vRA server using the `cloudadmin@corp.local` account that has the **tenant administrator** role and the **IaaS administrator** role in the `vsphere.local` tenant. The following code is similar to the code in the preceding section, *Connecting to vRA servers*. First, we will save the server name, username, password, and tenant name in variables, using the following commands:

```
PowerCLI C:\> $vRAServer = 'vra-01a.corp.local'
PowerCLI C:\> $Username = 'cloudadmin@corp.local'
PowerCLI C:\> $Password = 'VMware1!'
PowerCLI C:\> $Tenant = 'vsphere.local'
```

We will create a JSON here-string to store the username, password, and tenant name in the variable `$Body`, as follows:

```
$Body = @"
{
  "username":"$Username",
  "password":"$Password",
  "tenant":"$Tenant"
}
"@
```

We save the URI in the variable $Uri, using the following command:

```
PowerCLI C:\> $Uri = "https://$vRAServer/identity/api/tokens"
```

We call the Invoke-RestMethod cmdlet with the POST method and save the output in the variable $Response, as follows:

```
PowerCLI C:\> $Response = Invoke-RestMethod -Uri $Uri -Method POST
-Body $Body -ContentType 'application/json'
```

The bearer token and other properties will be saved in the $DefaultvRAServer variable, using the following command:

```
$DefaultvRAServer = [pscustomobject]@{
  Server = $vRAServer
  Token = $Response.id
  Expires = $Response.Expires
  Tenant = $Response.tenant
  Username = $Username
}
```

We create a new hash table containing the bearer token and save the hash table in the variable $Headers for later use, with the following command:

```
$Headers = @{
  Accept = "application/json"
  'Content-Type' = "application/json"
  Authorization = "Bearer $($Global:DefaultvRAServer.Token)"
}
```

The URI, using the vRA identity service, is saved in the $Uri variable, as follows:

```
PowerCLI C:\> $Uri = "https://$vRAServer/identity/api/tenants/
vsphere.local/subtenants"
```

We call the Invoke-Restmethod cmdlet with the GET method and save the response in the $Response variable using the following command:

```
PowerCLI C:\> $Response = Invoke-RestMethod -Uri $Uri -Method GET
-Headers $Headers
```

The business groups are in the $Response.content property. Evaluating the $Response.content property will show us the business groups, as follows:

```
PowerCLI C:\> $Response.content
```

You can see the output of the preceding command in the following screenshot.

In the screenshot, you can see that there are two business groups in the `vsphere.local` tenant. One business group is named **Development**. The other business group is named **Content**.

Managing vRA reservations

Reservations in vRealize Automation are resources, such as CPU, memory, storage, and network port groups reserved for the business group. You have to create a business group before you can create a reservation. In the following sections, *Creating vRA reservations* and *Retrieving vRA reservations*, we will create and retrieve reservations.

Creating vRA reservations

To create a reservation, you have to create a JSON string that specifies the properties of the reservation. In the following code, we will make a here-string containing the specification of the reservation we are going to create. We will save the here-string in the variable $Body. The specification includes properties such as `name`, `reservationTypeId`, `tenantId`, `subTenantId`, and `ExtensionData` that contains the reserved values for the reserved networks, memory, compute resources, and storages. The here-string is too big to include in this chapter. Please download the code from the Packt website `https://www.packtpub.com/`.

It can be challenging to create a valid JSON string.

> You can use the JSON validator at `http://jsonlint.com/` to check the JSON code.

We will save the URI in the variable $Uri, as follows:

```
PowerCLI C:\> $Uri = "https://$vRAServer/reservation-service
/api/reservations"
```

Finally, we call the `Invoke-RestMethod` cmdlet with the URI, the `POST` method, the JSON here-string, and the headers to create the reservation, with the following command:

```
PowerCLI C:\> Invoke-RestMethod -Uri $Uri -Method POST
-Body $Body -Headers $Headers
```

The preceding command does not return any output.

Retrieving vRA reservations

To retrieve reservations, we use the same URI as we used in the preceding section, *Creating vRA reservations*, to create a reservation. We save the URI to the variable $Uri, as follows:

```
PowerCLI C:\> $Uri = "https://$vRAServer/reservation-service
/api/reservations"
```

We will call the `Invoke-RestMethod` cmdlet with the `GET` method and save the output in the variable `$Response` using the following command:

```
PowerCLI C:\> $Response = Invoke-RestMethod -Uri $Uri -Method GET
-Headers $Headers
```

The reservations are in the `$Response.content` property. To retrieve only the `Reservation for Business Group Development` created in the preceding section, *Creating vRA reservations*, we pipe the output to the `Where-Object` cmdlet, as follows:

```
PowerCLI C:\> $Response.content | Where-Object {$_.Name -eq
'Reservation for Business Group Development'}
```

You can see the output of the preceding command in the following screenshot:

Managing vRA machines and applications

In vRA, new machines and applications are created by selecting them from the catalog, specifying the required settings, such as the number of machines or applications to create, and submitting a request to create the machines or applications. In the following sections, *Retrieving entitled catalog items*, *Retrieving a template request for an entitled catalog item*, *Creating vRA machines*, *Viewing details of a machine request*, and *Retrieving provisioned resources*, we will walk you through the workflow to provision new machines or applications.

Retrieving entitled catalog items

We will use `devuser@corp.local` user account to deploy a `CentOS 6.6` machine. First, we have to connect to the vRA server with the `devuser@corp.local` account using the following code we have used before in the section *Connecting to vRA servers*:

```
$vRAServer = 'vra-01a.corp.local'
$Username = 'devuser@corp.local'
$Password = 'VMware1!'
$Tenant = 'vsphere.local'
$Body = @"
{
  "username":"$Username",
  "password":"$Password",
  "tenant":"$Tenant"
}
"@

$Uri = "https://$vRAServer/identity/api/tokens"
$Response = Invoke-RestMethod -Uri $Uri -Method POST -Body $Body -
ContentType 'application/json'
$DefaultvRAServer = [pscustomobject]@{
  Server = $vRAServer
  Token = $Response.id
  Expires = $Response.Expires
  Tenant = $Response.tenant
  Username = $Username
}

$Headers = @{
  Accept = "application/json"
  'Content-Type' = "application/json"
  Authorization = "Bearer $($Global:DefaultvRAServer.Token)"
}
```

We have to use the catalog service to retrieve the catalog items the user is entitled to use. We save the URI in the variable `$Uri`, as follows:

```
PowerCLI C:\> $Uri = "https://$vRAServer/catalog-
service/api/consumer/entitledCatalogItemViews"
```

The `Invoke-RestMethod` cmdlet is called using the `GET` method. We will save the in the variable `$Reponse`, with the following command:

```
PowerCLI C:\> $Response = Invoke-RestMethod -Uri $Uri -Method GET
-Headers $Headers
```

The entitled catalog items are in the `$Response.content` property. Using the following command, we will only retrieve the names of the catalog items the `devuser@corp.local` user is entitled to use:

```
PowerCLI C:\> $Response.content.name
```

You can see the output of the preceding command in the following screenshot:

You can see in the screenshot that the `devuser@corp.local` user is entitled to six catalog items including `CentOS 6.6`. In the following command, we will select only the `CentOS 6.6` catalog item and save it in the variable `$CatalogItem`:

```
PowerCLI C:\> $CatalogItem = $Response.content | Where-Object
{$_.Name -eq 'CentOS 6.6'}
```

By evaluating the `$CatalogItem` variable, we can see the value of its properties, as follows:

```
PowerCLI C:\> $CatalogItem
```

You can see the output of the preceding command in the following screenshot:

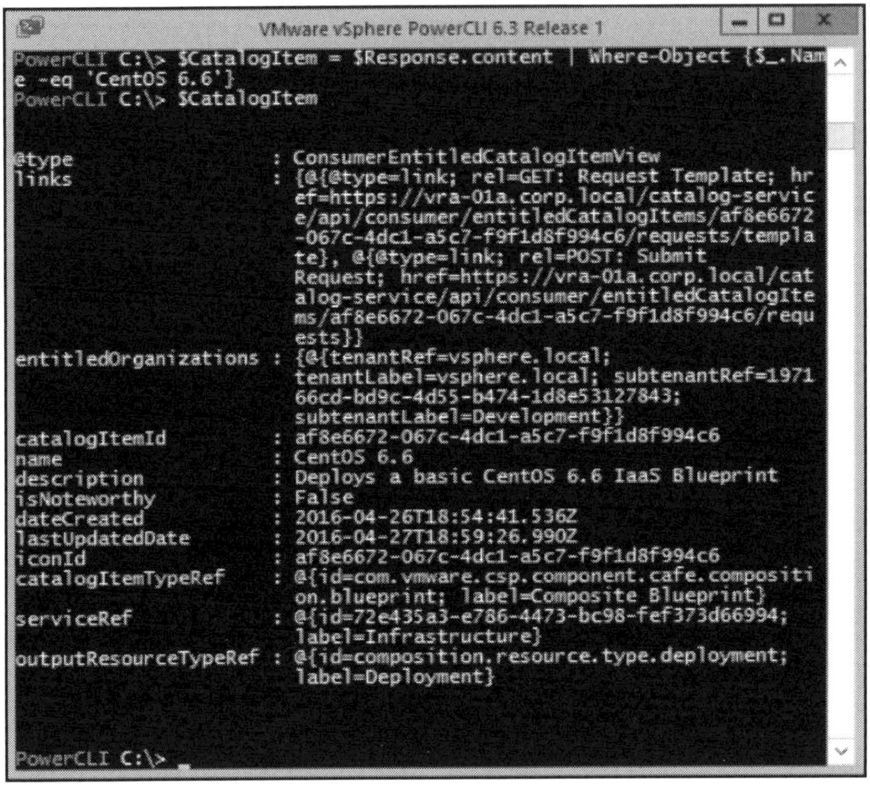

Retrieving a template request for an entitled catalog item

A catalog item contains URIs you can use to retrieve the template and submit a deployment request. The URIs are in the `links` property. The following command will use the `CentOS 6.6` catalog item retrieved in the preceding section, *Retrieving entitled catalog items*, extract the URI to retrieve a template and save the URI in the `$Uri` variable:

```
PowerCLI C:\> $Uri = ($CatalogItem.links | Where-Object
{$_.rel -eq 'GET: Request template'}).href
```

We retrieve the template with the `Invoke-RestMethod` cmdlet and the `GET` method using the URI saved in the `$Uri` variable and save the output in the `$Template` variable, as follows:

```
PowerCLI C:\> $Template = Invoke-RestMethod -Uri $Uri -Method GET
-Headers $Headers
```

By evaluating the `$Template` variable, we can see the properties of the template:

```
PowerCLI C:\> $Template
```

The output of the preceding command can be seen in the following screenshot:

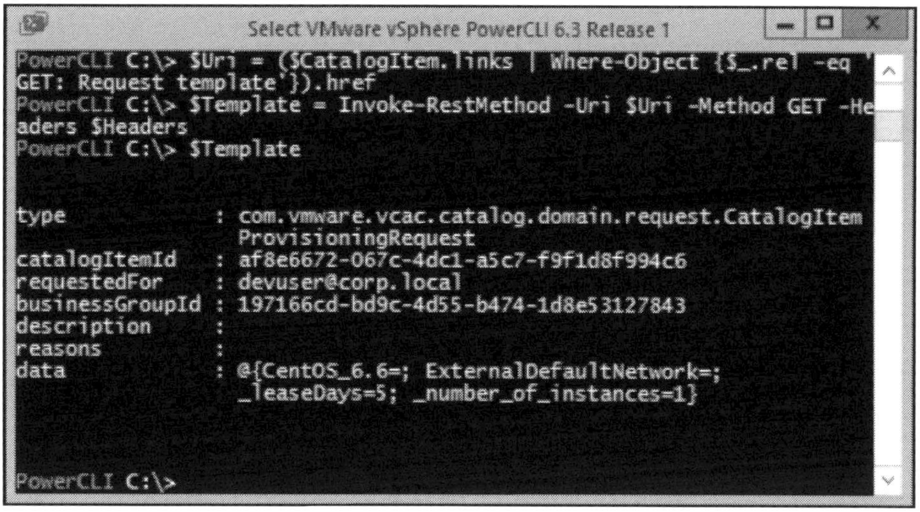

Creating vRA machines

We will use the PowerShell `ConvertTo-Json` cmdlet to convert the object in the `$Template` variable to JSON. The `ConvertTo-Json` cmdlet has the following syntax:

```
ConvertTo-Json [-InputObject] <Object> [-Compress]
[-Depth <Int32>] [<CommonParameters>]
```

The default value of the -Depth parameter is 2. Because the depth of the object in the $Template variable is more than two, we have to specify a larger value. We don't know the exact depth of the template object, so we will use a large enough value, 999, to be sure the entire object will be converted to JSON.

> If the ConvertTo-Json -Depth value is too low, the Invoke-RestMethod cmdlet will return the following error message:
>
> **Invoke-Restmethod : {"errors":[{"code":50505,"message":"System exception.","systemMessage": "java.lang.String cannot be cast to java.util.Map","moreInfoUrl":null}]}**

The following command converts the object in the $Template variable to JSON and saves the output in the variable $Body:

```
PowerCLI C:\> $Body = $Template | ConvertTo-Json -Depth 999
```

We will extract the URI needed to submit the deployment request from the entitled catalog item object links property, as follows:

```
PowerCLI C:\> $Uri = ($CatalogItem.links | Where-Object {$_.rel
-eq 'POST: Submit Request'}).href
```

We call the Invoke-RestMethod cmdlet with the POST method to submit the deployment request and save the output in the variable $Request, using the following command:

```
PowerCLI C:\> $Request = Invoke-RestMethod -Uri $Uri
-Method POST -Body $Body -Headers $Headers
```

By evaluating the $Request variable, we can get the properties of the request, as follows:

```
PowerCLI C:\> $Request
```

You can see the output of the preceding command in the following screenshot:

In the preceding screenshot, you can see that the request has **state SUBMITTED**. It takes about 10 minutes for the deployment to complete.

Viewing details of a machine request

To know when the deployment has finished, we have to retrieve the request status. If the status is **SUCCESSFUL**, we are aware that we did a successful deployment. To retrieve the details of a request, we have to specify the request ID in the URI. We will save the URI in the variable $Uri, as follows:

```
PowerCLI C:\> $Uri = "https://$vRAServer/catalog-
service/api/consumer/requests/$($Request.Id)"
```

The Invoke-RestMethod cmdlet is called using the GET method, and the output is saved in the variable $Request, with the following command:

```
PowerCLI C:\> $Request = Invoke-RestMethod -Uri $Uri -Method GET
-Headers $Headers
```

We will evaluate the variable $Request to retrieve its content, as follows:

```
PowerCLI C:\> $Request
```

You can see the output of the preceding command in the following screenshot:

You can see in the preceding screenshot that we have successfully deployed a basic `CentOS` `6.6` IaaS Blueprint.

Retrieving provisioned resources

After successful deployment of machines or applications, you can retrieve the resources you have deployed with the following URI that we save in the variable `$Uri`, as follows:

```
PowerCLI C:\> $Uri = "https://$vRAServer/catalog-service
/api/consumer/resources"
```

We will call the `Invoke-RestMethod` cmdlet with the `GET` method and save the output in the variable `$Response`, using the following command:

```
PowerCLI C:\> $Response = Invoke-RestMethod -Uri $Uri -Method GET
-Headers $Headers
```

The provisioned resources can be found in the `$Response.content` property. In the following command, we will pipe the output of the `$Response.content` property to the `Where-Object` cmdlet to filter for the `CentOS 6.6` machine deployed in the preceding section, *Creating vRA machines*:

```
PowerCLI C:\> $Response.content | Where-Object
{$_.name -like 'CentOS 6.6*'}
```

The following screenshot shows you the output of the preceding command:

In the preceding screenshot, you can see the name, status, owners, lease expiration date, costs, and destroy date of the resource.

Summary

In this chapter, you learned to use REST APIs from PowerCLI with examples from VMware NSX and vRealize Automation. You saw how to connect to NSX servers using basic authentication and to connect to vRealize Automation servers with a bearer token. The NSX examples used XML and the vRealize Automation examples used JSON.

We discussed managing NSX logical switches, logical (distributed) routers, and edge services gateways. The vRealize Automation examples were about managing vRA tenants, reservations, and resources.

In the following chapter, you will learn how to report with PowerCLI.

15
Reporting with PowerCLI

Creating reports is the task that most new PowerCLI users start with. If your boss wants a report of all the new virtual machines created last month or a list of all the datastores that are over 90 percent full, PowerCLI will make it easy for you to create such a report and save it as a CSV or HTML file. In this chapter, you will learn some techniques to create reports.

The following topics are covered in this chapter:

- Retrieving log files
- Creating log bundles
- Performance reporting
- Exporting reports to CSV files
- Generating HTML reports
- Sending reports by e-mail
- Reporting the health of your vSphere environment with vCheck

Retrieving log files

ESXi servers and vCenter Servers generate log files. Some of these log files can be retrieved using PowerCLI. The Get-LogType cmdlet can be used to retrieve information about the available log file types on a virtual machine host or vCenter Server. The syntax of the Get-LogType cmdlet is as follows:

```
Get-LogType [[-VMHost] <VMHost[]>] [-Server <VIServer[]>]
[<CommonParameters>]
```

There are no required parameters. If you specify a value for the -VMHost parameter, the available log types on the host will be retrieved. If you omit the -VMHost parameter, the available log types on the default vCenter Server will be retrieved.

In the first example, we will retrieve the available log types on the vCenter Server:

```
PowerCLI C:\> Get-LogType
```

The output of the preceding command is as follows:

```
Key                                Summary
---                                -------
vpxd:vpxd-13.log                   vCenter Server log in 'plain' format
vpxd:vpxd-alert-12.log             vCenter Server log in 'plain' format
vpxd:vpxd-alert.log                vCenter Server log in 'plain' format
vpxd:vpxd-profiler-12.log          vCenter Server log in 'plain' format
vpxd:vpxd-profiler.log             vCenter Server log in 'plain' format
vpxd:vpxd.log                      vCenter Server log in 'plain' format
vpxd:vpxd_cfg.log                  vCenter Server log in 'plain' format
vpxd-profiler:vpxd-profiler-1...   vpxd-profiler
vpxd-profiler:vpxd-profiler.log    vpxd-profiler
```

In the second example, we will retrieve the available log types on the ESXi server 192.168.0.133:

```
PowerCLI C:\> Get-LogType -VMHost 192.168.0.133
```

The output of the preceding command is as follows:

```
Key            Summary
---            -------
fdm            fdm
hostd          Server log in 'plain' format
vmkernel       Server log in 'plain' format
vpxa           vCenter Server agent log in 'plain' format
```

Now that you know the available log types, you can use them as input for the Get-Log cmdlet and retrieve entries from these logs or the entire bundle of log files. The Get-Log cmdlet has the following syntax. The first parameter set is for retrieving log files:

```
Get-Log [-Key] <String[]> [[-VMHost] <VMHost[]>] [[-StartLineNum]
<Int32>] [[-NumLines] <Int32>] [-Server <VIServer[]>]
[<CommonParameters>]
```

The second parameter set is for retrieving a log bundle. VMware technical support may ask for a log bundle after you submitted a *Support Request*.

The `-Key` parameter is required to retrieve the log files:

```
Get-Log [[-VMHost] <VMHost[]>] [-Bundle] [-DestinationPath] <String>
[-Server <VIServer[]>] [-RunAsync] [<CommonParameters>]
```

The `-DestinationPath` parameter is required to retrieve a log bundle.

In the following example, we will retrieve the last two lines of the `vmkernel` log file from the host `192.168.0.133`:

```
PowerCLI C:\> Get-Log -Key vmkernel -VMHost 192.168.0.133 |
>> Select-Object -ExpandProperty Entries |
>> Select-Object -Last 2
```

The output of the preceding command is as follows:

```
2017-02-04T21:18:54.880Z cpu1:33061)NMP: nmp_ThrottleLogForDevice:
3298: Cmd 0x12 (0x439d802037c0, 0) to dev "mpx.vmhba1:C0:T0:L0"
on path "vmhba1:C0:T0:L0" Failed: H:0x0 D:0x2 P:0x0 Valid sense
data: 0x5 0x24 0x0. Act:NONE
2017-02-04T21:18:54.882Z cpu0:32785)NMP: nmp_ThrottleLogForDevice:
3298: Cmd 0x1a (0x439d802037c0, 0) to dev "mpx.vmhba32:C0:T0:L0"
on path "vmhba32:C0:T0:L0" Failed: H:0x0 D:0x2 P:0x0 Valid sense
data: 0x5 0x20 0x0. Act:NONE
```

The VMware Knowledge Base article, *Interpreting SCSI sense codes in VMware ESXi and ESX (289902)* at `http://kb.vmware.com/kb/289902` will give you a detailed explanation of the SCSI code that is in the output of the preceding command.

If you want to search a log file for certain strings or patterns, you can use the PowerShell `Select-String` cmdlet to do so. The syntax of this cmdlet is as follows:

- The first parameter set is for searching for text in files specified by the `-Path` parameter. Wildcards in the value of the `-Path` parameter, such as `*.log`, are permitted:

  ```
  Select-String [-Pattern] <String[]> [-Path] <String[]> [-AllMatches]
  [-CaseSensitive] [-Context <Int32[]>] [-Encoding <String>] [-Exclude
  <String[]>] [-Include <String[]>] [-List] [-NotMatch] [-Quiet]
  [-SimpleMatch] [<CommonParameters>]
  ```

  The `-Pattern` and the `-Path` parameters are required.

- The second parameter set is for searching for text in `String` type objects specified by the `-InputObject` parameter:

```
Select-String [-Pattern] <String[]> [-AllMatches] [-CaseSensitive]
[-Context <Int32[]>] [-Encoding <String>] [-Exclude <String[]>]
[-Include <String[]>] [-List] [-NotMatch] [-Quiet] [-SimpleMatch]
-InputObject <PSObject> [<CommonParameters>]
```

The `-Pattern` and the `-InputObject` parameters are required.

- The third parameter set is for searching for text in files specified by the `-LiteralPath` parameter. The difference between the `-Path` parameter in the first parameter set and the `-LiteralPath` parameter is that the characters in the value of the `-LiteralPath` parameter are not interpreted as wildcards:

```
Select-String [-Pattern] <String[]> [-AllMatches] [-CaseSensitive]
[-Context <Int32[]>] [-Encoding <String>] [-Exclude <String[]>]
[-Include <String[]>] [-List] [-NotMatch] [-Quiet] [-SimpleMatch]
-LiteralPath <String[]> [<CommonParameters>]
```

The `-Pattern` and the `-LiteralPath` parameters are required.

The value of the `-Pattern` parameter can be a regular expression. If you use the `-SimpleMatch` parameter, the value of the `-Pattern` parameter is not interpreted as a regular expression.

As an example of the preceding `Select-String` cmdlet syntax, you can use the following command to retrieve the last two lines from the `vmkernel` log file in the host `192.168.0.133` that contain the word `WARNING`:

```
PowerCLI C:\> Get-Log -Key vmkernel -VMHost 192.168.0.133 |
>> Select-Object -ExpandProperty Entries |
>> Select-String -Pattern 'WARNING' |
>> Select-Object -Last 2
```

The output of the preceding command is as follows:

```
2017-02-04T19:39:18.100Z cpu1:33355)WARNING: DOM memory will be
preallocated.
2017-02-04T19:39:18.932Z cpu1:33405)WARNING: FTCpt: 476: Using
IPv6 address tostart server listener
```

If you omit the `Get-Log -VMHost` parameter, you will retrieve vCenter Server log files. In the following example, we will retrieve the contents of the `vpxd:vpxd_cfg.log` file:

```
PowerCLI C:\> Get-Log -Key vpxd:vpxd_cfg.log |
>> Select-Object -ExpandProperty Entries
```

Because the output of the preceding command is very long, it is omitted from this book.

Creating log bundles

VMware technical support might ask for a log bundle when you submit a support request. You can create a log bundle from the vCenter Server's log files with the following command:

```
PowerCLI C:\> Get-Log -Bundle -DestinationPath c:\
```

The output of the preceding command is as follows:

```
Data
----
C:\vcsupport-52387fc8-52de-113b-7f28-1908e9ffa0d7.zip
```

In the following command, we will create a log bundle from the log files on the host `192.168.0.133`:

```
PowerCLI C:\> Get-Log -VMHost 192.168.0.133 -Bundle
-DestinationPath  c:\
```

The output of the preceding command is as follows:

```
Data
----
C:\vmsupport-52348fab-b7a7-97f1-bf2a-719b91ab84b3.tgz
```

Performance reporting

If your users complain that their virtual machines are running slowly, you may want to find the reason for their complaints. You also want to know how your vSphere environment is performing, to see if additional hosts are necessary to keep your systems running smoothly. In PowerCLI, you can use the `Get-Stat` cmdlet to retrieve statistical information that is available on ESXi hosts and vCenter servers.

VMware vCenter servers keep statistical information about the performance of the virtual machines, hosts, resource pools, and so on. This statistical information is retrieved by the hosts in real time and aggregated in four **statistical intervals** on the vCenter servers. The real-time information is collected by the hosts with a collection frequency of 20 seconds and kept for 1 hour. The aggregated information is stored in the database of the vCenter server.

Retrieving the statistical intervals

Information about the statistical intervals can be retrieved using the Get-StatInterval cmdlet. The syntax of this cmdlet is as follows:

```
Get-StatInterval [[-Name] <String[]>] [[-SamplingPeriodSecs]
<Int32[]>] [-Server <VIServer[]>] [<CommonParameters>]
```

There are no required parameters. Without parameters, the Get-StatInterval cmdlet gives information about all of the four statistical intervals. The default output is in seconds. To make the output more useful, we can use calculated properties to convert the output Sampling Period to Minutes and the Storage Time to Days using the following command lines:

```
PowerCLI C:\> Get-StatInterval |
>> Select-Object -Property Name,
>> @{Name='Sampling Period (Minutes)'
>>    Expression={($_.SamplingPeriodSecs)/60}},
>> @{Name='Storage Time (Days)'
>>    Expression={$_.StorageTimeSecs/(60*60*24)}}
```

The output of the preceding command is as follows:

Name	Sampling Period (Minutes)	Storage Time (Days)
Past day	5	1
Past week	30	7
Past month	120	30
Past year	1440	365

The sampling period for the real-time interval is 20 seconds. As you can see in the preceding output, the sampling periods for the statistical intervals increase from 5 minutes in Past day to 30 minutes in Past week, 2 hours in Past month, and 1 day in Past year. This means that, if you retrieve an average CPU usage value in the past day's statistical interval, the value is an average of 5 minutes.

During the aggregation process, the data from the previous statistical interval is taken to create the data for the next statistical interval. For example, to calculate an average value for the past week's statistical interval, the average value calculated is an average of the six average values from the same time period in the past day's statistical interval.

Performance data is retrieved for **metric groups**, such as CPU, datastore, disk, memory, network, power, and system.

Depending on the **statistics level** of a statistical interval, the approximate number of metrics is aggregated and stored in the vCenter server database. Statistics Level 4 stores all metrics, while statistics Level 1 stores the least metrics.

The following screenshot of the vSphere Web Client shows the **Statistics Intervals** settings in **vCenter Server Settings**, with a different **Statistics Level** for each statistics interval:

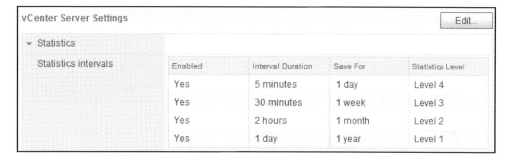

A statistics level must have the same value as the statistics level of the previous interval, or a lower one.

The statistics levels in the screenshot are just an example and are not recommended values! Try to keep the statistics levels low. Otherwise, your vCenter server database will grow larger, and the aggregation rollup jobs will take a lot of time to complete. The default setting is 1 for every statistics level interval! Higher levels include more metrics. Each statistics level includes all of the metrics of the lower statistics levels and includes additional metrics. Statistics level 4 contains all metrics that are supported by the vCenter server. More information about the statistics levels and the metrics included in each level can be found in the VMware vSphere documentation at the following link:
`http://pubs.vmware.com/vsphere-65/index.jsp#com.vmware.vsphere`
`.monitoring.doc/GUID-25800DE4-68E5-41CC-82D9-8811E27924BC.html`

Retrieving performance statistics

The `Get-Stat` cmdlet retrieves the statistical information available on a vCenter server system. The syntax of this cmdlet is as follows:

```
Get-Stat [-Entity] <VIObject[]> [-Common] [-Memory] [-Cpu] [-Disk]   [-
Network] [-Stat <String[]>] [-Start <DateTime>] [-Finish  <DateTime>] [-
MaxSamples <Int32>] [-IntervalMins <Int32[]>]   [-IntervalSecs <Int32[]>] [-
Instance <String[]>] [-Realtime]   [-Server <VIServer[]>]
[<CommonParameters>]
```

The `-Entity` parameter is required. The value of this parameter must be the object whose performance statistics you want to retrieve.

In the following example, we will retrieve the performance statistics for the host `192.168.0.133` and for every metric ID only 1 sample is shown:

```
PowerCLI C:\> Get-Stat -Entity (Get-VMHost -Name 192.168.0.133)
-MaxSamples 1
```

The output of the preceding command is as follows:

MetricId	Timestamp	Value	Unit	Instance
cpu.usage.average	2/4/2017 1:00:00 AM	3.37	%	
cpu.usagemhz.average	2/4/2017 1:00:00 AM	181	MHz	
mem.usage.average	2/4/2017 1:00:00 AM	33.43	%	
disk.usage.average	2/4/2017 1:00:00 AM	77	KBps	
net.usage.average	2/4/2017 1:00:00 AM	15	KBps	
sys.uptime.latest	2/4/2017 1:00:00 AM	965	second	

In the following example, three samples of the real-time values for the `cpu.usage.average` metric are shown for the host `192.168.0.133`. This host has two CPUs, instance `0` and instance **1**. The rows in the following output where the instance is empty are average values of the two instances:

```
PowerCLI C:\> Get-Stat -Entity (Get-VMHost -Name 192.168.0.133)
-Stat  cpu.usage.average -Realtime -MaxSamples 3 |
>> Sort-Object -Property Timestamp -Descending
```

The output of the preceding command is as follows:

MetricId	Timestamp	Value	Unit	Instance
cpu.usage.average	2/4/2017 11:05:00 AM	0.42	%	1
cpu.usage.average	2/4/2017 11:05:00 AM	0.47	%	
cpu.usage.average	2/4/2017 11:05:00 AM	0.52	%	0

```
cpu.usage.average 2/4/2017 11:04:40 AM  0.31 %    1
cpu.usage.average 2/4/2017 11:04:40 AM  0.51 %
cpu.usage.average 2/4/2017 11:04:40 AM  0.71 %    0
cpu.usage.average 2/4/2017 11:04:20 AM  0.34 %    1
cpu.usage.average 2/4/2017 11:04:20 AM  0.57 %
cpu.usage.average 2/4/2017 11:04:20 AM   0.8 %    0
```

The preceding output shows a time difference of 20 seconds between the intervals. 20 Seconds is the sampling period for the real-time interval. The times in the `Timestamp` column are the times when the interval finishes.

The following screenshot shows a realtime summary performance graph report from the vSphere Web Client for the **CPU** usage of host `192.168.0.133`:

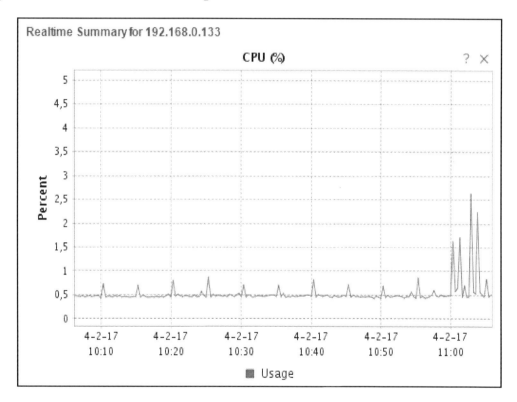

Retrieving metric IDs

If you want to know which metric IDs are available for an object in a certain statistical interval, you can use the Get-StatType cmdlet to retrieve them. The syntax of the Get-StatType cmdlet is as follows:

```
Get-StatType [[-Name] <String[]>] [-Entity] <VIObject[]> [-Start
<DateTime>] [-Finish <DateTime>] [-Interval <StatInterval[]>] [-Realtime]
[-Server <VIServer[]>] [<CommonParameters>]
```

The -Entity parameter is required to retrieve metric IDs for clusters, virtual machine hosts, resource pools, or virtual machines.

In the following example, we will retrieve the available metric IDs for the host 192.168.0.133 in the real-time statistical interval and return them after sorting:

```
PowerCLI C:\> Get-StatType -Entity (Get-VMHost -Name 192.168.0.133)
-RealTime |
>> Sort-Object
```

The output of the preceding command is as follows:

```
cpu.coreUtilization.average
cpu.costop.summation
cpu.demand.average
cpu.idle.summation
cpu.latency.average
cpu.readiness.average
cpu.ready.summation
cpu.reservedCapacity.average
cpu.swapwait.summation
cpu.totalCapacity.average
cpu.usage.average
cpu.usagemhz.average
cpu.used.summation
cpu.utilization.average
cpu.wait.summation
```

I have aborted the output of the preceding command after the CPU counter group (or the metric group) in this chapter because the command returned 178 metric IDs in total. The following are other counter groups besides CPU: datastore, disk, hbr, mem, net, power, rescpu, storageAdapter, storagePath, sys, and vflashModule.

Exporting reports to CSV files

If your boss asks for a report, they probably want it in the form of a spreadsheet. The easiest way to create a spreadsheet from a PowerCLI report is to export it to a CSV file. This CSV file can be imported into a spreadsheet. Another use case for CSV files is creating export files of one system that you can use later to import into another system. For example, you can use CSV files to export the settings of a vCenter Server and import them in another vCenter Server. PowerShell contains the `Export-CSV` cmdlet to create CSV files. The syntax of the `Export-CSV` cmdlet is as follows. The first parameter set can be used to specify a delimiter to separate the property values:

```
Export-Csv [[-Path] <String>] [[-Delimiter] <Char>] [-Append] [-Confirm] [-
Encoding {Unicode | UTF7 | UTF8 | ASCII | UTF32 | BigEndianUnicode |
Default | OEM}] [-Force] -InputObject <PSObject> [-LiteralPath <String>] [-
NoClobber] [-NoTypeInformation] [-WhatIf] [<CommonParameters>]
```

The second parameter set can be used to use the list separator for the current culture as the item delimiter:

```
Export-Csv [[-Path] <String>] [-Append] [-Confirm] [-Encoding {Unicode |
UTF7 | UTF8 | ASCII | UTF32 | BigEndianUnicode | Default | OEM}] [-Force] -
InputObject <PSObject> [-LiteralPath <String>] [-NoClobber] [-
NoTypeInformation] [-UseCulture] [-WhatIf] [<CommonParameters>]
```

The `-InputObject` parameter is required and accepts input from the pipeline `ByValue` and `ByPropertyName`.

In the following example, we will create a CSV file containing the virtual machines in your environment. The output of this script has some problems that will be discussed later in this section:

```
PowerCLI C:\> Get-VM | Export-CSV -Path c:\VMs.csv
```

If you open the `c:\VMs.csv` file in Notepad or with the `Get-Content` cmdlet, you will see that the first line contains the type of the objects in the file:

```
#TYPE VMware.VimAutomation.ViCore.Impl.V1.VM
.UniversalVirtualMachineImpl
```

Your boss doesn't want to know this. You can prevent the creation of this first line by using the `Export-CSV -NoTypeInformation` parameter.

The second problem is the comma that is used as a delimiter between the columns in the CSV file. In a lot of cultures, the default delimiter for a CSV file is another character. For example, the default CSV file delimiter in the Netherlands, where I live, is a semicolon. There are two possible solutions for this problem:

- You can use the `-Delimiter` parameter and specify the delimiter character as a value, for example:

```
PowerCLI C:\> Get-VM |
>> Export-CSV -Path c:\VMs.csv -Delimiter ';'
```

- Another and in my opinion better solution is to use the `-UseCulture` parameter. This creates the CSV file with the correct delimiter for the current culture on the system where the script is running. Combined with the `-NoTypeInformation` parameter, the command becomes something such as this:

```
PowerCLI C:\> Get-VM |
>> Export-CSV -Path c:\VMs.csv -UseCulture -NoTypeInformation
```

The last problem with the `Export-CSV` cmdlet is that the values of properties that contain array objects are not shown in the CSV file. The file only shows the type of the property. For example, the `DatastoreIdList` column is filled with the following value:

```
System.String[]
```

You can use the .NET `[string]::Join()` method to solve this problem. This method requires two parameters. The first parameter is a character used as a delimiter. The second parameter is the array of objects you want to join.

The following example shows you how to get the datastore IDs in the CSV file. You now have to use the `Select-Object` cmdlet to specify all of the objects you want to return in the CSV file. For the `DatastoreIdList` column, you have to create a calculated property. The following example will only save the name of the virtual machines and the datastore IDs in the CSV file:

```
PowerCLI C:\> Get-VM |
>> Select-Object -Property Name,
>> @{Name="DatastoreIdList";Expression={[string]::
Join(',',$_.DatastoreIdList)}} |
>> Export-CSV -Path c:\VMs.csv -UseCulture -NoTypeInformation
```

The following screenshot shows the exported CSV file after its imported in a spreadsheet. The virtual machines are from my home lab that I used to write this book:

	A	B
1	Name	DatastoreIdList
2	VM10	Datastore-datastore-112
3	VM2	Datastore-datastore-15
4	vcenter	Datastore-datastore-15
5	VM7	Datastore-datastore-15
6	VM4	Datastore-datastore-15
7	VM3	Datastore-datastore-15
8	VM1	Datastore-datastore-15

Generating HTML reports

CSV files are nice, but HTML files are more impressive. This section will show you how to create nice-looking HTML files from your reports. PowerShell gives you the ConvertTo-Html cmdlet to do this. The syntax of this cmdlet is as follows.

The first parameter set creates an entire HTML page:

```
ConvertTo-Html [[-Property] <Object[]>] [[-Head] <String[]>]  [[-Title]
<String>] [[-Body] <String[]>] [-As {Table | List}] [-CssUri <Uri>] [-
InputObject <PSObject>] [-PostContent <String[]>]  [-PreContent <String[]>]
[<CommonParameters>]
```

The second parameter set creates only an HTML table and omits the HTML, HEAD, TITLE, and BODY tags:

```
ConvertTo-Html [[-Property] <Object[]>] [-As {Table | List}] [-Fragment] [-
InputObject <PSObject>] [-PostContent <String[]>] [-PreContent <String[]>]
[<CommonParameters>]
```

There are no required parameters.

In the first example, you will create a report about the connection state of the hosts. The `ConvertTo-Html` cmdlet doesn't have a `-Path` parameter to specify a filename. This problem can be solved by piping the output to the `Out-File` cmdlet, as shown in the following code:

```
Get-VMHost |
Select-Object -Property Name,ConnectionState |
Sort-Object -Property Name |
ConvertTo-Html |
Out-File -FilePath c:\VMHosts.html
```

You can open the `c:\VMHosts.html` file in a browser using the following command:

```
PowerCLI C:\> Start-Process -FilePath c:\VMHosts.html
```

 Be warned that the first time you use the `ConvertTo-Html` cmdlet, you might be disappointed because the output doesn't look nice by default.

The following screenshot shows the output of the preceding command:

Name	ConnectionState
192.168.0.133	Connected
192.168.0.134	Maintenance

To make the output look nicer, it is better to create an HTML fragment from the script and make the HTML header yourself. To make an HTML fragment, you have to use the `ConvertTo-Html -Fragment` parameter. To create the HTML header, you can use a PowerShell here-string.

In the following example, an HTML header and tail are created with here-strings. The table is created using `ConvertTo-Html -Fragment`. If the host's connection state is **Connected**, the color of the text is changed to *green*. If the connection state is **Disconnected**, the color is changed to *red*. A **Cascading Style Sheet** (CSS) is used to provide background and foreground colors for the HTML body and table. After creating the HTML page, a web browser is started to display the page:

1. First, we store the path to the HTML file in the `$FilePath` variable:

   ```
   $FilePath = 'c:\VMHostsConnectionState.html'
   ```

2. Now we create the HTML header as a here-string and store it in the `$Header` variable:

   ```
   $Header = @"
   <!DOCTYPE html>
   <html>
     <head>
       <title>VMware vSphere Hosts ConnectionState Report</title>
       <style>
         body  {background-color: lightgray}
         table {background-color: white}
         th    {color: white; background-color: darkgray}
         tr    {background-color: white}
       </style>
     </head>
     <body>
       <h2>VMware vSphere Hosts ConnectionState Report</h2>
   "@
   ```

3. The connection state of the ESXi hosts is retrieved using the `Get-VMHost` cmdlet and converted into an HTML table fragment that is stored in the `$Fragment` variable:

   ```
   $Fragment = Get-VMHost |
   Select-Object -Property Name,ConnectionState |
   Sort-Object -Property Name |
   ConvertTo-Html -Fragment
   ```

4. The tail of the HTML page is created and stored in the `$Tail` variable:

   ```
   $Tail = @"
     </body>
   </html>
   "@
   ```

5. The HTML header, table fragment, and tail are combined into one HTML page that is stored in the $HTML variable:

```
$HTML = $Header
$HTML += $Fragment
$HTML += $Tail
```

6. The Replace() method of the System.String object is used to replace **Connected** into an HTML code that displays Connected in green color. **Disconnected** is replaced by an HTML code that display Disconnected in red color:

```
$HTML = $HTML.Replace('<td>Connected</td>',
  '<td style="color: green">Connected</td>')
.Replace('<td>Disconnected</td>',
  '<td style="color: red">Disconnected</td>')
```

7. The generated HTML page is stored in the location defined by the $FilePath variable:

```
$HTML | Out-File -FilePath $FilePath
```

8. Finally, we will use the Start-Process cmdlet to open a web browser and display the page:

```
Start-Process -FilePath $FilePath
```

The following screenshot shows the output of the preceding script:

Do you agree that it looks much better than the first HTML report?

Using fragments, you can easily create one report with different segments for hosts, virtual machines, networks, and so on.

Sending reports by e-mail

After creating a report, you might want to send it to your boss or to yourself. The PowerShell `Send-MailMessage` cmdlet can send e-mail messages using an SMTP server. The syntax of this cmdlet is as follows:

```
Send-MailMessage [-To] <String[]> [-Subject] <String> [[-Body] <String>]
[[-SmtpServer] <String>] [-Attachments <String[]>] [-Bcc <String[]>] [-
BodyAsHtml] [-Cc <String[]>] [-Credential <PSCredential>] [-
DeliveryNotificationOption {None | OnSuccess | OnFailure | Delay | Never}]
[-Encoding <Encoding>] [-Port <Int32>] [-Priority {Normal | Low | High}] [-
UseSsl] -From <String> [<CommonParameters>]
```

The `-From`, `-To`, and `-Subject` parameters are required to send a report by e-mail. You can use the PowerShell `$PSEmailServer` preference variable for the SMTP server. If the `$PSEmailServer` variable is not set, you have to use the `-SmtpServer` parameter.

You can send a report by putting it in the body of the e-mail or as an attachment. If the report is an HTML document and you want to send it in the body of the e-mail, you have to use the `-BodyAsHtml` parameter.

In the first example, the HTML report file that was created in the preceding section, *Generating HTML reports*, is sent in the body of an e-mail. In this example, we will use splatting to specify the parameters. The PowerShell `Out-String` cmdlet is used to create a single string from the HTML content.

The SMTP server used in this environment does not require authentication or SSL and uses the default port 25. Additional parameters may be required in some environments:

```
$Parameters = @{
  From = 'admin@blackmilktea.com'
  To = 'manager@blackmilktea.com'
  Subject = 'VMware vSphere hosts Connection State report'
  Body = Get-Content -Path 'c:\VMHostsConnectionState.html' |
        Out-String
  BodyAsHtml = $true
  SmtpServer = 'smtpserver.blackmilktea.com'
}
Send-MailMessage @Parameters
```

 You don't have to create a file before you can send an e-mail. You can also use the content of a variable.

In the second example, we will use the content of the $HTML variable (created in the preceding section, *Generating HTML reports*) as the body of the e-mail:

```
$Parameters = @{
  From = 'admin@blackmilktea.com'
  To = 'manager@blackmilktea.com'
  Subject = 'VMware vSphere hosts Connection State report'
  Body = $HTML
  BodyAsHtml = $true
  SmtpServer = 'smtpserver.blackmilktea.com'
}
Send-MailMessage @Parameters
```

In the third example, we will send the HTML report created in the preceding section, *Generating HTML reports* as an attachment:

```
$Parameters = @{
  From = 'admin@blackmilktea.com'
  To = 'manager@blackmilktea.com'
  Subject = 'VMware vSphere hosts Connection State report'
  Body = 'VMware vSphere hosts Connection State report is attached
  to this email.'
  Attachment = 'c:\VMHostsConnectionState.html'
  SmtpServer = 'smtpserver.blackmilktea.com'
}
Send-MailMessage @Parameters
```

Reporting the health of your vSphere environment with vCheck

In this section of the book, I want to introduce a PowerCLI script that every vSphere admin should use. The **vCheck** script written by Alan Renouf can check your vSphere environment for various configuration issues and report them in HTML format. The vCheck script reports several issues, such as VMs having CD-ROMs connected, VMs with CPU or memory reservations configured, VMs ballooning or swapping, VMs with less than 100 MB free space on a disk, VMs with an old hardware version, and VMs that do not have VMware Tools installed. These are just a few examples. The script reports many more issues.

The script is written in a modular way, and it uses a plugin for every check it performs. It is very easy to write plugins and add them to the script. There are plugins created to check other technologies such as Microsoft Exchange, vCloud Director, vCloud Air, **System Center Virtual Machine Manager** (**SCVMM**), and Cisco UCS. Reading the vCheck plugins is a good way to see how the checks are implemented and to learn from PowerCLI scripts created by other people in the community. The vCheck script is meant to run daily as a scheduled task so that you can receive the results in your mailbox.

You can find Alan's blog post about vCheck at the following link:

```
http://www.virtu-al.net/vcheck-pluginsheaders/vcheck/
```

The vCheck script is now maintained at GitHub and can be downloaded from the following link:

```
https://github.com/alanrenouf/vCheck-vSphere
```

In the following screenshot, you will find some of the issues the vCheck script in my home lab found:

VMs in Inconsistent folders 4

The Following VM's are not stored in folders consistent to their names, this may cause issues when trying to locate them from the datastore manually

VM	Path
VM7	[Datastore2] VM3
VM1	[Datastore2] VM5
DNS1	[Datastore2] vm7
test2	[Cluster01_Vmfs01] test1

NO VM Tools: 7

The following VMs have No VMTools installed, for optimal configuration and performance these should be installed

Name	Status
DC1	toolsNotInstalled
VM2	toolsNotInstalled
DC1	toolsNotInstalled
VM4	toolsNotInstalled
VM1	toolsNotInstalled
DNS1	toolsNotInstalled
WindowsServer2012	toolsNotInstalled

Summary

In this chapter, you learned techniques to create reports with PowerCLI. You saw how to create log files and log bundles using the `Get-Log` cmdlet. Performance reporting using the `Get-Stat` cmdlet was discussed. CSV files and HTML reports were created using the `Export-CSV` and `ConvertTo-Html` cmdlets, and they were sent by e-mail using the `Send-MailMessage` cmdlet. Then you were introduced to the vCheck script to report about common issues in your vSphere environment, and finally, you learned how to use PowerGUI.

This was the last chapter of the book. I hope that you enjoyed reading this book and I hope that you will use PowerCLI to make your job as a vSphere administrator easier.

If you have questions about PowerCLI or PowerCLI scripts that you are writing, the best place to ask your questions is the PowerCLI community in the VMware VMTN Communities at `http://www.vmware.com/go/powercli`.

Go to the **Discussions** tab and click on **Start a Discussion**, or use the PowerCLI command `Get-PowerCLICommunity` to open the PowerCLI community from your PowerCLI session. You may get an answer in a few minutes.

You can also help other people by answering their questions. Answering questions is a great way to improve your PowerCLI skills.

Index

95915401R00313

Made in the USA
San Bernardino, CA
17 November 2018